RUSSIA IN THE AGE OF MODERNISATION AND REVOLUTION 1881–1917

LONGMAN HISTORY OF RUSSIA
General Editor: Harold Shukman

*Already published

Russia in the Age of Modernisation and Revolution 1881–1917

HANS ROGGER

LONGMAN
London and New York

Longman Group Limited
Longman House, Burnt Mill, Harlow
Essex CM20 2JE, England
Associated companies throughout the world

Published in the United States of America
by Longman Inc., New York

First published 1983

British Library Cataloguing in Publication Data
Rogger, Hans
Russia in the age of modernisation and revolution 1891–1917.
– (Longman history of Russia)
1. Russia – History – Nicholas II, 1894–1917 I. Title
947.08'3   DK246

ISBN 0-582-48911-3
ISBN 0-582-48912-1 Pbk

Library of Congress Cataloging in Publication Data
Rogger, Hans.
Russia in the age of modernisation and revolution, 1881–1917.

(Longman history of Russia)
Bibliography: p.
Includes index.
1. Soviet Union – History – Alexander III, 1881–1894.
2. Soviet Union – History – Nicholas II, 1894–1917.
3. Soviet Union – History – Revolution, 1917–1921 – Causes.
I. Title.   II. Series.
DK241.R63 1983   947.08'2   83-714
ISBN 0-582-48911-3
ISBN 0-582-48912-1 (pbk.)

Printed in Singapore by
Kyodo Shing Loong Printing Industries Pte Ltd.

Contents

List of maps

Preface

I have emphasized in the present book what I take to be the central issue of the history of late Imperial Russia — the relationship between state and society and how it affected politics, economics, and class relations. I have also tried to indicate, by devoting a chapter each to foreign affairs and the non-Russian nationalities, the importance (international as well as domestic) I attach to the empire's role and interests as a great power and to its character as a multi-national state.

This has meant neglecting cultural and intellectual history, a subject which deserves better and more detailed treatment than could have been given it in the space allotted to me.

Dates are given according to the Julian calendar which in the nineteenth century was twelve, and in the twentieth century, thirteen, days behind the Gregorian calendar. Where necessary, dates are given in both styles (as in the discussion of foreign relations). The transliteration system is that of the Library of Congress. I have omitted the diaeresis on ё as well as soft and hard signs. In a few instances, consistency has yielded to familiarity, e.g., Alexander rather than Aleksandr, Nicholas instead of Nikolai, Soviet rather than Sovet, Witte rather than Vitte.

The author of a work of synthesis must, inevitably, draw widely and shamelessly upon the writings and researches of many colleagues. My debt to them is only partially recognized in the Notes and Bibliography, and I ask the pardon of those whose contributions to my thinking and writing on Russian history I have failed to acknowledge. I want to give special thanks to colleagues who answered specific queries, clarified obscure points, or provided their unpublished or just-published books and papers: M. Hagen, H. Heilbronner, R. G. Hovannisian, D. Lieven, D. T. Orlovsky, D. K. Rowney, L. Siegelbaum, R. G. Suny, T. Taranovski, E. C. Thaden, J. M. Thompson, G. L. Yaney and last, but not least, my patient editor and good friend, H. Shukman. None of them is to be held to account for my mistakes of fact, judgement, or omission. In the preparation of the manuscript I have had the invaluable and expert help of Teri Coleman and Joan Waugh.

vii

The book is dedicated to Claire Rogger, critic and comrade of many years, whose sharp eye and pencil improved every page.

HANS ROGGER
University of California
Los Angeles
April 1982

CHAPTER ONE

Prologue

The terrorist bomb which on 1 March 1881 killed Alexander II was the most extreme statement of a question agitating all thinking Russians. That question was not simply whether the reforms begun with the abolition of serfdom in 1861 should now be carried forward, but whether the autocracy which had initiated the work of renovation could remain untouched by the changes it had so cautiously introduced into selected areas of Russian life: local government, the courts, the armed services, education. By removing autocracy's head and embodiment, the revolutionists hoped to sow fear and confusion among its defenders and to provoke a popular rising. They wished also to make Russians ask whether the institution which had since the days of Peter the Great been the chief engine of their country's progress was not now the most important barrier to its welfare and happiness.

In that intention they succeeded. For most of its remaining years the monarchy's character, powers, personnel, and policies dominated political debate. The last two tsars judged nearly all their acts and measures by the effect these would have on the maintenance of the existing political order, which most often meant the preservation of political authority and control in their own hands. Even those opponents of the tsarist regime – the Marxists foremost among them – who saw Russia's burning problems as being of a more fundamental economic and social nature than its political superstructure, had to confront the reality of autocracy. The opposition, especially its liberal wing, had also to dispute autocracy's claim that it alone was sufficiently above party and selfish interest to give evenhanded justice to all and to keep a vast, diverse, multinational empire from breaking up and becoming the prey of more advanced competitors.

Because autocracy and its instruments had for so long loomed so large on the Russian scene, there was a tendency to overrate either its positive or negative role. From this tendency historians have not been free, especially those who wrote of the monarchy's failures a short time after its fall. More recent studies of the Russian crisis have stressed what are thought to be its deeper sources. They have probed cultural and economic backwardness, the agrarian problem, social conflict, and the utopian impatience of revolutionaries more

1

often than the institutions and personnel of government.

Yet, to examine the materials of Russian history for the years 1881 to 1917 for purposes of a general study is to come away with a sense of the extra-ordinary influence the character and conduct of government had on the way Russia's problems were treated or perceived. This is not to suggest that autocracy was the source of all problems or that a more liberal polity and more enlightened rulers would have assured their solution. It is difficult, however, not to share the feeling of most articulate Russians – including those who were not committed revolutionaries – that their country's multiple crisis was exacer-bated and its resolution complicated by the absoluteness of power claimed by their rulers. This, they felt, made for the inflexibility, the unresponsive-ness, and the incompetence of the regime, and most particularly of its top layers.

Students and professors in the universities; teachers, agronomists, and econ-omists; doctors, lawyers, and businessmen agreed in private and, when they were permitted, in public that the professional or technical problems they faced were difficult of solution as long as the political system was not reformed. Even the landed nobles, the regime's most favoured and generally conservative supporters, complained that it crudely violated their rights or did not attend to their needs. The critics overstated their case and disagreed on the desired remedies. But knowledge of the past, personal experience, and comparisons with Western Europe made educated Russians uncomfortably aware of the state's intrusions into their lives and of its jealous defensiveness in the face of real or presumed attacks on its vast powers and prerogatives. The result was growing estrangement and friction between an authoritarian state and a restive society.

It is an underlying theme of the pages which follow, that the nature, course, and outcome of this confrontation were decisively affected by the govern-ment's policies, personalities, and institutions. The attempt here will be to give these their proper weight in the story, not to slight other aspects of history. Such an approach seems justified not merely because we are dealing with a political system in which the impulses for action or reaction came from a few men who often isolated themselves from the swift historical currents that swirled around them. It is forcefully suggested also by Western experience which serves as a reminder that the way men are governed and how they feel about their governments and leaders, the extent of their trust and confidence in them, help to determine whether there shall be social peace or conflict, consensus or disaffection, hope or despair. If that is so in countries with repre-sentative institutions, some of them neither backward nor poor, how much truer must it have been where autocracy had always claimed to be the best and only agency for achieving national security and public welfare and failed to make good that claim.

Consciousness of that failure had towards the end of his life and a lost war reached even the 'knight-errant' of absolutism, Nicholas I (1825–55), and led his son, Alexander II (1855–81), to enact reforms that would allow the system to survive by partial liberalization but leave its essence, autocracy, intact.

Indeed, Alexander felt that the reassertion of autocracy's monopoly of power and initiative became all the more important as the serfs were freed (1861), the universities given a large measure of autonomy (1863), the judiciary made independent (1864), rural and urban communities granted limited self-government (1864, 1870) and press censorship relaxed (1865). It seemed to him a necessity of national survival and a precondition of orderly progress that there be no growth of faction or party, no splintering of authority or purpose along lines of class, region, or nationality.

The achievement of serf-emancipation by the sovereign will, especially when compared with the agony that slave liberation had cost America, confirmed the emperor in this view. There would be no sharing of the tsar's power by representative bodies of estates, citizens, or even by permanently constituted agencies of government, such as a cabinet with collective responsibility for the formulation and execution of policy. Alexander II, as did his successors, preferred to deal with individuals, autocrat to bureaucrat, rather than institutions. This placed on him a burden which was bound to undermine the practice of autocracy as well as its theory. It was the weight of that burden, combined with the educated public's demand for some role in the running of the country and repeated attempts on his life, that at last made the tsar heed those who urged conciliation of the public in order to isolate the revolutionaries.

In January 1881 his Minister of Interior, Count M. T. Loris-Melikov, addressed himself to this task. He disavowed any intention of introducing representative, constitutional government or of reviving the assembly of estates (*zemskii sobor*) that the Muscovite tsars had on occasion summoned before the days of Peter the Great. What he envisaged was much more modest and could be justified on the grounds that no group of men as self-contained and remote as were the autocrat and his servants in the central administration could have adequate knowledge to deal with the range of problems before them. To make up for these deficiencies, Loris-Melikov proposed the inclusion, in two specialized governmental commissions, of a few invited public figures of relevant competence, as well as members of appropriate state agencies. These commissions – one administrative and economic, the other financial – would examine only questions that the government put before them. Any legislative proposals would go to a purely advisory General Commission (meeting for no longer than two months) in which elected representatives of local governments would sit.

Before being accepted or rejected by the emperor, the commission's projects, as did all laws, would have to pass the Council of State, an appointive assembly of elder statesmen and senior bureaucrats whose number might, if the tsar wished, be enlarged by ten to fifteen voting representatives of public institutions with special knowledge, experience, and outstanding abilities. Loris-Melikov reassured his master that his power would not be diminished, that he alone would continue to decide whether the commissions met, what they discussed, and whether their draft bills became law. On 17 February 1881 Alexander approved what came to be known as the 'Loris-Melikov Constitution'. On the day of his death he had agreed that his ministers should meet with him on 4 March to discuss how it was to be implemented and announced.

Satisfied as to the integrity of his authority, the emperor wondered whether 'the loyal elements of society' would be content with what they had been offered. He was right to wonder, for the Loris-Melikov project, precisely because it was not a constitution, would soon have raised more urgently the issues it left unresolved: the reach and sources of supreme power and its relationship to the increasingly vocal groups asking for some protection from government or a share in it. In short, the adoption of the non-constitution was likely to whet appetites and prepare minds for a real one. Alexander III, who rejoiced that this 'criminal and hasty step' was not taken, certainly thought so.[1]

As events were to show, the desire remained strong for subjecting the legislative and administrative activities of the state to public control and accounting. At the very least, the constitution of Loris-Melikov could, as he hoped, gain time for a government faced by pressing problems and conflicting demands. And if it had led to fruitful cooperation between the monarchy and spokesmen for the public, future concessions might have been made more easily by the former and received with greater trust by the latter. Twenty-five years later Nicholas II had to pay a heavy price for the inflexibility of his father.

When he ascended the throne, Alxander III was not yet certain what his wisest and safest course would be. The son of a self-indulgent and often vacillating father, the new tsar took pains to give the impression of decisiveness and a strong will. But initially he hesitated, as did some of his advisers. Their hesitation was part of the crisis of confidence that had afflicted the government since the late 1870s and had caused Alexander II to countenance the Loris-Melikov project and his son to consider it briefly. The assassination was bound to deepen the crisis for no one could yet be sure of the extent of the revolutionary conspiracy. In this area at least, firm and comforting measures of defence could be taken and soon showed that the danger had been exaggerated.

In the political sphere, however, continuing irresolution testified to an awareness that terror was only one aspect of the trouble; equally important were those who used words rather than bombs, the very people whom Loris-Melikov had tried to appease. Far from being stunned into silence by the killing of the tsar-liberator or by attempts to saddle them with moral responsibility for the crime, the non-revolutionary opposition refused to view it as an indictment of the liberalizing steps that Alexander II had taken or as a refutation of its own ideas for the improvement of the system. Even among some highly-placed courtiers and guards officers, the conviction was growing that a constitution might be the only way of winning over the moderates and undercutting the 'nihilists'.

In the higher spheres in which it circulated, such a conclusion may have been the result of a failure of nerve. Elsewhere it continued to be the expression of liberal convictions or practical considerations for broadening the basis of government, improving its effectiveness, and bringing it closer to the people. The conservative assumption that the deed of 1 March would so immediately and totally discredit the advocates of liberalization that they could henceforth be ignored, proved false. Far from thinking that the Great Reforms had gone too far, most moderates (and, naturally, the radicals) blamed the inadequacies of what had been granted in the previous reign for the breach between government and society. One of the prime movers of the reforms, Minister of War D. A. Miliutin, looked upon the fourteen years before 1880 as years of reaction, implying that it could hardly have been the one year of new beginnings following 1880 and the appointment of Loris-Melikov that had prepared the ground for the revolutionaries.[2]

On 10 March 1881 the Executive Committee of the People's Will, which had planned the murder of Alexander II, demanded in an open letter that his son call a national assembly of freely elected representatives to reorder the nation's social and political life from top to bottom. This could be dismissed in view of its source and scope. Not so the more moderate demands which addressed themselves to the issues of a constitution or some form of representation. In the days after the catastrophe, six of the country's major newspapers and an equal number of its more important provincial assemblies (*zemstva*) called upon the government and the tsar not to yield to the easy temptation of a policy of repression. That, it was pointed out, had been given an adequate trial. A more generous course was indicated that would turn subjects into loyal citizens by meeting them with trust and establishing institutions which could tell the ruler of their needs and desires. Only an expression of the will of the people, a St Petersburg newspaper wrote, could show the road the new monarch had to take, while another recommended that a public body serve alongside the government to work for the public welfare. A third, disingenuously yet boldly, concluded that the best way of assuring the monarch's safety was to lessen his responsibilities, make him a symbol of national unity, and charge the people's representatives with the conduct of domestic policy. 'Why must the Leader of the Russian Nation be held personally accountable for all that is done in Russia – from economic mistakes . . . to Siberian exile?'[3]

Arguments that did not raise the sensitive point of the imperial prerogative were also made, discreetly, by a few prominent men who eschewed the idea of a constitution as either premature or harmful. One of these was Boris Chicherin, a jurist and philosopher, professor of Moscow University and former tutor to the tsar's late brother. Chicherin's liberalism was concerned in the first instance with the protection of property and persons from arbitrary authority. It was further tempered by his belief that there could be no limiting of the supreme power at a time of turbulence and by his distrust of popular assemblies and popular sovereignty. A constitution, although it was probably inevitable, should be introduced only when the monarch thought it necessary.

Chicherin none the less proposed that delegates of provincial gentry assemblies and of elected local governments sit, as of right, in the Council of State. That was the only way of introducing healthy elements into the state organism, of creating a non-parliamentary forum in which men and ideas could be developed and safely tested. For the time was past, even in Russia, when the autocratic state could govern only through its own instruments.[4]

There was, apparently, no avoiding the central question whether Russia, in the late nineteenth century, could be ruled by principles and methods (ideally, those of enlightened despotism) that had served her well a century earlier. A growing number of educated Russians thought not, including many who were deeply attached to the monarchy, anti-liberal, opposed to the copying of Western models, and fearful of letting the untutored and resentful masses play a political role. In order to continue the exclusion of the masses and the repression of the revolutionaries, to prevent radical changes or to control its speed and direction, government, the well-to-do, and the well-educated had to make common cause and to trust each other.

The issue of trust was a crucial one for Konstantin Pobedonostsev, to whom Chicherin had sent his reflections on 11 March, hoping that Pobedonostsev would gain a hearing for them in the Committee of Ministers. Like Chicherin a jurist and former professor of law, Pobedonostsev had entered the state service after playing an important part in the judicial reforms of 1864. In 1880 he had been appointed *Ober-Prokuror*, or lay director of the Most Holy Synod, the government office in charge of the country's ecclesiastical establishment. To that post he brought an increasingly bureaucratic outlook on the governing of both Church and State, the regrets he had developed over his role in the Great Reforms, and the belief, striking in its simple consistency, that Russia's salvation in the midst of the giddy inconstancy of modern life lay in strict hierarchy, obedience, and authority. Men were not to be trusted and had, therefore, to be restrained – the lower orders because of their ignorance and brutishness, the upper classes because of selfishness and moral weakness.

Chicherin was mistaken to look for help in that quarter. Personal closeness to Alexander III, whom he had tutored in earlier years, made Pobedonostsev an influential figure in the new reign. But he used his position and the tsar's initial confusion to oppose Loris-Melikov and his chief allies, Miliutin and Finance Minister A. A. Abaza, because they personified the weak-willed and weak-minded liberalism he had come to abhor.

Alexander III had given no sign of sympathy for the governmental reforms he had inherited along with their author Loris-Melikov; neither had he rejected them. As late as mid April 1881, a month and a half after his accession, he had not yet revealed his mind. The outcome, therefore, of the high-level conferences which were reviewing the project already approved by the late emperor was far from predictable. Sensing a possible shift in the prevailing winds, Loris-Melikov decided to move matters along and elicit a clarification of his own status by giving the monarch a comprehensive governmental programme which retained but de-emphasized the key elements of his constitution. He started out with practical recommendations for improving state security which were designed to appeal to the emperor as well as to placate the public. Balancing concession and control, the programme dealt with the organization of the police, with local administration, education, press censorship, peasant taxation and migration.

Broader perspectives were drawn by suggesting that success in most of these areas depended on harmony in the central administration – namely, a unified cabinet – and on the inclusion of knowledgeable non-governmental advisers in the bureaucratic bodies that would draft the necessary legislation. But Loris-Melikov had been careful not to spell out how these advisers were to be selected or what form their participation was to take. All that could be settled if and when the principle of participation had been accepted. There was nothing really new here, he told the tsar, nothing certainly that could be regarded as threatening or diminishing his authority. Loris-Melikov had staged a tactical retreat by weakening the political provisions of the constitution and had reason to hope that this retreat would serve its purpose. His supporters in the government and the imperial family were more numerous than his enemies, and Alexander himself had authorized his chief ministers to meet without him on 28 April and to submit their collective view on the great questions of governmental policy and restructuring that still awaited resolution.

There could be no better illustration of the defects of autocratic rule than was supplied by the events of 28 April. The meeting held that evening led to agreement on a number of Loris-Melikov's lesser proposals; prospects for a similarly favourable reception of the rest of his programme appeared excellent. Pobedonostsev's was the only dissenting voice. But as the gathering broke up at one o'clock in the morning of the 29th, there came news that an imperial manifesto was being distributed in the city which was a direct negation of all that the ministers had agreed to. The manifesto's high-flown language, its appeal to divine command and providence, its vow to uphold and preserve the autocratic power undiminished and unimpaired, left no doubt of its authorship. Pobedonostsev admitted to his colleagues – some speechless, some nearly hysterical – that it was he who had drafted the declaration and quickly left their presence. He did not tell them that he had been the author not only of the text but of the very idea and that he had belaboured the tsar for nearly two months to stand fast and not to listen to the liberal siren song of the Petersburg politicians. The country, the simple people were waiting for a sign of firmness from the throne, he had told Alexander on 26 April in a note accompanying the draft manifesto which he successfully urged him to publish without consulting anyone else.

To give the appearance of firmness, the tsar had retreated before the hectoring of one individual from a policy to which he had seemingly committed his government only days before. Beyond the defeat of Loris-Melikov and his adherents, beyond their resignation or dismissal, the manifesto undid an essential first step to assure orderly government and restricting personal and accidental influences on the ruler. As long as gaining the monarch's ear and favour could settle matters of high policy, policy was bound to have an element of unpredictability and capriciousness about it, with the confidence of the tsar the chief criterion of a minister's performance.

The reaffirmation of the principle of personal government and the practice of favouritism survived the Revolution of 1905 and the limitations which were placed upon the crown in its wake. Even after the constitutional change of

1906, the opinion of an individual who might or might not have an official function or position, or even the private intuition of the emperor, could be as influential in the making of policy as the advice of all or any of his ministers. Such a state of affairs led many Russians to think or say that their country was run by cliques of changing composition, outlook, and influence.

Pobedonostsev's *coup de théâtre* (as Miliutin called it),[5] while it spelled the demise of the 'liberal' members of the government, Loris-Melikov, Abaza, and Miliutin, as well as of their hopes, did not put an end to irresolution at the top or to calls from below that the gap between rulers and ruled had to be narrowed. The editor of the arch-conservative *Moskovskie Vedomosti* ('Moscow Gazette'), M. N. Katkov, greeted the Manifesto of 29 April as an end to wavering and a decisive rejection of false and alien beliefs, as did the Slavophile writer and publisher Ivan Aksakov. Almost everyone else was perplexed or shocked by its harshness of tone and lack of clarity which, as Chicherin pointed out to Pobedonostsev, did little to reconcile the two worlds which faced each other in hostility or incomprehension – Petersburg officialdom and that part of society which was represented in the organs of local government. Pobedonostsev admitted that he had miscalculated and that the majority of the intelligentsia, the state servants, and even the officer corps were dismayed by the manifesto and doubted its value. 'But the simple people are satisfied', he comforted himself, although how he, shut off in the capital by paper, protocol, and a forbidding personality, could know remains a mystery. This did not keep him from speaking in the name of the *narod*, the mass of simple, untutored, and uncorrupted people who had kept their religious and dynastic faith.[6]

That mystical entity, the narod, would for forty years be invoked by defenders of the status quo to counter liberal or radical arguments, although the actual appearance of the people in politics was resisted, especially by Pobedonostsev. His indictment of the greatest of the Great Reforms shows what he thought of the people and foreshadowed the treatment they were soon to receive. Emancipation had given the peasants their freedom but left them without proper supervision 'which the dark masses require. And to make matters worse, taverns were opened everywhere, so that the poor people, left to themselves, with no one to look after them, began to drink and to idle. As a result, they fell into the hands of publicans, usurers, and Jews.'[7]

The assassination of Alexander II was the excuse, not the cause, for the illiberal policies pursued by those who felt that the reforms had been ill-advised, that they were tantamount to a revolution, that they had pushed the country onto a wrong road, and that there was now a chance to undo some of the harm that they had done.

The Slavophiles, while on the conservative side of the political spectrum in their rejection of the West and its parliaments, constitutions, and parties, were far removed, however, from Pobedonostsev's authoritarianism. It was to them another evil of the alien bureaucratism begun by Peter the Great, the perversion of a truly Russian, patriarchal monarchy. In their romantic vision of the past, tsar, nobles and peasants had once been members of a genuine national family whose harmonious balance they sought to recover. If Aksakov and his few followers, therefore, were at one with Katkov and Pobedonostsev in rejoicing over the fall of Loris-Melikov and his plans, they also helped to swell the chorus of those who believed that Russia could not be governed by a strong hand alone, that the country had to be heard and in some way involved in running its own affairs.

The Slavophiles' stance was not a political but a religious and moral one, as had been their advocacy of emancipation and judicial reform; but even they did not ignore the force of pragmatic considerations. For some Slavophiles these were strong enough to move them away from a self-contained view of national traditions that denied the relevance of Western experience. 'Let Russians enjoy the rights enjoyed by the citizens of the entire enlightened world.' Thus A. I. Koshelev expressed the uncharacteristic view in 1882 that if Russians, as did citizens in the entire enlightened world, could freely and responsibly voice their opinions and feelings, there would be neither nihilism nor many of the other ailments afflicting the Russian body politic. 'In only two European countries', he wrote, 'is arbitrary power now above the law.'[8] The institution in which the nation's 'trusted members' could express its needs and opinions was the gathering of the land, the *zemskii sobor*, idealized by the Slavophiles. Aksakov urged the convocation of this body upon the new Minister of Interior, Count N. P. Ignatev. Meeting at the time of the coronation in the old capital, Moscow, with over 2,000 elected delegates from Russia's traditional estates – nobles, merchants, clergy and at least a thousand peasants – such a gathering would dramatically demonstrate the nation's unity, its loyalty to the throne, and its superiority over all other nations.

Aksakov's Russian answer to what Koshelev recognized to be a universal yearning was as unrealistic as the revolutionaries' call for a democratic assembly. Nor would the Russian label attached to an assembly of estates insure against the risks inherent in any body which represented the country and spoke for it. If it did not speak, and remained only a colourful decoration for the coronation festivities, it could hardly justify Aksakov's hopes of nullifying 'all foreign, liberal, aristocratic, nihilistic and other such intentions'.[9]

Pobedonostsev saw risks as well as contradictions in Aksakov's ideas, and had as little use for them as for those of Loris-Melikov. The meeting of the estates would be revolution, the end of government and of Russia, he warned the tsar, and prevailed once more. In the process, Pobedonostsev also sealed the fate of Ignatev only a year after securing his appointment, because the minister had made himself the spokesman for the Slavophile 'constitutionalists'.

Ignatev's embracing of the zemskii sobor stemmed from a mixture of vanity and political romanticism. Close to the Slavophiles and their conservative populism, he thought of himself as a saviour of the fatherland, a maker and a mover of history. Yet for all his exalted notions, he showed during his year in office (May 1881 to May 1882) an awareness of the country's distemper and of the inadequacy of strong deeds. Besides his unpublicized advocacy of the zemskii sobor there was his promise on taking office to let 'elected local people' take part in the discussion of certain administrative matters. He invited two commissions of 'experienced men' (including zemstvo delegates) to advise the government on peasant affairs. Although the members of these commissions were appointed rather than elected, their very presence conceded the principle of public participation. This had been the beginning of Pobedonostsev's disenchantment with the man whom he had once praised for possessing 'Russian instincts and a Russian soul' and the admiration of the healthy part of the nation.[10] Ignatev was succeeded as minister of interior by Count Dmitrii Tolstoi, Pobedonostsev's predecessor at the Holy Synod.

The appointment of Tolstoi, who was unhappily remembered for an earlier tenure of the Ministry of Education, achieved what the Manifesto of 29 April 1881 had not: the recovery of a sense of control and direction in the administration and an end to hopes for political reform in society. With Tolstoi the new reign and the definition of its profile really began. His programme, he said, could be summed up in one word: 'Order'.[11] There was no further experimentation with consultative or advisory bodies, large or small, elected or appointed, no admission that they were desirable or necessary.

That the autocracy intended henceforth neither to ask nor to accept the help of any outside force or group was made clear when in late 1883 Tolstoi suppressed one of the strangest organizations to appear in tsarist Russia. The Holy Company (*Sviashchennaia druzhina*) was formed in March 1881 to guard the life of the new tsar and to fight the revolutionaries with some of their own weapons – conspiracy, infiltration of the enemy camp, and propaganda. Founded by a few highly placed aristocrats, bearers of some of Russia's most illustrious names, the Holy Company eventually counted about 700 'companions' in an interlocking series of secret cells and 14,000 members in an auxiliary organization, the Volunteer Guard. The exalted sponsorship of the Holy Company, which included the assistant minister of interior, was largely responsible for its toleration by the police. But its existence was also an admission of inadequacy by the regularly constituted organs of state security. Their having to accept the help of a force they had not created and did not control was enough to assure the Company's dissolution.

An elected council of 228 of the capital's substantial citizens, summoned by the prefect of St Petersburg, N. M. Baranov, to help maintain public order, was even more quickly shut down. This so-called 'Baranov Parliament' (also referred to as the 'Parliament of Sheep', in a play on the word *baran* – sheep) was another sign of the disorientation that seized official Russia after the first of March and led to frantic searches for a wider base and public role in the state's battle against the revolutionary threat.

Among the Holy Company's leaders there were men who thought that lasting safety from terror was not to be had by counterterror and advocated structural changes in government. A constitution or some form of popular representation, Count A. A. Bobrinskii believed, was the means of defence which providence itself had indicated. His fellow 'companion', Count P. P. Shuvalov, wished to make elected delegates of the propertied classes permanent members of the Council of State. Pobedonostsev, with his keen sense for the slightest hint of unorthodoxy, had been among the first to grow suspicious and by late 1882 had made up his mind that a stop must be put to the whole hazardous business. 'I am more and more convinced', he wrote to Alexander. on 23 November, 'that however great the danger to Your Majesty from evil plotters, the danger from the Company is greater still.'[12]

Tolstoi also viewed the Holy Company as a seat of 'noxious liberalism' and a nuisance.[13] If he had not closed it, it would probably not have lasted very much longer. There was little need any more for unorthodox methods to battle a revolutionary monster that turned out to be a paper tiger; protection from such a threat could safely be left in the hands of soldiers and policemen. Propaganda, the Company's other main purpose, had been difficult to produce and largely ineffective. An internal report attributed failure in this area to the fact that most writers and journalists were radicals or liberals and that there were no serious and attractive conservative publications. That state of affairs even government funds could not have remedied, for it had deeper roots than the temporary disorientation caused by the killing of an emperor.

The nature of those roots was suggested in an appeal for Christian love and forgiveness which the writer Lev Tolstoi addressed to Alexander III on behalf of his father's murderers. To apply the death penalty to revolutionaries, the great preacher of non-violence pleaded, was useless, for it was not their numbers but their ideas that counted. 'To fight them, you must meet them on the ground of ideas. Their ideal is universal well-being, equality, liberty. To combat them some other ideal must be advanced, superior to theirs, larger than theirs.'[14]

It was the lack of such an idea, of a comprehensive and affirmative faith, that afflicted the autocracy and its defenders. It robbed them of confidence in the future, made them defensive in the present, and filled them with anxiety over their ability to control and survive. Their fear, which made for rigidity, half-measures, or grudging concessions, had manifold sources, not all of them obvious.

There was, most visibly, a kind of historical pessimism, a feeling among the Pobedonostsevs, Tolstois, and Katkovs of a loss of mastery over a world that was moving too fast for their tastes and abilities. Its disintegration could, at best, be postponed but not prevented by the protective dikes they were forever erecting and repairing. There is much testimony to their despair, to loss of belief in their own cause, to premonitions of their ultimate defeat. Pobedonostsev was not the Torquemada his enemies saw. He was not a fanatic – if he had been he might have found a faith and a following – but a pessimist, perhaps even a sceptic. A friend said of him that he had not once given an indication of what he would put in place of what he anathematized.

Dmitrii Tolstoi lacked confidence that 'nihilism' and the 'Hebrew leprosy', those twin symbols of modernity, could be stamped out; at best they could be contained. The minister of education, I. D. Delianov, a friend and protégé of Pobedonostsev, told an acquaintance in 1887 that Russia stood where France had been ten years before her revolution. And Katkov, absolutism's most militant spokesman, told a circle of intimates not long after hailing the government of Alexander III as the embodiment of his ideals, that their 'party' was inferior to the liberals in boldness, discipline, and talents and was not likely ever to amount to much.[15]

Underneath the public assertions of the uniqueness and superiority of Russia, it is not difficult to detect a consciousness of her estrangement from a Europe that all these men had once admired. If that model of civilization had now moved beyond them, if Bulgarians and Serbs took their ideas and institutions from the West rather than from their Russian sponsors, if even some Slavophiles, like Koshelev, came to see as relevant for Russia the experience of the 'civilized world', then the proponents of autocracy were bound to get a heightened sense of their isolation within Russia as well as from Europe.

There was more to this than pessimism or cultural estrangement. There was also social isolation. Pobedonostsev betrayed it when he referred to himself in his ideological loneliness as the last of the Mohicans; Katkov confessed to it when he said that he saw little hope for the future in any stratum of Russian society. Attempts to portray Alexander III as the 'peasant tsar' testify to it, as does the simultaneous and slightly more realistic wooing of the landed gentry. The official ideology's poverty, its lack of self-confidence and resonance, stem in part from the regime's lack of a social basis, from its failure to identify itself with a vital social or historical force from which it could have drawn political and moral justification.

Even if the autocracy had found a social grouping or class strong enough to be of help and weak enough to pose no threat, it would have been difficult to embrace as an ally. Tsarism had become the prisoner of its own rhetoric. It wanted to appear as a government of all the people, above class and party, and was left without solid support anywhere. Ironically, what the monarchy feared most might have contributed most to its survival – albeit in a changed form. Political debate and organizations, if permitted before the trauma of revolution, could conceivably have led to the emergence of autonomous political forces on which the state might have leaned, which it could have played off against each other, among which it could have found allies or scapegoats for public hostility. Imperial Russia suffered from a scarcity of political resources to help enlist society for the enormous tasks ahead. Without social cohesion or a unifying ideology, civil and political liberties and some degree of political participation, for all the risks they posed, were necessary to clarify the nation's goals and gain acceptance for them.

To immobilize a few revolutionary terrorists who had as yet no mass following or substantial organization was relatively easy. But this would neither prevent the appearance of new groups of revolutionary activists nor evoke the creative collaboration and positive loyalty the regime needed to solve the country's many problems and to keep its opponents from winning the allegiance it was losing. Acute nihilism, an observer of the post-1881 period noted, had decreased. 'The number of firebrands who are ready to sacrifice themselves in perpetrating criminal acts has become smaller, but the mass of the discontented . . . constantly increases.'[16]

The calm which settled over public life when the government of Alexander III finally embarked on its reactionary course did not stop the erosion of its moral and political authority. This process continued into the next reign and into the years following the Revolution of 1905. All the institutional changes it brought are less of a watershed, therefore, than would at first appear. The years before 1905 are the more important ones in our story, for it was then that the patterns of distrust and contention that divided government and society were laid down.

All of which is another way of saying that Russia's was a crisis of authority; it had many causes but manifested itself in a waning of respect for established rules and those who enforced them. While there was no inevitability about the outcome of the crisis, there is much evidence that the actions which Russia's leaders took or failed to take narrowed their options and hardened lines of confrontation, with a loss of flexibility on all sides. Perhaps the old regime's rigidity, its lack of boldness, its reluctance to experiment were born of a more realistic appraisal than its critics made of the limits imposed by the country's poverty and backwardness and by concerns for its survival. If that was so, there was all the more reason for Russia's leaders to take the country into their confidence – and to win it. And if it was to be done without a basic transformation of political institutions, then Russia's prospects depended even more on the quality of her government and the men who staffed it.

REFERENCES

1. Leonard Schapiro, *Rationalism and Nationalism in Russian Nineteenth-Century Thought* (New Haven, Conn., and London, 1967), p. 126.
2. D. A. Miliutin, *Dnevnik*, IV (Moscow, 1950), p. 57.
3. L. A. Tikhomirov, *Konstitutionalisty v epokhu 1881 goda* (St Petersburg, 1895), p. 87.
4. B. N. Chicherin, *Vospominaniia: Zemstvo i Moskovskaia Duma* (Moscow, 1934), pp. 120–32.
5. Miliutin, op. cit., p. 63.
6. R. F. Byrnes, *Pobedonostsev* (Bloomington, Ind., 1968), pp. 139–64.
7. E. A. Perets, *Dnevnik E. A. Peretsa, gosudarstvennogo sekretaria (1880–1883)* (Moscow-Leningrad, 1927), p. 39.
8. A. I. Koshelev, *Chto zhe teper? Avgust 1882* (Berlin, 1882), p. 34.
9. Stephen Lukashevich, *Ivan Aksakov* (Cambridge, Mass., 1965), p. 155.
10. Byrnes, op. cit., p. 151.
11. H. L. von Schweinitz, *Denkwürdigkeiten* (Berlin, 1927), II, 203.
12. *Pis'ma K. P. Pobedonostseva k Aleksandru III* (Moscow, 1925–26), I, 396.
13. Stephen Lukashevich, 'The Holy Brotherhood: 1881–1883', *American Slavic and East European Review* 18 (Dec. 1959), pp. 491–509.
14 Henri Troyat, *Tolstoy*, trans. N. Amphoux (Garden City, NY, 1967), p. 405.
15. J. F. Baddeley, *Russia in the Eighties* (London, 1921), pp. 184–90; Hans Rogger, 'Reflections on Russian Conservatism' *Jahrbücher für Geschichte Osteuropas* 14 (June 1966), pp. 195–212; Richard Graf von Pfeil, *Neun Jahre in russischen Diensten unter Kaiser Alexander III.* (Leipzig, 1907), p. 209.
16. Hermann von Samson-Himmelstjierna, *Russia under Alexander III*, trans. J. Morrison (London, 1893), pp. 63–4.

Tsar, autocrat, and emperor

Russian autocracy was not an ancient despotism in which neither law nor custom protected persons and property from a totally arbitrary authority. And compared with the murderous excesses of twentieth-century totalitarianism, pre-revolutionary Russia looks tolerant, even idyllic. After Stalin and Hitler, it appears remarkable that only the five regicide conspirators of 1881 were hanged and that many more of their comrades of 'The People's Will' were merely imprisoned or exiled. Some, like Vera Figner, survived to become heroes to a new generation of revolutionaries or to rejoin the battle against autocracy.

That Russians measured their government by the standards of a less cruel age is but one reason why so many of them found it oppressive, capricious, or unresponsive. They also compared it unfavourably with what they knew of law and politics in the West where the participation of solid citizens in public life was tolerated or encouraged. A Russian professional or landed proprietor who felt as civilized as any European, could hardly be flattered on learning that at the accession of Nicholas II, Turkey, Montenegro, and Russia were the only European countries without a parliament. He could, moreover, judge his government by rules it had laid down for itself.

The Fundamental Laws of 1832 proclaimed: 'The Russian Empire is ruled on the firm basis of positive laws and statutes which emanate from the Autocratic Power.' There was, then, a standard by which to gauge the legality of its acts, especially since the Council of State, established in 1810, had to review all legislation originating in the administration before it was submitted for the emperor's approval. That Alexander I as well as Alexander III confirmed the minority view in one third of the decisions on which the Council was divided illustrates that the monarch was supreme over institutions as well as laws. His supremacy was anchored in the first article of the Code of Laws which set forth the unlimited authority of the autocratic sovereign. It was further buttressed by the fact that until 1906 an imperial decree (*imennoi ukaz*) as well as commands and verbal instructions had the force of law.

Independent courts and judges introduced in 1864 restricted monarchical and administrative interference in the processes of justice and widened the area of the citizens' security beyond the protection they already enjoyed from arbitrary taxation, state interference in family affairs, and the deprivation of life, honour, noble status and privileges. But in many areas of public life – including the courts, when the security of the state was felt to be at stake – the monarch's will was law, as were the dispositions of those who acted in his name.

Observance of legality depended ultimately on the will and intentions of the tsar and his agents. If this made Russia's a government of men rather than laws, it was pre-eminently the government of one man. Even the new Fundamental Laws of 1906, which gave the people's representatives an equal share with the sovereign in the making of laws, left to him alone the right to initiate changes in the constitutional order. His power as head of state, its administration and armed forces, was great also because the state controlled, or was involved with, the Church and education, industry and transport, local government, public health and welfare. Before 1906, and to a considerable degree after that year, the emperor's political preferences and prejudices, his qualities of mind and character, the appointments he made and the advice he took, the information he received and how he acted upon it, were key elements of Russian life.

Alexander III (1881–94) and his son Nicholas II (1894–1917) held to their ancestors' personal and paternalistic conception of their office and duties. They felt confirmed in that style of rule by the fact that most of their subjects had but recently emerged from serfdom and were sullenly resentful over past and present injustices. The task of controlling and organizing this often recalcitrant mass for defence and development had in their view to be concentrated in a few hands. Society, its vocal segments felt, had since the Great Reforms acquired abilities and institutions for 'self-activity' that made superfluous the preponderance of the autocratic state in the life of the nation. There were, as yet, few calls for its abolition. But there was growing resentment when autocracy treated even loyal and distinguished citizens like troublesome children. Such treatment – for example the removal of Chicherin as mayor of Moscow for the mildest of criticisms – raised doubts about the wisdom of unchecked power and its ability to distinguish between revolutionary challengers and loyal critics.

In the reign of Alexander III, external peace and internal quiet temporarily obscured the widening gap between the pretensions of autocracy and its performance, as did certain personal qualities of the ruler which appeared to conform well with the autocratic idea. Alexander subscribed to Pobedonostsev's dictum that 'the whole secret of Russia's order and prosperity is in the top, in the person of the supreme authority',[1] and he disapproved of those of his father's acts (including the liaison with Princess Dolgorukaia) that in his view diminished the monarchy's esteem and strength. Intellectually unadventurous and ill-equipped, he was not disposed to experiment with new governmental arrangements, a disposition which his father's inconsistency and fate, his mentor's teachings, and the confusion of the first year of his reign had reinforced. If they thought his mind ordinary, there were, none the less, contemporaries who respected Alexander. They saw in him sufficient strength and stature to vindicate the system, to prolong its lease of life, and to supply the impetus for its advance in power and prosperity. They described him as a man of noble aspirations and sincere religiosity, honest, upright, and thrifty, true to his beliefs and to the men who served him. His minister of finance, Sergei Witte, admired him for upholding the historical force which was alone capable in Russian conditions of mustering the energies and resources necessary for economic modernization. Yet by praising Alexander's steady commitment to that goal in order to point up the shortcomings of his son, Witte also made clear the defects of a system which left so much to the chance of heredity and personality.

If Nicholas was weak-willed and devious, if he had so little confidence in his own judgement that he distrusted his ministers and failed to back them up, was this not as much an indictment of autocracy as of the autocrat? Many Russians, including Witte, came to think so. No individual, however well-equipped or motivated, could alone bear the responsibility for governing a vast empire. Yet there would be no prime minister or cabinet with sufficient power or prestige to pose even an implicit challenge to a central tenet of autocracy: that the tsar cannot divest himself of ultimate authority, that he alone can know his people's needs and be the just arbiter of their concerns.

Neither Nicholas nor Alexander was well trained for a difficult and arduous job. Nor was the father so much superior to the son in character or abilities as to justify the hopes of admirers that, had he lived longer, so would the monarchy have. In both cases institutional and personal shortcomings combined to reveal autocracy's flaws even to those who thought that it was still needed to supply leadership, unity, and stability.

The impression of strength and self-confidence Alexander conveyed derived in large part from stubbornness, a massive physique, and brusque manner. When his minister of war likened the emperor to Peter the Great with his cudgel, a friend retorted that he was only the cudgel without the great Peter.[2] Although his generalship in the Russo-Turkish war of 1877/78 had not been distinguished, Alexander, like all the male Romanovs, had an absorbing interest in military matters, especially in uniforms, which he changed to a more 'Russian' look.

Thirty-six years old on his accession, he had in 1866 married a Danish princess, the fiancée of his older brother who had died a year earlier. This brother, a man of charm, had been his father's favourite, and as heir apparent had received a better education than Alexander. Until his twentieth year the future tsar's training had been casual. Lectures by Sergei Solovev in history and Pobedonostsev in law fortified his patriotism and conservatism but did little to expand his knowledge of Russian life and thought. After a year he received his teachers only irregularly. Although introduced to various branches of the higher administration, his participation in their work was neither systematic nor prominent.

Alexander was more inclined to physical than to mental exercise and preferred conviviality to sustained discussion of affairs of state. An adjutant and drinking companion called him 'a very simple and a very good child with little regard for the opinions and feelings of others'.[3] 'He is more and more becoming the autocrat,' Count V. N. Lamzdorf, an official of the Foreign Ministry wrote in 1889, noting that he seemed also to be developing a dangerous sense of his own infallibility. Lamzdorf attributed the emperor's 'drunkenness with power' to the absence in his entourage of men with enough courage and independence to speak the truth. The imperial couple, he complained, disliked serious conversation with educated and well-bred people. 'They prefer commonplaces, anecdotes, banter.' Even Pobedonostsev once deplored Alexander's habit of simply giving orders without consultation or discussion.[4]

Other courtiers and functionaries discovered that their chivalrous tsar could be ungrateful, meddlesome, small-minded and less than straightforward. Chicherin believed that the habit of unquestioned command inherent in absolutism had combined with the tsar's native coarseness to make him such a hard master. But he saw this hardness as being without larger purpose, such as Peter the Great had had; autocracy was becoming confused with the ruler's personal prejudices and prerogatives, and serving limited or petty aims.[5]

Viewed in his own right, not measured against his ill-fated son, Alexander does not look quite so formidable. Witte admired him for his firm support of industrialization and Witte's biographer called him the last Romanov to make his will felt throughout the government.[6] Yet Witte, becoming minister of finance in 1892, had that support for only the last two years of Alexander's life. If he had ruled as long as his son, twenty-two years instead of thirteen, if he too had been bedevilled by wars and revolutions, he too might have revealed deficiencies of character and intellect that were obvious to astute and close observers. The Grand Duke Mikhail Nikolaevich, Alexander's uncle and President of the Council of State, had a simple summary of that body's proceedings prepared for his nephew since he doubted the latter's patience and penetration. A German diplomat thought that the emperor was poor in ideas and held tightly to those he had because he was very uncertain of himself.

There is much to make one wonder whether he was superior to Nicholas in the comprehension and handling of vital issues: his unthinking anti-Semitism; his denigration of all that he disliked in art or politics as dishonest or vicious; his reluctance, at first, to admit that the famine of 1891 was more than a local crop failure exaggerated by meddlesome persons; his temperamental conduct during the Bulgarian imbroglio of 1885–6, when he ignored the advice of his foreign minister, complicated relations with Germany and Austria, and out of personal pique opposed a pro-Russian prince only to see him replaced by an unfriendly one on the Bulgarian throne.

Nicholas was not lacking in firmness or, depending on one's view, obstinacy. Where the father appeared to some to be strong, direct and certain, the son was said to be weak, shifty, and faltering. Yet when it came to the integrity of his power or the defence of cherished prejudices, this slight young man – he was twenty-six on his accession in 1894 – with the shy smile and the gentle eyes, could be as determined as his bear of a father. The problem was rather an excess than a want of firmness; more precisely, an inability to distinguish between flexibility and weakness, strength and mulishness.

Even more poorly prepared than his father for the burdens of kingship, Nicholas had no knowledge of the world or of men, of politics or government, to help him make the difficult and weighty decisions that in the Russian system the tsar alone must make. His training was adequate only for the one role he would not play – the ceremonial one of constitutional monarch. The only lodestars he recognized were an inherited belief in the moral rightness and historical necessity of autocracy, and a religious faith, bordering on fatalism, that he was in God's hands and his actions divinely inspired. Such exalted notions were bound to have an unsettling effect on an unformed mind and character.

Except to a few intimates aware of his intellectual and emotional immaturity – a state prolonged by isolation from serious studies or real work – Nicholas was an unknown quantity at his accession. As always when there was a new tsar, there was new hope and speculation. Hope sprang from the belief that the tranquillity of the last reign made possible the resumption of reforms; speculation centred on the likelihood of the young tsar's departing from his father's rigidities. A famous liberal hailed Nicholas as the source of 'all our hope, all our faith in the future'.[7] A more realistic contemporary said: 'We do not know whether we are on the eve of reforms, of reactionary measures, or of a regime of no principles.'[8] The answer was not long in coming.

At a reception in January 1895 for delegates from zemstvo, town, and nobility assemblies who had come to offer their good wishes, Nicholas thanked his visitors for their expressions of loyalty and the sincerity of their sentiments, and read them a small lecture on autocracy as he understood it. Referring to the voices that had asked for the right to tell the government of the people's needs and thoughts, Nicholas dismissed them as 'the senseless dream of participation by zemstvo representatives in affairs of internal administration. Let all know that I . . . shall safeguard the principles of autocracy as firmly and unswervingly as did my late, unforgettable father.'[9] So sharp a reaction to a modest proposal had a chilling effect. No matter how it was interpreted – as a slip of the tongue (Nicholas had meant to say unrealizable instead of senseless); as the work of Pobedonostsev; as an overreaction to what had been an indirect call for a constitution by only one zemstvo – the rebuke was taken to be an indication of deeply held feelings.

Nicholas had not reflected on the consequences of his step. Such disregard for political considerations remained a feature of his rule. The result was that within less than a decade the prestige of the autocrat who would not listen had been critically damaged; and with it that of the autocracy. Petr Struve, a future leader of liberalism, predicted as much in an open letter to Nicholas which called his remarks a challenge issued to Russian society as a whole. An autocracy, he warned, that rested on bureaucratic omnipotence and public silence was digging its own grave.[10]

All that an incurious Nicholas saw, all that it was arranged for him to see, all that a sovereign shielded by ceremony and security could see, confirmed his prejudices. A simple man himself, he was convinced until the very end that the simple people were on his side and that this made him the best judge of the country's mood. Protest and dissent were temporary aberrations, traceable to agitators, Jews, or selfish politicians. Typical of his inclination to wishful thinking was the conclusion he drew from the cordial reception he was given in France in 1900. Delighted by the warmth with which the crowds had greeted the head of an allied power, he expressed the opinion that they would some day restore their monarchy. When his minister of interior told him in late 1904 of the need for an elected national representation, he retorted that all that was wanted in government was good people.

Even after the Revolution of 1905 had wrung from him a popularly elected legislature, the Duma, Nicholas tried to narrow its sphere of competence. He never was reconciled to the idea of representative government, limited as its Russian version was, and by repeated displays of regret over what he had granted raised doubts of his sincerity. He told a German visitor that the Duma was a useful place for letting off steam, that it might even have a role to play in examining legislation and advising on it, but that the decisions were his. 'There can be no other system with half developed nations; a crowd wants a firm and rough hand over it . . . I am the master here.'[11] And again, in 1909, to the assistant minister of war: 'I created the Duma so that it would advise, not order, me.'[12]

Such talk, while it expressed genuine sentiments, need not all be taken at face value. Some of it was swagger, not meant for public or home consumption. But there was enough substance and echo to it to influence all but the most independent-minded members of the government in their attitudes to the Duma and the country. A return to the pre-1905 situation was, however, impossible; for that, strength and determination were lacking, so that the main effect of the emperor's remarks was to give heart to a few right-wing politicians and to irritate nearly everyone else. He lacked courage and support to reverse what he had come to consider a mistake and the wisdom to live with it gracefully.

In 1913 Nicholas went so far as to consider taking all legislative rights from the Duma, making it purely advisory, and returning to 'the former peaceful course of lawmaking . . . in accordance with the Russian tradition'.[13] A minister who was sympathetic to the emperor's plan convinced him of its risks. Only a day before his abdication in 1917 he explained his refusal to heed the Duma's call for a ministry of public confidence by saying that he distrusted profoundly the abilities, intelligence, and integrity of people who were said to enjoy the confidence of the public.[14] He may have been right to reject popularity as a proof of excellence. But he had no reason to trust people simply because he, rather than the Duma or the electors, had chosen them — and, in fact, he did not.

Nicholas brought nothing to the job of kingship that would help to explain why the regime survived as long as it did and functioned as well as it did. The empire's last head was without virtues or talents commensurate with his role. If he had virtues, they were minor or private ones. He was a conscientious and industrious monarch in the first half of his reign, sitting for long hours over reports and papers of state, annotating them and issuing instructions on a host of matters. One must question whether such devotion to his duties was a virtue in view of the insignificance of the matters that occupied much of the emperor's time, while issues of high policy went unattended, except at moments of crisis. Sustained deliberations of plans and policies with the tsar's participation were rare. The attention Nicholas paid to the minutiae, to the routine and rituals of his office, looks more like an avoidance than a meeting of problems.

The role the sovereign played as chief clerk of his empire had long been cause for concern among men who were close to the throne. Ministers of Alexander II had sought permission to submit only major questions to the emperor who refused to let anyone else determine what was major or minor and, like his successors, was burdened by a mass of petty business. He approved the leave requests of imperial pages and the assignments of grenadiers to guard his palace. Loris-Melikov suggested to Alexander III that the Council of Ministers relieve the emperor of such tasks as the appointment of provincial midwives and present for his decision only what ministers had agreed to be of sufficient importance. Loris-Melikov failed, and Nicholas was still required to approve a supplemental appropriation for repairs at an agricultural training school. The examples cited are extreme, but they do not distort the reality of a situation in which the sovereign 'ruled and administered'[15] and final decisions were his.

Since he was unable to decide everything and was faced by intractable problems, Nicholas's industry flagged and became more fitful. Yet he never made a formal or systematic delegation of his authority. This led in the last years of his reign to a near-paralysis of initiative at the centre. Not himself an expert in anything and reluctant to take informed advice which clashed with his preferences, Nicholas increasingly let things slide or simply threw up his hands in resignation. The ruler as clerk gave way to the ruler as gentleman or family man, the political amateur who disdained trying to find his way through the discord and contention that had grown up around him and to which he reacted with distaste and removal, psychological as well as physical.

There were ever more frequent diary entries of yachting trips, of hunting and hiking, of swimming and tennis, of picnics and picture taking, of long stays in the Crimea which were escapes from St Petersburg. Although his chief minister thought the emperor's presence was needed in the capital, Nicholas found its atmosphere, its scandals, its press and politicians unbearable. 'You probably envy me,' he told V. N. Kokovtsov in early 1912, 'but I not only do not envy you, I simply pity you, that you are staying in this swamp.'[16] In the midst of the First World War he almost boasted of his ignorance of economics, as if a basic understanding of scarcity and its effects were below his dignity. 'It is the most perplexing problem with which I have ever had to deal. I was never a businessman and haven't the least understanding of these questions of supplies and provisions.'[17] His father had once said something like it to a minister who talked to him about the exchange rate of the ruble. Nicholas's assumption of personal command over the armies in the field in

1915 may have been a flight from complexity rather than an act of sacrifice or solidarity with the troops. When he returned for the last time to army headquarters from the capital in early 1917, he was homesick for his children, played solitaire and dominoes, and wrote in his diary: 'My head is resting here – no ministers, no wearisome questions to trouble one.'[18]

The family which claimed so much of Nicholas's time, monopolized his affections, and showed him at his most attractive, consisted of his German-born English-bred wife Alexandra, four daughters, and a son. It was a close-knit family whose members delighted in each other's company and in simple pleasures. The happiness of the imperial couple, who were married just after the bridegroom became tsar, was clouded by the young empress's failure to produce an heir, the strain this put on her high-strung temperament, and by the tragedy which befell them when after ten years of prayers a male child was finally born.

The boy, named Aleksei, turned out to be a bleeder, the sufferer of an incurable and painful disease, haemophilia, transmitted by the mother, in which the blood clots slowly, haemorrhaging is difficult to control, and death may follow after injuries or operations. After medical men had failed them, the distraught parents turned to a self-proclaimed holy man, the peasant Grigorii Rasputin. Rasputin, while he did not cure Aleksei, was able to mitigate his suffering and to cheer the child and his parents. Whether his success was attributable to coincidence (that is, to the normal cessation of bleeding at or shortly after Rasputin's appearance), to quasi-hypnotic powers, or simply to the roughly affectionate way in which he distracted the child, must remain a matter of conjecture. The parents, especially the mother, were grateful.

Proximity to the court opened doors and opportunities for Rasputin in the church, in society, and, it was believed, in government. His name became a byword for intrigue and sinister influences in high places. Hinting that they were closer than in fact they were, Rasputin made use of his connections to win favours for friends and an expansive style of life for himself. But those who thought him the real power behind the throne were wrong. Although the religious intoxication and mystical mood of the empress made her increasingly receptive to the 'man of God's' oracular advice, especially during the difficult days of the First World War, Nicholas was capable of resisting it. Nor was Rasputin's counsel inspired by larger aims or organized interests, such as a separate peace with Germany or a reactionary clique at home. His person and activities were, in any case, unsavoury enough to reduce still further the country's respect for its monarchs; he cannot, however, be made to bear a major share of responsibility for their unhappy end.

Rasputin, Nicholas's fatalism and vagueness, Alexandra's hysteria, become easier to understand against the background of a child's affliction. But sympathy cannot change the historical judgement of the parents' political immaturity and of their failure to draw the necessary conclusions from their terrible predicament. Because it was a near certainty that Aleksei would die at an early age and an absolute certainty that he could never be an active and energetic ruler, his parents should have given serious thought to the abandonment of a form of government which made no sense without a real autocrat. Nicholas and Alexandra lacked the good sense to protect Russia *and* their son by shedding the power and lessening the burdens they wished to bequeath to him undiminished.

'For Baby's sake', Alexandra wrote in 1916, 'we must be firm as otherwise his inheritance will be awful, as with his character he won't bow down to others but [will] be his own master, as one must in Russia whilst people are still so uneducated.'[19] When she kept exhorting Nicholas to be terrible like Ivan and great like Peter; when, like him, she dismissed the oppositional mood of the capitals as exceptions on the map of an otherwise devoted fatherland; when she told her husband at the front that she was fighting at home for his throne and Baby's future – Alexandra demonstrated by her fantasies as Nicholas had demonstrated by his physical removal, their own and the monarchy's isolation from the real world.

Long before Aleksei had made obvious the unworkability of autocracy by his physical disability, Nicholas had done so by his failings. 'There no longer is an autocracy in Russia,' a respected latter-day Slavophile had exclaimed shortly after the beginning of the reign.[20] His poor impression of the new tsar soon came to be widely shared. In the salons of St Petersburg the witticism circulated that Russia did not need a constitution to limit the monarchy since she already had a limited monarch.[21] Even when there was a strong ruler and no Rasputin, there were doubts of the effectiveness of the system. A high official asked in 1888: 'Where is the autocracy? I see no autocracy, I see only administrative anarchy. Each department usurps some of the autocratic power. Ministers . . . make war upon each other or make peace. All that I see; but the autocracy – where is that?'[22]

That autocracy was not a fact, perhaps could not be, made reluctant liberals or constitutionalists of many conservative or apolitical Russians. Prince Sergei Trubetskoi, a highly regarded philosopher and critic of the radical intelligentsia, wrote in 1900:

There is an autocracy of policemen and land captains, of governors, department heads, and ministers. A unitary, tsarist autocracy in the proper sense of the word does not and cannot exist. A tsar, who in the present state of governmental and economic life can know of . . . the needs of the people, of the condition of the country and the different branches of state administration only what it is considered impossible to conceal from him; a tsar who learns of the country only what can reach him through a complicated system of bureaucratic filters, is limited in his power more fundamentally than a monarch informed about his country's needs by its elected representatives.[23]

Neither in the case of Alexander III nor in that of Nicholas II was the conscientious industry of the sovereign an adequate substitute for what an unfettered public opinion or a genuinely representative body might have told him. Nor was either man an effective coordinator of the machinery of state with its many and often clashing parts. In that role, as chief executive, arbiter, and leader of his government, the autocrat, it could be argued, might have been more useful than as clerk, figurehead, or leader of men in battle. Does not every political system, every large public or private enterprise, require the managerial and executive talents that are loosely described as 'leadership' and rarely the product of specialized training or expertise? Why should not a tsar supply such leadership as well as a president or prime minister? Was autocratic monarchy intrinsically incompatible with the character and needs of a modern state and a modernizing society?

In the Russia of the turn of the century the answer must, for many reasons, be 'yes', the most basic one being the principle of hereditary succession, for it conflicts most directly with the tests of ability, popularity, and performance which are employed to select and judge the non-hereditary leader. Even if Nicholas, equipped with better genes and better training, had met these tests, his son could never have done so. No solution was ever proposed for the problem which was a pressing one in the reign of Nicholas and would have become pressing in that of Aleksei; how to modify a system to whose successful operation the leadership of the monarch was essential when he not only failed to supply that leadership but was the single most important obstacle to its assumption by others.

A modification of autocracy which could have solved that problem would have been tantamount to its abolition. The fact that the word 'unlimited' was struck from the imperial title after 1905, while 'Autocrat' was retained along with sole executive and other wide powers for the emperor, illustrates the dilemma faced by all whom habit, fear, or loyalty kept from admitting that effective leadership and autocracy were indeed incompatible. Proponents of autocracy who clamoured loudly for its retention and, after 1905, for its restoration – while conceding privately that with Nicholas their cause was lost – should, for the sake of consistency or patriotism, have wished either for a parliamentary government or for a *coup d'état*.

Only in late 1916 could a few generals and politicians bring themselves to think of removing Nicholas and making his brother, the Grand Duke Michael, regent for Aleksei. Their thought was carried out by other, and rougher, hands – the striking workers and mutinous soldiers of Petrograd. When it fell in February 1917, tsarism found few defenders and Nicholas abdicated for himself and for his son. Six months later, his chief of staff, General M. V Alekseev, told a liberal politician – who had wanted for the sake of legitimacy and national unity to preserve the dynasty with Michael as its head – that he was against the monarchy because he knew it so well.[24]

In view of this, its longevity is baffling. What can account for such resilience in the face of criticism, indifference or disaffection? A complex of deeply rooted traditions and feelings is part of the answer, as are more tangible interests whose satisfaction depended upon survival of the old regime. There was also the progressive, modernizing role the monarchy had played in the past and, it was hoped, would play again. Relatively efficient instruments of control and repression also played their part, along with the political immaturity or apathy of the peasant majority of the nation which cared less for forms of government than for the satisfaction of its material needs. At the same time it was these dark untutored masses – whether settled on the land or becoming proletarians in the cities – who kept a large proportion of the country's educated and privileged classes loyal to the regime for a surprisingly long time.

Their loyalty was not given freely or generously; it was inspired by fear of what the masses in their resentment over centuries of injustice might do if the restraints of habitual obedience and deference were lifted. The tsar – the mystical unity of his person and office – was thought to be the linchpin of the system, and willingness to contemplate his removal and the social upheaval which was expected to follow from it divided revolutionaries and radicals from moderate liberals and liberal conservatives who wished, in Chicherin's phrase, for 'liberal reforms *and* a strong state authority', that is, for a gradual extension of political rights to 'society' (*obshchestvo*) while the masses were either being educated for citizenship or kept away from it.

Russia's upper classes had a strong sense of being a thin layer of privilege, education, and civilization resting insecurely on a volcano of mass grievance, resentment, coarseness, and ignorance. More than once that volcano had erupted and the fury of serf and peasant had turned against friend and enemy alike, against that small percentage of the nation which did not toil in its fields or factories, paid a disproportionately low share of its taxes, and enjoyed most of its benefits – education, preferment in civil and military service, social distinctions, and the state's financial assistance in agriculture and industry. The fears induced by the peasant risings of Razin in the seventeenth century and Pugachev in the eighteenth were kept alive by repeated outbursts of violence against landlords, Jews, or factory owners and by agrarian disorders which, as happened before and during the Revolution of 1905, could seize whole regions.

That much of the landowning nobility, mindful of the legacy of serfdom and isolated in a sea of peasants, should have clung to the autocracy for protection from such a threat is not surprising. That the country's industrialists, recipients of the state's benefactions, did so to keep the workers in check is also understandable, although they were at the same time resentful of the government's tutelage over economic and political life. But what must come as something of a surprise is the recognition by part of the professional and intellectual classes, including, after 1905, some of the critical intelligentsia, that they too had been protected by the autocracy. When the intellectual historian M. O. Gershenzon wrote sadly in 1909 that only the 'prisons and bayonets' of the state still stood between the intelligentsia and the popular wrath,[25] he anticipated the industrialist A. I. Putilov who knew in 1915 that the days of tsarism were, deservedly, numbered yet feared the anarchy which would follow. 'The times of Pugachev will return, and perhaps it will be even worse than that.'[26]

Autocracy, the creator of national unity and greatness, was seen by many as the barrier to national and social disintegration, the only focus for a common loyalty in a multi-national state, and the only agency for enforcing that loyalty if it should not be given freely. Whether they were conscious or not, fears of anarchy and a massive social upheaval that would sweep away all of

Russia's hard-won cultural achievements and her status as a great power along with the autocracy, helped to prolong its life beyond what appears to have been its natural term. What made autocracy vulnerable also helped to ease its disappearance – its intimate identification with the person of the autocratic monarch. When Nicholas abdicated his throne under pressure, the system collapsed, regretted by few and defended by none.

The liberal lawyer and politician V. A. Maklakov (born, like Lenin, in 1870) was to write in his memoirs 'for my generation the problem of autocracy stood at the centre of political thought.'[27] In the years leading up to 1905 this was eminently true; in those that followed it was less true. As an intellectual problem autocracy was then no longer a preoccupation of political thought. But autocracy as a problem of practical politics, autocracy as an institution or synonym for the powers which the emperor retained and how he used them, troubled Russian political life until February 1917 to an excessive and quite unnecessary degree. Russia's real problems lay elsewhere; their solution was made more difficult by the emphasis autocracy's head and defenders put upon its prerogatives and duties. Their exercise, especially when they violated the civil liberties and political rights granted in 1905 and 1906, was used by the revolutionaries to justify their own illegal acts and excesses.

Autocracy's moderation or modification, or even its disappearance if it had not taken place in the midst of foreign defeat and domestic turmoil, could hardly have created greater complications than those which its remaining claims and powers caused and left behind. The deep distrust of all state authority; the contempt for that side of politics which is the search for accommodation and compromise; the widespread lack of administrative experience in the population, coupled with a weak and brief tradition of self-government, autonomy, and diversity in public life; the absence of leaders and social institutions sufficiently independent and popular to mediate the conflicts between classes and between state and society, or to uphold the former when it crumbled under internal and external blows – all this was part of the legacy of autocracy and contributed as much to the failure of the Provisional Government that replaced it as did the attacks of Germans and Bolsheviks.

REFERENCES

1. A. E. Adams, 'Pobedonostsev and the Rule of Firmness', *Slavonic and East European Review* 32 (Dec. 1953), p. 134.
2. V. N. Lamzdorf, *Dnevnik, 1891–1892* (Moscow, 1934), p. 342.
3. Karl Stählin, *Geschichte Russlands* (Königsberg and Berlin, 1939), IV/1, p. 539.
4. V. N. Lamzdorf, *Dnevnik, 1886–1890* (Moscow, 1926), pp. 230–1; A. A. Polovtsov, *Dnevnik gosudarstvennogo sekretaria A.A. Polovtsova* (Moscow, 1966), I, p. 376; II, pp. 191, 246.
5. B. N. Chicherin, *Vospominaniia: Zemstvo i Moskovskaia Duma* (Moscow, 1934), p. 299.
6. T. H. Von Laue, *Sergei Witte and the Industrialization of Russia* (New York, 1963), p. 68.

7. G. V. Adamovich, *Maklakov: Politik, Iurist, Chelovek* (Paris, 1959), p. 40.
8. Thomas Riha, *A Russian European: Paul Miliukov in Russian Politics* (Notre Dame, Ind., and London, 1969), p. 26.
9. H. Seton-Watson, *The Russian Empire 1801–1917* (Oxford, 1967), p. 549; A. V. Bogdanovich, *Tri poslednikh samoderzhtsa. Dnevnik* (Leningrad, 1924), p. 189.
10. R. E. Pipes, *Struve. Liberal on the Left, 1870–1905* (Cambridge, Mass., 1970), p 125.
11. Ernst Seraphim, *Russische Porträts* (Zürich-Leipzig-Vienna, 1943), I, p. 250.
12. A. A. Polivanov, *Iz dnevnikov i vospominanii . . . 1907–1914* (Moscow, 1924), p. 69.
13. V. P. Semevskii, (ed.), *Monarkhiia pered krusheniem* (Moscow-Leningrad, 1927), p. 92; *Padenie tsarskogo rezhima* (Leningrad, 1924–27), IV, pp. 195–6.
14. George Katkov, *Russia 1917. The February Revolution* (New York, 1967), p. 356.
15. V. A. Maklakov, *Vtoraia Duma* (Paris, 1947), p. 76.
16. V. N. Kokovtsov, *Out of My Past. The Memoirs of Count Kokovtsov*, trans. L. Matveev (Stanford, Cal., and London, 1935), p. 304.
17. Stählin, op. cit.; IV/2, p. 1101.
18. Ibid., pp. 1123–4.
19. Bernard Pares (ed), *The Letters of the Tsaritsa to the Tsar* (London, 1923), p. 305.
20. S. Ia. Elpatevskii, *Vospominaniia* (Leningrad, 1929), p 264.
21. Bogdanovich, op. cit., p. 299.
22. W T. Stead, *Truth About Russia* (London and New York, 1888), pp. 199–200.
23. O. N. Trubetskaia, *Kniaz S. N. Trubetskoi* (New York, 1953), p. 38.
24. V. A. Maklakov, Introduction to *La chute du régime tsariste* (Paris, 1927), p. 86.
25. Boris Shragin and Albert Todd (eds), *Landmarks. A Collection of Essays on the Russian Intelligentsia. 1909*, trans. M. Schwartz (New York, 1977), p. 81.
26. Maurice Paléologue, *An Ambassador's Memoirs*, trans. F. A. Holt (London and New York, 1923–25), III, pp. 349–50.
27. V. A. Maklakov, *Vlast i obshchestvennost na zakate staroi Rossii* (Paris, 1936), pp. 10–11.

CHAPTER THREE

Corridors of power: the tsar's ministers

'What is the use of your new ministerial institutions? Why do you write laws', the historian N. M. Karamzin asked Alexander I in 1811. 'Men, not documents, govern.' This dictum became a central tenet of Russian governmental conservatism. Its emphasis on men rather than the machinery of state (or laws to regulate its personnel and operation), was the logical extension of a highly personal, centralized system of rule. Seek men, Karamzin exhorted the ruler: fifty wise and conscientious governors will accomplish more than councils or regulations. Pobedonostsev told an acquaintance that it was necessary only that the sovereign be firm and good and that he have a knowledge of men.[1]

When his former pupil became tsar in 1881, the essence of the copious advice Pobedonostsev gave was contained in the admonition 'Cherchez des capables!' 'Institutions are of no importance,' he repeated in 1884. 'Everything depends on individuals.' This first rule of government he imparted to Nicholas II, who learned it well. In the midst of revolution, in 1905, the tsar told his mother that all would be well if only the governors of the provinces were honest and capable. A few years later he reiterated that the choice of suitable ministers would decide the outcome of Russia's crisis.[2]

Skilful, conscientious, trusted and honest administrators were indispensable to the effective functioning of a centralized monarchy. The prominent place its top officials occupy in memoirs and diaries reflects their importance to state and society. The memoirists, who were themselves at or near the heights of power, shared the beliefs of Karamzin and Pobedonostsev; they also found most occupants of the great offices of government devoid of the qualities that would have validated these beliefs. Even when allowance is made for the distortions born of envy or malice, the cantankerousness of old age or the loss of position, the constant chorus of complaints sung about tsarism's grandees by those who knew them best comes as a surprise. That chorus was not merely a phenomenon of the regime's final agony; it was the steady accompaniment of the reigns of the last two Romanovs and preceded the convulsions of the twentieth century. Pobedonostsev himself joined the chorus in 1881. He decried the calling of the zemskii sobor because it would be folly to assemble hundreds of people to deliver speeches when it was difficult to find even one intelligent person. Ideological disagreements were not the only source for his contempt for other high functionaries. In 1904, complaining that the emperor had not been listening to him but to adventurers and scoundrels, he told the minister of war, A. N. Kuropatkin, that even in Japan (which Russians regarded as a backward tyranny), there was a council of elders to advise the monarch. It was a strange observation by a man who had fought against institutionalizing the relationship between the sovereign and his counsellors.[3]

A former interior minister, P. A. Valuev, took an equally dim view in mid 1881 of what he called the hastily composed government of political dilettantes, armchair generals, inept bureaucrats, and the sexton Pobedonostsev. In 1884 the imperial secretary agreed with the emperor's brother that there was disarray in the administration and that it lacked clear views and plans. In 1892, Lamzdorf found the majority of ministers to be of mediocre ability and more or less addicted to graft, greed, and intrigue. He blamed low social origin or standing for their shortcomings, as did the publisher of the country's biggest conservative newspaper, A. S. Suvorin. In 1893 Suvorin attributed the scarcity of good men to Russia's lack of a genuine ruling class or aristocracy; in 1904 he concluded that if the government had no friends, this was because it was composed of fools and dolts, extortionists and thieves. Without necessarily going so far, other members of the 'establishment' thought that there were not enough good men to fill high offices, that there was no one for the emperor to turn to, that he was either misled or given stupid and incompetent advice.[4]

This supposed poverty of human resources rarely caused a critical re-examination of inherited truths. Instead, there was always the call for new and better men, the hope that a fresh face, someone unknown or untried, could supply the needed energy and excellence. Only outside of the establishment was the unavoidable lesson drawn from the weakness of the state's human material. In such conditions, Chicherin believed, limiting the autocracy became an urgent necessity.[5]

If ministers were judged harshly and frequently unfairly, it was because they were assumed to have great opportunities for doing good as well as evil and because they often served as lightning rods for him who was beyond criticism. They were, in fact, superior clerks as well as makers of policy, if they had their master's backing. In this relationship to the tsar lay the ambiguity of their situation, its difficulty, and its limitations. Regarded by much of the world as lesser tsars in their own spheres of authority, the heads of ministries or chief departments (Interior, War, Navy, Foreign Affairs, Finance, Education, Justice, the Holy Synod, Agriculture, Trade, Transport) were servants of the crown and might be treated as such.

Valuev recalled that Alexander II had dealt with ministers as if they were grand domestics rather than great state servitors and addressed them with the familiar *ty*. Although Alexander III ended this practice, his foreign minister for twelve years prepared for his weekly audiences like a schoolboy for his examinations. The minister of education did not even enjoy the privilege of a regular reporting day and had to request it in writing. Kokovtsov, who ended a decade of devoted duty in 1914 as chairman of the Council of Ministers, was let go, one of the grand dukes said, like a domestic. Sergei Witte, perhaps the ablest man to serve the last two tsars, at times behaved in their presence like a junior officer – bowing excessively, his hands at the seams of his trousers, and displaying little of his bold and independent mind. 'In Russia, even responsible ministers do not have the right to speak out,' Foreign Minister S. D. Sazonov told his colleagues in 1915.[6]

Ministers could and did, of course, speak out, but at some risk to their position, their reputation for loyalty, and to chances for preferment, pay, or pension. The monarch's favour had a direct bearing on perquisites and salaries, and differences in the latter were great. This was no small matter, since few ministers in our period came from the aristocracy of landed wealth. More often they belonged to the military or service nobility or were members of the gentry who had taken state employment out of ambition or need. While 72 per cent of the great servitors of state were nobles by birth – of the 345 highest central officials only 7 were sons of merchants – only 30 per cent had significant holdings of land.[7]

To avoid endangering income and status, or out of respect for the principles of autocratic rule, a minister might vote against his own proposal in the Council of State if the emperor disapproved of it. Resignations of protest were practically unheard of; interest and duty made ministers stay to carry out measures they opposed. In most cases they did not have that choice, for a change of policy normally brought a change of incumbent. This was most true at the Ministry of Interior, the most sensitive and important of the chief bureaus of government and the one to whose occupant the country looked for a sign of the ruler's intentions.

Because it controlled the ordinary and political police; issued the required internal passports; licensed businesses and public entertainment; supervised press, posts and telegraph, local government, the rural economy and gentry affairs, medical and veterinary services, peasant resettlement (until 1905), prisons (before 1895), and recruit levies; managed famine relief, Duma elections, and much else, Interior impinged most often and most directly on the lives of Russians. The minister, therefore, was the object of much fear or hope, the recipient of numerous pleas and petitions, the last resort in a multitude of petty or weighty affairs, the signer of hundreds of documents he could not possibly have studied with care. Like other ministers, and to a still greater degree, he affected a kind of patriarchal accessibility which was meant to suggest that government had at its centre a human heart which could and did care for its charges.

Unless they were too frequent targets for terrorists, ministers regularly received the public, admitting to their antechambers anyone who wanted to hand in a petition or make a verbal appeal. While more prominent visitors would be taken into the ministerial presence, His Excellency, accompanied by note-taking assistants, would make the round of other petitioners in the reception room, addressing a few words to each and listening to requests for pensions or commercial concessions, for clemency or jobs. This custom could remedy only isolated problems; it could also give a minister the mistaken impression that he was really learning of the country's ills and attending to them. More likely, it took precious hours away from the study of basic issues. It was said of Tolstoi, for example, that he picked such bad governors for the provinces because he did not have the time to interview candidates before appointing them and that he had difficulty afterwards fitting them into his crowded schedule. Ignatev made himself so readily available to callers that he saw each of them only briefly. Russia's last minister of finance saw from fifty to sixty people at his weekly receptions. Much of a minister's work, obviously, was turned over to assistants who were themselves, out of necessity or indolence, accomplished passers of paper to lower levels of the hierarchy.[8]

Alexander III's first appointee as minister of interior, like the man he replaced in May 1881 – Loris-Melikov had spent nearly all his life in the military – had no training and little background in domestic affairs. Ignatev, as did almost a third of the administrative elite, began his career in the military. The son of a general, he was a student in the Corps of Pages, passed next into a life guards regiment, then the General Staff Academy and the army. An assignment as military agent in London led to a diplomatic career, to the directorship of the Foreign Ministry's Asiatic Department, the embassy in Constantinople, and a key role in the diplomatic history of the Russo-Turkish War of 1877/78. The Treaty of San Stefano that followed was largely his work. When Russia had to disavow some of its gains under pressure from the European powers, Ignatev retired. In 1879 he was sent to Nizhnii-Novgorod as governor-general, and in March 1881 Loris-Melikov brought him into the government as minister of state domains, possibly to appease his critics on the right.

A military and diplomatic past did not necessarily incapacitate Ignatev for leadership of Russia's civil government. Even liberal critics conceded that besides repressing the Jews and civil liberties, he favoured economic aid to the peasantry (ending the 'temporary obligations' of 1.5 million ex-serfs to their masters by compelling their purchase of land allotment; reducing redemption payments and cancelling debts), improvements in rural administration, and public consultation in these matters. Ignatev had not, however, been chosen for his administrative talents, but because Pobedonostsev – who had great influence over the emperor – could not find an experienced civil servant who had sound political convictions and was also acceptable to the country at a critical time. After only a year, Ignatev was dismissed. His sponsor now called him an intriguer, a liar, and a chatterbox.[9]

After the unpredictable Ignatev and his toying with the dangerous idea of a consultative assembly, Dmitrii Tolstoi came as a relief to advocates of firmness and discipline. Katkov called his very name a manifesto and a programme.[10] But even supporters of a strong hand felt the minister went too far in his quest for authority 'not restrained by excessive formalism' when he tried to make the elective zemstvos into subordinate bureaucratic agencies. To Chicherin, that 'scoundrel' Tolstoi was a challenge flung in the face of all thinking and feeling Russians. Koshelev thought his appointment mocked or insulted society.[11]

Tolstoi had this advantage over Ignatev: he had spent many years in the bureaucracy, knew its workings intimately, and identified its retention of control over most areas of national life with the country's and the dynasty's welfare. His earlier service had been in the simultaneous directorship of the Holy Synod and the Ministry of Education. His infringement of university autonomy and the rights of students and professors had earned him the hatred of educated Russians and he was blamed by the chief of gendarmes for the younger generation's hostility to government. Tolstoi's imposition of a classical curriculum on secondary schools to insulate pupils from the political temptations that modern history and languages might offer was resisted and resented. His years at the Synod had been marked by a decline in the vitality of the Church for which Pobedonostsev, its hierarchs and well-wishers blamed Tolstoi's religious indifference. Colleagues rated his abilities as an administrator very low or average. Witte was one of the few who thought him a strong-willed, efficient administrator who kept his department running smoothly. But he too saw dangers in Tolstoi's ultra-conservatism and held him responsible for the disaffection that issued in the Revolution of 1905. Pobedonostsev taxed him with having neither plan nor system and simply living from day to day.[12]

An attitude of conservative pessimism or negativism was common among Tolstoi's successors. The fact that they were chosen most often from among the personnel of the ministry, or related branches of the civil service, shows that greater stress was placed on a mastery of bureaucratic routine and the instruments of control than on broad perspectives or bold programmes. When Tolstoi died in 1889 he was succeeded by the man who had been assistant minister for four years, director of charities in His Majesty's Own Chancellery for three, and a provincial governor for a decade before that. Having neither great wealth nor talents, I. N. Durnovo owed his rise, after service in the artillery, to his capacity for pleasing superiors and a cheerful amiability. He was ever ready to see callers and to promise what was asked of him, without necessarily intending to keep his word. There is no dissent from the contemporary view that he was, at best, a mediocrity.[13]

If Durnovo had plans or opinions of his own, he did not reveal them. He followed the measures Tolstoi initiated because the emperor approved of them and because Durnovo, too, believed that the initiative of private or voluntary agencies must be fenced in. In 1895 he subjected the Committees of Popular Literacy to the 'moral control' of the Ministry of Education because he trusted neither them nor the censorship to keep harmful literature from the lower classes.[14] It is not clear why Nicholas discharged such a compliant agent of autocracy in 1895. There was talk that the Dowager Empress was displeased with him for intercepting her mail, an accusation Durnovo denied. Whether he did so or not, it was common practice for the Police Department to open letters sent through the mails, whoever the addressee.

Durnovo's replacement, I. L. Goremykin, occupied several key posts in fifty-five years of service. He was chosen, after some hesitation, perhaps because he supported as assistant minister of justice the partial undoing of the judicial reforms, perhaps because Pobedonostsev, when Nicholas asked his opinion of the only other serious contenders for the post, called one a fool and the other a scoundrel. Goremykin was dismissed in 1899, in part because he favoured the qualified extension of the zemstvos to the western provinces, in part because of interministerial rivalries. Yet he was head of the Council of Ministers for three months in 1906, and from January 1914 to January 1916, as a very old and very cynical man, he was entrusted once more with the same responsible position – pulled out of mothballs, he said.[15]

Both these appointments offended public opinion and Goremykin's retirements were necessary concessions to it. He had long since become the personification of the lazy, time-serving bureaucrat who believed in nothing and took nothing very seriously, except the orders of his master, his own comfort and the advantages of high office. Although he was recognized in his early years as an experienced administrator (especially in peasant affairs), a capable jurist, a man of intelligence and honesty, a conservative critic said of him that it would be hard to find a worse minister of interior but that the feat had been managed with the appointment of Sipiagin.[16]

D. S. Sipiagin was the 'fool' who had been bypassed in 1895. Pobedonostev's judgement of his intellectual limitations was widely shared, which did not keep this old-fashioned and affable country squire from reaching the top of the ministry he had entered as a young man in 1876. He was not so foolish as to be unaware of discontent and protest – he even spoke of Russia being on the verge of revolution – but thought of no better response than repression. Sipiagin considered trial by jury a tool of lawlessness, favoured the cutting back of local self-government, closed or curbed associations of writers, lawyers, and economists, and tightened censorship. A fellow bureaucrat wrote of him that during his ministry no measures of general importance had been studied or carried through. When Witte objected to his proposal that the government protect workers from 'the arbitrary impact of economic phenomena' by improving their living and working conditions, he retreated to an exclusive reliance on the police. Nicholas thought that he employed it with insufficient severity, and when Sipiagin was shot by a revolutionary in April 1902 the policy of the firm hand was made firmer still.[17]

The choice to carry it out fell on V. K. Pleve, the 'scoundrel' who had missed out on the ministry a few years earlier. When he entered the post to which thirty-five years in government pointed – especially those as state prosecutor, director of the Police Department, and assistant minister of interior – he was destined to fill it for little more than two years. In July 1904 he was assassinated by a Socialist Revolutionary, the third of Nicholas's ministers to fall victim to a political murder. Many other functionaries succumbed to bombs or bullets afterwards – including the tsar's uncle in 1905 and the chairman of the Council of Ministers, Stolypin, in 1911. The death of none had such political and psychological impact as that of Pleve, whose end was greeted with manifestations of joy. A minister who could in only two years lay up such a store of hatred for himself was an unusual phenomenon even in Russia. The reason was not Pleve's reputation for harsh inflexibility alone, but the war with Japan and the various crises that came to a head during his ministry.

There was extensive looting and burning of gentry estates in three provinces in 1902 and 1903. The crisis of a multinational empire that helped to create the disaffection it feared by national and religious discrimination announced itself in Armenian and Finnish resistance and in the pogroms of Kishinev (blamed on Pleve) and Gomel for which the regime's anti-Jewish policies were at least morally responsible.

The problem of the working class exploded in 1903 in the greatest wave of strikes the country had yet seen. The existence of a crisis of confidence, the distress of the rural population, and the disturbed state of the nation were recognized in an imperial manifesto of 26 February 1903 which promised reforms in peasant legislation and announced freedom of religious belief. It also reaffirmed the fullness of autocratic power, which alone could assure the welfare and rights of all, and charged that performing this task had been made impossible by ill-disposed enemies and the carriers of alien ideas.

This ambiguous admission of trouble, and the way in which it was proposed to deal with it, showed the mind and hand of Pleve. He was too intelligent to deny that Russia was convulsed by serious difficulties and was prepared to countenance partial reforms. In his capacity for seeing reality he was superior to the monarch and most of his colleagues. In private he even conceded that representative government was bound to come sooner or later. But not only did he prefer that it be later, he also belied his intelligence by not bringing it to bear on the concrete issues facing him. But it was one thing to recognize that history was moving in a certain direction and that Russia was fated to move along with it; quite another for the man who was responsible for law and order to act boldly on that knowledge and allow unfettered discussion or trial of ways in which the future could be met.

In a conversation between Pleve and his great rival Witte in 1902, the latter tried to impress upon his colleague that agitation was not the only source of public unhappiness and that it was vain to think that police measures could cure it. The nation's distemper could be traced as far back as the reforms of Alexander II and their incompleteness. 'The building has been reconstructed,' Witte said, employing the liberal formula for a national legislature, 'but the cupola has been left untouched.' Society now wanted some role in law-making, some checks over the bureaucracy, and if there was no concession to that desire it would, Witte warned, take illegal forms. The state could not continue to ignore public opinion since it needed the educated classes. Whom else could it rely on? The masses? The conservative belief in the peasants as a pillar of the regime Witte dismissed as mere phrase-making.

Pleve agreed that dissatisfaction had deep roots, that it was not the result of artificial stimulation alone. Russia might indeed be on the eve of great upheavals, and precisely for that reason the state had to defend itself and battle against threats to its existence. 'If we are incapable of changing the course of historical events which will shake the state, then we are obliged to dam the current, to hold it back, not to swim with it or try always to keep abreast of it.' Witte himself, Pleve said, had shown that reforms were best carried out by the government, often against the wish of society and without need of a constitution. The government had experience, tradition, and the habit of rule behind it; it was above factions and could avoid the passions, jealousies and disappointed promises that were sure to follow the opposition's coming to power and cause its early downfall. 'And then, there will come to the surface, led by the Jews, all the harmful, criminal elements that yearn for Russia's ruin and dissolution. What will happen then? It is hard even to imagine it.'[18]

Pleve imagined only too vividly the consequences of letting down the barriers that protected authority and order. He had been a policeman too long to think that trust and goodwill could lead to accommodation and saw the relationship between state and society as a contest in which it was important to keep the advantage of control and constraint. Witte, on the other hand, had come to believe that the autocracy and its subjects had to trust each other and work together to make Russia a strong and prosperous power.

Witte was not a liberal and was as loyal to autocracy as any man. It was he who had proposed formation of the Holy Company and had in 1899 argued against Goremykin that the extension, indeed the very existence, of the zemstvo was incompatible with autocracy. Asked his thoughts on the constitutional changes of 1905–6 which he had helped to bring about, Witte replied: 'I have a constitution in my head, but in my heart I spit on it.'[19] Whatever its emotional or intellectual sources may have been, Witte gave pragmatic explanations for his devotion to autocracy. It was simply the most efficient agency for reform and economic modernization, the only one capable of holding together a largely illiterate people of many nationalities and languages. 'If the tsar's government falls, you will see absolute chaos in Russia . . . .'[20] Parliamentary institutions would only make the government's job harder. If he eventually moved towards a grudging acceptance of an elected legislature and constitutional restrictions on the autocrat, it was because of disenchantment with the latter rather than conversion to the former.

As minister of finance from 1892 to 1903 and prime mover of the country's industrialization, Witte was driven to see that autocracy (as practiced by Nicholas) and bureaucracy (as administered by Sipiagin and Pleve) straitjacketed enterprise and initiative. His debate with Pleve was symptomatic of a larger debate between the two men and their ministries. Theirs was no mere contest over budgets and spheres of influence, but a deep disagreement over the degree and rate of change that was compatible with the preservation of the political system and its supports. Witte, invoking economic rationality and necessity, saw an end to the predominance of agriculture and the nobility, as well as changes in autocracy's mode of rule, as indispensable for autocracy's survival and Russia's remaining a major power. Pleve believed in change too, or so he said, but change so controlled, so protective of traditional groups and values as to be hardly distinguished from immobility.

Finance reached nearly as deeply and painfully into the lives of Russians as did Interior. It assessed and (after 1899) collected taxes and customs duties; prepared the national budget and administered the alcohol monopoly; it dealt directly or indirectly with such diverse matters as railroad rates and foreign loans, exports and imports, patents and weights and measures, stock companies and stock exchanges, factory inspection and legislation; it subsidized shipbuilding and shipping companies, maintained technical schools and institutes, collected and published statistics and technical information – in sum, it was involved in or responsible for a host of matters having to do with the commerce, industry, and finances of the empire. It was the single most important agency dealing with Russian economic development and well-being and the most progressive and expertly run. Like Transport, Agriculture, and (after 1905) Trade and Industry, it attracted and sought technical specialists who were valued for their training and abilities by their superiors as well as the public which distinguished between them and the law and order bureaucrats of Interior and Justice or the favourites and courtiers of the emperor. Finance was headed by men who, for the most part, enjoyed long terms of office. Nikolai Bunge, whom Alexander III had appointed in 1881, served for nearly six years, as did his successor Ivan Vyshnegradskii. Witte was minister for eleven, Kokovtsov for nine, and Petr Bark for three years. Bunge came to government after an academic career in economics in Kiev, service in the administration of that city, and participation in governmental commissions on peasant affairs. He was a thorough, decent, and enlightened man who enjoyed the good opinion of his contemporaries, thought that the nobility was a dying class, reduced the tax burden on the peasantry, took the first steps to protect workers from exploitation, but was unable either to find enough money to balance the budget or to invest in future growth.

When he resigned in 1887 – Tolstoi had told the emperor that Bunge was surrounded by 'unreliable people'[21] – he was replaced by another newcomer to the bureaucracy. Vyshnegradskii had been a professor of engineering and director of the St Petersburg Technological Institute whose experience of economics had been acquired as a director of railway and other companies. It was rumoured that he had been bought by the Rothschilds when negotiating a loan and that he was more interested in filling his own pockets than in general welfare. Vyshnegradskii may, on occasion, have profited from knowing how the international money market or the stock exchange would react to measures he had taken in his official capacity. But this was not the same thing as designing policies for his own benefit. To restore Russia to financial health, he pursued an orthodox course of cutting expenditures, increasing revenues, and pushing grain exports.

Vyshnegradskii's unpopularity stemmed less from a lack of probity than from stringent fiscal measures that helped to bring the country's budget and foreign trade into favourable balance. While the high taxes and tariffs which achieved this feat benefited the treasury and selected industries, they were a burden on consumers and peasant agriculture. When twenty provinces were hit by drought, crop failure, famine and cholera in 1891/92 and it was realized that high taxes and the export drive had left the peasants without reserves of money or grain, it was charged that budget and trade surpluses had been achieved at their expense. The cost of famine relief ate deeply into the savings the state had accumulated; the political costs were to prove even higher. It was in the midst of this débâcle that Witte took over the Ministry of Finance.

He too represented a new type of functionary. Although well born and well connected, Witte did not prepare for the military or civil service but took up the study of mathematics. Told by an uncle that this was inappropriate for someone of his class, Witte gave up the academic career he had contemplated and took employment with the state railway administration, then with private railroads, and in 1889 as head of the Railway Department in the Ministry of Finance. He became minister of transport in early 1892 and of finance later that year. Prepared to speak bluntly and act boldly, to make his own way from railway ticket office to great power and prestige, to work hard and to respect others who did, whatever their rank or religion, Witte was yet a transitional figure and in some ways surprisingly unmodern.

Opposed to the nobility's social and economic claims, he also tried to satisfy some of these and paid deference to titled courtiers. He sought acceptance in high society and at court for his wife (a divorcee), nearly venerated one emperor and could be timid in the presence of another. Exceedingly sensitive to slights to his dignity and person, he was so deeply moved by the honour of a ministerial appointment that he celebrated it with a divine service. This sensible, businesslike realist and railwayman even went so far as to review, on horseback and in a specially designed uniform, the detachments of border guards that were under his authority. These contradictions in his make-up did not keep Witte from asking searching questions about the character of Russia's institutions and the quality of her government.

He did so in an 1899 memorandum to Nicholas which pointed out the incompatibility of autocracy with a substantial measure of self-government because the latter would undermine the unitary character of the central authority and its capacity for unchallenged and enlightened leadership. In an exchange with Sipiagin he held that autocracy did not mean the infallibility of the emperor or silent acceptance of his orders when a minister felt that a contrary view must be argued for the sake of the country. He also called for a streamlined government that would be subservient to law, responsive to the country's needs, flexible and self-confident enough to loosen the tight rein on which it held the intelligent and enterprising part of the nation.

Asking that government trust society – only then could it win its confidence and feel secure – Witte himself was distrusted by almost every segment of opinion and interest. His policies, which advanced and speeded industrialization, also deepened the agrarian crisis and increased the burdens the general population had to bear. Agrarian conservatives, socialists, and liberals disliked what he was doing while the business community he favoured was not yet sufficiently strong or numerous to gain him popularity. At court and in high society, Witte's unorthodox definitions of autocracy caused him to be suspected of being a 'revolutionist with secret, malevolent intentions'.[22] His caustic tongue and vast influence, his masterful ways and quarrels with other ministers, made Witte an uncomfortable adviser and an easy target for attacks from all quarters. Nicholas, who had weighed the step for some time, dismissed him in August 1903. The blow was softened by promotion to the chairmanship of the Committee of Ministers, a powerless post which offered little scope for Witte's ambitions and did not even confer the privilege of a regular audience with the monarch.

Stolypin, chairman of the Council of Ministers and minister of interior from 1906 to 1911, was the only statesman of the period who could compare with Witte in clarity of outlook and independence of judgement. Stolypin accepted the new state of affairs in which basic civil liberties and political rights had been proclaimed, in which there was a popularly elected legislature, and in which government needed allies, not merely clients. He wished to part 'with the old police order of things'[23] and to collaborate with the Duma. Yet he was in an older tradition, that of the masterful enlightened bureaucrat who preferred to promote and control reforms from above, and had little taste or talent for politics.

A relative stranger to the inner workings of St Petersburg officialdom, Stolypin was trained in mathematics and natural science, and had attracted attention while serving in the provinces, most recently as governor of Saratov during the disturbances of 1905. He was an old-fashioned, almost chauvinistic patriot and deeply devoted to the monarchy. He suffered as much as had Witte from the hostility of reactionary opponents of change, from the suspicions of liberals and, naturally, from the hatred of revolutionaries whom he repressed with fierce effectiveness. Above all, he suffered from the limitations and weakness of the monarch, which restricted his freedom of action, and ultimately from his ingratitude. Only an untimely death at the hands of a young socialist turned police informer spared him from the dismissal which would surely have followed an obvious lack of favour. Stolypin may not have been the Russian Bismarck his admirers saw, but he loomed very large on the Russian scene.

If it was difficult for any Russian monarch to have as leader of his government a statesman of great calibre – for fear of being overshadowed or overpowered – it was doubly difficult for Nicholas II. Only an exceptional tsar could long tolerate an exceptional chief minister. As the reign of Nicholas neared its end, his cabinet choices fell more and more often on men of lesser and lesser status. The result was a constant loss of respect for the government and instability at its helm. After Pleve, there were eleven ministers of interior in twelve years; after the assassination of N. P. Bogolepov in 1901, ten ministers of education in sixteen. When the competent A. S. Ermolov lost his post as minister of agriculture in 1905 (he had told Nicholas, 'at the present time we have no government'[24]), he was followed by nine others. During the eleven years of its existence, the Ministry of Trade and Industry had eight chiefs and a full year without one. During the First World War, these changes reached such dizzying proportions that the right-wing politician V. M. Pur-ishkevich described them as 'ministerial leapfrog'.[25] From July 1914 to Feb-ruary 1917 there were four chairmen of the Council of Ministers; six ministers of interior; four ministers each of justice, war, and agriculture; and four directors of the Holy Synod. The top officials of tsarism became during its final crisis the laughing-stock of the nation. But their real or supposed short-comings, their foibles and failures, had long been the subject of malicious gossip as well as of more serious criticism. The problem of providing coherent policies, unified management, and effective leadership did not arise as a con-sequence of the war and its extraordinary demands and pressures; nor was it primarily attributable to the sinister influence of Rasputin or the meddling of the empress. It had deeper roots which made the tragic farce of the final years possible.

The emperor's part in the selection and retention of ministers, as well as in the approval or disapproval of their initiatives, remained decisive until the last. His choices were not necessarily worse than those made by the elected head of a parliamentary regime who had to give representation in his cabinet to diverse interests. But having to win and keep the monarch's favour for men who had no independent power or constituency was a serious inhibition even for those who had an independent mind. Thus, Witte overstated his case against the zemstvos in order to gain the tsar's backing against Goremykin, and Stolypin withdrew a cabinet project for easing Jewish disabilities because Nicholas opposed it. If a minister's pliability counted for so much, then tsar-ism was no better than those liberal regimes where cabinet posts were rewards for subservience to party, politicians, or fickle public opinion. There was this difference: the preferences to which a tsarist minister had to conform were not those of a party or parliament, but of one very fallible individual whose judge-ments were apt to be received as if they were infallible.

A close student of Russia's administration has concluded that ministers' dependence on the favour of the tsar, and in particular the latter's backing of a favourite minister, were a necessity and an advantage when decisive action was wanted and departmental disagreements blocked it.[26] Witte's introduction of the gold standard in 1897, when a hostile State Council was bypassed, is cited as a case in point. On this view it was not the mysticism or narrowness of the tsars, their whims or character, nor their advisers' political or personal faults that made for institutional defects in the supreme organs of state. It was rather the unprecedented tasks they faced, and the weakness of a legal system in which lower levels found it difficult to interpret the law, that explain contradictory policies, the appearance of disorder, the recourse to *ad hoc* procedures and to favourites.

Even if too much weight has been given to the failings of individuals and too little to the magnitude of their problems, the ruler's favour and periodic interventions could not compensate for the lack of law and rationality in institutional and political life. When there was no clear favourite to impose his will or when the tsar, as in the last two reigns, was not an active proponent of policy, there was bound to be drift, confusion. discontinuity. The machinery of government lacked a coordinating mechanism and moved slowly. Special commissions were formed, mountains of material gathered, and projects drafted only, in most cases, to be shelved or disappear from view years later. Ironically, deleteriousness could have its positive sides as well, as in the reversal of the judicial reforms first contemplated in 1885. Alexander III, Katkov, and Pobedonostsev agreed that irremovable judges, independent courts, public and jury trials undermined the authority of the state and its ability to maintain order. Not until two ministers of justice had been dismissed and a more suitable one found in 1894 was a Commission for the Revision of Laws Concerning the Administration of Justice set up and not until September 1905 were its recommendations buried. By then they had been so thoroughly modified – Finance found them too strong, Interior too weak – that they bore little resemblance to the aims of their sponsors.

There were officials who said, perhaps half-seriously, that interministerial conflict kept the worst from happening and that lack of unity was a kind of constitution or charter of liberties. But most found it a serious drawback. Even in foreign affairs, where the emperor was pre-eminent and his minister little more than his *rapporteur*, conflicting policies were pursued. N. K. Giers, Alexander's foreign minister for thirteen years, complained in 1887 that there were three governments: himself, the domestic departments, and Katkov; the emperor, he added, was a government to and by himself. Without a cabinet or other means of coordination, a joint policy could never be counted on. Each minister reported separately to the tsar and his appointment did not require the agreement of his colleagues. This could go so far as Nicholas naming an assistant minister of interior in 1905 without the knowledge of his chief, A. G. Bulygin. The latter offered his resignation, which Nicholas curtly refused: in Russia ministers did not resign, he said, they were dismissed.[27]

While the minister of interior was normally and by virtue of his importance first among equals, he was far, however, from being a prime minister or head of government. He could not, therefore, play the role of coordinator, form a unified ministry, or expect the cooperation of like-minded colleagues. The Committee of Ministers, formed in 1802 and abolished in 1905, did not meet the need for coordination, although its function was to arbitrate conflicts and concert joint action between departments. It did so less frequently than it was used by ministers who wanted to circumvent the Council of State which had become something of a guardian of legality. Certain of resistance in the Council and confident of the emperor's support, Ignatev brought his 'regulation' of special state protection to the Committee. The fact that it never found solidarity on issues the emperor opposed indicates the Committee's insignificance, as does the decline in the amount of business that came before it. When Witte was named to its chairmanship the appointment was correctly seen as a demotion.

The revival in October 1905 of the Council of Ministers (established in 1865 but not summoned since 1882) with a president or chairman (*predsedatel*) as its clearly designated head, was expected to change all that. The Council would at last provide the coherence for which even Pobedonostsev had asked at its activation in 1885. But neither in law nor in practice was the goal of governmental unity reached. The statute setting up the new post-1905 Council of Ministers provided in article 16 that matters pertaining to the imperial court, to crown lands, to foreign affairs and questions of state defence could come before the Council only with the sovereign's permission, when heads of the departments listed considered their introduction necessary, or when they touched upon the interests of other departments.

It is clear what a reasonable interpretation of the law would have required in foreign affairs and defence. Yet as chairman of the Council of Ministers, Stolypin (who had first been selected as minister of interior in the Goremykin Cabinet not by its head but by Nicholas) protested angrily during the Bosnian crisis of 1908 that the foreign minister had not kept him informed of its background and had not submitted the measures he had taken to the Council which was by law charged with directing and coordinating policy. The experience caused Stolypin to prepare a governmental reorganization project which would oblige the minister of foreign affairs to keep the chairman of the Council of Ministers informed of the international situation and of the state of Russia's relations with the major foreign states. He also proposed – and this was the crux of the issue of cabinet autonomy and solidarity – that its head select the members, subject to the tsar's approval, and that they report to the tsar only after prior agreement with the president of the Council who would also be responsible for the actions of all ministers before the emperor.[28]

The proposal, drafted in the year of Stolypin's death, came to nought. Kokovtsov repeated all of Stolypin's complaints: that he never succeeded in creating a unified government, that ministerial changes were made with little regard for his wishes, and that he had to evade foreigners who wanted to talk to him on matters of external policy because this was the prerogative of the tsar and the minister of foreign affairs. With the return of the aged and feeble Goremykin to the chairmanship of the Council in early 1914, and even more with the coming of war and the assumption of vast powers and responsibilities by the military, the situation deteriorated still further. Even the best of Nicholas's ministers were frustrated in their best efforts, while the worst bowed to his wishes.

It is, of course, all too easy to find fault with men whom events have already condemned; essential to remember that Russia's monumental difficulties might have defeated the inspired efforts of a phalanx of virtue and genius; and important, for the sake of perspective, to keep in mind that in more fortunate countries, too, positions of political leadership did not and normally do not fall to 'the best and the brightest' who are more often found at the level of the devoted but anonymous expert or specialist. These were a small group in Russia, but one which was growing in size and importance.

It is possible that the empire's ministers have been judged unfairly, that their intentions, particularly towards peasants and workers, were better and their possibilities narrower than the negative assessments of contemporaries and historians have allowed, and that these may yet be proved wrong. If that should happen, it still remains to be asked why most ministers' reputations were so low and why so much of the blame for the nation's descent into revolution, chaos, and tyranny was attached to them.

One of the more important answers to that question must surely be the great responsibilities and powers that ministers possessed or claimed and declared to be necessary for the effective and speedy solution of national tasks. When, unavoidably, they failed or fell short of their goals, they exposed a gap between pretensions and performance that invited not merely questions about the latter but basic challenges to the legitimacy of the former. The very role assigned to them promised (or threatened) more than they could possibly deliver, and was bound to cause either derision or disappointment. A more modest statement of their functions and authority would have served them better.

While none of Russia's ministers had enough effective power to carry through comprehensive programmes of social, economic, and governmental reorganization, they had sufficient means and authority for intruding into many aspects of the country's life and for irritating its citizens. What a one-time assistant minister of interior said of Pleve has wider application.

During his entire term of office, Pleve did not effect one single decisive measure in any field; yet the discontent and grievances he inspired in individual persons, in the public at large, and even in national organizations was very great. He touched almost every phase of public life in some way – and in every case he aroused discontent. Threats, leniency, favours – all were intermixed and, in consequence, threats did not frighten and favors did not excite gratitude.[29]

The cumulative effect of these irritations was annoyance with all levels of a bureaucracy whose heads were not too sharply distinguished from the subordinates who acted in their name and were given as little respect.

REFERENCES

1. R. E. Pipes, *Karamzin's Memoir on Ancient and Modern Russia: A Translation and Analysis* (Cambridge, Mass., 1959), pp. 193–4; A. A. Polovtsov, 'Dnevnik, 1877–1878', *Krasnyi Arkhiv* 33 (1929), p. 178
2. R. F. Byrnes, *Pobedonostsev: His Life and Thought* (Bloomington, Ind., 1968), p. 312; G. L. Yaney, *The Systematization of Russian Government* (Chicago and London, 1973), p. 276; Ernst Seraphim, 'Zar Nikolaus II. und Graf Witte. Eine historisch-psychologische Studie', *Historische Zeitschrift* 161 (Jan. 1940), p. 298; Arthur Levin, 'Russian bureaucratic opinion in the wake of the 1905 revolution', *Jahrbücher für Geschichte Osteuropas* 11 (Dec. 1963), p. 8.
3. H. Heilbronner, 'The administration of Loris-Melikov and Ignatiev, 1880–82' (Ph.D. Diss. University of Michigan, 1954), p. 298; 'Dnevnik A. N. Kuropatkina', *Krasnyi Arkhiv* 5 (1924), p. 88.
4. P. A. Valuev, *Dnevnik, 1877–1884* (Petrograd, 1919); A. A. Polovtsov, *Dnevnik gosudarstvennogo sekretaria A. A. Polovtsova* (Moscow, 1966), I, p. 167; V. N. Lamzdorf, *Dnevnik, 1891–1892* (Moscow, 1934), p. 310; A. S. Suvorin, *Dnevnik* (Moscow-Petrograd, 1923), pp. 25, 327.

5. B. N. Chicherin, *Vospominaniia: Zemstvo i Moskovskaia Duma* (Moscow, 1934), p. 260.

6. Valuev, op. cit., p. 194; Lamzdorf, op. cit., p. viii; V. D. Novitskii, *Iz vospominanii zhandarma* (Leningrad, 1929), pp. 163–4; Hans Rogger, 'Russia in 1914', *Journal of Contemporary History* 1 (Oct. 1966), p. 96; S. S. Fabritskii, *Iz proshlago* (Berlin, 1926), pp. 66–7; M. Cherniavsky (ed.), *Prologue to Revolution* (Englewood Cliffs, NJ, 1967), p. 94.

7. D. Field, 'Three new books on the imperial bureaucracy', *Kritika* [Cambridge, Mass.] 15 (Spring 1979), pp. 125–8.

8. E. M. Feoktistov, *Vospominaniia* (Leningrad, 1929), p. 231; P. L. Bark, 'Glava iz vospominanii', *Vozrozbdenie* [Paris] 43 (July 1955), pp. 13–14; I. F. Koshko, *Vospominaniia gubernatora* (Petrograd, 1916), p. 15; H. N. Neelmeyer-Vukassowitsch, *Das Russland der Gegenwart and Zukunft* (Leipzig, 1883, pp. 125–6.

9. P. A. Zaionchkovskii, *The Russian Autocracy in Crisis 1878–1882*, trans. G. M. Hamburg (Gulf Breeze, Fla., 1979), pp. 212, 299.

10. P. A. Zaionchkovskii, *The Russian Autocracy Under Alexander III*, trans. D. D. Jones (Gulf Breeze, Fla., 1976), p. 83.

11. Chicherin, op. cit., p. 223; A. I. Koshelev, *Zapiski, 1812–1883* (Berlin, 1884), p. 264.

12. Polovtsov. *Dnevnik* I, p. 172: II, pp. 67, 189–92, 245; S. Iu. Vitte, *Vospominaniia* (Moscow, 1969) I, pp. 298–303; K. F. Golovin, *Meine Erinnerungen* (Leipzig, 1911), pp. 145, 223–4; 262–3; Allen Sinel, *The Classroom and the Chancellery: State Educational Reform in Russia under Count Dmitry Tolstoi* (Cambridge, Mass., 1973), p. 59.

13. Polovtsov, *Dnevnik* II, p. 243; Chicherin, op. cit., p. 286; A. V. Bogdanovich, *Tri poslednikh samoderzhtsa Dnevnik* (Leningrad, 1924), pp. 119, 155; Golovin, op. cit., p. 320; Lamzdorf, op. cit., p. 105.

14. Jacob Walkin, *The Rise of Democracy in Pre-Revolutionary Russia* (New York, 1962), p. 137.

15. Byrnes, op. cit., p. 240; V. N. Kokovtsov, *Out of My Past* (Stanford, Cal., and London, 1935), p. 439.

16. Bogdanovich, op. cit., p. 277.

17. V. I. Gurko, *Features and Figures of the Past*, trans. L. Matveev (Stanford, Cal., and London, 1939), pp. 85–6; Vitte, op. cit., II, pp. 202–4.

18. D. N. Liubimov, 'Otryvki iz vospominanii', *Istoricheskii Arkhiv* 6 (1962), pp. 82–3; D. N. Shipov, *Vospominaniia i dumy o perezhitom* (Moscow, 1918), pp. 171–97; A. N. Kuropatkin, 'Dnevnik', *Krasnyi Arkhiv* 2 (1922), pp. 43–4, 82; N. B. Weissman, *Reform in Tsarist Russia* (New Brunswick, NJ, 1981), chs II–III.

19. Bernard Pares, *My Russian Memoirs* (London, 1931), p. 184.

20. H. D. Mehlinger and J. M. Thompson, *Count Witte and the Tsarist Government in the 1905 Revolution* (Bloomington, Ind., and London, 1972), p. 327.

21. Zaionchkovskii, *Russian Autocracy Under Alexander III*, p. 46.

22. D. M. Wallace, *Russia*, (New York, 1961) p. 510.

23. Pares, op. cit., p. 126.

24. 'Zapiski A. S. Ermolova', *Krasnyi Arkhiv* 8 (1925), p. 55.

25. Bernard Pares, *The Fall of the Russian Monarchy*, (New York, 1961), p. 397.

26. G. L. Yaney, op. cit., pp. 242–3; 272, 279–80.

27. G. F. Kennan, *The Decline of Bismarck's European Order* (Princeton, NJ, 1979), pp. 345–6; Gurko, op. cit., p. 360.

28. A. V. Zenkovskii, *Pravda o Stolypine* (New York, 1956), pp. 111–12; Kokovtsov, op. cit., pp. 214–18; 349ff.
29. Gurko, op. cit., p. 237.

CHAPTER FOUR

Bureaucrats, policemen, and public servants

One reason for the low regard Russians had for so many of their ministers was that they saw them less as great officers of state – men of wealth, power, lineage, or ability – than as *chinovniki*, superior to run-of-the-mill civil servants in nothing but rank. When an admirer of Stolypin wanted to stress his uniqueness he described him as 'an unusual type of minister, not the bureaucrat who floats with the current in pursuit of personal well-being'.[1]

There was social as well as intellectual condescension for bureaucrats high and low; but snobbishness was not the prime source of disdain for that seemingly ubiquitous figure, the *chinovnik*, the man of rank (*chin*), who occupied one of fourteen (later twelve) rungs or grades on the ladder of state service above the level of clerk. When Peter I established a Table of Ranks for the Civil and military services in 1722, his purpose had been fourfold: to make the civil service as·attractive as the military; to tie pay and honour to office and duty; to require the latter of all well-born citizens;[2] and to reward the ability and diligence of all free subjects who served the monarch and state. Initially, ascent to commissioned rank in the army and navy and to the eighth *chin* of the civil services conferred hereditary nobility; personal nobility in the latter came with rank fourteen. Thus, state service became a duty for the rich and noble, a source of income and importance (as well as an obligation) for the merely noble, and an opportunity for commoners to become noble and rich. rich.

Originally, *chin* defined the office and the rank of its occupant, but in time that connection was ended, as was the service obligation Peter had imposed on the gentry. By the end of the eighteenth century it had freed itself of the legal requirement to serve while having its special rights in, and to, service recognized. The time for promotion to a certain *chin* was reduced for nobles; the rank which conferred hereditary nobility was raised in 1856 to the fourth in the civil and to the sixth in the military services and its attainment made more difficult between 1892 and 1900 for merchants, descendants of personal nobles, holders of grade five and certain decorations. Thus automatic ennoblement through the Table of Ranks was effectively ended. But the monarch never yielded to the gentry's clamour for closure, and reserved the right to raise deserving servitors to that estate. Until 1906, when appointments were made independent of class, nobility, along with length of service, conferred formal advantages – and informal ones after that date.

The relaxation of Peter's rules, which caused the awarding of ranks to be divorced from office or duty, also brought a lowering of quality in personnel. The examinations introduced by a reforming minister of Alexander I for attaining the eighth rank were fought by the nobility and abandoned by 1834. A rank and salary in state service had become a sought-after goal, especially when the end of serfdom deprived the gentry's debt-ridden majority of income and comforts. For the untrained scions of lesser gentry, a government post and pension were a necessity and they succeeded in preserving the advantages of birth in entry to and advancement in the bureaucracy. Although the gentry in the nineteenth century regarded state service less often as a burden to be shunned than a class right to be protected, the bureaucracy did not become a noble preserve and service in it was no guarantee of social distinction or individual respect.

The success of the gentry in keeping professionalism to a minimum is one reason for the paradox which made so many members of the class seek state employment, while an equal number looked upon it as demeaning. Matters were beginning to improve in our period, but the empire's civil servants were never a corps of officials with clearly defined rights, responsibilities, and skills. The typical chinovnik, with important exceptions at the top and in certain specialized fields, had little authority either in the sense of power or in the sense of expertise. He also had a relatively low salary, for the monetary benefits of service were unevenly distributed.

An ambassador could receive as much as 50,000 rubles per year; ministers from 18,000 to 23,000; their directors of department, bureau chiefs, and heads of desks about 7,000, 2,500, and 1,500 respectively. Members of the Council of State, governors, and city prefects might have anywhere from 12,000 to 20,000 rubles; a police chief from 3,000 to 4,500. Often there were allowances for living quarters, equipment, or uniforms. Salaries could range up or down from those mentioned, depending on location, seniority, position in the Table of Ranks, ministerial or imperial favour. When Witte was offered the Railway Department his reluctance to leave the directorship of a private railroad, with its independence and 50,000 rubles, for a post in expensive St Petersburg which paid 8,000, prompted Alexander III to assign him an additional 8,000 out of his own pocket. He also advanced him from the ninth *chin* (titular councillor) to the fourth which carried the title of actual state councillor and the appellation 'excellency'.[3]

Only about a fifth of the 'men of the twentieth', as popular speech called them in reference to pay-day, received more than 1,000 rubles a year. In Saratov in 1899, low-level civil servants fared little better than printers. With 700–1,000 rubles considered a minimum for a middle-class style of life, the twentieth of the month must have been eagerly awaited. A salary that was essential but did not make for comfort, especially in the larger cities, created envy, inhibited professional solidarity and pride, and deepened the average chinovnik's sense of insecurity. Although his superior was enjoined by the rules of the service to have cause, a civil servant could be dismissed without a reason having to be given. Staying in the good graces of one's chief was obviously important. The novelist Ivan Turgenev described a friend of change-able convictions as something of a chinovnik. The reasons Nikolai Gogol, the author of *Dead Souls*, had given in the 1820s for leaving the state service were still applicable to many of its non-technical branches in 1900: 'What kind of happiness is it to reach your fiftieth birthday in a service . . . and have a salary barely sufficient to keep yourself decent and not have the power to bring a kopek's worth of good to Humanity?'[4]

Many families of old lineage or wealth looked down on bureaucrats and preferred to serve their country in the elite regiments of the guards, the elec-tive posts of gentry assemblies and zemstvos, or to enter the professions. As a result, state offices were more and more filled with a new breed of official who wished to make a career in government and was conscious of owing his benefits and allegiance to monarch and state. Many of these people came from the lower nobility or were of non-noble origin, so that service, with its dis-tinctions and rewards, marked off the career bureaucrat from the rest of the nobility. A chinovnik might be a noble by birth or have become one through service. But in the eyes of most educated Russians he was a chinovnik first and a nobleman last.

The opening of the bureaucracy to non-nobles in the nineteenth century was made necessary by its expansion and by new tasks. In the last half of the century its personnel grew fourfold, with one half to two thirds being of non-noble origin. In 1897, 78 per cent of officials in the bottom five ranks were born into a non-noble estate. New functions required new techniques and skills, and these were less likely to have been acquired by impecunious rural gentry seeking public employment than by ambitious children of clergy, lead-ing merchants, civil servants, or professionals. Service privileges reserved for nobles were gradually extended to these categories of citizens, as well as to specialists in finance, transportation, medicine, agronomy, communications, law, mining, and forestry. By 1900 many positions could be filled by open hiring. After 1906 advanced training in one of these specialties outweighed the claims of birth in appointments to the lower half of the Table of Ranks. Religion or nationality were nominally no bar, except for Jews, unless they held advanced degrees. In practice, they were almost totally excluded, whereas the number of Catholics (who were most often Poles and therefore thought unreliable) was severely limited.

None the less, there were considerably more educated Russians outside officialdom than in it – a fact not worth remarking had it not meant the reversal of an earlier condition.[7] The educational level of bureaucracy changed slowly. More than half of 4,339 appointees in 1894/95 had neither a higher nor secondary education and 8.12 per cent had no schooling. Of 1,609 indi-viduals taken into the ministry of finance at the same time, only 17 per cent had a higher education, while 10.32 per cent had a secondary and 72.68 per cent a lower education.[6] In all but the most technical services, social origin or connections, seniority, political reliability, the favour of superiors, and a mastery of routine continued to be valuable. Men who met some or all of these criteria could be shifted from one sphere of administration to another or recruited from outside. The coexistence of old and new ways is illustrated by the extension of *chin* equivalency and seniority rights to individuals in certain non- or quasi-governmental bodies – some higher educational institutions, the executive boards of town councils and zemstvos. Designed to facilitate transfers into the bureaucracy, the practice was not followed for individuals in industry, business, or the professions. The continued employment of military men in civil posts, although inhibited by law, is added evidence of the survival of old habits and traditions.

Russia's emperors thought of themselves more as leaders of armies than bureaucracies, and since they liked the simple directness of military men, they frequently entrusted difficult areas of government to soldiers. Loris-Melikov had served in the guards and as army commander in the Caucasus before becoming a governor and minister of interior. Two generals became ministers of education, another, assistant minister of interior, and a large number served as provincial governors. Many more ex-officers were city prefects, district police chiefs, or rural land captains. General V. A. Sukhomlinov, minister of war from 1909 to 1915, admitted that he was unprepared for the post of governor-general of Kiev to which he was appointed in 1905, that he had never been anything but a soldier, and neither knew nor wanted to know anything of civil affairs. Nicholas II placed special trust in the soldierly virtues and was convinced that those who embodied them would right what was wrong with the civil administration. He said in 1903 that the state could not do without the services of military men, especially in the Ministry of Interior, and that they were better disciplined and able to deal with the people than their civilian counterparts.[7]

Opponents as well as proponents of the monarchy charged that the bureaucracy had become a power in its own right, that it had interposed itself between people and ruler and was subverting the good intentions of the latter or the best interests of the former for its own security and profit. But the bureaucracy was incapable of playing the role of which it was suspected, for it lacked unity, homogeneity, security and a precise system or code to regulate and coordinate the operations of its various sectors. It remained the executor of the monarch's will. That will, it is true, was not always firm, clear, or self-generated, but the last word of approval or negation was always the emperor's. Since ministers served at his sole pleasure and represented departments that often worked at cross-purposes, and since coordination of the governmental machinery was poor, eyes were always fixed on the emperor for the clue or signal that would indicate basic political directions. All too often this caused the avoidance of initiatives or decisive action.

Autocracy in Russia remained strong and rigidly conservative not so much because of excessive bureaucratization but because there was 'no homogeneous, efficient, alert and politically conscious policy-making bureaucracy comparable to the Prussian, French, or even Austrian. The Russian bureaucracy was unable to create a *Rechtsstaat*, the *sine qua non* of orderly bureaucratic government, and as a result, the arbitrary and capricious personal power of the Russian autocrat remained undiminished until 1905.'[8] And, it may be added, extensive even after that.

'When he has put on his long blue-grey overcoat', a frequent English visitor to Russia in the years before 1917 wrote of the tsarist official, 'he is often a machine assiduously and painfully obeying instructions of which he may not be able to see the bearing.'[9] This was most true at the middle and lower levels of agencies which were charged with the control and supervision of citizens, but that is where most contacts and conflicts occurred. Chinovniks, therefore, were commonly seen as soulless or brainless pushers of pens and passers-on of paper who were isolated from real life and dreaded responsibility. Their critics said that men who saw reality in paper and affirmation of their worth in the approval of superiors were bound to be indifferent to the concerns of the people.

Widespread as such a picture was, it was not entirely fair or accurate. No bureaucracy is popular, least of all one carrying out the laws and orders of an unpopular government. From the perspective of the late twentieth century, it appears that as bureaucracies go, the Russian one was no more addicted to paper than most; its inefficiencies were a saving grace that left some loopholes for the individual to slip through; and what was perceived to be its indifference to the welfare of its charges was largely the natural outgrowth of unrealistic expectations, of differing interpretations of needs and priorities, of inadequate means, training, and manpower.

The Western traveller to Russia never failed to remark on the great number of officials he ran up against and how they helped or hindered his progress – mainly the latter. But the foreigner crossing frontiers, seeking permits to travel, reside, or do business in Russia, particularly if he was a journalist, was apt to get a distorted impression of the frequency with which most Russians, who were rural dwellers, came in contact with officialdom. According to a 1912 figure, there was one chinovnik per 60 persons in towns and one per 707 in the rural districts.[10] Anyone who opposed or criticized the regime, or was suspected of doing so, was likely to have more attention paid to him by agents of the government than he wished, but this was hardly true for the majority of the population. Against the common impression it is possible to argue that Russia may have been undergoverned rather than overgoverned. In the words of a German historian, the country was too much governed at the top and too little administered below.[11]

The manner of Russia's growth as a unified state led to an early and impressive concentration of control at the centre. It was exercised in the seventeenth and eighteenth centuries by full or part-time servitors of the crown who secured the taxes, recruits, and obedience the state required to develop its might. Measured against the country's human and economic resources and vast spaces, this was a great achievement. It was not enough to render those services the people increasingly required and that the civil services of Western Europe were beginning to perform with growing sophistication and effectiveness. While the empire's servants had been successful in the very difficult task of enforcing national unity and order, they had failed to convince literate town dwellers and illiterate peasants alike that they were as much interested in advancing the citizens' well-being as that of the state or that they treated with fairness poor and rich alike. The peasants in particular suffered from the inadequacies of government services. Until the 1890s, for example, the police were the only agents of the central administration in rural Russia who were represented below the level of the *uezdy*, the districts into which each province (*guberniia*) was divided.

There is, of course, no universally accepted standard of what constitutes an appropriate number of officials. Comparison is complicated by uncertainties of definition. In Russia, as elsewhere, some doctors and engineers, professors and architects were state functionaries and might be included in a listing of civil servants, as might the employees of local government, military officers, and teachers. Nor is there agreement on what the lower limit of inclusion is. For Russia, P.A. Zaionchkovskii has defined officialdom as the upper and middle levels of the state apparatus holding graded rank, omitting such categories as clerks, tax collectors, and rural police who were part of the government machine but not officials or bureaucrats in the Table of Ranks.

For all the differences of nomenclature, it appears that Russia – that homeland of the arch-bureaucrat, of Gogol's 'Inspector General', Tolstoi's Karenin, and swarms of chinovniks in the pages of Mikhail Saltykov and Anton Chekhov – had fewer civil servants in proportion to population than other European countries, three to four times fewer in the middle of the century. A French writer estimated in 1910 that for every 10,000 inhabitants Belgium had 200 public officials, France 176, Germany 126, the United States 113, and England 73. For the European part of Russia the figure, calculated by a Russian statistician, was 62, while a German journalist estimated 40 for the empire as a whole. Zaionchkovskii's definition yields a figure of 336, based on a total number of chinovniks in 1903 of 384,000, but included in this figure were state railway and bank employees, as well as teachers. [12]

Estimates of the number of persons in 'public service' vary from about 500,000 (384,000 plus non-ranked individuals) to nearly a million on the eve of the war. More instructive are the less comprehensive figures that are available. The 1897 census listed as being employed in 'Administration, Courts, and Police', a total of 225,770. Of that number, 48,646 held class rank (chin) in civil government or the courts, 393 served in diplomatic posts, 10,425 were officers (*ofitserskie chiny*) in the gendarmerie and police, and 4,490 were attached to the imperial court. The total number of chinovniks, strictly speaking, was 63,954 at the most. The remainder were clerical staff in the various chancelleries (46,453), maintenance personnel, guards (21,214), and the lower ratings of the police, gendarmerie, and fire brigades (94,150). Together these totalled 161,817 persons who may have been in public or civil service but who were not chinovniks or bureaucrats, except in a loose interpretation of these terms. The number of officials in the classes of the Table of Ranks employed in central government was approximately 23,000 in 1880 and 52,000 in 1914, those serving in the provinces numbered, respectively, about

12,000 and 16,000. These were the relatively few men whose character and performance gave the Russian bureaucracy its reputation, for the postal clerks, policemen, foresters, and railway guards who account for the larger estimates were not the literary prototypes of the typical chinovnik, although in their uniforms and officiousness they too appeared to be such to the lower classes of the population.[13]

The paper ranks of the public service may also have been swelled by the inclusion of the doctors, veterinarians, agronomists, teachers, and other specialists working for municipalities and zemstvos. About 65,000 to 70,000 of these were employed by the latter in 1903 and 85,000 in 1912, the majority teachers, of whom there were some 80,000 in 1914. A breakdown for an earlier period which covers the zemstvos of 34 provinces shows a total of 52,000: 3,000 doctors, 1,000 veterinarians, 1,100 agricultural experts, 1,000 insurance agents, 1,400 medical assistants and midwives, and 45,000 teachers.[14] The growth of this group somewhat made up for the disproportionate expansion of the state bureaucracy and did a great deal to supply much-needed services. Hired by the organs of local self-government, their job was less to control and supervise than to help and advise, and while peasants were no more happy to pay the taxes of the zemstvo than those of the more distant authority, they appreciated the services rendered. Since many zemstvo employees had chosen their work as a way of dedicating themselves to the betterment of 'dark' rural Russia, their probity in money matters was high. The villagers did not always understand or like this – one of Chekhov's peasants thinks that it is his failure to pay enough of a bribe that makes a doctor refuse an illegal request – but public opinion exempted zemstvo employees from the charge of venality raised against those of the state.[15]

For all the literary testimony we possess, it is not possible to render a reliable verdict of official corruption. Bribe-taking was common especially among lower officials who regarded it as a legitimate salary supplement, and it probably helped to humanize the system and to make it more tolerable. But it is far from certain that corruption in the larger sense – the constant and intimate involvement of officialdom in economic activities – was as frequent in Russia as in representative systems which are more responsive to changing political pressures and fortunes. No definitive study of that particular problem has been made and none may be possible at this late date; that it existed and grew with the spread of capitalist enterprise can, however, be shown.

The role of the state as licenser and purchaser made producers and sellers seek the assistance of well-placed bureaucrats with gifts of money or promises of profit. A law of 1885, recognizing that the temptations offered were great, prohibited officials of the three highest grades, as well as directors of departments and chief administrations, governors, prefects, and others, from participating in the management of industrial and commercial firms. No limitations were placed on the ownership of stocks or the right of officials who owned real estate to put it at the disposal of manufacturing companies. Since officials were not obliged to declare their shareholdings, the possibility of conflicts of interest remained. Although bureaucratic participation in firms in leading industries was widespread, proven and egregious violations of the law were few. Nor does the movement between private business and the public sector appear to have been as easy or frequent as in the United States. The success of organized business, the Association of Trade and Industry, for example, to mould government policy was limited.[16]

To contemporaries it was not, in any case, bribery – nor even incompetence and ineffectiveness – that constituted the worst indictment of the bureaucracy. It was the corruption of power that most troubled Russians who expressed their thoughts on how they were governed. There was indulgence for the lowly clerk or policeman who in exchange for a gratuity helped to expedite a petition or closed an eye to an expired residence permit, cab licence, or missing railroad ticket. When it came to the holder of a higher office – a governor, police chief, or department head, especially one who carried out his duties harshly or interpreted regulations narrowly – there was much less tolerance for bribe-taking which at that level occurred less often and less visibly than below. Without power to set policy, these levels of the bureaucracy yet had a great deal of leeway in its application, and in that area arose what the bureaucracy's critics called *proizvol*.

By this they meant arbitrariness, the infringement of law by those called to uphold it, the lack of a clearly defined system of legal rules of administration, the violation of rules that did exist, and the near-impossibility of a speedy redress of grievances when authority was abused. There were established ways of bringing charges against state officials for malfeasance, but whether an indictment was brought and the putative offender turned over to a court depended not on the judicial authorities but on the consent of the individual's superiors. The questions which could be put to the government in the Duma from 1906 made possible the publicizing of administrative abuses as did the greater latitude allowed the press. Still, the Duma's right of interpellation did not change the situation in essence and a bill it adopted in April 1913 to fix the responsibility of officials and facilitate their prosecution was turned down by the Council of State, the conservative upper house. This left control of the administrative apparatus where it had been throughout the nineteenth century: in the hands of its own organs or in the Senate.

The Senate was the country's highest court of review and interpreter of its laws; it also supervised the work of the administration, heard complaints against officials, and sat as an administrative court. Senators – high-ranking civil servants who were appointed by the tsar and served at his pleasure – were delegated to inspect the performance of the government's provincial agencies when evidence of mismanagement or dissatisfaction became too obvious. The Senate's usefulness as an independent organ of control was limited by exempting from its jurisdiction several ministries (War, Navy, Justice, Foreign Affairs) and other state agencies and by requiring that complaints pass through the administrative hierarchy before the Senate, in a two thirds or unanimous vote, could act on them. The offender was likely to end up with no more severe punishment than an honourable retirement or transfer to another post. This was particularly true for governors who, although subordinates of the minister of interior, often had independent influence at court and, especially if they were military men, could count on an imperial pardon or silent dismissal of their case. Baranov, for example, survived the disgrace of being cashiered from the navy for false claims of heroism during the Turkish War of 1877/78 to become a colonel in the army, prefect of the capital and, in spite of the ridicule of the Sheep's Parliament, governor of three provinces in succession.

The most important and powerful of the state's servitors in the provinces, the governor, was also the most frequent target of public censure. The writer Maxim Gorkii could find no better way of describing Lev Tolstoi's tendency to intellectual or moral dominance than to compare the great novelist and preacher of non-violence to that official. 'He says he is an anarchist. To some extent, yes. But although he destroys some regulations, he dictates others in their place, no less harsh and burdensome. That is not anarchism; it is the authoritarianism of a provincial governor.'[17] Whereas central government suffered from overlapping jurisdictions, ill-defined areas of competence, and an excessive dependence on direction from above, too much of provincial administration was in the hands of the governor or required his participation. He was at one and the same time the personal representative of the tsar and the agent of the minister of interior and as such vested with wide authority over the organs and personnel of local self-government as well as the local branches of several central state agencies.

To deal with difficult and potentially dangerous situations, governors and equivalent officials in 78 provinces and 22 other large administrative units (the numbers refer to 1914) had vast responsibilities and duties. The great weight and discretion they carried by virtue of their office and as guardians of the law – which required them to see that it was observed by their subordinates as well as by elected officials and ordinary citizens – was increased further by the adoption in August 1881 of a 'temporary' regulation which allowed for the imposition of 'reinforced' or 'extraordinary' states of protection. Initially imposed on ten provinces for three years, it still applied in 1913, the year of its expiration, to some of the most populous regions of the country, including all of the provinces of St Petersburg and Moscow. A Moscow newspaper claimed in January 1912 that all but 5 million Russians were not living under some form of 'exceptional measures'.[18]

The 'Regulation on Measures for the Safety of the State and the Protection of Public Order' was not a law or an imperial decree but an ordinance presented by Ignatev to the Committee of Ministers and approved by it and the tsar. Not enacted by the Council of State or even brought before it, the Regulation was none the less incorporated into the Collection of Laws as an addition to an existing statute from which it was kept distinct by being set in smaller type. It loomed large as a symbol of official arbitrariness and was a source of annoyance, or worse, in the lives of individuals. A state of reinforced protection allowed a governor, without recourse to the courts: to impose imprisonment for up to three months and a money fine of 400 rubles; to hand troublemakers over to military tribunals; to expel citizens from their home province and, with the consent of the minister, banish them to live under police surveillance in other parts of the empire; to order domestic searches; to close businesses and schools temporarily and prohibit private and public gatherings, including the sittings of town councils and zemstvos whose politically 'unreliable' employees he could dismiss summarily. The proclamation of a state of extraordinary protection could bring even more severe restrictions of civil rights: the suspension of newspapers, detention of suspects for up to three months, fines of up to 3,000 rubles, the removal of zemstvo deputies, or the shutting down of an entire zemstvo.[19]

Measures taken on the basis of the 1881 ordinance could not be appealed to the Senate which was not allowed to hear complaints in these cases. Although governors could be reprimanded, fined, or prosecuted with imperial permission, an official report testifies to their near-total immunity from punishment for abuses of office. Nicholas II in the first eight years of his reign approved the disciplining of one governor, his father that of two in ten years. From 1875 to 1884 there were ten such cases, and in each of the five decades from 1825 to 1874, 45, 95, 50, 26, and 17 governors were penalized in unspecified ways. Their risks appear to have declined as their authority grew. Even if they exceeded it, as happened both before and after 1905, under weak as well as strong ministers, their careers suffered no lasting damage.[20]

His opponents and victims were not above exaggerating the 'tyranny' of the local 'satrap'. But even when his actions were merely annoying and offensive rather than cruel and vicious, sober and solid citizens resented them greatly. The fact that one individual could reach so deeply and ruinously into public and private life; the fact that he was known, that he could not hide behind a faceless organism and had to initiate or authorize repressive acts himself; the lack of ready recourse against dispositions that might bring personal catastrophes – all this made governors detestable even for their lesser misdeeds. Reports and anecdotes of gubernatorial injustices and blunders are more numerous than testimonies to their efficiency and humanity.

One governor was accused of halting all traffice to facilitate his progress through his provincial capital; another ordered that no theatrical performance he planned to attend start before his arrival; a third used police informers to eavesdrop on the deliberations of a panel of judges; still another prohibited the adoption by town and rural councils of resolutions honouring the memory of Lev Tolstoi. There were instances in which governors misused their police powers in civil cases and charges that they did so to settle personal scores. Because much depended on how a discriminatory law or regulation was interpreted and applied, national and religious minorities were easy targets of gubernatorial caprice or zeal, as were 'politically unreliable' elements. Ivan Petrunkevich, a liberal zemstvo leader, was kept out of his native Chernigov province for twenty-five years by gubernatorial order, until Pleve's successor, Prince Sviatopolk-Mirskii, restored his right to reside anywhere in Russia. Three governors were assassinated and attempts were made on the lives of several more. In 1917 the Provisional Government abolished an office which had existed for over 200 years.[21]

For some time it had been recognized, even within the government, that the very institution of the governorship, with its excessive authority and responsibilities, had led to the abuse of the former and the neglect of the latter. A man who was required to chair some twenty or more committees, to make or take part in weighty decisions concerning the welfare of peasants and the levying of recruits, as well as political, medical, educational, and security matters, to issue commands and warnings, to be the emperor's personal reporter and the minister's eyes and ears, to confirm or veto the personnel and actions of a number of agencies – such a man could hardly do all that was expected of him and do it well. He would inevitably be tempted to conserve time and energy by acting quickly and decisively, and therefore with insufficient care or caution, or to act not at all.

Complaints against proizvol and the more violent protests of terrorists had assumed such proportions by the second half of 1904 that they could no longer be ignored. Sviatopolk-Mirskii told the emperor in November that Moscow (where the tsar's uncle, the Grand Duke Sergei, was governor-general) was to all intents and purposes without law and that it was necessary to assure citizens everywhere that they could not simply be shipped off to Siberia by the wilful act of a governor. An imperial decree of 12 December, addressed to the Senate and inspired by Mirskii's representations, admitted that not all authorities were abiding by the law or held accountable for their acts. The Senate was also instructed to review the temporary regulations of 1881 – 'the application of which has been attended by a marked expansion of the discretionary power of administrative authorities' – and to restrict the number of localities subjected to them.

There was agreement in the Committee of Ministers that something had to be done: P. N. Durnovo, who would in 1905 gain an unsavoury reputation as a repressive minister of interior, spoke of the degree to which the regulations for the protection of public order were being misused, a change of governors, or even a governor's change of mood, leading to different interpretations. 'There is no citizen who can be certain that his home will not be subject to administrative search and he himself be arrested.' Witte's was another voice from inside the highest levels of government which echoed what was said in the drawing-rooms of society, in the offices of lawyers and editors, in scholars' studies, and even in the boardrooms of banks and corporations.[22]

That the regime's radical and liberal critics were saying that Russia was becoming a police state (as did Petr Struve in Osvobozhdenie – 'Liberation' – the left-liberal organ being published abroad) was less significant than that partisans of autocracy did. A Countess Vorontsova told the emperor that 'all Petersburg' was aware of its letters being read by the police, and critical ones being shown to him. Nicholas denied it and promised to fire any minister who did such an underhand thing, but the practice continued, as did the complaints. One came from a most unusual source: Prince V. P. Meshcherskii, publisher of a reactionary newspaper and personal friend of Nicholas. He wondered whether a police apparatus which spent so much time inquiring into people's views and lives was the most effective guardian of the system and whether it was not neglecting what was going on among the terrorists.[23]

Much of the blame was put on Pleve, the arch-bureaucrat and arch-police-man, and on the clumsiness of his minions. In this, too, there was a large dose of aristocratic contempt for the grubby and devious work of the police, as well as anger at its lack of discrimination. People of quality were not nor-mally mixed up with the police, shunned service in its ranks, and expected to be free of its attentions. But as the Prince knew and remarked, since the time of Nicholas I there had been in Russia a political or security police, com-monly referred to as 'The Third Section', which was charged with the sur-veillance of political suspects and the ferreting out of disloyal thoughts and deeds. Inevitably such an assignment led to invasions of the private and per-sonal sphere, to snooping, and to offensive meddling in perfectly legitimate or relatively harmless activities. It was also feared by revolutionaries and ter-rorists and for most of the nineteenth century managed to keep open political opposition in check.

The 'Third Section' had, in fact, been abolished in 1880, because its very name had become odious, but the Corps of Gendarmes, its arm and army, continued to function under the Ministry of Interior's Department of Police. An assistant minister was commander of this formation which had some 13,000 men in its uniformed ranks in the late 1870s and as many as 50,000 towards its end. Their work was assisted by even more special and secret security detachments, the *okhrannye otdeleniia*, or *Okhrana* for short. Its branches, which eventually numbered twenty-six in various Russian cities and abroad, carried out political intelligence and counter-revolutionary operations and like the gendarmerie were part of the Department of Police which in 1893 established a 'Special Section' to coordinate the campaign against subversion.

Both Okhrana and gendarmerie enjoyed considerable independence from other government agencies; they were responsible directly to their chiefs and a local procurator (state attorney or public prosecutor) could do no more than report their illegal actions to the minister of justice; they were explicitly exempt from the authority of governors and governors-general and at times ignored even the minister of interior. As a result they magnified fears and fantasies. These were understandably greatest where the Okhrana was con-cerned. It maintained 'black cabinets' at post offices in seven large cities, intercepted mail, checked on the trustworthiness of persons entering St Peters-burg, and employed a variety of agents – from waiters and cabmen to house porters and former revolutionaries – for shadowing suspects, reporting sus-picious individuals and activities, and infiltrating actually or potentially subversive organizations.

Unpopular as gendarmes and secret policemen were, they were not so ruth-less or efficient as to paralyse the radicals or to silence malcontents. The tsarist political police were not a state within a state whose victims quietly disap-peared from view for years on end or for ever. The regime showed a curious inconsistency in the treatment of its political enemies. They were harassed, embittered, imprisoned, or exiled; they could also be permitted a surprising degree of personal freedom and public activity. Petrunkevich, for example, was not debarred from playing a prominent role in the zemstvo of another province and Lenin, although expelled from the University of Kazan and the brother of an executed state criminal, obtained by examination at the University of St Petersburg the degree which made it possible for him to practice law.

Most political exiles (about 3,900 in 1901) were permitted, even under difficult conditions in remote regions, to study or work; many escaped or returned after serving their sentences. Clandestine meetings grew more frequent in the reign of Nicholas and contraband literature circulated inside the country and across its frontiers with relative ease. Hundreds of thousands made use each year of the freedom to travel abroad and the special status of Finland made it, although part of the empire, a haven for revolutionaries. The instruments of repression and control were, like the rest of the bureaucracy, not as numerous, ubiquitous, and formidable as they were thought or felt to be, although they were on occasion ruthless and devastating to individuals and whole categories of people.

The ordinary police too were not as effective as suggested by the notion of the police state. While it cannot be taken as the last word, a calculation is startling which gives a ratio of police to population seven times greater for Britain and five times for France than for Russia. St Petersburg in 1897 had fewer policemen, proportionately, than London or Paris and only one third as many as Moscow in 1980 – one for each 510 inhabitants as compared with one for 160. The proportions were worse in smaller cities, and even more so in the countryside, where the police were ill-trained, ill-paid, and few – only about 7,500 in 1903. Russia was policed poorly, and contempt for the police, even before they put down strikes and demonstrations, stemmed from their inability to perform with even-handed efficiency their numerous and unpleasant duties.[24]

A contemporary article on the regulations which required citizens to carry an internal passport when they left their place of permanent residence and to present it for the police *en route* or on arrival at their new home, claimed that false or forged passports were so easily available as to make requiring them quixotic.[25] This did not, of course, lead to an end of the requirement. The potential for graft and friction was in any case great where the police took an interest in many aspects of the people's life and work. In 1896, for instance, in the capital city of 1.2 million inhabitants, the police detained 115,000 people: 46,000 for criminal activities; 23,000 for passport violations; 16,000 for beggary; 23,000 for 'idleness' (presumably an inability to prove regular employment); 7,000 for unlicensed prostitution; 200 for vagrancy and desertion.

The police were not merely charged with the preservation of law and order, the prevention and detection of crime. They collected government taxes and other dues from the peasants until 1899 and acted as the executive arm of local governments in town and country that had no other way of having their overdue payments brought in or their sanitary regulations enforced. The police supplied statistics and the certificates of good conduct and political reliability required for employment in the professions or in government. In the districts of each province, the administration's top official was the *ispravnik* or police chief, a policeman in effect occupying the post of sub-governor. A summary of scholarly criticism of the police concluded in 1898 that their powers and functions, their accountability to the courts and higher administration, were inadequately defined and regulated by law; that their relationship to the judiciary and elected public bodies was an adversary one; that they treated persons of different social categories differently; that they were assigned inappropriate tasks – such as certifying in certain districts to the blameless performance of private tutors and teachers; and, finally, that their numbers, pay, and training had not kept pace with the expansion of their duties or the growth of cities.[26]

Supervision and censorship of the printed word by the Interior Ministry's Chief Press Administration, with help from the clerical censors, was another irritant to the advanced segments of society. The citizen of a totalitarian state would be amazed by what it was possible to print and read in tsarist Russia. The first volume of Marx's *Capital* appeared in Russian in 1872, before it was translated into any other language. Lenin wrote his *Development of Capitalism in Russia* while he was in jail or Siberia and in 1899 had it published legally during his last year of exile. Less abstruse Marxist writings did not fare so well, nor did a new edition of *Capital* in 1894, works of Mill, Spencer, Darwin, Heine and Flaubert, or those of many Russian thinkers and novelists. As late as 1904 a list of forbidden works included Spinoza's *Ethics*, the *Leviathan* of Hobbes, and Lecky's *History of Rationalism*. Tolstoi was forced to make 500 changes in the text of *Resurrection* (1899) to get it past the censors; his *Power of Darkness* was allowed in print but not on the stage; newspapers were ordered to refrain from comment when he was excommunicated from the Orthodox Church in 1902. The sixth volume of the works of the conservative novelist N. S. Leskov was ordered destroyed because it mentioned corruption among the clergy. A short play of Chekhov's was banned as too gloomy in 1885. Chekhov, a non-political man, must have spoken for many when he wrote, on visiting Vienna in 1891: 'It is strange that here one is free to read anything and to say what one likes.'[27]

The relatively liberal censorship regulations of 1865 – which allowed books in general and periodical publications in St Petersburg and Moscow to be printed (but not distributed) without prior approval – were amended in 1873 to provide, 'in cases of urgent necessity', for ministerial prohibition of press discussion of such sensitive problems as the resignation of three ministers in 1881, the anniversary of peasant emancipation in 1885, strikes of students or workers, pogroms, public scandals, and much else. 'Urgent necessity' had arisen 564 times by January 1905. In August 1882 'temporary' regulations were adopted to muzzle a press which had for the most part been on the side of reform. These and earlier regulations could and did lead to warnings, fines, suspensions (for up to eight months), to the removal of books and journals from public reading rooms, to the denial of licences for new publications, to outright suppression (as in the exceptional case of the monthly *Otechestvennie*

Zapiski ('Fatherland Annals') or to the reimposition of preliminary censorship, which proved ruinous to at least one daily newspaper, the liberal *Golos* ('Voice'), in 1883. In the provinces rules were more stringent and censors less independent, less sophisticated, and more cautious than their colleagues in the two capitals. Zemstvo boards complained that they were unnecessarily restricted in the bulletins they published for the instruction of the rural population, that communications taken from the *Pravitelstvennyi Vestnik* ('Government Gazette') had been deleted from their pages, and that complaints to higher authorities as well as requests to be free of preliminary censorship went unheeded.

When preliminary censorship was at last abolished in 1906, considerable discretion still remained in the hands of the Press Administration, except that the courts were now supposed to determine when existing laws or regulations had been violated. With the wide application of the exceptional laws of 1881 and such vaguely defined offences as the 'spreading of misinformation concerning state agencies and officials' or 'favourable comments on criminal acts', that was not much of a safeguard. In December 1906 and January 1907 alone – admittedly a critical period – no fewer than 337 newspapers and pamphlets were suppressed. From 1905 to 1910 periodicals suffered 4,386 penalties as compared to 82 from 1900 to 1904; in over one thousand cases they resulted in closure. In one year alone, 1907, 175 editors and publishers were imprisoned. A conservative member of the Octobrist party said in 1908 that the press laws were in conflict with the October Manifesto and in tranquil 1910 his party demanded that governors be denied their special rights to interfere with the press and impose administrative banishment. The issue was still alive in 1913 when the Ministry of Interior submitted a new press law to the Duma which recommended the restoration of preliminary and the retention of foreign and clerical censorship, larger fines and penalties, and an increase in the discretionary powers of censors. Things improved greatly after the 1905 Revolution, but real limits remained, and as long as they were shifting and might be narrowed again, they served rather as a constant reminder of freedoms denied than of rights won.

Literate Russians were annoyed and offended by the unpredictability and stupidity of the censorship which could, in any case, be circumvented with enough determination, resourcefulness, or money. Newspapers and journals could hire a 'sitting editor' to go to prison while the real one continued publication; they could start again under a new name, as did the Bolshevik *Pravda* ('Truth'); or they could avoid the red pencil by speaking of 'legal order' instead of 'constitutional government'. Neither their determination nor inventiveness was matched by the censor's. Pleve is reported once to have asked the socialist literary critic, N. K. Mikhailovskii, why he was so much interested in freedom of the press when he could say all that he wanted to say 'between the lines'.[28] It is unknown what Mikhailovskii, a man of principle, answered. But he might have said that articulate and self-respecting Russians were less interested in the regime's occasional closing of eyes to cautiously or obscurely expressed oppositional sentiments than they were in firmly fixed and recognized rights.

* * * *

Between 1881 and 1905 a major arena of conflict and much chafing against the leading strings in which the bureaucracy tried to hold the country was that of local self-government. Its achievement under Alexander II had been taken as a hopeful sign that the scope for society's 'self-activity' would grow. The reasons for setting up elected zemstvos in thirty-four provinces of European Russia by 1878, as well as in the ten or so districts of each province, were mainly pragmatic: with the end of serfdom, the manorial authority of the nobility had to be replaced and the state lacked resources to do so on its own.

Yet when the zemstvo statute of 1864 was followed in the same year by the reform of the judiciary and in 1870 by the introduction of municipal councils (*dumy*) in 423 cities, it was believed that the state had committed itself as a matter of principle to public participation in public affairs and, given time, to its extension. When that belief was disappointed, when there was a narrowing of the sphere of self-government, there was scepticism about the compatibility of autocracy and local autonomy and about the motives for introducing it. These had, indeed, been mixed, with some members of the higher bureaucracy viewing the new institutions as subordinate parts of the central administration, others as independent of it but concerned with purely local affairs. Not until 1911/1912 were zemstvos installed in nine additional provinces; neither they nor the town councils reached Siberia or most non-Russian territories of the empire. From 1890 to 1905 the restrictive sides of the reform were seen most clearly, with the bureaucracy frequently determining what were permissible activities for local councils and watching them closely.

This is where difficulties and differences arose. Given extensive responsibilities in many fields (roads, prisons, hospitals, asylums, sanitation education, poor and famine relief, fire prevention, insurance, and agricultural advisory services), the zemstvos were at the same time limited in their ability to tax, to operate in the *volost* or canton (a grouping of about twenty peasant villages below the *uezd*), and denied the executive and police power to enforce their own decisions. This the government had reserved to itself, along with a veto over the election of the chief executive officers of zemstvos and municipalities, approval of formal contacts or joint activities by zemstvos of more than one province, and censorship over the publication of their proceedings. When a minister of education preempted the zemstvos' role in educational policy and management; when a minister of interior stopped the zemstvos of two neighbouring provinces from concerting measures to combat a plague of locusts or tried to increase administrative control over local medical institutions; and when a governor suspended the ordinances or members of a zemstvo executive (*uprava* – board), they seemed to prove the point made by Chicherin in 1883 in a speech for which he was deposed as mayor of Moscow: that the revolutionary underground was successful only because the 'legal' part of society was not allowed to speak, to organize, or to develop the independence and self-government that the country needed to prosper and to advance.[29]

In 1883 the part of society that was represented in town councils and zemstvos of provinces and districts was not yet prepared to speak and was far from being the spearhead of the constitutional movement it became two decades later. Most zemstvos, although they were 'all-class' institutions, were dominated by apolitical or conservative gentry; meeting in general assembly only once a year (for twenty days in the province and ten in the district) and electing their executive boards once every three years, they suffered from lack of interest and participation and were hardly the tireless champions of the people's rights and welfare pictured by their admirers. None the less, the zemstvos started to emerge in the 1890s as centres of opposition to the bureaucracy and eventually of autocracy as well; they began to resist encroachments of their activities and funds and to expand their services to the peasantry. This was so because a vocal, politically conscious minority had the sympathy of a majority of landed nobles who felt that the government and its agents were indifferent to the interests of their class.

In setting up the zemstvos and municipal councils, the state had parted with little of its authority, while divesting itself of many burdensome and costly tasks. The performance of these – consisting of contributions in money or services for the quartering of troops and the maintenance of roads, for mails and jails, for police and transportation – took from 40 to 50 per cent of zemstvo income until 1890, when this proportion began to decline markedly, until it reached about 5 per cent in 1912. But in the very year in which the flow of local revenues to the centre began to be reversed, local autonomy and initiative came under attack. The framers of the so-called 'counter-reforms' of 1890 (for the zemstvos) and 1892 (for the towns), Minister of Interior Tolstoi and his assistant A. D. Pazukhin, were quite open about viewing zemstvo functions as state functions, thus feeding doubts about whether genuine local self-government existed.

Under the new dispensation the elected members of zemstvo boards became government officials and subject to approval by the governor who was given increased authority to discipline them and to veto their decisions. Peasant deputies to the district zemstvo assemblies were no longer elected by their fellows but appointed by the governor from a list made up by a *volost* peasant meeting – a practice followed until 1906. The already disproportionate share of noble deputies (the only ones elected directly) was increased to 55.2 per cent, as compared with 42.2 per cent before 1890. Peasant representation was reduced from 38.5 to 31 per cent and that of others (merchants, clergy, etc.) from 19.3 to 13.8 per cent. In the provincial zemstvos the disparity was even greater. This further shift in favour of the nobility did not, however, signify an increase in its actual class power. The benefits of the counter-reforms accrued to the bureaucracy and its local agents, whose interventions in zemstvo affairs were encouraged by the new law. Before 1890, there had been five cases in which a governor had withheld confirmation of a zemstvo executive's elected chairman; by 1909 there were eighty-one, and six in which the entire membership of an executive board was vetoed by the governor of a province. If non-confirmation of an individual or a whole board occurred twice, the government could fill the vacant posts by appointment. This ultimate sanction was rarely employed, but it was a useful deterrent to the election of men who were considered unreliable.[30]

The technical specialists hired by the zemstvos were also subject to gubernatorial approval, and since many were educated men and women who saw their service as the only form of public duty open to them, they were suspected of harbouring unorthodox ideas. They did, in fact, help to push the zemstvos towards greater political and social activism in the years before 1905. The vice-governor of Samara referred to these experts as the 'Third Element' – the other two being appointed officials and elected board members –, perhaps implying a certain similarity with the third estate of pre-revolutionary France. The governor of Orlov province declared all zemstvo statisticians to be dangerous socialists and would not allow them to carry on their work. Pleve called them a cohort of *sans-culottes*, blamed them for peasant riots, and had the governors of several provinces keep them from carrying out statistical surveys.[31]

The widest latitude for bureaucratic interference was opened up by that section of the zemstvo statutes that empowered the governor not only to question the legality of decisions adopted by the zemstvos but also to stop those he considered to be in conflict with the public good, the interests of the state, or the welfare of the local population. And where a governor's veto could earlier be appealed directly to the Senate, after 1890 this had to be done through the newly established Guberniia Office for Zemstvo and Municipal Affairs, of which the governor was chairman and which contained a majority of state officials.

If the new rules for the zemstvos were designed to inhibit their potential for political activity, because a few of them had become strongholds of that gentry liberalism which asked for continuing the Great Reforms and even for a national zemstvo, they failed in their purpose. In this, as in other respects, the government's bark was worse than its bite. While voicing political aspirations was made more difficult after 1890 and the zemstvos turned to practical tasks, they were not silenced. Nor did the counter-reform markedly hinder their work in health, education, welfare and the improvement of agriculture and crafts. Between 1890 and 1900 the number of agronomists increased from 29 to 197 and expenditures for primary schools, public health and veterinary services alone more than doubled. The chief result of the bureaucracy's enlarged role in this area of Russian public life – and the most fateful one politically – was that it brought benefits neither to the state nor to the zemstvos, only new frictions and irritations.

Because of the large role that businessmen careful of their money played in them, the municipalities were not as enterprising as the zemstvos, nor did their members have as great a sense of public responsibility as did the professional experts or independent-minded local nobles of the zemstvos. By 1892, when the 1870 statute was revised, interest in municipal affairs had declined so much that absenteeism at council meetings made their work difficult. The new law narrowed the basis of public participation, tightened bureaucratic control, and increased apathy on the part of the electorate. The number of meetings a municipal assembly could hold was now regulated; mayors, assistant mayors, and board members were henceforth considered state servitors, and elections of the latter had to be confirmed by the authorities; if they were not, others could be appointed in their place. Higher property qualifications reduced the electorate in St Petersburg (a city of 1.2 million in 1897) from 21,000 to 8,000; from 20,000 to 7,000 in Moscow (population 1 million), from 6,900 to 2,300 in Kharkov (out of 175,000), and from 5,400 to 800 in Rostov-on-Don which had 120,000 inhabitants. The minister of interior or a governor could confirm a council's minority candidate for mayor, remove him, city councillors or other town officials, and veto their decisions. Between 1900 and 1914 the elections of 217 mayors and of board members of 318 councils were annulled.[32]

At a time when Russian cities were growing at a rapid rate, such hobbling hindered their dealing with the problems of growth and particularly the influx of large numbers of workers who were soon to prove a troublesome element in the urban centres. Few had the amenities of larger European cities and many were overgrown villages of wooden houses lacking running water, adequate sanitation, paved streets and public transportation. In many cities state obligations for the billeting of troops and police subsidies consumed from a third to a half of the budget which was already lower by two to five times than that of Austrian, French or German cities.

Unable to perform the many services the country needed, the bureaucracy was yet reluctant to let others take its place. There was more to this, of course, than fear or jealousy alone. There were, as noted, problems of adequate quality and quantity of staff, of service morale and independence, and also of scarce resources which, so the central administration felt, had to be allocated centrally. Any substantial sums collected by local governments and expended for local needs would be lost to the state. As there was never enough to go round in the first place, additional diversions of funds were a serious matter. The limits placed on the taxing powers of cities and zemstvos were motivated by such financial considerations as was Witte's insistence before the Council of State that property taxes raised by the latter could not be increased without the express approval of the central government. In the event, the Council modified his proposal to apply only to increases in excess of 3 per cent per year. But this went along with an extension of the governors' authority to approve or reject budgets requiring exemption from the new law. This proved to be a handicap mainly for the poorer zemstvos since in most the yearly growth rate had averaged 4 per cent. As late as 1914 local government expenditures came to only 14 per cent of the national budget, whereas in some European countries they exceeded it.[33]

Although among the most able and enlightened of tsarist bureaucrats, Witte was as concerned as the most anxious traditionalist over encroachments on the executive power by the zemstvos and was convinced that they would in time challenge it. In such a contest, the autocracy's ability to reform, to modernize and guide the country might be impaired. Witte was not, he said in his memorandum of 1899 on 'Autocracy and Zemstvo', for the abolition of the latter, but argued against their extension and for the transfer of still more zemstvo functions to the state. Local needs were likely to be selfish needs. A modern, dependable and capable civil service would be in a much better position to fix priorities with an eye to the general welfare. It would also, Witte believed, guard individual rights and in that way help rather than hinder the growth of initiative in all spheres of national life.[34]

Witte knew that the kind of civil service he wanted to take charge of Russia's social and economic development did not exist. In fact, he blamed the strict administrative supervision of local government for its anomalous and 'most pitiful' condition. But his success in organizing the railroad and financial administrations, and training their personnel, gave him confidence that the entire state apparatus would in time function with a like spirit and efficiency. His optimism was shared neither by those who saw no ready alternative to a bureaucratic autocracy nor among advocates of local autonomy or representative government. The latter were convinced by the disastrous famine of 1891 of the shortcomings of officialdom. Improvements made in the imperial civil service in its remaining quarter century of existence never extinguished the memory of what was thought to have been its fearful bungling in that crisis. The memory was kept alive by prejudice and magnified by other famines and failures, particularly in the management of the military effort and the home front in two wars.

The nearly unanimous view that the bureaucracy was by turns callous and helpless in 1891 is as little justified as the picture of the zemstvos clamouring for aid and attention from an indifferent St Petersburg and of private relief efforts being blocked by a too cautious government. The administrators, it has been shown, probably did as well as they could, given the magnitude of the catastrophe and the paucity of means to deal with it. Nor were the government's agents at the central, provincial, and local levels insensitive to the plight of the stricken peasants, an impression that was created by bureaucratic defensiveness and discretion. And while there was friction with the zemstvos, they were not seriously hampered in carrying out a task that was legally theirs but also beyond their capacity – provisioning the hungry people of their districts. Indeed, they had occasionally to be prodded into greater energy by an activist governor. It is true that the administration did not like students raising money in the universities and setting up soup kitchens in the villages, society ladies arranging benefit concerts, or Lev Tolstoi and Chekhov collecting food, seed grains, and horses for the peasants. Yet because its own resources were inadequate it tolerated and even encouraged public aid to the affected provinces and their inhabitants. Still, failure there was and although it was exaggerated by the regime's critics it was deeply rooted in the nature of the system which did not draw the lessons of 1891.[35]

The experience of combating the famine and its consequences revealed a lack of cohesion and control in a governmental apparatus that had always claimed to possess these advantages as against decentralization or local self-government. The Committee of Ministers, which was supposed to coordinate the government's efforts in just such crises as this one, did not have the machinery or the leadership to do so. Nor did the Ministry of Interior, whose head, Durnovo, had not enough energy, ability, or standing to impose a unified policy. Even a better man and administrator would have been without adequate information on which to base policy or a reliable chain of command reaching to the villages to carry it out. This was not only because some governors defied ministerial directives, and local representatives of the ministries in their turn ignored the governors. It was also the result of not having enough officials in the countryside to whom a minister could entrust the execution of his orders. That gap the zemstvos too could not fill; not merely because the government suspected their political pretensions, but because they were organized to function mainly at the provincial and *uezd* levels and did not have the men or the money to operate in a sustained way in the villages or cantons (*volosti*). Moreover, the zemstvos had no nationwide organization that could have supplemented or replaced the activities of government, and for that the latter's political anxieties were responsible.

These defects of the bureaucratic structure – the lack of policy coordination; the absence of firm links between centre and localities; shortages of information and personnel in the countryside – were not remedied in the wake of 1891. A commission chaired by Pleve attempted to improve famine relief and food supply, but its recommendations to take these tasks out of the hands of the zemstvos would only have placed additional burdens on an already creaky administrative machinery. Another famine in 1898 led the state to give up this plan, although in 1900 it tried once more. But when there was crop failure and hunger again in certain localities in 1901, and the central authorities had to recognize that they could not cope with it unaided, they retreated from the 'temporary' rules they had just issued and instructed governors to apply them only in 'normal' times. In this way the bureaucracy tacitly admitted its own inability to deal with any but normal situations. And normalcy would very soon become an exceptional state of affairs.[36]

Thus, during the Russo-Japanese War of 1904/1905, the zemstvos of fourteen provinces, in order to assist the army's overburdened medical services, joined in an All-Zemstvo Organization to equip and send field hospitals to the Far East at their own expense. Since Pleve saw in such joint activity a dangerous precedent for common political action by the zemstvos, he instructed governors of provinces whose zemstvos had not joined the Organization to prevent their doing so. This, in effect, made zemstvo efforts on behalf of the wounded illegal and caused them to be carried out discreetly. With help coming from inside the bureaucracy, Pleve's opposition was circumvented, and the hospitals were sent anyway. Yet not until the Ministry of Interior under Sviatopolk-Mirskii gave explicit permission to all the zemstvos to participate in the work begun by fourteen of their number, could it go forward unhindered.[37]

Eventually the government saw itself forced to accept the permanent organization of non-governmental assistance to supplement its limited capabilites for meeting calamities. This happened when the Japanese War was followed by another famine year during which state relief funds were channelled through the combined zemstvos of the affected provinces. In general, relations between central and local governments improved after 1906 — with increases in subsidies paid by the former and a reduction in contributions from the latter. The war that broke out in 1914 would show once again how much the bureaucracy depended on the assistance of the public, organized in the first instance through the municipal and rural councils, and how incapable it was of accepting the help of outsiders without suspecting their motives or interfering with their methods.

When Chicherin had been removed as mayor of Moscow without being given a chance to defend himself, he commented that too many of his friends were inclined to blame the minister of interior or the governor-general of Moscow for the abominable conduct of the administration. They, he said, had only played the parts assigned to them; it was the monarch who approved such conduct and had to bear the moral responsibility for not living up to his high calling.[38] Article 80 of the Fundamental Laws also spelled out his legal responsibility: 'The power of administration in all its extent belongs to the Emperor. In matters of supreme administration it acts directly, while in matters of subordinate administration, a limited amount of power may be entrusted by him to offices and persons acting in his name and according to his commands.' The fact that until 1917 the bureaucracy was ultimately accountable only to an emperor who was its real head and guiding spirit was bound to damage both. 'The autocrat was identified on the one side with God, and on the other . . . with the lowest of his police corporals. This involved a double responsibility which no system in the world could adequately discharge',[39] least of all one which failed so often in some basic tasks.

Private philanthropy, voluntary or cooperative organizations, although they had begun to make an appearance, were yet too few and feeble to step into the breach. Neither could the church play the dual role it had filled with some success in most of Europe's old regimes: pillar and preacher of the established order; helper and mentor of its flock. Subordinate to the state and deprived of its independence, it had, like the bureaucracy, been made more responsive to orders from the centre than to the needs of its charges. Since the time of Peter the Great, when the office of Patriarch of Moscow and all the Russias was allowed to lapse, the Orthodox Church had been headed by a synod of ecclesiastics of which a layman appointed by the tsar was the director. Together with a loss of vitality, church and clergy suffered a loss of respect as a result of their close embrace by the state. They tried to distance themselves from it in 1905, when Pobedonostsev was forced to resign as Procurator of the Holy Synod after twenty-five years.

The hierarchy also wished to restore the patriarchate and to call the first church council since 1682 in order to elect a patriarch, decentralize administration, and reform parish and school. Nicholas declared this to be premature and in December 1906 dissolved a commission of bishops and lay experts who had prepared an agenda of reforms, to be discussed by a council, which would, among other things, have reduced the procurator's authority. Another pre-council conference was called in 1912. It had as little success as the liberal churchmen who proposed the abolition of the procuracy, the democratization of the parish, and greater lay participation in church affairs. After 1907 the government made extensive use of hierarchs and clergy as propagandists and electoral agents for rightist parties, and the prestige of the church declined even further. Only when the monarchy fell did the Holy Synod feel free and bold enough to declare its independence and to welcome the liberties that revolution had brought.

These failed efforts at reform provide part of the explanation for the church's inability to be a better support of the state with which it was so closely linked. It was not merely that it routinely preached to an increasingly rebellious people what it practised: obedience to the powers that be. The Synod and the pre-conciliar committee also learned, or learned again, of the practical problems that kept the clergy in town and country from carrying out its mission of charity and the cure of souls – problems of quantity and quality not unlike those that plagued the bureaucracy.

By the end of the nineteenth century Russia had only about half as many churches for every 100,000 Orthodox inhabitants as there had been two centuries earlier – 52 as compared to 106, and the lack was greatest in areas of greatest population growth, among uprooted peasants and workers in cities and factory towns. Odessa, a city of almost half a million, had only five parish churches, two cemetery churches and several private chapels. The industrial settlement of Orekhovo-Zuevo had but one church for 40,000 people, a factory town of 6,000 near Tver had none. Many church buildings were close to ruin because parishioners could not or would not contribute to their repair; many were so-called 'cold churches' because there was no money to heat them; others, in Western Russia, had to be closed because means for maintaining clerics were lacking. One priest reported that when at last his congregation of 2,400 peasants agreed to donate 25 kopeks per farmstead to replace his ragged vestments, a third refused when it was time to pay.

The poverty of communicants, particularly in the villages, was matched by that of their shepherds. Although the latter were given state salaries, these were too small – from 250 to 400 rubles per year and less for deacons and psalmists – to free them of an embarrassing dependence on the 'voluntary' gifts, fees in money, kind or service from their flocks. The haggling that arose over assessments and collections lowered the dignity of the clerical calling.

The married village priest who struggled to provide for his large family – only monastic clergy were celibate – was too much like the peasants to inspire respect and in most cases had not taken his vows out of choice or dedication. He had been born into the clerical estate, the son of a priest who could gain admission for him to a seminary but could not afford to send him to a secular institution. In the early years of the twentieth century about 80 per cent of seminarists came from clerical families, and before 1905 most were barred from shifting to a university. Many, therefore, entered the priesthood unwillingly; following necessity rather than a vocation, they performed their offices indifferently. More than a third of 47,000 priests (in 1904) had not completed a full seminary education. The infrequency with which they preached sermons may have been related to their inability to do so.

Growing numbers of seminary graduates either left the priesthood, especially after 1905, or shunned the difficult and lowly life of the rural pastor. In Siberia in particular there was a shortage of priests. In the diocese of Omsk alone, twenty parishes were without a curate, and the bishop of Mogilev, in Western Russia, complained in 1905 that he had to fill twenty vacancies with priests who had not completed a seminary education. The bishop of Smolensk considered better priests and better conditions for their life and work to be indispensable prerequisites for the revitalization of the parish. He thought that the promise every priest had to give even before his ordination – to abide by the instructions and prohibitions of the secular authorities – diminished his service to the church and his flock. Forbidden, under pain of severe penalties, to 'involve himself' in the most pressing needs of the peasants, their pastor was obliged to ignore their distress. Those who disobeyed were disciplined by the church or lost to it.[40]

* * * *

'When we have open and independent courts, when local society is called to participate in self-government, the rightlessness of the individual before administrative licence (*proizvol*) is a strange anachronism . . . .'[41] That a text on public law containing these words was passed by the censor in 1899 is, in a way, more revealing than the fact that they were written. The tsarist government, while it could be brutal to its enemies, was not so totally or consistently repressive as to extinguish, or even want to extinguish, human or property rights, legality, or the consciousness of these. And the survival of these values and practices made their infringement all the more reprehensible and difficult to bear. A sense of injustice in the face of *proizvol* was decisive in shaping attitudes towards the bureaucracy among the articulate and educated members of society. Its other shortcomings might have mattered less if it had shown a greater regard for the law. It is possible that the clamour for political rights might have been muted if civil rights had been assured. Since they were not, the political struggle came to be seen as one way of securing them as well as a more responsive and effective civil service.

REFERENCES

1. S. E. Kryzhanovskii, *Vospominaniia* (Berlin, n.d.), p. 209.
2. The nobility (*dvorianstvo*) of Russia, although a legal estate (soslovie), was more open and fluid than that of other countries. The very concept of nobility, implying a high degree of corporate consciousness, organization, and power, may not be entirely applicable here. Many American and English historians, therefore,

have preferred to use 'gentry' for the land- and (before 1861) serf-owning class of the empire. The term is indeed preferable, but it tends to understate the element of heredity in the prestige and the prerogatives of the class, an element of aristocratism and exclusiveness that was stressed increasingly from the late eighteenth century on by members of the class and, to a lesser extent, by the ruler. Nor does gentry, with its suggestion of 'landed', allow for those nobles whose primary source of income and status was the state rather than the land. If this is remembered, gentry and nobility can be used interchangeably. See pp. 88 –95 below.

3. P. A. Zaionchkovskii, *Pravitelstvennyi apparat samoderzhavnoi Rossii v XIX v.* (Moscow, 1978), pp. 85–90; S. Iu. Vitte, *Vospominaniia* (Moscow, 1969) I, pp. 208–209.

4. P. V. Annenkov, *The Extraordinary Decade. Literary Memoirs*, trans. I. R. Titunik (Ann Arbor, Mich., 1968), p. viii; *Letters of Nikolai Gogol*, trans. C. R. Proffer (Ann Arbor, Mich., 1967), p. 32.

5. Philip Pomper, *The Russian Revolutionary Intelligentsia* (New York, 1970), p. 164.

6. Zaionchkovskii, op. cit., pp. 52–3.

7. V. A. Sukhomlinov, *Vospominaniia* (Berlin, 1924), p. 127; A. N. Kuropatkin, 'Dnevnik', *Krasnyi Arkhiv* 2 (1922), p. 59.

8. Marc Raeff, 'The Russian autocracy and its officials', *Harvard Slavic Studies* 4 (1957), pp. 77–91.

9. B. Pares, *Russia Between Reform and Revolution* (New York, 1962), pp. 146–7.

10. N. A. Rubakin, *Rossiia v tsifrakh* (St Petersburg, 1912), p. 64.

11. Otto Hoetzsch, *Russland* (Berlin, 1915), p. 270.

12. Zaionchkovskii, op. cit., p. 221; Rubakin, op. cit., pp. 62, 66; E. N. and A. P. R. Anderson, *Political Institutions and Social Change in Continental Europe in the 19th Century* (Berkeley and Los Angeles, Cal., 1967), p. 167.

13. Hugh Seton-Watson, *The Russian Empire 1801–1917* (Oxford, 1967), pp. 535–6; Alf Edeen, 'The Civil Service' in C. E. Black (ed.), *The Transformation of Russian Society* (Cambridge, Mass., 1960), p. 276; N. A. Rubakin, 'Mnogo li v Rossii chinovnikov?', *Vestnik Europy* 1 (Jan. 1910), pp. 111–34; L. K. Erman, *Intelligentsia v pervoi russkoi revoliutsii* (Moscow, 1966), ch. 1.

14. W. H. E. Johnson, *Russia's Educational Heritage* (Pittsburgh, Pa., 1959), p. 204; V. Trutovskii, *Sovremennoe zemstvo* (St Petersburg, 1916), pp. 47–8; 'Tretii element', *Sovetskaia istoricheskaia entsiklopediia*, XIV (1973), p. 393; A. Vucinich, 'The state and the local community', in Black, op. cit., p. 204.

15. W. H. Bruford, *Chekhov and His Russia* (London, 1948), pp. 56, 98; I. I. Petrunkevich, *Iz zapisok obshchestvennogo deiatelia* (Berlin, 1934), pp. 208–10.

16. I. F. Gindin, 'Russkaia burzhuaziia v period kapitalizma', *Istoriia SSSR* 2 (Jan.–Feb. 1963), pp. 72–8; and 3 (March–April 1963), pp. 54–8; Zaionchkovskii, op. cit., pp. 102–5, 268–73; J. P. McKay, *Pioneers for Profit* (Chicago, Ill., and London, 1970), pp. 268–73.

17. Henri Troyat, *Tolstoy* (Garden City, NY, 1967), p. 572.

18. Thomas Riha, 'Constitutional developments' in T. G. Stavrou (ed.), *Russia Under the Last Tsar* (Minneapolis, Minn., (1969), p. 98.

19. R. E. Pipes, *Russia Under the Old Regime* (London and New York, 1974), pp. 305–7; Anton Palme, *Die russische Verfassung* (Berlin, 1910), pp. 7–71; Samuel Kucherov, *Courts, Lawyers, and Trials Under the Last Three Tsars* (New York, 1953), pp. 202–5; George Vernadsky *et al.*, (eds), *A Source Book for Russian His-*

tory (New Haven, Conn., and London, 1972), III, pp. 680–1.

20. Russia, Komitet ministrov, *Istoricheskii obzor deiatelnosti komiteta ministrov* V (St Petersburg, 1902), p. 3.

21. N. Voronovich, *Vechernyi zvon. Ocherki proshlogo* (New York, 1955), pp. 16–17; Petrunkevich, op. cit., p. 244; V. M. Khizhniakov, *Vospominaniia zemskogo deiatelia* (Petrograd, 1916), pp. 87–93, 180–1; B. N. Chicherin, *Vospominaniia*: *Zemstvo i Moskovskaia Duma* (Moscow, 1934), pp. 209–210; 'Iz materialov o L. N. Tolstom', *Krasnyi Arkhiv* 4 (1923), pp. 361–2; A. D. Golitsyn, 'Vospominaniia', book V (manuscript in Archives of Russian History and Culture, Columbia University, NY).

22. 'Dnevnik Kn. E. A. Sviatopolk-Mirskoi, 1904–1905', *Istoricheskie zapiski* 77 (1965), pp. 258–9; V. I. Gurko, *Features and Figures of the Past* (Stanford Cal., and London, 1939), pp. 319–21.

23. Gurko, op. cit., pp. 120–1; 'Dnevnik Sviatopolk-Mirskoi', op. cit., p. 241; *Osvobozhdenie* 20–21 (18 April/1 May 1903), p. 357.

24. Arsène de Goulevich, *Czarism and Revolution* (Hawthorne, Cal., 1962), pp. 38–9; N. B. Weissman, *Reform in Tsarist Russia* (New Brunswick, NJ, 1981), p. 11, 23, 206–7; G. B. Sliozberg, *Dorevoliutsionny stroi Rossii* (Paris, 1938), pp. 177–90; 'Politsiia',*Entsiklopedicheskii slovar* XXIV (St Petersburg, 1898), pp. 327–37; Sidney Monas, 'The Political Police' in Black, op. cit., pp. 164–81.

25. 'Pasport', *Bolshaia Entsiklopediia* XIV (St Petersburg, 1914), p. 731.

26. 'Politsiia', op. cit., p. 332.

27. W. H. Bruford, *Chekhov and His Russia: A Sociological Study* (London, 1947), p. 106.

28. Seton-Watson, op. cit., p. 481.

29. Chicherin, op. cit., pp. 234–45; George Fischer, Russian Liberalism (Cambridge, Mass., 1958), pp. 7–13; Sergius Gogel, *Die Ursachen der russischen Revolution* (Berlin, 1926) pp. 48–9; Khizhniakov, op. cit., pp. 177–8; V. Iu. Skalon, *Mneniia zemskikh sobranii o sovremennom polozhenii Rossii* (Berlin, 1883), p. 13.

30. L. G. Zakharova, *Zemskaia kontr-reforma 1890 g.* (Moscow, 1968), pp. 157–67; J. Melnik (ed.), *Russen über Russland* (Frankfurt, 1906), pp. 140–150.

31. T. I. Polner, *Zhiznennyi put Kn. G. E. Lvova* (Paris, 1932), pp. 55–6; A. N. Naumov, *Iz utselevshikh vospominanii, 1868–1917* (New York, 1955), pp. 259–62; Gurko, op. cit., pp. 234–6.

32. N. I. Astrov, *Vospominaniia* (Paris, 1949), p. 257; P. P. Gronsky and N. I. Astrov, *The War and the Russian Government* (New Haven, Conn., 1929),pp. 134–7; V. N. Kokovtsov, *Out of My Past* (Stanford, Cal., and London, 1935), p. 396.

33. M. F. Hamm (ed.), *The City in Russian History* (Lexington, Ky., 1976), pp. 91–113, 182–200; Sliozberg, op. cit., pp. 211–12.

34. S. Iu. Vitte, *Samoderzhavie i zemstvo* (Stuttgart, 1903); T. H. Von Laue, *Sergei Witte and the Industrialization of Russia* (New York, 1963), pp. 157–61.

35. R. G. Robbins, *Famine in Russia 1891–1892* (New York and London, 1975).

36. A. A. Kizevetter, *Na rubezhe dvukh stoletii: vospominaniia, 1881–1914* (Prague, 1929), pp. 198–200, 321–2; M. T. Florinsky, *Russia* (New York, 1953), II, p. 1167.

37. T. I. Polner *et al.*, *Russian Local Government* (New Haven, Conn., 1930), pp. 7–8, 33–4.

38. Chicherin, op. cit., p. 246.
39. B. Pares, *Russia Between Reform and Revolution* (New York, 1962), p. 156.
40. See the works by Curtiss, Immekus, and Simon in the bibliography for Chapter four.
41. N. M. Korkunov, *Russkoe gosudarstvennoe pravo* (St Petersburg, 1899), I, p. 429.

CHAPTER FIVE

Peasants and nobles: the problems of rural Russia

Although peasants[1] might be vexed by the treatment they received at the hands of government agents, proizvol was not their main complaint. It was, as they saw it, lack of land. In the core provinces of the empire its most direct and visible cause was the neighbouring squire and the fields, once worked by his serfs, he had kept at the emancipation. When peasants took up clubs and torches in the disturbances of 1905–06, they were concerned first and foremost with the land; 'they did not usually march against some local official of the government, but toward some manor house'.[2] The appearance of an official personage was fairly rare in the villages, but the policeman, recruiting officer, or excise inspector was no more popular for being rare. Yet he was a less readily available target for the discontent and frustration of former serfs and state peasants than the noble landlord or the peasant functionaries who were charged with a variety of administrative chores for which they had little aptitude or training.

At first blush the structure of authority in the countryside looks exceptionally democratic. It seemed to give wide scope to local self-government and custom and to avoid the formalism and legalism that illiterate or semi-literate peasants have at all times and places found remote, incomprehensible, and difficult. At the lowest level, the village community (*selskoe obshchestvo*), acting through the assembly of heads of households, exercised much of the authority formerly vested in the landlords or, in the case of state peasants, in the Ministry of State Domains. The village community elected and paid its elder and scribe, set local dues, apportioned state taxes or other obligations and saw to their collection. It selected the required number of conscripts for the military; admitted, banished or released members; decided on divisions of households and property in large families; apportioned the arable and common lands among member households, and for each ten of the latter sent one delegate to the assembly of the canton (*volost*). There they elected the office-holders in some 10,000 cantons, each embracing several villages and from 300 to 2,000 male peasants, who were responsible to the government organs of the district for the maintenance of order and tranquillity. They also kept records and vital statistics, called out peasants to work on schools and roads, to fight fires and floods.

But the elected officials of village and canton – elders and their deputies, clerks and tax-gatherers, the judges of cantonal courts who heard civil cases involving no more than 100 rubles and punished minor offences – accepted their posts with more resignation than joy. Having to do the state's work took them away from fields and families and did nothing to make them popular with their fellows. These could be flogged at their order, deported to Siberia for 'vicious conduct', denied a passport to leave the community or hired out to make good their share of its financial obligations.

Nor did peasants think of themselves as favoured and protected by an administrative and legal system to which they alone were subject. Village government was based on their separateness from other citizens and on a customary law that was far from clear, uniform, or stable. It denied peasants some of the statutory safeguards of the Civil Code of 1864 and helped to perpetuate their distinctness and inferiority. The village functionaries were not the peasants' representatives and protectors. Contemporary accounts are full of complaints about them: that elders had men whipped for insolence; that clerks (often the only literates in rural government and therefore powerful) cheated and insulted peasants; that since the best men shunned village posts, the worst took them up for selfish reasons, and that a bucket of vodka or other bribe could influence elders or judges.[3]

During the ministry of Tolstoi, the central government, concerned over maintaining order in the countryside, also noted the shortcomings of peasant administrators: their squandering of public funds, abuses of authority, or avoidance of responsibility. Tolstoi did not see the remedy in extending to village and volost the zemstvo elected by all classes in district and province or the general system of courts with their regularized procedures and safeguards. He wished to preserve the existing structure and to tighten the government's control over it. This was done by creating in 1889 the office of land captain (*zemskii nachalnik*) who was to check the arbitrariness of peasant over peasant by carrying the bureaucratic arbitrariness of St Petersburg to all.

Where the volost elder had the right to impose fines of up to one ruble and forty-eight hours of arrest, the land captain could fine five rubles and imprison for seven days. The *zemskii*, as he was called, was to watch over the rights of villagers and to their share of the land (*nadel*) assigned to the community at the emancipation; he was also to preserve public order, decency, and safety. To that end he could review the actions taken by village and canton assemblies, courts and officials, suspend the latter and recommend their dismissal. It was he who appointed as volost elder one of the two men elected to that post and half the number of candidates chosen for the cantonal court. He made his weight felt also in determining the issues brought before peasant assemblies and in the cantonal elections of deputies to the district zemstvo. After 1905 it was his job to see that 'unreliables' did not become electors or deputies to the Duma. The zemskii acted as judge in certain civil and lesser criminal cases that had previously come before elected justices of the peace who decided matters that went beyond the competence of cantonal courts on the basis of laws valid for all citizens. Until justices of the peace were restored in 1912, peasants wanting to appeal against the verdict of a zemskii had no recourse to the courts, only to administrative agencies.[4]

It is difficult to know what peasants thought of the new official who appeared among them after 1889, or whether he made a great difference in their lives. Pares reported that no other official was so unpopular, and the minister of agriculture remarked in 1897 that land captains who made it difficult for peasants to migrate to Siberia were suspected of working hand in glove with landowners who did not wish to lose cheap labour. In 1907 N. N. Kutler, a former minister of agriculture, attacked the captains as a wasteful expenditure and an instrument of social oppression. During zemstvo elections in 1909–10 the peasants tried hard to defeat candidates favoured by the zemskii. At the time of the 1912 Duma elections, however, several governors agreed that the land captains could do little to influence peasant votes, suggesting that they had too little power or too little respect. There were those who maintained that things had changed very little and that only doctrinaire liberals or romantic idealizers of peasant virtues believed that the zemskii carried into the village more arbitrariness or violations of rights than had always been there. The main problem, it was widely felt, was one which plagued the entire governmental apparatus – a lack of good men. It was not, an assistant minister of interior thought, proizvol but laziness and indifference that were the chief sins of the land captain.[5]

To urban and upper-class Russians he was a controversial figure, even if they admitted that he made volost administration more orderly and efficient. Conservatives saw in the very need for such an official another sign of the decline of patriarchal authority in the countryside; to liberals he stood for the 'counter-reforms' in law and local government that were whittling away the gains of the previous reign. When Tolstoi proposed the new institution, the majority of the State Council thought it wrong to correct rural mismanagement by endowing with both executive and judicial powers a bureaucrat who dealt only with peasants and without reference to the general laws; all strata of the population, all types of communities needed better management and the rule of law. The Council's negative vote of 39 to 13 was a rebuke to the minister of interior for continuing to treat peasants as wards of the state. Since the emperor shared it, the minority view prevailed.

The impression that peasants were to remain a distinct and inferior category was reinforced by the requirement that applicants for the new post who were hereditary nobles of the locality be given preference and that gentry marshals be consulted on their appointment. This led to protests that what was contemplated was a form of outdoor relief for the nobility; that serfdom was being restored in a new guise; and that the disciplinary powers vested in the zemskii gave him an unchecked personal authority over the peasants. Even in the time of serfdom, a member of the Council of State protested, no decent landlord would have allowed himself the kind of interference in their property rights that was permitted to the zemskii. How, it was asked, could peasants develop a respect for the law, for government, and for the rights and property of others if their own rights were settled not in the courts, not on the basis of law, but by administrative fiat?

The official answer was that educated noble landowners, dedicated to the peasants' welfare and familiar with their needs, would do more for them than impersonal codes. But the call for such men was not met in sufficient numbers, and after 1905 a zemskii needed no longer to be a noble. The ideal of a firm, paternal supervisor of peasant affairs who knew local conditions turned out too often to be a run-of-the-mill functionary who took the post for want of a better one and had little prior knowledge of the rural masses, their customs and problems. There were approximately 2,000 land captains in 1895 and from 5,000 to 6,000 twenty years later, each supposedly overseeing 200,000 peasants. Fewer than a third of these were local nobles; another third or more were civil servants and up to 40 per cent former officers. While their forceful way of dealing with subordinates pleased the Emperor Nicholas, this did not endear them to the peasants or to critics of the institution.

From the government's point of view, the zemskii looked like a useful innovation. In 1898 he was introduced to Siberia, where serfdom and the serf-owning landlord had never existed, and in 1901 to the guberniias of Vilna, Kovno, and Grodno. He remained a feature of the countryside until the Revolution. Proponents said that there were not enough land captains, and that the size of their territories diminished their effectiveness. Yet even doubling their numbers could not have prevented the localized agrarian riots of 1902 and the massive ones of 1905–06.

Whatever his virtues or vices, the zemskii was the first official of the central administration who dealt with the peasants directly, on their own ground, and tried to do so on the basis of local custom rather than laws or prescriptions developed elsewhere. Whether his function was to keep order or to facilitate the collection of dues and taxes, to protect the interests of the state or those of the peasants, he provided a closer link between a majority of the tsar's subjects and their government than had existed before. This gave the government a fund of information and experience that it had lacked, that no other group of Russians possessed, and that would before long play a part in rural reform.[6]

Peasants were much pitied or praised by their privileged and literate countrymen from all parts of the ideological spectrum, but they were little known even by those who made an honest effort to study them. The young men and women from the cities who had 'gone to the people' in 1874 to live among their lesser brothers in the villages, either to serve or to revolutionize them, were shocked by the gulf of misunderstanding that separated them from those they championed. Disraeli's image of two nations vastly different in numbers, benefits, duties, and ways of life was more applicable to Russia than to England.

After even bolder attempts to rouse the people, culminating in the assassination of Alexander II, had failed, repression made sustained contact between urban intellectuals and the rural masses impossible. The peasant became still more of an abstraction, an emblem of suffering and of virtue born of suffering.

After 1881 reaction, the caution or quietism to which it condemned reformers and radicals, and urban Russia's commercial and industrial preoccupations combined to let the former serf and his plight recede to the background for a decade. The drought and crop failure of 1891 caused a famine which lasted into the next year and together with outbreaks of cholera and typhus claimed 400,000 victims. Their sufferings awoke privileged Russia from its political apathy, revived vocal criticism of the regime and served as a reminder of the stubbornness of the peasantry's troubles. The famine once again focused attention on the villages, stirred consciences, and was for many a second 'going to the people'. For some, like Petr Struve, it was a confirmation of Marx's prediction that backward, agrarian Russia was not immune from the inroads of capitalism; its iron laws were driving marginal producers off the land to create a rural middle class and a more productive and progressive economy. The hunger of 1891–92 did more to make him a Marxist, Struve said, than the reading of *Capital*.[7]

The aid which government and public gave to the sufferers was described by Lev Tolstoi as a case of the parasite feeding the host.[8] Witte, a few years later, told Nicholas II that disarray in the rural economy brought joy to all enemies of the autocracy.[9] Whether concern was stimulated by conscience or calculation, by a wish to maintain agriculture's ability to provide taxes and exports, or by the fear of mass violence, the famine and what it revealed of conditions in the countryside led eventually to a major re-examination of the state's agrarian policy. It was hastened also by the agrarian riots of 1902, but signs of trouble were visible before then. The events of 1891 were not isolated, only the most catastrophic. Whereas between 1871 and 1890 relief expenditures had been 12 million rubles, 1891 cost the exchequer 144 million in loans and aid, with another 95 million for food and seed grain needed in the decade 1893–1902; of the latter amount the state recovered only 8.5 million rubles. A further 268 million were paid out for relief from 1901 to 1906.[10]

Although the fiscal policies of Vyshnegradskii were widely blamed for 1891, they could not by themselves and in the few years since their adoption (1887) have had such a devastating effect. The troubles of the peasantry had multiple causes: too much or too little state guidance, too many taxes and not enough land were only partial explanations of the problems afflicting most of Russian agriculture. 'Landowners, peasants, and grain traders alike are lost in a maze of debts and arrears,' spokesmen for the nobility of twenty-seven provinces agreed in 1896, 'with no way out, since no one pays attention to their needs and problems.'[11] This was not, in fact, true, since the state, for economic as well as political reasons, could not afford to ignore the plight of most of the population. But neither could it offer swift remedies that would have satisfied peasants and gentry without also diminishing resources for industrial development and for security needs at home and abroad.

The most immediate and visible sign that the government recognized the gravity of the situation was the transformation in 1894 of the Ministry of State Domains into the Ministry of Agriculture and the appointment as its head of Aleksei Ermolov. A graduate of the St Petersburg Agricultural Academy who had served for over twenty years in the Ministry of Finance, Ermolov was the author of several highly regarded works on agricultural economics. His study of the famine identified communal land tenure as one of its more important causes. During the rest of the decade the government initiated a series of conferences, commissions, and investigations to examine the rural economy. But not even the most ambitious and prestigious of these, summoned by Witte in 1902 – the Special Conference on the Needs of Agriculture, with its hundreds of local committees and thousands of participants (of whom only 2 per cent were peasants)[12] – did more than recommend palliatives. It served as a forum for exploring solutions to the crisis and reviewing the elements that went into its making.

To begin with, there *was* a land shortage, even if it was relative. The real problem was low productivity to which the answer was better capitalization and tools, more intensive farming methods, crop diversification, and easier access to markets. Although Russian peasants held and worked more land per person than the farmers of almost every other country, their plots were smaller than those they had cultivated before the emancipation, as was the overall amount allotted to them at that time. There had been gains for certain regions and groups (former state peasants, for example); but in most of the leading agricultural regions of European Russia and Ukraine they were outweighed by losses of from 10 to 40 per cent, being highest in the fertile and unruly black-soil provinces of the middle Volga and northern Ukraine. The average loss for thirty-six provinces was around 25 per cent. Although some of this was made good by purchases in subsequent decades, the overall situation did not change; nor did the peasant's feeling that the fields 'allotted' to him, the *nadel*, were only part of what was rightfully his.

The gains made by the peasantry as a class, although statistically impressive, were not enough to satisfy those who most hungered for land, or to keep pace with the explosive pressure of population. From 1877 to 1897 the rural population grew by 25 per cent and did so again in the next twenty years. Land in peasant possession had increased only by 15 per cent in 1905 and 19 per cent in 1916. The average size of an allotment held by peasant households declined from 13.2 desiatinas in 1887 to 10.4 desiatinas in 1905 (one *desiatina* = 2.7 acres). Calculated on the basis of average allotment size per male peasant, the loss was 47 per cent between 1860 and 1900. What allotment land there was and what was purchased in addition had to be divided among households whose number rose in the half century after 1861 from 8.5 million to 12.3 million. According to another calculation for the same period: population grew by more than 50 per cent; the amount of additional land acquired through purchase by 10 per cent.[13]

The peasant's sense of having been cheated – the so-called cut-offs (*otrezki*) kept by the former masters were roughly one sixth the area they surrendered – was deepened by the frequently poor quality and location of holdings and the retention by his noble neighbour of woodland and meadow. The peasant was also made to 'redeem' his allotment. He had to repay the state for the compensation the latter had made to the gentry (and to itself in the case of state peasants) for losses of land and labour. The redemption payments – fixed above market value of the land and stretched over forty-nine years (forty-four for former state peasants) – were a reminder of servile status; so was the village community in which title to the allotted land was vested along with joint responsibility for dues and taxes.

The *muzhik* (literally, the little man) was no longer subordinate to the serf-master or an agent of the Ministry of State Domains. He was not yet a free individual who could move or dispose of his property at will. Allotment lands could be distributed or redistributed among members of the community, but they could neither be sold nor mortgaged. Redemption dues and taxes were a heavy burden. Together with over-population, a low level of agricultural techniques, an exhausted soil, inadequate rainfall, frequent crop failures, a slump in grain prices and a steep rise in land values, they were the classic ingredients of what had become a deep-seated depression of most of peasant farming.

The readiest measure of the depression, and one of which the government was as painfully aware as the most fervent advocate of the rural masses, was the mounting indebtedness of village communities, the fiscal obligations on which their members had defaulted. For the years 1876–80 direct tax arrears averaged 22 per cent of expected collections; they reached 119 per cent in the period 1896–1900. Arrears on redemption dues in 1903 were 138 per cent.[14] There was a social aspect to this problem which was of sufficient gravity to be officially recognized: the system of direct taxation had for centuries rested on a class basis; even after emancipation the law distinguished between privileged and unprivileged Russians, between those who did and those who did not pay certain taxes.

Only peasants and townsmen of the lower classes were subject to the poll- or head-tax which had first been imposed by Peter I and became a main source of state income. A salt tax, particularly onerous to peasants, had been abolished at the end of Alexander II's reign; the poll-tax, providing a falling share of ordinary revenues, could be abandoned in European Russia by 1886–87 and by 1899 in Siberia; the redemption debt was reduced by about a fourth in the same decade. Some tax arrears were forgiven altogether as signs of imperial grace on festive occasions, and in 1881 there was a symbolic raising of the peasants' civic status when they were allowed for the first time since serfdom to take the oath of loyalty to the new tsar. Gentry properties had been made subject to the land tax in 1875, but until 1906 peasant land remained in a special category which might pay up to ten times more than did land held by other classes.[15]

Indirect taxes, however, were the largest single source of state income. If their inequitable impact was not to be worsened, additional direct taxes had to make up for those that had been dropped. Bunge, finance minister from 1881 to 1887, had the best of intentions, for he knew that a destitute peasantry could not help to balance the budget, reduce the state debt, and stabilize the ruble. But his lowering of the peasants' fiscal obligations by some 25 per cent, and his introduction in 1882–85 of taxes on inheritances, on industrial and commercial profits, and on the income from securities, savings and bank accounts, brought only modest and short-lived benefits. Subsequent taxes on urban dwellings (1893) and on businesses (1898) did not permanently change the basic relationship of direct to indirect levies which was 16.8:83.2 in 1887; 14.5:85.5 in 1897; and 16.6:83.4 in 1913. In that year Englishmen paid four times as much in direct taxes as did Russians. Faced with bankruptcy at the time of the great famine, Vyshnegradskii considered an income tax; there would be none until 1916.[16]

Even if the tax burden had been more equitably distributed and the privileged had borne their share through a graduated income tax, higher death duties, the curbing of luxury expenditures, and restrictions on non-essential imports and foreign travel, it is open to question how much the lot of the largely marginal peasant producer would have improved without also diverting funds from the military, the railroads, and industry. There were limits, of a practical and prudential kind, to what a restructuring of the tax system could have accomplished under Russian conditions. Placing greater burdens on those better able to bear them could have led to the flight of capital abroad, a consideration which had kept the 1885 tax on dividends and interest low. Prohibiting foreign travel, on which Russians spent as much between 1881 and 1897 as the state took up in foreign loans, would have antagonized the upper classes. And as late as 1907, fewer than 700,000 individuals would have had to pay the progressive income tax that the government in that year proposed to levy on all incomes of more than 1,000 rubles. They were a very small number, compared with the masses of town and country who, almost unknowingly, made a contribution to the exchequer whenever they purchased items of basic necessity.[17]

Whatever it was that kept the state from tackling a fundamental reform of the tax structure – fear of alienating the upper classes; the wish to attract capital to high risk and high profit ventures; or simply the convenience of collecting imposts on items of mass consumption – the latter continued to furnish the bulk of tax revenues. Bunge's successors, Vyshnegradskii and Witte, committed to a sound, convertible currency to attract and service foreign loans and, especially in Witte's case, to industrial expansion, relied heavily on indirect taxation of this kind. The sale of matches, vodka, tobacco, sugar, tea, and kerosene brought in, by 1900, five sixths of the taxes collected. Some of the most heavily taxed items were close to being essentials. The excise on sugar, a staple element in peasant and worker diets, was raised by 100 per cent; that on matches and kerosene by 106 and 50 per cent respectively. In 1899 per capita consumption of sugar in England and the United States was seven to ten times that in Russia, and Englishmen drank more than seven times as much tea as did Russians. To what extent peasant poverty accounted for these differences is shown by an urban–rural comparison. City dwellers in Russia consumed nearly six times as much sugar as did their rural countrymen and drank anywhere from seven to twenty times as much tea.[18]

During Vyshnegradskii's ministry (1887–92) fiscal pressures were tightened again and fell most heavily on the subsistence sector of agriculture, that is, the majority of peasant households. There was an increase in land taxes, in stamp duties, a more energetic collection of arrears and, in 1891, a high tariff (the highest in Europe) which drove up the cost of farm implements. In purely budgetary terms, these rigorous measures bore fruit. The 3.5 million ruble deficit of 1887 became a 65.9 million ruble surplus by 1890. Witte, who pursued his predecessor's policies even more energetically and who achieved a threefold improvement in the nation's trade balances, claimed that higher tax yields also reflected higher levels of consumption. His claims were challenged by conservative agrarians who disliked high tariffs and resented the favouring of industry; they were also disputed by liberals and radicals who contended that even if present policies made Russia a great industrial power, their cost was too high. They could point to the fact that by 1895 direct taxes were a good deal higher than in 1881, before Bunge's reductions; that all taxes had climbed 29 per cent between 1883 and 1892 when population had grown by only 16 per cent (the corresponding figures for the 1893–1902 period were 49 and 13 per cent respectively); or that in the forty years of fairly stable prices before 1900, indirect taxes rose 4.5 times, direct taxes doubled, but population rose only 78 per cent. Arrears too were up again. An associate of Witte's admitted that foreign loans were used to cover up budgetary difficulties.[19]

That such loans were available was, of course, a tribute to the policies of Vyshnegradskii and Witte. The former's insistence on exporting grain, even if there was not a domestic surplus, made possible the accumulation of a gold reserve and the adoption of the gold standard in 1897. This made the ruble freely convertible for the attraction of foreign investors and the settlement of international obligations, but also devalued it, boosting exports while raising the cost of imports. And at the same time as sales of grain rose to nearly half of all exports, its price fell, forcing the producers of Russia's Centre and South to sell or work more to pay the taxes which Vyshnegradskii had collected after the harvest, when prices were depressed. It was a vicious circle in which peasants and, ultimately, the whole country, were caught. If Russians were to eat as much bread, the mainstay of their diet, as did Germans, not only would grain exports have to be stopped, as was done temporarily after the 1891 famine; an amount equal to 10 per cent of the harvest would have had to be imported each year.[20]

A largely peasant agriculture of overpopulated holdings lacked the markets, the capital, and the technology either to improve output to keep pace with the fertility of the peasants, or to produce large enough internal savings on which the state could draw for an economic development of sufficient magnitude and speed to absorb the surplus labour of the villages. That surplus was estimated at from 4 to 6 million and as high as 23 million persons (1900), or half the rural labour force.[21] How to break out of that predicament became an ever more pressing economic and moral question as greater and lesser crop failures belied whatever statistical evidence might be brought to show that 'on the whole, in general, in the long run' things were improving. Nor could the government ignore evidence that in 1890 about 64 per cent of peasants called up for the army were declared unfit on grounds of health and that this figure rose to 78 per cent after the famine of 1891.[22] Productivity improved by 10 per cent or more between 1883 and 1903, population and the price of land rose very much higher and faster, while yields remained one third those of Western Europe.[23] With the revival of political debate and opposition in the 1890s, the agrarian question also acquired political dimensions and risks. These increased measurably when in the new century the peasants themselves gave violent expression to their discontent. Then it was no longer possible to deny that the special laws and institutions governing the peasants were inadequate as controls and served instead to spread their grievances and to foster their solidarity.

The peasant or field commune (*obshchina*) was the most important institution of rural Russia. It was usually, but not always, coterminous with the village community and controlled 83 per cent of allotment lands and nearly half of all arable in the European provinces of the country. Its practice of communal land tenure, with periodic redistribution according to family size, quality of the soil, and distance from the village, had also become the subject of fierce debate when the commune was made a legal institution at the time of emancipation. Title to the peasants' land had then been vested in the obshchina (or its successor, the village community) primarily for fiscal reasons and only for the duration of the redemption operation. There had been no intention of making communal tenure, repartition, or membership in the obshchina obligatory and permanent. Once communal obligations to the state were discharged, the latter would not oppose, indeed would favour, the emergence of a prosperous, individualistic peasantry. But the emancipation settlement, and factors which those who drafted it could neither foresee nor prevent, made that impossible. In addition to being an administrative and fiscal convenience, the commune became a repository for conservative hopes for rural tranquillity and for escaping the problems that a mass of landless rural proletarians would have posed.[24]

Warnings which had been sounded at the emancipation were heard again when it appeared that the peasant problem might be a lasting one: it made little sense to tie the peasant to an institution that gave him no incentive to improve land not fully his and that made the industrious bear the greater share of the collective debt. Under such conditions even the most energetic and enterprising were kept from breaking out of the cycle of poverty, low productivity, and high population density that was three to eight times greater in central Russia and Ukraine (1897) than in Iowa, Kansas, and Nebraska (1920).[25] As early as 1885 Bunge recommended that the commune's joint responsibility for meeting its members' monetary obligations end together with the head-tax. The Ministry of Interior's interest in the presumed political and social benefits of the commune through an 'egalitarian' land distribution prevailed over the economic rationality propounded by the minister of finance. Instead, the scope of communal and administrative authority over its members was widened and their rights narrowed.

Individual dependence on the commune for land allotments was reinforced by a law of 1886. It took from heads of households the right to approve the division of a family's allotment into smaller holdings (usually for an elder son) and vested it in a two-thirds majority of the village meeting and, after 1889, in the land captain. A law of December 1893 forbade the selling or mortgaging of allotment land and repealed the provision of the Emancipation Statute that allowed families who had paid all their redemption dues to withdraw from the commune and to assume title to their land in full ownership. Withdrawal was made subject to approval by two thirds of the village meeting and the land captains of the district. This additional barrier to individual tenure simultaneously removed an inducement to family limitation, since the amount of land assigned to member households usually reflected their size. A law adopted in June of the same year revealed divisions in the official mind over the benefits of equalizing holdings by periodic redistributions. It set a minimum term of twelve years for these, required the agreement of meeting and land captains, and incorporated a proposal of Witte's that a peasant who had improved his land should keep it or be compensated for his efforts. Thus, while the commune was preserved and even strengthened — the law had the unintended effect of reviving partitions where the practice was no longer observed — the advantages of individual and continuous cultivation and, implicitly, ownership, were recognized.[26]

Some historians believe that the vast majority of Russian peasants were anxious to preserve communal land tenure with its underlying ideas of equality and collective ownership. So, for different reasons, did the *narodniki*, or populists, Russia's non-Marxist socialists. If they were right — and the growing number of legal and illegal repartitions suggests that they were — it was merely another indication that the majority of peasants were poor and feared having to fend on their own without the minimal security afforded them by their right to a portion of communal land. That peasants were instinctively or traditionally egalitarian or, even less probably, socialist (as many narodniki believed) is disproved by the exclusion of homesteads and kitchen gardens from communal farming and by the fact that every family cultivated its own land and kept its own cattle.

Economists (the Marxists foremost among them) who saw economic and class differentiation in the village as signs of capitalism may have overstated their case, for they measured family economies producing primarily for subsistence by standards borrowed from more rational enterprises. But they were right in pointing out, near the turn of the century, that from 17 to 18 per cent of peasant households (perhaps as many as 25 per cent by 1908) could be classified as well-to-do, had enough land, some livestock, machinery, and possibly a little money in a savings bank; and that at the other end of the scale 11 per cent of the peasantry were without any arable or livestock. Clearly the field commune, collective responsibility, and an egalitarian instinct (if it existed) had not prevented the splitting off from the mass of the peasantry of a very poor and a relatively prosperous group.[27]

If there was rural socialism it extended at best only to ownership of the land, and even then but incompletely. Since it took account of changing family size and labouring ability, periodic repartition should, in theory, have led to equal economic opportunity or at least to the avoidance of great inequities. In reality some families or individuals managed by dint of industry or luck (which could come in the form of sturdy sons or a favourable location of fields) to improve their situation over that of their neighbours; their voices would naturally carry added weight when the community discussed the assignment of lands and obligations and in that way the accidental inequalities of fortune might be perpetuated and enlarged.

Yet they were kept within bounds, and the overwhelming majority of villagers continued to receive a fair share of communal land. As a result the number of holdings rose sharply, while the pattern of tenure and cultivation changed little; so did the proportion of poor to prosperous families. The additional 10 per cent of land acquired through purchase – mainly by well-to-do peasants – in the half century before 1905 compares with an increase of 50 per cent in a population which simply divided what was available into smaller units. These averaged 2.6 desiatinas per male peasant in 1900, down from 4.8 in the 1860s. Famine grants, costing the treasury 33.5 million rubles in 1901 alone, offered only partial or temporary relief, as did putting meadow or grazing land under the plough. Using more grain for sale or consumption meant less fodder for animals, therefore less cattle and natural fertilizer, fewer work horses, and a decline in yields.

Where the peasants did not depend on state aid it was subsidiary occupations, handicrafts, cottage industries, and wage work that kept them going, posing the question whether it made sense to assure every member of the commune of his bit of land if that land could not sustain him and if his poverty made him as marginal and possibly as bitter as if landlessness had driven him out of the village. As early as 1882, when about a quarter of nine million households was reported to be without working horses, a conservative newspaper was led to conclude that one quarter of Russia's peasants could no longer be regarded as independent agriculturalists. By 1900 about 29 per cent of 11 million households in European Russia were without horses and perhaps a third had only one; 35 per cent had no cow; barely half were producing enough to feed themselves; and only 16 per cent had a surplus. According to one estimate, that figure dropped to 10 per cent in 1905.[28]

What under such circumstances did it mean – in economic and social terms – to be a cultivator and part-owner of the soil? Maintenance of communal tenure (and of a peasant estate whose allotments were inalienable) might still be useful as a kind of relief programme. But even its proponents were beginning to ask whether it was not the crux of the agrarian problem, the basic cause of rural poverty, of underproduction and underconsumption, and therefore of industrial backwardness as well. There was concern also that treating the peasant as a second-class citizen was likely to sharpen the disgruntlement caused by his misery.

Witte, who had initially favoured the commune as a product of the national character and tradition – a preference which was strengthened when he became finance minister by the difficulty of collecting taxes from millions of households with an inadequate bureaucracy –, came very close to calling for its dissolution by the end of the century. It was time, he told Nicholas in 1898, to make the peasant, who was but half a person, into a full one, to eliminate or lessen the legal peculiarities and administrative tutelage to which he was subjected, to end communal responsibility for the monetary obligations of individuals and the corporal punishment from which nobles (in 1762), merchants (in 1782) and all others (in 1863) had been freed. Witte's reluctance to go the whole way probably stemmed from a mixture of ideological, practical and tactical considerations. Only a few years earlier he had argued against allowing certain categories of peasants to leave the commune. A sudden reversal might have given pause to the suspicious Nicholas whom others were trying to convince that it was desirable and necessary to maintain the 'social distinctiveness of the peasant estate, the inviolability of the communal structure, and the inalienability of peasant allotment lands'.[29]

That was the formula propounded, also in 1898, by Pleve who was echoing the social conservatism and the security concerns prevailing in the Ministry of Interior. The police still shared in the job of collecting arrears from the communes; for this and other reasons Witte wished to avoid a head-on clash. Yet in 1902, spurred by the disorders of that year, he spoke decisively for the abolition of the commune. Pleve, now minister, also changed his tune, but with reservations and his customary caution. He admitted 'that collectivism and communal tenure are nonsense, leading only to chaos. But I cannot permit the immediate extension of full citizenship rights to the peasant; this must be done gradually.' And he still insisted that it was essential to keep a significant portion of peasant land inalienable, so that Russian peasants should not become merely hired hands on large latifundia.[30] Pleve's opposition and the natural hesitancy of a conservative government fearful of the unpredictable social and political consequences of basic changes in policy, overcame the advocates of dissolution. It was not until the even more serious disturbances of 1905–06 and the accompanying revolution in the cities that the administration left behind its fears and heeded the advice of those who had all along warned that the commune was no guarantee of rural stability. A new agrarian policy was to be the work of new hands. Until they took over, there were palliatives that amended rather than changed the status quo. In 1903 collective fiscal responsibility ended and so, in 1904, did corporal punishment for peasants.

An American student of the obshchina concludes that it prevented the application of rational policies in agriculture, a more flexible allocation of resources, and increased output.[31] Communal tenure inhibited individual initiative and prevented the consolidation of holdings that for the sake of equalizing quality were scattered in thirty to forty strips throughout the village fields. It also helped to perpetuate antiquated farming methods, the three-field system in which one third of land lay fallow at all times, and the underinvestment of care and capital on plots that might, at the next division, be given to another family. Having granted the largely economic indictments of its critics, one must also concede that too much blame was placed on the commune. It is possible to dismiss the claims of populists for its egalitarian and cooperative virtues as born of their aversion for a selfish, competitive capitalism from which Russia should and could be spared. There is justification also for scepticism in face of the belief that the 'collective spirit' of the commune would permit large-scale undertakings (draining swamps or processing raw materials) that were beyond the capability of private owners, or for distrusting the faith that the custom of collective decisions by the village meeting would help rather than hinder the spread of innovative techniques. Yet the commune's defenders were right when they put much of the blame for the country's stagnant agriculture on the government's failure to give more help to the nation's most important industry. Precise figures are hard to come by, but before 1905 little public or private capital was invested in the rural economy, and less in its peasant sector.[32]

With or without the commune, the villages needed help and resources that could come only from elsewhere. Government experts, liberals, and many populists were agreed on a number of steps that would at least relieve the poverty of the masses and might even raise the productivity of their fields. There was need for relief from tariffs, taxes and redemption dues, for cheap credit and the resettlement of excess population, for better roads and supports for grain prices, for a lessening of administrative supervision, for an improvement of the terms which governed peasant rentals of gentry land, and for a less frequent division of allotments. What was necessary above all – and before any complicated technology or machinery could even be thought of – was to instruct peasants in the many improvements in fertilizer, seed, implements, crop rotation and diversification that could have been made fairly simply and quickly.[33]

This required a faster spread of literacy, of free literature, and agricultural advisory services than the government was undertaking or the zemstvos were capable of supplying. The problem was at least recognized and a decree of 1883 provided for a system of 'lower agricultural schools' to spread generalized and special farming techniques. Five years later thirteen such schools had been set up, with an enrolment of 397 students. In 1890 there were forty-three agricultural schools with a total of 2,715 students and three agricultural colleges for the entire empire. After 1890 model fields and farms were set up in one third of district zemstvos as well as hundreds of depots for the sale of agricultural machinery. According to the census of 1897, 37 per cent of male peasants between the ages of twenty and fifty-nine were literate; not all of them could read with ease, others worked in the cities. There would be advances in literacy as well as in farming techniques in years to come, but for most of our period peasant illiteracy and peasant poverty went hand in hand.[34]

Lacking instruction, incentives, and capital, the peasants, as always, saw more land as the solution to their problem and the state tried to meet their desire part way by founding the Peasant Land Bank in 1883. It was to help the purchase of land by individuals as well as by communes and peasant associations, but in the initial years of its existence its operations were modest and its loan requirements too stringent to benefit those who were most in need of credit. Interest rates were comparatively high (5.55%), repayments had to be made within $24\frac{1}{2}$ or $34\frac{1}{2}$ years, and only one quarter to one half the purchase price was advanced by the Bank. Since its debtors were often delinquent in their payments, they were as often foreclosed. Many prospective buyers, therefore, turned to private banks and acquired with their help three times as much land as the 2.4 million desiatinas bought through the Peasant Land Bank from 1883 to 1895. Public and private credit had the further effect of driving up land prices (doubling them in the case of land bought through the Peasant Land Bank), and making it appear once more that every step helpful to some peasants was bound to bring harm to still more. After 1894, when with a falling grain market more estate owners needed cash and were ready to part with their property, the Peasant Land Bank stepped up its activities in order to help them and, incidentally, the peasants. From now on it advanced from 90 to 100 per cent of the purchase price, reduced interest rates, and extended the loan period to more than fifty years. In the ten years before November 1905, Bank credit helped peasants to buy 5.3 million desiatinas of land, or 2.5 times as much as in the first thirteen years of its operation.[35]

In order to judge of the scale of the Peasant Land Bank's operation it is useful to mention that the amount of land bought by the peasantry without its assistance reached 17 million desiatinas for the years 1877–1905, and that the Gentry Land Bank (established in 1885) lent to its clients at 4.5 per cent, twice the amount advanced to peasants. Public as well as private credit went for the most part to the wealthier peasants. The poverty of the rural masses was not fundamentally affected by the mobilization of gentry lands and their transfer to the peasantry. From 1877 to 1905 land owned by the peasants (communally or individually) increased from 32 to 40 per cent of the total area held by all categories of owners, including the state; the area actually cultivated by them grew by 24.3 per cent. But population grew by 27.8 per cent, while the proportion of allotment (i.e. communal) land held steady at around one third of the total, suggesting that basic patterns had changed very little.

It is true that confiscation and distribution of all gentry lands would not have supplied enough additional acreage to still the land hunger of the peasants, that they or their communes already owned, by 1905, 69 per cent of all non-public lands as compared with the gentry's 22 per cent, or that the latter's share of the total land fund had sunk from 23 to 16 per cent by 1905. But this does not change the fact that estate farming continued to be important in the peasants' lives, especially in the areas of greatest poverty and population pressure. Of the total 219 million desiatinas held by peasants and gentry in European Russia in 1905 (not counting the holdings of other classes, crown and state property), 79.3 million or 36.2 per cent belonged to about 100,000 noble estates, whereas twelve million peasant households divided the remaining two thirds among themselves. Although by 1917 the gentry had lost approximately half of what it had owned at the emancipation, it still held over half of all privately owned land just before the Revolution.[36]

Gentry estates varied greatly in size, and while most (over 60,000) had fewer than 100 desiatinas each, they all, large or small, remained a powerful irritant and target for violence where hunger for land, or simply hunger, drove the peasant with an inadequate allotment to rent additional ploughland. Almost 40 per cent of all gentry land was rented out around 1900; another third was worked by peasants for a share of the crop or as payment in labour. Whatever the arrangement, it must have been a constant reminder of the days of serfdom. By 1905 fields rented either by peasants or their communes from neighbouring estates nearly equalled in extent those purchased by them. Since renting was costly and frequently did not pay for itself, it is an index of the economic compulsion behind it. When Stolypin was governor of Saratov guberniia – where peasants rented 47 per cent of noble land and sharecropped 10 per cent – he reported in 1904 that in a good year the harvests barely justified the high rental charges; in a bad or even average year the peasant exerted himself for nothing. 'This creates not only impoverishment but also hatred of one class for another and favourable soil for propaganda and agrarian riots which can spread with incredible speed. . . .'[37] Renting was usually for short terms, causing the soil to be used without care for its future fertility. Inadequate fertilization (due to the shortage of livestock and manure) and the concentration on grain crops contributed to the exhaustion of the land and to the peasants' never-ending search for more of it.

That search had taken 300,000 of them to Siberia and Turkestan in the quarter century after emancipation, but neither the prospects awaiting them nor the government's migration policies made this an attractive or realistic solution for any but a handful before 1889. In that year the government – which had earlier feared peasants leaving their communal obligations and surplus-producing estates losing their labour – passed a migration law. Although it was still restrictive and required proof that the prospective settler was not delinquent in his tax and redemption payments, it marked a turning-point in official attitudes and the beginning of assistance and guidance for what had largely been an unorganized or illegal movement. Even when the building of the Trans-Siberian Railroad and the wish to attract settlers to its route led to the encouragement of migration, the proportion of illegal migrants remained high among the yearly average (between 1895 and 1905) of about 130,000. On this, as on so many other issues having to do with agriculture and the peasantry, the government was of uncertain mind. As long as this remained true, and as long as communal tenure guaranteed some land to every villager, even the greater number of colonists could make little dent in the problem of over-population where it was worst – in the central, west-central, and southern provinces. At the end of the century the natural increase of population in European Russia was nearly fourteen times as great as the net loss which these guberniias incurred through migration. Only after 1905 did the government make a concerted effort to resettle significant numbers of peasants beyond the Urals.[38]

Outside of the forest provinces, where handicrafts supplied important side earnings, and those few areas where farming was profitable, most inhabitants of rural Russia who could not live by tilling their soil supplemented their incomes by working as agricultural labourers. At the turn of the century there were close to two million persons in this category on a permanent basis, and several million more who joined them temporarily at harvest time, often after travelling great distances at great cost. Poorly paid wage work, like renting, was for the peasant a reminder of his dependent and disadvantaged status. The introduction, in 1886, of work-books for hired hands and rules to prevent their leaving an employer before the expiration of contract, tells much about the conditions of rural labour. There were no limits on hours, and the average daily wage from 1882 to 1900 was from 50 to 60 kopeks, about 25 to 30 cents or one shilling. Where there were large reservoirs of labour, estate owners at times paid for the hire of hands by letting them and their families farm a portion of estate lands with their own implements. This was still another link in an unfortunate relationship in which one of the two parties seemed, as before 1861, to do all the work and the other to reap most of the benefits. The agrarian disturbances of 1905 were worst along the middle Volga and the central black-earth zone where the repartitional commune prevailed, where agriculture was stagnant, and where the big landowners let their lands for money, for labour, or for a share of the crop. If in the northern and western provinces rioters occasionally refused to pay their taxes and turned against local authorities, in the black-earth zone the anger of peasant renters or labourers was turned against the nearest estate which was struck, robbed, or burned out.[39]

Peasant poverty, it must be repeated, was not universal. There was a group of households, estimated at from 15 to 25 per cent of the total, that was relatively prosperous; there were regions, away from the crowded south-central one, where the conditions of the soil, the closeness of urban markets, or individualized tenure favoured intensified and diversified economies. There was the growth of cooperatives and, in Western Siberia, of a butter industry which was soon second only to Denmark's in exports. Towards the end of the 1890s, as prices recovered, harvesters and other machinery began to be acquired by about 20 per cent of wheat growers who had enough capital and 25 desiatinas or more of good land. There were districts, also, in which the noble manor and property were not disturbed in the violence of three revolutions. Indeed, a great deal of what has been said in these pages and elsewhere about peasant life and labour, views and feelings, can only be generalized approximations of a vast and complicated picture, varied as to time and place and often obscure for want of precise information.

The most recent re-examination of the available evidence on taxation, consumption, and grain production questions the very existence of an agrarian crisis in the late nineteenth century. It concludes that the worsening of living standards among the peasantry was confined to a minority in particular areas within the central black-earth provinces, and denies that the fiscal pressures of a state committed to industrial development 'ruined peasant husbandry by forcing the peasant to exhaust his soil, rent land, and flood the market with grain for export, in order to pay his taxes'.[40] The challenge to what for nearly a century has been the dominant view has not, in its turn, gone unchallenged; and the conclusion drawn by Simms from an eightfold increase in indirect tax returns between 1881 and 1899 – that since the peasant was the mass consumer his real income and buying power must have been growing – has been subjected to searching examination and found defective.[41]

The per capita intake of excise taxes, it has been calculated, rose only by 108.25 per cent; and although it did so faster than population or the tax rates, and per capita expenditures on matches, kerosene, sugar, and tea increased as well, the volume of consumption declined or remained static. The most important corrective of the view that tax collections denoted an improvement in the peasant economy is the finding that the main source of indirect revenue was not the villages but the burgeoning cities and industrial districts where bigger monetary incomes gave rise to consumption patterns different from those prevailing in the still largely natural economy of the countryside. The amount of goods purchased by the peasantry remained low; about three quarters of trade was concentrated in urban-industrial areas (with only 14 per cent of the population in 1912), and the 'average' peasant, with an annual cash deficit (in 1905) of 86 rubles, was not among the 3.5 million depositors in savings banks (up from 306,000 in 1886) who were mostly city dwellers. The off-farm wages of peasants who did not permanently join the industrial labour force, and especially those of agricultural labourers, did not rise enough in real terms to lift their families above the minimum subsistence level.

It must, none the less, be considered as established now that 'squeezing the peasants' by indirect taxation was not and could not have been the prime source of capital accumulation for industrialization, and likely that the effect of the state's fiscal policies on agriculture has been overestimated. Squeezing, often accompanied by a lowering of consumption, bore heavily on *all* the lower income groups, including a majority of peasants. They suffered both as producers and consumers from the preference given to industrial over agricultural investments. There was no substantial reordering of the state's priorities before 1905 and, as a result, little improvement in the standard of living of the rural masses, especially as compared with that of other countries. Tax collections tell only part of the story. A description of agrarian policies and problems must also mention a per capita use of wheat and rye which was a third lower than American wheat consumption; a death rate (attributable mainly to infant mortality) nearly twice England's; annual increases in agricultural productivity of 0.3 per cent compared with industry's 2.7 per cent; and greater yields on private than on communal lands.[42]

Whether one does or does not agree that there was a crisis in peasant Russia or prefers to call it stagnation or depression, it is certain that whatever term is used cannot be a faithful reflection of the lives of millions of human beings. Trends, averages, estimates, and comparisons are, at best, only suggestive of a reality that was enormously complex and requires still more and better evidence and investigative tools to do it justice.

* * * *

This applies as well to a much smaller group of Russians, the nobles, with whose fate that of the peasants was so intimately linked for so long. Many peasants and radicals still saw them as serf-masters in a new guise, exploiters and oppressors of the poor, the main buttresses and beneficiaries of autocracy. And since noble privilege was such a frequent target for its critics and opponents, the government of Alexander III began to think of the nobility as a sturdier ally than it could possibly be in the future or had, in all likelihood, been in the past.

What is often called the feudal or noble reaction of the 1880s was indeed a reaction – to the regime's sense of isolation and to the economic decline of a class whose help was still felt to be needed for the maintenance of internal security. This pro-gentry policy was not, however, designed to restore it to independent vitality and cohesion. The nobility (or gentry – in Russian, *dvorianstvo*, see p. 67, ref. 2) had long drawn most of its strength from the state and had never achieved enough common purpose, interest, or consciousness to develop political and economic power on its own. What independent strength or importance there had been was being eroded in the years after emancipation when the gentry annually lost on average one per cent of its lands (or 41 per cent in the 43 years before 1905) through sale or foreclosure. The *dvorianstvo*, as a result, faced the state, the other classes of Russian society, and the future with little agreement as to goals or even grievances.[43]

Collective purpose or corporate consciousness would have been difficult to achieve in any case, for the legal definition of membership in the noble estate (*soslovie*) took no account of the many divisions within that very broad category. There were hereditary nobles and 'personal' ones, most of the latter civil servants. The 1897 census counted some 1.2 million individuals who were hereditary and about 630,000 who were lifetime nobles, or $1\frac{1}{2}$ per cent of the population altogether. There were rich nobles and poor ones, rustics and urbanites, reactionaries and liberals, capitalist operators of large estates, employers of hired or tenant labour (the majority of the landed gentry), rentiers, civil servants, officers, and professionals (one fifth or more) who, at best, kept a tenuous foothold or summer home in the countryside. Half the nobility was non-Russian, and the 28.6 per cent who were Poles and discriminated against by the state hardly contributed to the solidarity of the class.[44]

The largest single group, some 120,000 families of landed gentry, had shared an important function until 1861: administering and controlling the life and work of the serfs who then made up about half the country's rural population. For many nobles it was always a minor task since 41,000 properties had fewer than twenty-one male serfs. For their former owners and their sons, state service became a matter of economic necessity, since an insufficiency of capital, skills, or land kept the gentry from becoming the organizers of an efficient, market-oriented agriculture. The connection between state service, land ownership, and noble status was broken. In 1897 only 51 per cent of the officer corps and 30 per cent of civilian officials were nobles by birth. A shrinking proportion of state servitors, even in the highest four ranks, were heirs or holders of patrimonial estates – only about a third in 1888. Of 3,490 chinovniks in this group in 1901, 70 per cent had fewer than 100 desiatinas of land or none at all; in 1858 it had been 20 per cent. Among the hereditary nobility 12 per cent were without land in 1858 and 55 per cent in 1905.[45]

Although the number of nobles nearly doubled after 1875, the number of noble estates declined to 107,000 in 1905. Only half of these (representing 3 per cent of gentry land) were large enough (over 100 desiatinas) to be economically significant. The nobility, which had received about half of all privately owned arable at the emancipation, lost nearly half of it by 1905 and was to lose still more. For the time being, land – renting it out, sharecropping it, or working it with hired hands – still constituted an important source of gentry wealth and income. Moreover, 9 per cent of owners had estates of over 1,000 desiatinas (or nearly three quarters of gentry and 60 per cent of private land) and more than half of gentry holdings was in properties of more than 5,000 desiatinas. Such a degree of concentration, particularly pronounced in certain regions (e.g. the Baltic, White Russian, and Southern provinces), was an economic and, after 1905, a political factor. Yet neither the productivity nor the number of large estates was great enough to allow their owners, as a class, to play a dominant political or economic role. Soviet scholars estimate that gentry agriculture produced only 12 per cent of all bread grains on the eve of the First World War, and although half of that amount was sold, gentry grain provided no more than 21.6 per cent of the market total. The bulk continued to come from the peasantry; half from the well-to-do, the remainder from the so-called middle and poor peasants who consumed most of what they grew.[46]

Neither the few hundred large latifundia, like those belonging to the Iusopov family or to the Duke of Mecklenburg, which employed hired labour and complicated machinery, nor the nobles who successfully raised industrial crops or built refineries, mills, and distilleries had much to offer the peasantry by way of example. The average estate was as backward and undercapitalized as most peasant farms and did little to justify official hopes that the gentry would serve as teachers of advanced methods of cultivation. Salesmen for the McCormick Harvesting Machine Company complained to the home office that cheap and plentiful labour made their job difficult. One of them sold in 1892 one binder, 29 reapers, and 21 mowers in a territory four times the size of Ohio. In 1901 the American consul at Odessa reported that many estates of thousands of acres had not a single harvester or binder. A revision of tariffs in 1898 and increased domestic output made farm machinery less expensive and more available. But as late as 1911 all of European Russia had only 66,000 reapers (to W. Siberia's 36,000) and 166 tractors to America's 14,000.[47]

What the novelist Mikhail Saltykov-Shchedrin had written towards the end of the 1870s was still true a decade or more later. 'Doom seems to hang over some families. This is particularly true among the minor gentry scattered all over Russia, with nothing to do with themselves, divorced from the stream of life and without a position of leadership. Under serfdom they could subsist, but now they simply sit in their ramshackle estates, waiting to disappear.'[48] The monarchy tried to keep them from disappearing altogether in the reign of Alexander III – partly because they were thought to be needed (especially in the villages) as leaders of society and servants of the state; partly because they might otherwise be recruited into the ranks of the opposition (as was already happening); partly because the tsar felt it his duty to rescue a class whose well-being and glory had been an ingredient and reflection of his own. Besides, there was no other socio-economic group more willing than the nobility to make common cause with the state and none less likely to exact political concessions for its support and loyalty. The nobility's economic weakness condemned it, however, to being the state's client, and like all dependent allies it was both distrustful and distrusted.

There was something almost quixotic in the hopes the administration of Tolstoi placed in the nobility as the peasantry's moral leader, political guide, and economic exemplar. According to official figures, two thirds of the gentry in forty-five provinces were without lands at the beginning of the twentieth century. A liberal monthly pointed out that in the northern and eastern provinces there were hardly any resident gentry left; that Arkhangelsk, for example, had only four noble landowners; that in the central provinces they were in extremely poor financial shape and many estates in the hands of non-noble speculators, and that even in the richer agricultural areas of the south the nobility played a minor role. Moreover, the journal contended, there were only about 1,000 properties which assured the financial independence of their owners who did not, as a rule, live in the countryside; in only twenty-eight provinces were the nobility still numerous enough to be truly influential in local life. Conservatives said much the same thing, deplored the gentry's massive flight from their rural homes and pursuits and the loss of class solidarity.[49]

Perhaps Tolstoi and his associates knew all this; yet their efforts to arrest the nobility's decline and to strengthen its public role were too cautious to achieve those ends while their feudal rhetoric only offended or frightened politically aware Russians. A government which prohibited commemorations or even mention of the twenty-fifth anniversary of serf emancipation while it celebrated the centenary of Catherine's Charter to the Nobility (1785) was justifiably suspected of wishing to turn back the clock.[50] The charter had given the nobility a number of exclusive privileges; preferential access to state service; class courts whose judges were elected by the nobility itself; a measure of self-administration for the class; freedom of physical mobility and from corporal punishment; the right to organize district and provincial assemblies which met every three years to discuss common concerns and needs, to communicate these to the government, and to elect spokesmen or marshals (who had direct access to the emperor) as well as a number of officials to serve as district police officers and justices or in local branches of state agencies. But the right of petition was limited to local matters and the nobility had no corporate organs beyond the guberniia which would have given it a voice in national affairs. When several assemblies of nobility asked the government to convene a meeting of guberniia marshals to prepare for the forthcoming centenary, Tolstoi refused: the assemblies had no business to address the subject and the law did not provide for congresses of marshals.[51]

Tolstoi was less intent on buttressing the gentry than the state. The imperial rescript of 1885, which proclaimed that the nobility must, as in the past, play the leading role in the military, in local administration and justice, in caring for the educational, moral and material needs of the people, brought no lasting benefits to the noble estate. Access to it by service, although restricted, was not closed, as many of its members wished. The officer corps (except in the guards regiments) and the bureaucracy remained open to commoners and became more so as both grew in size, even if high birth facilitated advancement. The educational counter-reforms of 1884 and 1887 failed to change the social composition of student bodies in secondary schools or universities and the proportion of nobles in both continued to decline. In the area of peasant administration, the land captain turned out to be more often an ordinary functionary than a respected local notable, whereas the call for greater gentry weight in the zemstvos was a device to bring these elective organs of local government more firmly under bureaucratic control. The law of 1890 assured the nobility's continued dominance of the zemstvos; it did nothing to increase their powers or autonomy. As before, resolutions of zemstvo assemblies needed gubernatorial (or ministerial) sanction to take effect.

The most concrete boon of the 1885 rescript was the setting up of the Gentry Land Bank, with interest and amortization rates lower and loans larger (and easier to obtain) than those of the Peasant Land Bank. By 1904 the bank had given 707 million rubles of credit, or nearly twice the amount lent by the Peasant Bank (380 million). But its generosity did not halt trends going back at least to 1861 – noble indebtedness, loss of lands, waning importance and numbers in the countryside. 'There is cause to fear', Tolstoi's head of chancellery, A. D. Pazukhin, the chief architect of the 'noble reaction' and a former district marshal of nobility, had warned in 1886, 'that left to its own devices, the gentry will be unable to occupy that position in the country which is demanded by state needs. The landowning gentry in certain localities has so declined in numbers, that without the infusion of new and strong elements it will not be in a position to maintain itself and carry out its obligations. . . .'[52] The diagnosis was correct, but the remedies prescribed failed to achieve their goal. The 57.1 per cent of seats in district zemstvo assemblies assigned by law to the gentry could not always be filled, and in some cases elections to the gentry curia could not be held for an insufficiency of electors. In Tver guberniia the number of nobles with properties large enough to vote directly dropped from 853 to 475 between 1891 and 1912. In one district there were 20 electors to choose 16 deputies; in others the proportion was 21 to 14, or 32 to 18; in some from one fourth to one third of gentry seats remained unoccupied.[53]

Even the marshals of nobility who represented their class and its interests in various public bodies, the men whom Alexander III had told the peasants to obey and who sat on innumerable local boards and committees – even they were more the unpaid agents of the state than the guardians of corporate rights. The marshals performed a great deal of the government's business, but real power lay elsewhere.

The Marshal is consulted on the appointment of Land Captains, but his advice is not necessarily taken. He presides over them when they meet at the District Sessions. He regulates their leave of absence. Officially, he takes precedence over the Police Colonel [*ispravnik*] and presides on all local committees, such as those which deal with recruiting, maintenance of prisons, upkeep of schools, and public temperance; but he is always overweighted by official votes. His chief real responsibility is the presidency of the local zemstvo assembly, in which the atmosphere is far more free. He has the entry of the Court, but it is of little use to him as a representative of his class or of the population. . . . If he satisfies the Ministers, he may be appointed to some high post, and that is the real importance of his office.[54]

Chicherin believed that by appointing the land captains the state had undermined the prestige of the gentry marshals and taken all local administration into its own hands. A good many marshals agreed, and neglected their duties; about a third did not even live in their districts at the turn of the century.[55]

The great praise and small favours bestowed upon the nobility in the reign of Alexander III guaranteed neither its economic immunity from the depression of the 1890s nor its solidity as a conservative political force. They only raised expectations that the state was not prepared to meet. Thus, when in 1888 gentry petitions were permitted to raise issues of state policy affecting the class, there were pleas for more privileges, for places in local and central government and in the military, for special class courts, pensions, and educational institutions and for financial assistance. These calls for help led in 1897 to the convening of a Conference on the Problems of the Nobility, chaired by I. N. Durnovo, then head of the Committee of Ministers, who, along with A. V. Krivoshein, a future minister of agriculture, told Nicholas that the autocracy must, in the interest of its own survival, assure that of the landed gentry. The peasantry, Krivoshein warned, was no pillar for the regime, since it played no active political role in combating the 'internal enemy' and, lacking leadership, was open to all kinds of harmful influences. But neither was the gentry given an active political role to play. The Conference gave little satisfaction to advocates of the gentry cause.[56]

Resistance to the gentry's pretensions was as much financial as political. Witte, aside from minor concessions, had no intention of shifting public resources from railroads and factories to rescue a largely unproductive class. 'Again promises, and again hopes that cannot be fulfilled, if for no other reason than that they are limitless and therefore bound to be disappointed.' He pointed out that over half of gentry lands were free of debt; that nobles who still owned property were not as badly off as they claimed, since the value of their land had nearly doubled; that selling, leasing, or mortgaging land benefited from this appreciation; and that the loss of noble acres was taking place mostly in districts of absentee ownership, where the process of alienation (spurred by a favourable market) was well under way before the emancipation. By indicating that the gentry's impoverishment and disappearance varied by region, Witte implied that the process was natural and that government should not interfere with it. He told the Conference that his concern was with the well-being of the nation as a whole. Unexpected support came from Pobedonostsev. He told Witte in March 1898 that for decades the peasants had been neglected and that this had caused chaos and poverty in the villages.

Then the nobility, which itself required curbing, was made to control and supervise the peasants; if this favouritism continued, Russia would end up with an oligarchic parliament and constitution.[57]

As had happened in the previous reign, what was done for the gentry was considerable but fell far short of its demands. Interest on short-term government loans was reduced to 3.5 per cent; a generous formula for land appraisals produced generous mortgages; special credits enabled noble landowners (unlike peasants) to withhold grain from markets until prices rose in the spring; the Gentry Land Bank facilitated the sale of estates and the reduction of debts; some small steps were taken to prevent the breaking up of gentry properties by entail and to enable the children of less wealthy rural families to board in towns where there were secondary schools. But in 1908 a gentry deputy in the Duma still complained that it was easier for a cook's son to get into a university than for the son of an average landowner. In his province, he said, 72 per cent of gentry families had fewer than 100 desiatinas and only rarely could they afford to send their children to secondary schools. A 1902 law reorganizing provincial gentry assemblies took away nearly as many rights as it conceded, and made collective appeals to the Crown more difficult. The largely symbolic 'gentry restoration' caused disgruntlement, mutual distrust, and recrimination. It led neither to reliance nor alliance. At a meeting of officials and gentry marshals in 1896 some of the latter had spoken favourably of a representative form of government. An associate of Pleve's recalled that reports of the critical public mood that reached his chief carried, for the most part, the names of respected nobles active in the loyal and largely conservative circles of the zemstvo and gentry assemblies. Pleve's reaction was to prohibit meetings of gentry marshals. The rightist gentry assembly of Kursk protested that he was violating the corporate rights granted by Catherine the Great.[58]

In the turbulent year and a half that followed Pleve's assassination and ended in the Revolution of 1905, the nobility proved to be as weak a reed for autocracy as Pobedonostsev had feared. Many nobles were prominent in the liberal movement although, unlike the zemstvo, the gentry as a corporation was not predominantly constitutionalist in sentiment and wanted to retain a strong monarchy. Gentry assemblies none the less spoke out for limiting the powers of the bureaucracy, for greater local autonomy, and for a consultative assembly elected along class lines.

The tsar promised such a body in February 1905 in hopes of staving off worse. At a conference called to consider how it should be elected, strong arguments were made for assuring the nobility's preponderance. At this the Grand Duke Vladimir Aleksandrovich exploded and recited a series of famous noble names whose bearers had led or joined the movement for constitutional or even parliamentary government. 'And to what class do the Dolgorukiis, Trubetskois, Golitsyns, Shakhovskois, Kuzmin-Karavaevs and Petrunkeviches belong, and what do they write and say?'[59] Whatever wing of the opposition they belonged to, they all wrote and said that things could not continue as they were. The Grand Duke's argument carried; nearly half the electoral votes were assigned to peasants and Cossacks, while urban workers and most of the intelligentsia were excluded from the franchise; the landed nobility was assigned a third of the seats in the new consultative assembly. It never met, in large part because the peasants were saying much the same thing as the nobles whose estates they were plundering and because they demonstrated in rather forceful ways that their political conservatism or indifference did not make them passive on the issue of land.

The widespread burning and looting of manors during the 1905 Revolution and the radicalism displayed in peasant ballots during the Duma elections of 1906 and 1907 drew the landowning gentry and the government closer together than they had ever been since 1861. Goremykin, chairman of the Council of Ministers in 1906, expressed pleasure that the nobles had been taught a lesson. Although the shock of peasant rebellion may have sobered them politically, it also served to frighten noble landowners and to weaken their hold in the countryside still more. During 1906–07 alone, the Peasant Bank acquired 1,891 estates, three times the number for the preceding eleven years. Anxious to leave a countryside in which their safety could only be assured by troops, the gentry sold over 10 million desiatinas or 20 per cent of its land after 1905. The fury the peasants directed against their noble neighbours left few of the latter with enough confidence in the security of their possessions and persons to invest much energy or capital in improvements. 'The manor and the village face each other like two warring camps', a newly formed political organization of nobles told Stolypin and sought for its members not merely physical safety but also compensation for losses suffered in money, in jobs, in preferential treatment of all kinds.

The revolution and the elections to the first two Dumas forcefully brought home to state and gentry the degree of their mutual dependence. It found expression in the electoral law of June 1907 and in the political activism of a class which began to think and act as such and was successful for the first time, through its disproportionate representation in the legislature and through its pressure groups, in blocking policies considered detrimental to the landed interest. In doing so, it clashed once again with a bureaucracy which, during Stolypin's tenure of office, hoped by measures of economic, social and administrative reform to prevent a recurrence of mass violence. Gentry resistance defeated many of these efforts, and in the villages the structure of authority and attitudes changed less than economic realities.

To the peasant, as well as to the soldier or worker recently come to the city, the nobleman, whether he was rich or poor, official, or operator of an estate, officer or judge, remained a noble. He was everywhere treated with a show of deference and continued to be, in the eyes of the masses of town and country, the representative and symbol of privileged Russia, the *barin* or lord. When another national catastrophe and official incompetence caused great suffering and misery, it was privileged Russia that was made the target of mass blame and anger, an anger that made little distinction between those who were noble and those who lived like them, looked like them or, as the nobility had done for centuries, commanded like them.

REFERENCES

1. Peasant (*krestianin*; pl. *krestiane*), like noble, was a legal term, denoting membership in a social estate and did not necessarily indicate occupation. Although the overwhelming majority of the peasantry – and of the country's population: 74 per cent in 1880; 72 per cent in 1913 – was engaged in agriculture and related pursuits, significant numbers of peasants did not work the land and spent part or all of the year away from their villages. In 1902, 67 per cent of Moscow's inhabitants were registered as peasants; in Petersburg it was almost 70 per cent in 1910. Total population, according to the 1897 census, was nearly 129 million; estimates for other years are (in millions): 1880–97.7; 1890–117.8; 1900–132.9; 1910–160.7; 1916–181.5. A. G. Rashin, *Naselenie Rossii za 100 let (1811–1913gg.)* (Moscow, 1956), p. 21.

2. G. T. Robinson, *Rural Russia under the Old Regime* (New York, 1932), p. 174.

3. Peter Czap, "Peasant class-courts and peasant customary justice in Russia, 1861–1912', *Journal of Social History* 1 (Winter 1967), pp. 149–78.

4. P. A. Zaionchkovskii, *Russian Autocracy under Alexander III* (Gulf Breeze, Fla., 1976), pp. 219–42; cf. T. S. Pearson, 'The Origins of Alexander III's Land Captains: A Reinterpretation, *Slavic Review* 40 (Fall 1981), pp. 384–403.

5. B. Pares, *Russia Between Reform and Revolution* (New York, 1962), pp. 68, 85, 387; D. W. Treadgold, *The Great Siberian Migration* (Princeton, N. J, 1957), p. 114; T. S. Hause, 'State and gentry in Russia', Ph. D. Diss., Stanford University, 1974, p. 211; V. N. Kokovtsov, *Out of My Past* (Stanford, Cal., and London, 1935),p. 337; V. I. Gurko, *Features and Figures of the Past* (Stanford, Cal., and London, 1939), pp. 144–7.

6. G. L. Yaney, 'Some aspects of the imperial Russian government on the eve of the World War', *Slavonic and East European Review* 43 (Dec. 1964), pp. 68–90; here, pp. 68–90; esp. pp. 80–81.

7. R. E. Pipes, *Struve. Liberal on the Left, 1870–1905* (Cambridge, Mass., 1970), p. 61; J. Y. Simms, Jr., 'The Crop Failure of 1891: Soil Exhaustion, Technological Backwardness, and Russia's "Agrarian Crisis"', *Slavonic Review*, 41 (Summer 1982), pp. 236–250, writes: 'The system, technological backwardness, and soil exhaustion were not to blame for the crop failure. Weather alone was the culprit.' (p. 240.)

8. E. D. Chermenskii, *Istoriia SSSR; period imperializma* (Moscow, 1959), p. 16.

9. M. S. Simonova, 'Borba techenii v pravitelstvennom lagere po voprosam agrarnoi politiki v kontse XIX veka', *Istoriia SSSR* 1 (Jan.–Feb.1963), p. 78.

10. *Ibid.*, p. 76.

11. G. M Hamburg, 'The Russian nobility on the eve of the 1905 revolution', *Russian Review* 38 (July 1979), p. 332.

12. H. T. Willetts, 'The agrarian problem' in E. Oberländer *et al.* (eds) *Russia Enters the Twentieth Century* (New York, 1971), p. 126.

13. F. M. Watters, 'Land tenure and financial burdens of the Russian peasant, 1861–1905', Ph.D. Diss. University of California, Berkeley, 1966, pp. 133–53; Jürgen Nötzold, *Wirtschaftspolitische Alternativen der Entwicklung Russlands in der Ära Witte und Stolypin* (Munich, 1966), pp. 41–3; Robinson, op. cit., p. 94.

14. Robinson, op. cit., p. 96; Chermenskii, op. cit., p. 15; D. M. Wallace, *Russia*, (New York, 1961), pp. 345–6; Simonova, op. cit., p. 75; Alexander Gerschenkron, 'Agrarian policies and industrialization: Russia, 1861–1917' in *Cambridge Economic History of Europe*, vol. VI, part 2 (Cambridge, 1965), pp. 769–70.

15. Watters, op. cit.; pp. 163, 170.
16. Zaionchkovskii, op. cit., pp. 77–8; Linda Bowman, 'Business Taxes in Imperial Russia', Ph.D. Diss., University of California, Los Angeles, 1982, ch. IV.
17. Nötzold, op. cit., pp. 131, 137; Arcadius Kahan, 'Government policies and the industrialization of Russia', *Journal of Economic History* 27 (Dec., 1967), pp. 461–6; Iu. N. Shebaldin, 'Gosudarstvennyi biudzhet Rossii v nachale XX v.', *Istoricheskie zapiski* 65 (1959), pp. 168–70; Robert Gorlin, 'Problems of tax reform in Imperial Russia', *Journal of Modern History* 49 (June 1977), pp. 246–65; C. A. Goldberg, 'The Association of Industry and Trade, 1906–1917: the successes and failures of Russia's organized businessmen', Ph.D. Diss., University of Michigan, 1974, pp. 228–31; Dietrich Geyer, *Der russische Imperialismus* (Göttingen, 1977), p. 196.
18. Eberhard Müller, 'Der Beitrag der Bauern zur Industrialisierung Russlands, 1885–1930', *Jahrbücher für Geschichte Osteuropas* 27 (1979), p. 202; I. Kh. Ozerov, 'Finanzpolitik' in Josef Melnik (ed.), *Russen über Russland* (Frankfurt, 1906), p. 224.
19. T. H. Von Laue, 'State and Economy' in C. E Black (ed.), *The Transformation of Russian Society*, (Cambridge, Mass., 1960), pp. 211–12.
20. Nötzold, op. cit., p. 159, n. 18.
21. Ibid., p. 41; A. P. Mendel, *Dilemmas of Progress in Tsarist Russia* (Cambridge, Mass., 1969), p. 50; A. M. Anfimov, *Krupnoe pomeshchiche khoziaistvo Evropeiskoi Rossii* (Moscow, 1969), p. 371.
22. R. C. Robbins, *Famine in Russia 1891–1892* (New York and London, 1975), p. 341.
23. Treadgold, op. cit., p. 56; Margaret Miller, *The Economic Development of Russia*, 1905–1914 (London, 1926 and 1967), p. 56.
24. On the village commune see F. M. Watters, 'The peasant and the village commune,' in W. S. Vucinich (ed.), *The Peasant in Nineteenth-Century Russia* (Stanford, Cal., 1968), pp. 133–57.
25. V. P. Timoshenko, *Agricultural Russia and the Wheat Problem*, Grain Economic Series, No. 1 (Stanford, Cal., 1932), p. 32.
26. Zaionchkovskii, op. cit., pp. 109–17.
27. Lazar Volin, *A Century of Russian Agriculture* (Cambridge, Mass., 1970), pp. 77–93; *Istoriia SSSR* V (Moscow, 1968), p. 303.
28. Nötzold, op. cit., pp. 46–7; Ozerov, op. cit., p. 213; Theodor Shanin, *The Awkward Class* (Oxford, 1972), ch. 3.
29. Simonova, op. cit., pp. 66, 77; A. N. Kuropatkin, 'Dnevnik', *Krasnyi Arkhiv* 2 (1922), p. 33.
30. A. A. Polovtsov, 'Dnevnik, 1901–1903', *Krasnyi Arkhiv* 3 (1923), p. 144.
31. Watters, 'The peasant and the village commune', in Vucinich, op. cit., p. 157.
32. H. Seton-Watson, *The Russian Empire, 1801–1917* (Oxford, 1967); pp. 402–3; Richard Wortman, *The Crisis of Russian Populism* (Cambridge, 1967), pp. 29–31, 46–7; Max Sering, *Russlands Kultur und Volkswirtschaft* (Berlin, 1913), p. 135; J. M Saltzgaber, 'The growth of mechanization in Russian wheat production', Ph.D. Diss., Syracuse University, NY, 1973, pp. 19–20.
33. In his most recent article (see ref. 7 above) Professor Simms has made a powerful argument that poor 'peasant technology was not as detrimental to productivity as has been alleged and was in fact appropriate to the dry farming requirements of the Russian grainlands. Thus, if a "crisis", that is, a distinct decline in the relative well-being of the Russian peasantry in general did exist . . . at the end of the

nineteenth century, it was not a decline predicated on soil exhaustion and technological backwardness.' For contrary views expressed at the time by Stolypin and a populist see (p. 250) L. I. Strakhovsky, 'The statesmanship of Peter Stolypin', *Slavonic and East European Review* 37 (June 1959), p. 350; N. V. Valentinov [N. V. Volskii], *The Early Years of Lenin*, trans. by R. Theen (Ann Arbor, Mich., 1969), p. 234.

34. K. F. Golovin, *Russlands Finanzpolitik*, trans. by M. Kolosovskii (Leipzig, 1900), pp. 165–7; A. A. Polovtsov, *Dnevnik* (Moscow, 1966), I, p. 488, n. 84; Saltzgaber, op. cit., pp. 304–5; Rashin, op. cit., p. 318.

35. Watters, op. cit.; pp. 198–201; B. Pares, op. cit., p. 68; K. F. Golovin, *Meine Erinnerungen* (Leipzig, 1911), pp. 311–14; B. D. Brutskus, *Agrarnyi vopros i agrarnaia politika* (Petrograd, 1922), pp. 52–4; 68–9; Yaney, loc. cit.; p. 75.

36. Robinson, op. cit., pp. 129–37; Terence Emmons. 'The Russian landed gentry and politics', *Russian Review* 33 (July 1974), pp. 270–71; Watters, op. cit., pp. 145–6.

37. 'K istorii agrarnoi reformy Stolypina', *Krasnyi Arkhiv* 17 (1926), p. 84; 'Iz istorii borby s agrarnym dvizheniem, 1905–1906', ibid. 39 (1930), p. 83; Timothy Mixter, 'Of grandfather-beaters and fat-heeled pacifists: perceptions of agricultural labor and hiring market disturbances in Saratov, 1872–1905', *Russian Review* 7 (1980), pp. 139–68.

38. Robinson, op. cit., p. 109; Treadgold, op. cit.; Zaionchkovskii, op. cit., pp. 105–9.

39. *Ibid.*, Zaionchkovskii, op. cit., pp. 110–12; Robinson, op. cit., pp. 105–8.

40. J. Y. Simms, 'The crisis in Russian agriculture at the end of the 19th century: a different view', *Slavic Review* 36 (Sept. 1977), pp. 377–98; and 'On missing the point: a rejoinder', ibid, 37 (Sept. 1978), pp. 487–90.

41. G. M. Hamburg, 'The crisis in Russian agriculture: a comment', *Slavic Review* 37 (Sept. 1978), pp. 481–6; Müller, loc. cit., pp. 197–219.

42. E. Immekus, *Die russische orthodoxe Landpfarrei zu Beginn des XX Jahrhunderts nach dem Gutachten der Diözesanen Bischöfe* (Würzburg, 1978), p. 173; Paul Gregory, 'Economic growth and structural change in Tsarist Russia: a case of modern economic growth?', *Soviet Studies* 23 (Jan. 1972), pp. 418–32; A. P. Nenarokov, *Russia in the 20th Century*, trans. from the Russian by D. Windheim (New York, 1968), p. 31.

43. A. P. Korelin, *Dvorianstvo v poreformennoi Rossii* (Moscow, 1979), p. 54.

44. Ibid., ch. I.

45. Ibid., pp. 76–105.

46. Ibid., p. 67; Emmons, loc. cit., pp. 270–1; Anfimov, op. cit., pp. 221–2; S. A. Zenkovsky, 'The emancipation of the serfs in retrospect', *Russian Review* 20 (Oct. 1961), p. 290.

47. G. S. Queen, 'The McCormick Harvesting Machine Company in Russia', *Russian Review* 23 (April 1964) pp. 164–81; *Historical Statistics of the United States* (Washington, DC, 1975), p. 469; Robinson, op. cit., p. 260; Nikolaus Poppe, 'The economic and cultural development of Siberia' in Oberländer, op. cit, p. 146.

48. M. E. Saltykov-Shchedrin, *The Golovlevs*, trans. by A. R. McAndrew (New York, 1961), p. 295. Cf. V. A. Obolenskii, *Ocherki minuvshago* (Belgrade, 1931), p. 263; N. Voronovskii, *Vechernii zvon; ocherki proshlogo* (New York, 1955), ch. 8.

49. E. M. Brusnikin, 'Krestianskii vopros v Rossii v period reaktsii', *Voprosy Istorii* 2 (1970), p. 36; *Vestnik Evropy* cited by V. Frank [H. von Samson-Himmel-

stjierna], *Russland* (Paderborn, 1888), p. 18; 'Obshchestvo "Sviashchennoi Druzhiny", Otchetnaia zapiska za 1881–1882 gg', *Krasnyi Arkhiv* 21(1927), p. 215.

50. P. A. Zaionchkovskii, 'Aleksandr III i ego blizhaishee okruzhenie', *Voprosy Istorii* 8 (1966) p. 132; L. G. Zakharova, *Zemskaia kontr-reforma 1890g.* (Moscow, 1968), p. 74.

51. Korelin, op. cit., p. 135.

52. Pazukhin quote from K. K. Arsenev, *Za chetvert veka* (Petrograd, 1915), pp. 170 –1; cf. Iu. B. Solovev, *Samoderzhavie i dvorianstvo v kontse XIX veka* (Leningrad, 1973), pp. 181–4.

53. Zakharova, op. cit., pp. 151–6; Golovin, op. cit., p. 353. For a similar picture in the local assemblies of the nobility see A. V. Bolotov, *Gospodin Velikii Novgorod. Vospominaniia* (Paris, 1925), pp. 74–5, and Korelin, op. cit., p. 142.

54. Pares, op. cit, p. 103.

55. B. N. Chicherin, *Vospominaniia: Zemstvo i Moskovskaia Duma* (Moscow, 1934), pp. 275–7; A. P. Korelin, 'Institut predvoditelei dvorianstva', *Istoriia SSSR* 3 (1978), pp. 31–48.

56. Solovev, op. cit., pp. 246–8.

57. 'Trebovaniia dvorianstva i finansovo-ekonomicheskaia politika tsarskogo pravitelstva v 1880–1890-kh godakh', *Istoricheskii Arkhiv* 4 (1957), pp. 123, 133; 'Perepiska S. Iu. Vitte i K. P. Pobedonostseva', *Krasnyi Arkhiv* 30 (1928), p. 101; Solovev op cit., pp. 229–35; Solovev, 'Pravitelstvo i politika ukrepleniia klassovykh pozitsii dvorianstva v kontse XIX veka', in N. E. Nosov (ed.), *Vnutrenniaia politika tsarizma* (Leningrad, 1967), p. 278; G. W. Simmonds, 'The Congress of Representatives of the Nobles' Associations, 1906–1916', Ph.D. Diss., Columbia University, NY, 1964, p. 64.

58. D. N. Liubimov, 'Otryvki iz vospominanii', *Istoricheskii Arkhiv* 6 (1962), pp. 72 –3; Korelin, op. cit., pp. 280–2.

59. *Petergofskoe soveshchanie o proekte Gosudarstvennoi Dumy* (Berlin, n.d.), p. 149.

CHAPTER SIX

Progress and poverty

The solution to Russia's agrarian problem was not to be found in agriculture alone. Improved patterns of tenancy and ownership, government aid, a reformed tax structure could not, by themselves, remedy rural overpopulation and backwardness, low yields and illiteracy. To draw underemployed hands from the land into trades and industries, to make them consumers of the products of a diversified and intensive agriculture, to raise the level of farming techniques required a quickened pace of economic development on a massive scale. In 1881 neither government nor society had yet committed themselves fully to the building of a modern industrial and commercial system. There were doubts of its desirability and fears of its political and social consequences.

The state had made a beginning with the emancipation of the serfs and other reforms to stimulate and give greater scope to the economic energies of its citizens. The Crimean defeat had driven home the fact of Russia's backwardness which contrasted so sharply with her standing and even more with her pretensions as a great power. In 1860 she was economically the least developed of the major states, with only some 860,000 of her 74 million people employed in industry and more than half the national income produced by the agricultural sector from which 85 to 90 per cent of the population drew their livelihood.[1]

The Great Reforms were the necessary precondition for industrialization. They began the removal of obstacles which had earlier made the mobilization of money, men, and property impossible or difficult and they established a legal framework designed to secure property rights and facilitate business transactions. But they did not set in motion a continuous march towards economic modernity. Serfdom, for example, had been abolished, but not the rules that made it difficult for peasants to leave their crowded villages. The number of long-term passports issued for work in the towns averaged only 60,000 per year during 1861–70, half as many as were issued for short terms of employment outside the villages.

The contradictions revealed in this example had their counterparts in other areas. Local self-government and independent courts did not necessarily lessen bureaucratic red tape and administrative interference with private enterprise, nor was the state's desire for a modern industrial and transport system rapidly translated into concrete action. For about a quarter century after 1861 the rate of industrial growth remained relatively low. Of the many reasons which may account for this one of the most important is the government's inability or unwillingness to lay down a clear line of economic policy and adhere to it. Uncertainty as to the unsettling political and social effects of industrialization, particularly on the peasantry, caused indecisiveness as to priorities and explains the state's failure to concentrate its slender financial resources on economic development.

A memorandum which Bunge addressed to Alexander III in March 1884 illustrates the problem which he and other ministers of finance faced in the absence of a clearly defined and proclaimed policy to guide the agencies of government. His colleagues at the War, Navy, and Transport Ministries had asked for supplemental appropriations to keep the empire from losing its place among the great powers. Bunge resisted, and justified his resistance by citing the need for bringing public expenditures and income into balance. A state which could not keep its financial house in order and meet its internal needs would be condemned to second-rate status as surely as one which lacked modern armaments and strategic railroads. In his view, the monarchy and the country would be served best by making the peasants better producers of crops and wealth, as well as better consumers, by lightening their tax burden.[2] For the moment, Bunge prevailed. But when he was unable to avoid deficits and had to have recourse to borrowing, he was replaced in 1886. The military expenses connected with the Bulgarian crisis of 1885–86 and campaigns in Central Asia (1882–84) defeated his hopes that fiscal reform would spur economic activity and create enough of a surplus to pay for industrialization at a moderate pace.

His successor Vyshnegradskii followed a different prescription to reach a similar goal. He, too, hoped to find the bulk of resources needed for industrial expansion at home, but expected to generate them by reducing, rather than stimulating, popular consumption, by squeezing the masses harder to produce more or, at least, to make them turn a larger share of their product over to the state. By curbing consumption, imports, and state expenditures he wanted to create the budgetary surpluses and gold reserves that would encourage domestic and foreign investment in Russian industry. He increased indirect taxes on articles of common consumption, greatly raised tariffs, and pressed the collection of arrears on the poll-tax and redemption payments. His orthodox and stringent policies allowed him to negotiate French loans on terms that made possible an interest reduction on foreign-owned bonds; helped by this and the revenues from state-owned railroads, he was able to claim success for five years in succession. The treasury was full and gold reserves more than doubled. But Vyshnegradskii was never able to realize the ultimate benefits and goals of all the squeezing and trimming that he had imposed on state and people, even going so far as to curtail railway construction. The consequences of the 1891 harvest failure were blamed on the man who had left the peasants without reserves of food or money to withstand such a catastrophe.

Bunge's programme demanded more time than it was given to bear fruit; on the part of government it presupposed belt-tightening and restraint in foreign affairs. Vyshnegradskii's plan required that the state continue the massive but risky fiscal pressures the benefits of which, as 1891 had shown, could be wiped out in one year. Vyshnegradskii resigned. The situation of a modernizing minister of finance in tsarist Russia was not unlike that of the peasant in the Russian story who believes he can get his horse used to not eating by gradually cutting down on its feed. The experiment would have worked, the peasant is convinced, if only the horse, in its stubbornness, had not died of starvation just when success was within reach. It was only when Witte replaced Vyshnegradskii in 1892 that a more coherent and determined policy of industrial expansion was adopted and, what is more, held to for nearly a decade, perhaps the most important decade in the economic history of pre-revolutionary Russia.

The great industrial spurt of the 1890s which largely coincided with Witte's administration cannot, however, be credited to him or to his policies alone. These only continued and intensified the various measures his predecessors, especially Vyshnegradskii, had employed. Their initial development of a railroad network, the creation of a stable ruble and of the export surpluses which enabled the government to borrow abroad, laid the basis for Witte's own achievements. What he brought to his post was unprecedented energy and the conviction that what was being done to free Russia from economic dependence on the advanced countries of the West had to be done very much more quickly and massively. While his sense of urgency was not shared everywhere, he managed to impart it to wider circles of officialdom and the general public than had ever before agreed that industrial development was essential and even desirable for Russia.

Witte's role as chief advocate and spokesman for the speedy build-up of Russian industrial might was as important as his management of that process. There was now some readiness to face the fact that, as Witte had warned, years and even decades might pass before the nation could enjoy the benefits of the exertions it was called upon to make. As a propagandist of industrialization and economic growth – through the press, the awarding of prizes, the encouragement of industrial exhibitions, technical education, and a merchant marine – Witte tried to overcome the opposition of agrarian conservatives and populists of all shadings who, for humanitarian, economic, or political reasons feared the growth of industrial capitalism and a factory proletariat. Unconsciously, perhaps, Witte tried in this way to give Russians the industrializing and modernizing ideology that most of them lacked, a faith in the future that would help to see them through the difficult years his programme would require.

What most distinguished Witte from his predecessors was his ability to create a climate conducive to industrial development and to commit governmental policy as well as considerable governmental resources to that purpose. Economic historians disagree on the size and on the adequacy of that commitment; some of them question whether the state took as active and leading a part in economic development and planning as it could or should have done. Others believe that the Witte years have been given too much importance and earlier developments neglected. But when expenditures for railroads are included, the years from 1894 to 1902 are those in which a higher proportion of public funds was assigned to industrial expansion than at any other time in the entire period from 1861 to the end of the monarchy.

At Witte's urging the state no longer merely encouraged the building of railroads and factories; it was no longer content to remove certain legal and institutional obstacles that stood in the way of achieving industrial growth; it looked even less than before to the market to supply either the customers or the capital to sustain the growth of heavy industry. The state itself became the prime mover of Russia's industrialization, especially by supplying needed capital or assuring its availability, by placing orders or guaranteeing profits for certain key industries at certain times. Although the state did not continue to play the role of prime mover after the fall of Witte, and did not complete the industrial revolution, its actions helped to create a momentum which, after the interruption caused by economic and political crises, could be resumed with a much smaller degree of state aid after 1906.

Witte's administration marked a departure also in the extent to which reliance was placed on foreign funds – in the form of state loans and private investments – to supply needed capital and to cover budgetary deficits. By the end of the century the state debt alone was 3.5 billion rubles, of which 1 billion was held abroad, making Russia's the world's largest foreign debt. The stabilization of the ruble and the adoption in 1897 of a convertible currency based on gold had made possible this influx of foreign funds, which were significant in financing industrial expansion. In the three years from 1893 to 1896 foreigners invested in Russian enterprises 40 million rubles more than did Russians (144.9 as against 103.7 million rubles). In the next triennium the gap grew wider, with Russians supplying 111.8 million and foreign investors – French, Belgian, German, English and Swedish – 450.7 million rubles.[3]

In the half century from the emancipation of the serfs to the First World War, the proportion of foreign investments in Russian corporations went from 13.4 per cent to one third. Even in the traditionally Russian cotton industry, a fifth of the capital was foreign; and nearly a third of the largest factories were entirely controlled by foreigners, who also owned almost all of the domestic cotton crop. Similarly, the Caucasian oil and Ukrainian coal and metallurgical industries were very largely in the hands of foreigners. A third of the capital in the big commercial banks was foreign. Foreigners controlled the largest parts of the embryo electrical, chemical and machine industries. They were the least influential but still played a role in woolens manufacture, insurance and maritime navigation.[4]

A major objection to Witte's policies was that they created a dangerous and shameful dependency on foreigners. To him, their large financial and technological contribution was both defensible and essential. Foreign borrowing on a large scale was, he argued, the only way of mitigating the sacrifices that Russians had to bring in the form of high taxes and tariffs. Even so the paying powers of the people would be strained to breaking point and their consumption reduced. Without the capital furnished by the developed countries the process of accumulating domestic savings in an agricultural economy would be too long, too costly, and too uncertain and could have the same dire results as Vyshnegradskii's policies had produced in 1891. Witte agreed that Russia's *economic* relationship to Europe was that of colony to metropolis, of supplier of raw materials to exporters of capital and finished products. Yet her might and military power were great enough to assure her political independence and, in the long run, her economic autonomy as well. In order to maintain her political and military strength, she had also to become industrially a great power – and that meant accepting as inevitable a temporary inferiority.

Foreign financing speeded and facilitated the growth of Russian mining, industry, and railroads, of credit and commerce, and there is evidence to show that Witte was right when he insisted that it need not lead to political or economic subjugation. Western as well as Soviet scholars[5] have come to discount the earlier view that Russia's creditors were able to dictate her foreign and domestic policies or that tsarism's siding with the Western allies during the First World War was ultimately determined by her financial dependence upon them, and France in particular. That political alliance and economic links reinforced each other may safely be assumed; the latter did not create the former. When Russian negotiators on occasion failed to secure a French loan or the participation of a Jewish banking house in an American one, this neither changed their country's discriminatory policy towards Jews, nor did sources of credit dry up. France's need of a counterweight to the German threat even gave Russian diplomats a measure of leverage over the French ally that belied the unequal nature of the relationship. During the Revolution of 1905, for example, the Russian government was helped through its crisis by being able to borrow abroad. Dependence there was, but it was mutual. With 27.5 per cent of French foreign investments placed in Russia in 1906 (90 per cent in state loans) – as compared with Germany's 15 per cent – it could not be otherwise.

Foreign purchasers of Russian bonds or investors in Russian enterprises sought a maximum return. They were not acting as agents of their governments seeking economic domination or given it. Thus the Russian state guaranteed the payment of dividends to foreigners who lent money for the construction of railroads but kept their control firmly in its own hands. By 1909–11 the proportion of foreign to domestic investment had been reversed, with the latter exceeding the former by more than three times (913 to 284 million rubles), testifying to the formation of native capital. At the same time the share of foreign capital in the Russian economy remained high (54 per cent in heavy industry; 62 per cent in construction and municipal enterprises; 34 per cent in banking; 45 per cent in the chemical industry), as did imports of capital. The belief that net foreign earnings had come to exceed net foreign payments and that Russia was close to entrepreneurial self-sufficiency by 1914[6] probably overstates the changes that had taken place, just as the revived thesis of a foreign policy shaped by the need of foreign credit goes too far in the other direction.[7]

As Witte had predicted, foreign borrowing was beginning to pay dividends: it was also costly and a mixed blessing. The service of the foreign debt and the outflow of profits were the negative sides of a relationship which could only be a partial remedy for Russia's shortage of capital and contributed to the uneven development of her economy. Agriculture continued to suffer from underinvestment; in some branches of production, costs were higher and quality lower than abroad; and the military still relied for much of its equipment on foreign suppliers – to the tune of 345 million rubles between 1901 and 1907. When the country was cut off from its trading partners (of which her enemy Germany was the most important) by the outbreak of hostilities in 1914, it was demonstrated how little Russia was yet capable of meeting some critical needs. More than a third of technical equipment and more than half of industrial machinery was still imported in 1913. None the less, Witte's policies improved Russia's ability to survive the military disasters of the early part of the war and to make significant progress in supplying her armies when the political order collapsed: they also laid the foundations on which the Soviets built a generation later.

All the statistics show the great difference that the ten years of Witte's vigorous management made to the growth of Russian industry. Much of this, as had been true in Western Europe, was stimulated by railroad building. Railroads were important in Witte's eyes as a force drawing together the country's vast spaces, its people, their farms and factories. They were agents of civilization and progress, linking Russia with Europe and Asia, where she would find the markets and profits that would end her financial dependence on Europe.

In 1855 there were only 850 miles of railroads. The Crimean defeat supplied the first great impetus for their expansion, and by 1885 there were some 17,000 miles of track. After a temporary slump, the tempo of construction greatly accelerated in the 1890s. By 1900, almost 13,000 miles had been added. Total mileage was about 40,000 in 1905, 48,000 in 1914. The single most impressive achievement of Russian railroad building – the Trans-Siberian line of almost 4,000 miles – was undertaken in 1891, when Witte was still minister of transport. Although it was to be twenty-five years before a journey to Vladivostok could be made entirely by rail, the line was basically completed in 1904. As did many of Russia's railways, the Trans-Siberian served strategic and military purposes (in its eastern sections) as well as social and economic goals, helping to develop Siberia and making its southern regions more easily accessible to peasant settlers. Its cost was extremely high (250 million rubles), a general feature of railroad construction in Russia and due largely to the high profits guaranteed to private entrepreneurs and suppliers. To encourage domestic producers these were paid double or triple what foreign manufacturers (of rails, for example) were asking.

The results, as was true in many sectors of the economy, were uneven. There was too much speculative construction in the 1870s and early 1880s, leading to overbuilding in some parts of the country and neglect in others. There were excessive costs and uneconomic lines, forcing the government eventually to take over most of them. There was insufficient density. In 1913 Russia ranked next to last, behind Bulgaria, Serbia, Greece and Romania, in a list of eighteen European countries in mile of track per square mile of territory. Yet in the end there was a system that for all its faults performed the functions that Witte, the former railroad man, had foreseen for it: a sophisticated industry turning out rails, locomotives, and rolling stock, some 3,000 stations, a lively traffic in goods and passengers and nearly half a million employees, more than were engaged in any other branch of industry.[8] To the populist N. F. Danielson, who feared that government-subsidized railroads were built to force agricultural exports through fiscal pressure on the peasants rather than to industrialize the country, Friedrich Engels wrote in 1892: 'On the day when railroads were introduced in Russia [the question of] the introduction of modern means of production was settled. You *must* be able to repair your locomotives, wagons, and rails yourself and this can be done cheaply only if you are also capable of building all that you need for that purpose.[9]

In Witte's vision the spread of railways was accompanied and followed by an expansion of heavy industry, by increased outputs of iron and steel, coal, oil, and machinery. Dramatic successes were made easier by the low starting level, the fact that most new investment went into heavy industry, and that the new plants and mines of Ukraine as well as the oilfields of Baku were larger and could use more modern equipment and techniques than many of their Western counterparts built decades earlier. The 'advantages of backwardness' through borrowing or copying advanced technologies showed in the Russian growth rates, which reached a yearly average of 7 to 8 per cent during the 1890s, and in some of those years went even higher. Such rates were little short of phenomenal. Even when all the years from 1885 to 1914 with their falls and rises are taken into account, the annual increase in industrial production averaged 5.72 per cent, exceeding the American, German and British percentages which were 5.26, 4.49, and 2.11 respectively. For the entire 1860–1913 period the increase in industrial output has been calculated as averaging probably 5 per cent per annum or 3 per cent per head of population. These rates are not considered exceptionally high in international comparison, but they were higher in relation to the rate of population growth than those of Germany and the United States and 'substantially greater than anything achieved in the United Kingdom even during the most rapid industrialization in the first half of the century'.[10]

Indices of industrial output do not tell the whole story. They give no certain indication of the degree to which the aim of catching up was achieved. While it is possible, for example, to say that iron smelting in Russia grew ten times faster than it did in England in the 1890s, it is also possible to put the matter in a less cheerful light and to point out that Russia lagged behind the United States as well as much smaller countries like England and Germany in the amount of iron produced. None the less, this constituted a respectable advance from the seventh place Russia had occupied in 1880. The empire was close to being the fifth largest industrial power in 1914, but labour productivity increased much more slowly than output. Per capita income, estimated at more than half the West European average in 1860, had fifty years later fallen to a third, and average growth rates for the economy as a whole (1860–1913) fell below the 2, 2.5 and 3 per cent of Germany, the United States, and Japan respectively. Every statistic could be made to yield optimistic or pessimistic assessments of the Witte system and its effects.

Russia's share of world steel output rose from 2 to 8 per cent between 1870 and 1900, putting her ahead of France – 4.8 vs. 4.6 million tons. Yet at that time she was still producing only one fifth as much iron and steel as the United States in absolute terms and on a per capita basis only one fifth the amount of steel turned out by German mills. Machine building and metal working made substantial progress; the chemical industry did not, with deleterious effects for an agriculture badly in need of chemical fertilizer. In the production of textiles too there was unevenness, with a highly mechanized and concentrated cotton industry moving to fourth place in the world and leaving an antiquated woollen manufacture far behind. The picture was mixed also in coal mining, where spectacular expansion in the Donets Basin contrasted with stagnation in the Urals and the Moscow region and with continued reliance on imports. The oil industry in the Caucasus saw an explosive growth in the 1890s, rivalling or overtaking that of the United States, but depletion of the most easily tapped wells, stiff foreign competition, and the effects of the 1905 Revolution, which raged with particular violence in Baku, caused a decline from which the industry did not fully recover. Altogether, the world-wide economic depression of the turn of the century, followed by agrarian riots, by war with Japan, by a political crisis and revolution, ended the expansion as well as some of the optimism of the 1890s. It was not until 1909 that production again reached the volume of 1900 and resumed its advance, though at slower rates.[11]

The sensitivity with which the national economy reacted to international economic disturbances and the continuing troubles in the Russian countryside – another famine in 1898–99 in the central Volga region, followed by peasant unrest in Kharkov and Poltava provinces in 1902 – confirmed Witte's opponents in their predictions of the ultimate failure of his policies. Witte himself had foreseen a difficult transition period before the third and final stage of his programme could be realized. After the build-up of heavy industry, stimulated by railway construction, there would be a growth of light industry with industrial and urban Russia as the market that would make for a prosperous agriculture which, in its turn, would be the consumer of domestically-produced manufactured goods. Even before the height of the economic crisis Witte had to admit, in a memorandum to Nicholas of 1899, that there were weaknesses in his scheme. They provided ready targets for attack and powerful arguments for softening the rigours of prevailing policies.

Russia has now an industry of tremendous size. The interests of our entire economy are closely tied to its future. This industry, however, has not yet reached such an extent and such technical perfection as to furnish the country with an abundance of cheap goods. Its services cost the country too dearly, and these excessive costs have a destructive influence over the welfare of the population, particularly in agriculture. [12]

That being so, how could the costs be reduced and the welfare of the people be increased? For the short run, Witte had only one answer: more of the same, seeing it through, more foreign borrowing, continued high tariffs and taxes. Otherwise his entire programme, including what had already been achieved, would be endangered by the resultant changes and wavering. 'Only by a system strictly sustained, and not by isolated measures, can a healthy development be guaranteed to our national economy.' Witte asked Nicholas that he stand firm in support of the present course, at least until 1904 when the issue of foreign capital and the protective tariff might be reviewed. Failing that, the emperor was to tell him what economic policy he should pursue. Nicholas did not like such talk, and Witte's 'or else' undoubtedly was a factor in his dismissal when the difficulties and critics of his system multiplied.

Did Witte really think that tariffs and capital imports could be substantially reduced in a matter of five years? It is certain that time was one of the indispensable ingredients of his system – time for all the changes that he saw as the products and preconditions of modern factories and business methods to take root. This meant changes in attitudes, laws and administration. It meant improved manufacturing techniques and management; economies of scale and mass production; lower prices for manufactured goods to capture markets at home and in Asia; a disciplined work force and an energetic entrepreneurial class, free of red tape. In short, what was needed, in Witte's words, were capital, knowledge, and the spirit of enterprise, and the best place to find these was – industry. He hoped and believed that industrialization would transform Russian society, but to become industrialized Russia had first to be transformed. At the least both processes had to move at comparable speeds, but this demanded that the country, its people and indeed the world hold still, so to speak, for an unknown length of time while industry performed its work of transformation. Tranquillity at home and peace abroad were essential, and the former especially would be difficult to maintain in the midst of the strains to which the country was being subjected.

It was a problem which all Russian reformers faced and one for which there was perhaps no solution short of the kind of coercion that twentieth-century dictatorships employed. Conceivably mass discontent, and the disaffection of articulate society which echoed it, might have been lessened by a more tolerant political order; political concessions might have created a measure of public support allowing the government to weather the storms of social protest for a longer period of time. Such an assumption was never tested. Even if it had been, even if there had been a greater supply of political intelligence or flexibility on the part of Russia's rulers, industrialization was bound to threaten political stability, and instability to endanger Witte's policies.

A restive peasantry was not the only source of danger. It was beginning to come also from a class of factory workers which was growing considerably, but not fast enough to relieve population pressure on the land. It was a class which retained strong personal, emotional, and economic links to the rural regions from which most of its members had come and in whom old and new grievances combined in an explosive way. As was true everywhere in the initial stages of industrialization, working conditions and wages were deplorably bad. Men in government were divided over whether their primary obligation was to foster enterprise and favour the employers or protect the workers from excessive exploitation. The state gave little help, therefore, to the disoriented and increasingly bitter men who were debarred by law from organizing unions until 1906.

Official neglect was caused also by the wish to ignore the political and social problems posed by an industrial working class and by perplexity and disagreement over the role the regime should play in the relations between owners and workers. An official report declared at the end of the 1880s that the labour question, in its West European form, did not exist in Russia. The government's raising it would only create expectations in the minds of the workers that the bureaucracy would back them against their bosses. When the Council of State in 1893 debated a bill that would have obliged negligent factory adminstrations to pay compensation for work-connected fatalities or injuries, Pobedonostsev denounced it as socialistic and designed to make proletarians out of Russian labouring men who were, essentially, still cultivators of the soil with strong ties to the land. Since the Russian peasant, in Witte's opinion, was much less demanding than the European or American worker, a low wage was for Russia's industries as much of a boon as her rich natural resources. As late as 1895 the Ministry of Finance denied the existence of a proletariat.[13]

Viewed in a statistical rather than ideological perspective, such attitudes do not appear entirely quixotic. In 1860 industrial workers formed 0.76 per cent of the total population. In 1900, after the changes wrought by the industrial upswing of the preceding decade, they still accounted for only 1.28 per cent (1.7 million persons) and in 1913 for 1.4 per cent (2.3 millions). Even the larger figures given by Soviet historians for the industrial working class (factory, mining, and railroad workers) of 2.2 millions for 1900 and 4.3 for 1913,[14] need not, at least in the earlier period, have forced a change of perceptions or priorities upon those who denied the existence of a genuine proletariat. Compared with the vast numbers who drew their livelihood from agricultural pursuits, and whom the country's rulers out of a mixture of fear and patriarchal obligation continued to regard as their first concern, factory workers were still a negligible quantity. This seemed all the more justifiable if one thought of Russia's workers primarily as peasants (the legal category to which most of them belonged) or as being peasants in outlook and expectations. These expectations were of official protection and care which the Ministry of Interior in particular felt constrained to extend against employers who in their search for profits were, in the ministry's view, guided neither by the landlord's sense of *noblesse oblige* nor by its own responsibility for preserving social tranquillity.[15]

Not surprisingly, the police were the first government agency to see the factory workers as a potential proletariat and their situation as a problem. In

1884 a Petersburg police official noted the existence of an urban working class which was different in outlook from its peasant brothers, which was receptive to 'all kinds of false doctrine', and could carry its factory-contracted infection back to the villages. The warning was echoed by the head of the Moscow police, who saw workers protesting their grievances as the primary school for their political education.[16] When a series of strikes culminated in an illegal walkout of 6,000 men at the Morozov textile plant in Orekhovo-Zuevo in 1885, it became a matter of concern at the highest levels of the administration. For this was more than merely an economic action; it gave every appearance of being an outburst of pent-up anger against managers, owners, and their property.

In letters to the emperor and to Bunge (the author of the first significant factory laws of 1882 and 1885), Tolstoi set forth what the Ministry of Interior took to be the causes of the work stoppages and disturbances in Vladimir and Moscow provinces in 1884 and 1885. Existing laws, dealing mainly with the labour of women and children, were inadequate. Although they had set up a factory inspectorate and thus inserted the state into the relations between management and labour, they did not keep the former from dealing with the latter in an arbitrary way. Excessive fines for minor or fictitious infractions of discipline had been imposed, exorbitant prices had been charged at company stores, and hours had been cut to save labour costs even where this violated contracts. In this way workers had been forced to make up for a fall in profits by having their wages cut by as much as 40 per cent (at a time when wage rates were already depressed by 20 per cent) and by paying for their food up to 45 per cent above prevailing prices. This had made it impossible for the workers to pay their taxes and feed their families, given rise to justified complaints and, eventually, to large-scale disturbances.[17]

The sequence in which Tolstoi listed the consequences of management's conduct was revealing, as was his omission of the political dimension of the labour question. He was not as prescient as the Petersburg policeman had been and was confident that his policy of firmness was keeping false doctrines and their carriers in check. They were not much in evidence during his ministry. He did no more, therefore, than to ask for more legislation of a paternalistic kind without expanding the workers' rights or seriously restricting those of the owners. The laws of 1886 forbade the use of money fines for any purpose other than workers' welfare, prohibited the lowering of contractually set wages, required the regular payment of wages in cash, not kind, set guidelines for labour contracts, introduced paybooks, and enlarged the role of the public authorities in the field of labour relations. Provincial factory boards were established on which the governor, vice-governor, police chief and representatives of local self-government sat together with factory inspectors whose investigative authority was widened. Given regulatory powers to ensure industrial peace, the boards appeared designed to make the state a permanent arbiter of the relations between management and labour.[18]

These measures, which were only gradually extended to sixty-four provinces, did not satisfy the workers' goal of decent wages, working conditions, and accident insurance. In the government's eyes they justified severe penalties for striking as well as continued denials of the workers' right to organize or even to assemble for the discussion of common concerns. With the state as their advocate, it was implied, they need not rely on mutual aid. The laws of 1886 were not nearly as impartial as the theorists of a fatherly autocracy would have it. By his indulgent attitude towards management, Vyshnegradskii soon weakened the limited protection the workers had obtained. When he prohibited publication of the reports of the factory inspectors he undercut even further the effectiveness of this dedicated but exceedingly small corps of men. In the search for industrial greatness the profits of private enterprise were as indispensable an ingredient as the export of grain. However humane or fearful, therefore, one or another segment of the bureaucracy might be, it could not consistently play the part of disinterested protector of workers or peasants. It took an explosion of major proportions to overcome the contrary pulls represented most often by the Ministries of Finance and Interior but at times even within one and the same ministry. That is what happened in the aftermath of the Morozov strike and in subsequent years as a consequence of further industrial strife and a prelude to government action.

That action as often took the form of repression as of concessions; indeed, the two 'remedies' might be applied simultaneously, in emphatic reaffirmation of the official determination not to reward troublemakers or violators of public order and factory discipline. This duality of approach diminished the moral victory and the concessions the workers had obtained; it also convinced them that the government was not a reliable defender of their interests. In the Morozov strike, for example, long before there were any new laws, there were the police and troops who brought about a resumption of work by mass arrests. Some 600 strikers were simply deported to their home villages, the strike leaders were brought to trial and their chief, when acquitted by a jury, was sent into distant administrative exile. In 1897 the minister of interior directed local authorities to use such extra-judicial ways of dealing with strikers because it would be difficult to prove in court that their offences constituted breaches of the law. In 1897, also, the factory inspectors were almost turned into police auxiliaries. They were pressured into informing on the workers, required to warn them of the punishment awaiting them if they struck, and ordered to make it possible for non-strikers to get to their jobs. A special factory police force was established in 1899 and its units stationed permanently in or near industrial establishments.[19]

These measures were a response to the greatest wave of strikes Russia had yet seen. In May 1896, and again in January 1897, 30,000 cotton spinners and weavers of St Petersburg walked out of their plants. They achieved a degree of solidarity, self-discipline and organization that forced the government to yield to their demand for a reduction of the work-day from thirteen to ten and a half hours. Their action also signalled the arrival of a genuine proletariat which was conscious of its identity and had shown itself capable of formulating its goals without much help from the socialist intelligentsia. The Marxists hailed that signal. It confirmed their hopes in the historical role of the proletariat and demonstrated the applicability of their theories to Russia. For populists and conservatives it called into question the likelihood of a separate path for Russia; some of the latter began to search for better answers to the labour problem than the old mixture of repression and concessions.

Made unavoidable by a rising curve of strike activity, a new look at that problem revealed not only a dramatic growth in the number of industrial workers; equally important were changes in the social characteristics of the men and women who were unmistakably becoming a working class. Between 1887 and 1897 the labour force engaged in manufacturing and mining industries increased from 1.3 million to 2.1 million persons and was expected at that rate to reach 2.2 million by 1907 and 5 million by 1917. The number of railroad employees was 215,000 in 1884 and had more than doubled by 1900. Although these trends did not develop quite as projected and although the proportion of all Russians who were wage workers in industry remained small, it became increasingly difficult to view them primarily as peasants who had temporarily left their villages. Nor were they a negligible quantity merely because they constituted but a small percentage of the population. Indeed, it was beginning to appear that the workers were already proving to be more consistently and deliberately troublesome than the peasants had ever been since the days of Pugachev, and that it was perhaps their peasant characteristics that instead of immunizing them helped to make them so.

The village, it is true, continued to claim most of them, both legally and emotionally. In 1900 about nine tenths of urban workers were still designated as belonging to the peasant estate (*soslovie*) in their passports. In light industries, such as textiles and food processing, as many as 4 million came to the factories seasonally and returned to the land in summer.[20] And even those who worked in plants and mines the year round retained membership in the village community along with the right to a share of its lands (usually tilled by a relative) and the duty (until 1903) to bear a share of its fiscal obligations. It was possible to see this link with the village as a form of social security. At least the Russian worker had a place to go when he was laid off or incapacitated by illness or old age. But it could also be argued that a man who sought the stupefying labour of mill or mine because poverty had driven him off the land was not likely to be comforted by the thought of having to return there. The smaller the area of sown land, the more time peasants spent in industrial occupations, suggesting what had dictated their movements. Possibly half of those who were recruited into the working class were young people between the ages of twenty and twenty-nine, without prospects or families of their own in the village, and for them leaving it was most often permanent.

For their older comrades, the heads of household who had gone away from lands and families only to return to them with their cash earnings, the link with the village made no more tolerable the miserable conditions under which they were forced to live. These men might make no lasting addition to proletarian solidarity, but contemporary observers stress their special hatred for the factory, an anger possibly greater than that of men who were forced to make a lasting adjustment to their new conditions of life and labour. There was, in any case, enough to embitter both categories of workers – those who took their grievances back to the village where they enlarged inherited if unorganized resentments, and those who stayed in city or town and were beginning to seek improvements in their lot through concerted action.[21]

The indignities and penalties to which factory hands were subjected by bosses and officials made them feel less than human; so did their loneliness (60 per cent lived without families) and the corner of a crowded room, factory barracks or shared bed that too many of them called home. A work week of 54 to 60 hours remained the norm, even with improvements after 1905, and wage increases of 20 per cent in the pre-war years, which brought the average in manufacturing to an annual 263 rubles in 1913, compensated only partially for higher prices. There were significant differences in pay (as well as living costs) between regions and industries. Machine builders and metal workers in the south and St Petersburg fared best (400 to 500 rubles), Moscow textile workers worst (200 rubles). The brutishness of the workingman's life tended to make him difficult and explosive.[22]

Around 1900 between one third and two thirds of those working in factories, mines and on railroads were the children of fathers who had done so before them; close to one half owned no land at all. Their rural outlook and attachments were bound to be waning. Even for those who were but recently enrolled in the industrial labour force, the change of occupation (and presumably of attitudes and aspirations) was apt to become permanent. Among metal workers recruited before 1905, 26 per cent had land; a decade later it was 19.4 per cent. As early as 1893 four fifths of workers in the Moscow industrial area were employed at their jobs all year. This was soon true of St Petersburg as well, though not of the newer industrial regions of the south.[23]

There were those who welcomed and those who feared these evidences of proletarianization. They spelled the growth of a distinct working-class consciousness, loyalties, and boldness, as well as adjustment to factory discipline and authority, the appearance of the steadiness and skills that management had found deplorably lacking among the peasants. Hopes and worries were both nourished by the concentration of large numbers of hands in a relatively small number of enterprises of great size. In 1895 plants with more than one thousand workers accounted for 31 per cent of those engaged in industry (as compared with 13 per cent in Germany); by 1907 that percentage was 39 and nearly 41 in 1914, or double the concentration of labour in American industry. That factories located in rural or semi-rural districts employed 70 per cent of all workers in 1900 gave little support to the belief that this would help to maintain patriarchal relationships in industry or protect workers from the evil influences of urban intellectuals and agitators. Concentration in what were essentially company towns furthered the spread of non-peasant concerns and attitudes, the emergence of leaders and collective action. The larger factories had more strikes and were favourable soil for the propaganda of socialists.[24]

However one might classify them in sociological terms, the men (and women – *circa* 25 per cent) drawn into industry during the Witte years did not remain raw peasants temporarily seeking to supplement their incomes by wage labour. They were not the carriers of proletarian revolution or even interested, for the most part, in political activity. But neither were they so disoriented, backward or frightened as to be unaware of their special interests and needs or to reject the help and advice the socialist intelligentsia was beginning to offer them. Male factory hands as a group were more literate than the population as a whole. The census of 1897 showed that 57.8 per cent of them could read, as compared with 28.4 per cent of Russians of both sexes between the ages of 9 and 49. Among the more highly skilled, such as the metal workers of St Petersburg, almost three quarters were literate. By 1913, it was 92 per cent. Men such as these knew what they wanted: better wages and working conditions, educational opportunities, and human dignity. They were also aware of what workers in other countries were doing, what they had achieved, and how.[25]

Strikes still involved only about half the workers in any given factory and, on the average, lasted no more than ten days. But along with their economic demands the strikers were beginning to sound political notes and to organize. There were strike committees and strike funds to which men in other than the struck branches of industry contributed, and since 1889 there had been a Central Workers' Circle in St Petersburg whose very few members tried to coordinate these various activities. Police vigilance frustrated organizational unity and permanence, but growing discontent and its articulation contributed to their eventual attainment. The secret meetings, open demonstrations, and leaflets celebrating May Day, the international holiday of labour, helped greatly to shape the workers' consciousness of their distinct needs and identity, particularly since they were invariably repressed. The slogans prepared for May Day – it was first observed in St Petersburg in 1891 – grew yearly more bold and more political, demanding the right to strike, political liberty, and an end to autocracy. Over 10,000 men marched in 1900 under red banners in the centre of Kharkov, demanding and securing the release of May Day demonstrators. May Day in St Petersburg led the next year to the 'Obukhov Defence' when steel workers for the first time in Russia erected barricades and defended them by force. In November 1902 there was a general strike in Rostov, with the workers calling for a nine-hour day and schools for their children. In 1903 general strikes broke out in the industrial south and in the Caucasus.

Marxist intellectuals were heartened. They tried, with some success, to make contact with the rebellious workers and, less successfully, to fuse their outbreaks into a movement. In 1894 a Union of Workers was established in Moscow and a year later the Union of Struggle for the Liberation of the Working Class in St Petersburg. Similar groups sprang up in other industrial centres and in March 1898 nine of their delegates (none of them workers) met to found the Russian Social Democratic Workers' Party.[26]

With eight of its nine founders arrested and its central organs destroyed in less than a year, the party's remnants led a shadowy existence. It was of little help to the workers, while being blamed by the police for stirring them up. It needed no agitators to demonstrate that a government which treated strikes as breaches of public order rather than economic acts was an ally of the bosses. Experience made the workers receptive to socialist arguments that the alliance of their oppressors was the inevitable outcome of a community of interest and privilege. A number of police officials argued that the socialists could be neutralized and the workers kept out of their clutches only if manufacturers were obliged to improve working conditions and wages. An inter-ministerial conference concluded in 1899 that such proposals were unwise and the existing labour laws adequate. In 1901 the chief of gendarmes warned that poor conditions in the factories were favourable soil for the propaganda of the radical intelligentsia.[27]

These were not, as noted, new thoughts in the state security organs. They were put most persuasively in a report on the strike movement by the head of the Moscow okhrana, Sergei Zubatov,[28] with the concurrence of that city's chief of police, General D. F. Trepov, in April 1898. Zubatov was an ex-revolutionary, Trepov an ex-officer of cavalry with appropriately chivalrous notions of the duties of rank and station. He believed, and said, that the Moscow workers were more poorly treated by their bourgeois masters than the serfs had been by their lords, and that if such treatment continued, it would endanger public order. Zubatov, for his part, believed that the government had to wrest the initiative from the socialists and take the wind out of their sails by meeting the just demands of the working people. But he had larger conceptions of a social monarchy which would restrain the greed and power of the factory bosses by coming to the aid of the insulted and oppressed. By holding the balance between competing social forces, the autocracy would also strengthen itself and enlarge its popular basis. It was the intervention of the Grand Duke Sergei, governor-general of Moscow, uncle of the tsar, arch-reactionary and anti-Semite which made it possible for the plans of Zubatov (who had once spoken of the 'crudity of the Jew-bosses') to go as far as they did and, finally, to be sanctioned, with considerable misgivings and scepticism, at the highest levels of government.

Zubatov's scheme was for the government to answer the workers' persistent yearnings for trade unions, for mutual aid, and education under police sponsorship and supervision. The educational activities began in early 1901 with lectures by liberal-minded professors (who were unaware of the nature of the enterprise) on such topics as mutual aid funds, labour exchanges, consumer cooperatives, cultural, or even political, themes. Zubatov next set up three societies, or unions, among the workers of different Moscow industries which were headed by men he trusted to follow his views and instructions. None the less, and perhaps unavoidably if they did not want to lose their following, the leaders of the unions began to act as genuine spokesmen for their members and forcefully presented their demands to employers who were in a number of instances made to yield by agents of the political police.

These successes increased the popularity and prestige of the Zubatov unions which began to spread to other cities. Their growth and activism (including strikes) alarmed the authorities as they were already alarming the employers, one of whom complained that he had been threatened by the police with deportation unless he granted the union's demands. Witte was outraged, stating that it was their political naivety that permitted the Grand Duke and Trepov to do things that even the French socialist leaders Jaurès and Millerand would consider risky. What, he asked, did they know of such complicated matters as the eight-hour day, wage determination by government, profit-sharing? Pleve was conscious of the risks inherent in what came to be called 'police-socialism', but he was not sufficiently worried or persuaded by Witte's arguments on behalf of the entrepreneurs to do more than tighten control over the unions.

Pleve's reluctance to put a complete stop to the Zubatov experiment was influenced by an extraordinary spectacle that took place in Moscow on 19 February 1902, the anniversary of the liberation of the serfs by Alexander II. On that day, which the Moscow newspapers had only a few years earlier been forbidden to mention, some 50,000 workers, turned out by Zubatov's men, had staged a peaceful march to the monument of the 'Tsar-Liberator' in a symbolic expression of their trust that the monarch would once again do justice to his lowliest subjects. Demonstrations of any kind – unless they were religious processions or illegal – were unheard of; as massive, disciplined, and loyal a one as this, by the usually turbulent factory workers, was hard to credit.

Among the officials reviewing this outpouring of the working class with the Grand Duke Sergei and General Trepov, was a high functionary of the political police, sent from St Petersburg to conduct an inquiry into the riotous student disorders which had rocked Moscow only weeks before. He could hardly believe his eyes and returned to the capital deeply impressed by what he had seen, a convert to Zubatov's methods. Here, in the urban masses, the autocracy might have an ally. Properly cultivated and handled, they could be a counterweight to all the radical students and socialists, liberal bourgeois, and oppositional gentry, whose political demands could be represented to the workers as a purely selfish wresting of power from an autocrat who was above parties and classes. For the moment the alarms of Witte and others that the Zubatovshchina threatened public order and the rights of private enterprise were ignored. It was not until July 1903, when a Zubatov union during a general strike in Odessa outran the control of its sponsors, that the experiment was abruptly terminated; its initiator was dismissed shortly thereafter.

What Zubatov called his idea of a 'pure monarchy' was not realized, then or later, but it was not entirely abandoned. Non-governmental adherents of the monarchy, in particular, felt that some positive action had to be taken to end its growing isolation from any vital social force, that more benevolence, more understanding, had to be shown the lower classes to wean them away from liberals and socialists. A St Petersburg priest and prison chaplain, Father Gapon, applied the Zubatov formula with resounding success and did so not only to aid the regime but also to bring pressure to bear upon it or, at least, to arouse the consciences of its leaders. Approved by Pleve in February 1904, his organization, the Assembly of Russian Factory Workers, began with tearooms and educational meetings. It culminated, and came to grief, with a march of 120,000 men, women and children – some of them bearing religious banners and icons – to the Winter Palace on 9 January 1905, 'Bloody Sunday'. Appealing to their tsar for a living wage and human working conditions, for civil and political rights, they were dispersed by rifle fire; some 150 were killed and hundreds more wounded. Their pleas went unanswered and what remained of the fiction of a kindly ruler kept in ignorance of the people's plight by heartless bureaucrats was shattered.[29]

Even after Bloody Sunday there were attempts to mobilize and make articulate the supposed monarchism of the masses, but they were few and timid, and they failed. To convert such loyalties as may have existed into an active political allegiance, tsarism had to become the genuine champion and defender of the poor against the rich and the powerful. It was debarred from doing so by its commitment to economic development along capitalist lines, by its fear of mass politics with all its unpredictable consequences, and by its own uncertainties. No longer confident of the efficacy of traditional methods of rule, Russia's rulers were yet fearful of exercising power in new ways and of seeking new allies to legitimize it.[30]

One such potential ally was the business class which tsarism, for all its toying with Zubatov and Gapon unions, backed consistently against the workers. For the most part, and for most of our period, Russia's capitalists supported a system of which they were the beneficiaries, but their support was of the passive kind. The few leaders of industry and finance who entered politics during or after 1905 were never trusted by a bureaucracy whose ability to rule they, in turn, came increasingly to distrust. They were not allowed a real share of political power or decision making and were driven against their will into opposition. The class as a whole never developed the sense of being, or speaking for, the nation that characterized the Western bourgeoisie. Fearful of the masses, tied to the state by fear and interest, the business class was not a political force in its own right, the autonomous ally who could have strengthened the state by becoming part of it.

In purely economic terms the manufacturers and entrepreneurs who had been gaining in numbers and importance since 1861, and especially in the 1890s, had little to complain of. The government was solicitous of their interests and bestowed upon them a wide range of favours designed to compensate for the shortage of capital, opportunities, and markets in an as yet underdeveloped country. Profits, while not uniformly exorbitant as maintained by Lenin, for example, were good; better in some industries than others, best for the organizers of new enterprises. In the iron industry net profits of 40 per cent were not uncommon; dividends in the cotton industry averaged 10 per cent and might reach 15 to 25 per cent; 7 to 12 per cent was considered a normal rate of return on capital.[31] In railroading, where profits were chancy and apt to be low, the government, in order to attract venture capital, acquired the majority of shares in private companies and guaranteed a high rate of return before, near the end of the century, buying most of the lines with generous compensation to private shareholders.[32] Taxes and tariffs were structured to benefit industry. There was no income tax until the war year 1916; regressive indirect taxes and excises weighed most heavily on the lower income groups while direct taxes (on land, buildings in towns, business licences, corporate capital and profits, income from securities, bank accounts, and inheritances) were moderate.[33] It was not simply to defend privilege that the regime resisted a more equitable distribution of the tax load. Shifting it to the propertied classes would antagonize these, discourage investments, yield insufficient revenue and still fail to satisfy the peasants and workers whose poverty made any tax seem excessive.

The government tolerated and occasionally encouraged the formation of syndicates and cartels to maintain prices or meet foreign competition.[34] When overproduction caused the price of sugar to fall drastically manufacturers combined in 1887 at the suggestion of government, agreed to restrict domestic sales and to export the surpluses. The oil industry was assisted to form a marketing syndicate and to compete with American producers. In periods of depression or difficulty the state also stepped in to save private banks and businesses from foundering, and by long-range orders it assured the existence and profitability of several firms, especially those connected with railroad construction. For many enterprises the treasury was the largest and most important customer; some worked on its orders only. There were few aspects of Russia's nascent industrial capitalism in which the state did not play at least a supporting role, and that fact had to be recognized as a boon by industrialists and financiers. As long as poverty and fiscal policy combined to keep the purchasing power of the people limited, the economic role of the state loomed large. As the Council of the Representatives of Trade and Industry put it in 1908: 'To dream of strengthening our iron and steel industry on the basis of horseshoes, axles, forged wheels, ploughs, and iron roofs . . . does not even enter the heads of practical men.'[35]

At the same time a policy of subsidies and assistance, purchases and protection, carried with it a degree of bureaucratic control that some industrialists began to resent. The state's deep involvement in the economy meant, moreover, that all its actions would affect the business community. Witte had made that point in pleading for a steady course in economic policy, for the utmost restraint in foreign affairs, for a softening of the police regime, and for improving the treatment of ethnic and religious minorities. His argument that the equilibrium of the entire economic organism could be upset by the wrong policies did not prevail. Administrative arbitrariness, interference with local government (especially of the cities, where commercial interests were strong) and discrimination against Jews were more and more felt to be hindrances to the normal conduct of affairs. A few notes of criticism became audible – Moscow merchants deploring the pogroms of 1881 or asking in 1893 that Jews be allowed to trade in their city. In 1900 Witte again pressed the emperor to remove the bureaucratic barriers blocking the advance of enterprise, to recognize that Russian laws and administrative practice were not attuned to an industrial age, its tempos and requirements. Uncomprehending or unsympathetic officials blocked economic expansion by adhering to outdated rules, and the petitions and visits to St Petersburg required to circumvent these discouraged all but the boldest or greediest entrepreneurs.[36]

Witte exaggerated. As his presence in it showed, a government which wanted and needed to develop the nation's potential had to pay some regard to the needs of industry. But this was not its first priority – the claims of army and navy, of administration and internal security still took precedence – as Witte's repeated pleadings testified. When the industrialization drive was slowed in 1899 by a slump which soon turned into a depression with unemployment, strikes, declining government orders and falling profits, the costs of the Witte system became intolerable to those who had all along been sceptical of it. Witte's opponents now gained the upper hand; he lost the support of the emperor and, in 1903, his post. Industrialists and bankers knew that they had been deprived of a powerful advocate in the councils of government; they feared that there was no longer a firm will or hand steering the ship of state in a direction they deemed desirable and correct.

Their fears were confirmed by the political crisis which developed alongside the economic one and by the autocracy's inept handling of both. The attitude of businessmen towards it began to change. The wave of protest that seized ever wider circles of the population made them fear that a general assault on the existing order might engulf them too. In the years immediately prior to the Revolution of 1905, there were scattered signs that the Russian business community was no longer solidly attached to its governmental sponsor and protector, that parts of it began to distance themselves from and to criticize the autocracy and its officials. Not until the revolutionary year itself did these critical notes take on political overtones. After Bloody Sunday associations of industrialists in Moscow, St Petersburg and the Urals, of iron producers, sugar refiners, and mutual credit institutions, petitioned the tsar for a strict observance of legality and personal security, for free speech, press, and assembly and, in some cases, for a voice in the determination of public policy. These, it was said, were the preconditions for domestic peace and for the prosperity which, in the long run, could only be attained by a self-reliant, literate and free people. Paupers made neither good citizens nor consumers.[37]

Judged by the temper of the times, these were moderate requests; measured by the previous history and conduct of Russian capital they suggested that its dependence on the state was waning and its confidence in it – shaken by police socialism and defeat in the Japanese war – no longer total. What Georgii Plekhanov, the 'father of Russian Marxism', had written, somewhat prematurely, in 1884, seemed now to correspond to reality.

Our bourgeoisie is now undergoing an important metamorphosis; it has developed lungs which require the clean air . . . of political self-government but at the same time its gills, with which it still breathes in the troubled water of decaying absolutism, have not yet completely atrophied. Its roots are still in the soil of the old regime, but its crown has already attained a development which shows that it absolutely needs to be transplanted.[38]

But was it accurate to speak of a bourgeoisie in Marxist terms? Were the manufacturers, bankers, and merchants who wanted a more efficient, orderly, and flexible tsarism in order to avoid a revolution that classic and conscious force that wanted to make one? Was there, in fact, a Russian bourgeoisie with enough economic strength, social cohesion, political sophistication and determination to deserve the name and to seek to replace absolutism by a liberal-bourgeois regime?

That question was as important, and as fiercely debated among all shades of opinion, as that of the proletariat and, of course, intimately linked with it. There were liberals writing in the monthly *Messenger of Europe* who affirmed with relief that since 'we have no bourgeoisie in the Western European sense of the word we also do not have a bourgeois [read: selfish] liberalism'.[39] Victor Chernov, speaking for a new generation of populists soon to be organized in the Socialist Revolutionary Party, thought that in Russia, where the bourgeoisie was a purely exploitative appendage of despotism, students and intelligentsia were the advance guard of progress.[40] The Marxist view of the question was stated most succinctly in the founding manifesto of the Russian Social Democratic Workers' Party of 1898. There it was said that the further east one moved in Europe, the weaker, the more cowardly, and the more base was the bourgeoisie in political affairs; consequently the task of leading the struggle for cultural advancement and political liberty that had elsewhere been conducted by the bourgeoisie fell in Russia to the working class.[41] Written by Struve, who soon abandoned Marxism for liberalism, the manifesto reflected accurately the contempt for the bourgeoisie that was near universal among the Russian intelligentsia. But it did not finally decide for Marxism or any segment of the opposition what its relation to the bourgeoisie in the political fight against autocracy was to be: to follow or to lead, to collaborate closely or to march separately.

Tactical disagreement on that score had doctrinal sources, creating difficulties of agreement on the very meaning of the term 'bourgeoisie'. These difficulties had roots also in the real problem of finding objective criteria for determining the sociological, economic, and political profile of the bourgeoisie. In the legal order of estates (*soslovie*) to one of whose categories every Russian subject belonged, there was a classification – *meshchane* – which is often translated as townsmen or burghers. But *meshchanstvo* was very far from being a middle class and a *meshchanin* was not a burgher, bourgeois or burgess, as the medieval estate order of Western Europe had known him. He belonged, like the peasant, to the non-privileged lower orders; he was a petty tradesman, shopkeeper, artisan, white-collar employee, possibly even a labourer or factory worker. And he did not necessarily live in a city; of the 13.4 million meshchane counted in the census of 1897, almost half did not. Of the other traditional estates from which a bourgeoisie might have come, the category of 'distinguished' or 'honoured' citizens, comprising 343,000 individuals (of whom 184,000 resided in urban areas), included a substantial number of professional people as well as businessmen of various types.

The closest equivalent to the European bourgeoisie were the Russian *kuptsy* (merchants), a 'middle' class between nobles and clergy, peasants and meshchane since medieval times. Forced like all other classes to render service to the state (such as collecting taxes and furnishing supplies), the *kupechestvo* (merchantry) had in return received favours (tax exemptions and monopolies) rather than rights. In the absence of self-governing cities before 1870 it had not developed an assertive, corporate consciousness or institutions, although it long clung to its own, old-fashioned values, life-styles, and business practices. The merchantry was Muscovy's business class, but it was neither numerous nor powerful enough to supplant the gentry or to be wooed as its counterweight by the monarchy. This had begun to change in the nineteenth century, but in 1897 there still were only 281,179 merchants (including families) of whom 225,660 were registered in the cities. It was not, even if half the distinguished citizens were added, an impressive number. There were roughly as many individuals in the clerical estate and three times as many nobles and officials.[42]

Still, it was from the merchantry, and particularly its upper segment, that most of Russia's native big businessmen and industrialists came, those who could be regarded as her capitalist bourgeoisie. It was a fluid group, however, made up of many disparate elements and late, therefore, in developing a common outlook or class organizations. There were, first of all, the Moscow cotton and wool industrialists, descendants of peasants or merchants, many of them members of the Old Believer sect which had split off from the state church in the seventeenth century. Kept by their religious disabilities from playing a public role or from rising into the gentry (as many wealthy merchants, abandoning trade for land, were apt to do), their thrift and sobriety had made them, like dissenters elsewhere, excellent traders and, in the nineteenth century, leaders of the financial and industrial life of the old capital. Their family enterprises having been transformed into corporations, the heirs of the great Moscow textile fortunes entered other businesses and soon dominated the city's banks, insurance companies and stock exchange. They or their grandsons also entered the professions, took up scholarly pursuits, became patrons of the arts or entered public life. A contemporary observer remarked in 1901 that a meeting of Moscow's city Duma resembled a board meeting of its banks.[43] During and after the Revolution of 1905 it was Moscow's prominent business and public men who began to speak and act as an identifiable group, to behave like a bourgeoisie, to found newspapers, to demand to be heard and heeded by government and in the national legislature. Having accumulated their capital early in the making and selling of consumer goods, Moscow firms were less dependent on government orders and subsidies than the heavy and transport industries of other regions.

Many of the latter were concentrated or represented in St Petersburg, the country's financial capital, its greatest port city, and home of shipyards, metallurgical and machine works. It was there that the links between business and the bureaucracy were closest, there that contracts and subsidies were to be had, there also that banks and bourse were most responsive to the needs of expanding corporate business and the requirements of new and speculative fields of investment. It was to St Petersburg that the heterogeneous elements that made up Russian capital had sooner or later to come and here that they could best be observed. Here were the headquarters of many companies, the

Department (after 1905 Ministry) of Trade and Industry and its advisory councils which were composed jointly of official and industry representatives.

So many of the chinovniks who had dealings with Russia's managers and captains of industry were being hired by them, that the practice of simultaneous public and private employment was prohibited by Alexander III. This did not keep civil and military engineers, specialists in transport, communications and mining, from taking leaves of absence from the government and entering key positions in private enterprise. Some did not return to state service and joined the growing numbers whose lives and interests revolved around business in one form or another. Lenin's 'Today a minister, tomorrow a banker',[44] was an exaggerated statement of what was, in fact, taking place. Members of the wealthier nobility of the capital were also becoming infected by the fever of stock speculation and the prospect of quick profits caused them to lend their names, their funds, or both, to newly formed corporations. There was a sizeable community of Germans – Russian subjects as well as nationals of the Reich – who were financiers, railroad magnates, and industrialists, as well as resident Englishmen, who were prominent in St Petersburg's textile and machine industries. There were representatives of Jewish capital – their numbers limited by residence restrictions – that were engaged in banking and railroads, the sugar refineries and commerce of Russia's Polish and southern provinces, as well as offices of the French and Belgian firms who were developing metallurgy and mining in the south.

Social, ethnic, and geographical diversity made it difficult for Russia's growing capitalist class to develop a common political outlook and positions. If Western experience had given rise to the assumption that the capitalist bourgeoisie would fight for representative government and political liberty, then the conduct of Russia's business class belied that assumption. Plekhanov himself was forced to note its political inertness, yet did not give up belief in the historical role that the bourgeoisie would be constrained to play by the inevitable clash between its economic goals and those of an autocratic, 'feudal' regime which inhibited their free and unhampered pursuit. But the activities and interests of capital did not, in fact, require systematic political activity for their advancement. For all its complaints against bureaucratic absolutism and its rigidities, Russian business was largely content. It had fared well at the hands of the state, and it was no more committed to economic than to political liberalism. It was, therefore, as much satisfaction as cowardice that made the capitalist class politically quiescent or illiberal and kept it from being or becoming a bourgeoisie in the classic sense of the word.

Cowardice there was too, or rather quite rational fears of what the irruption of disgruntled masses of workers and peasants into the political arena would mean. And it was that fear that led in 1905 to the defection of the business class from the shelter of a state unable to defend either itself, the country, or the property and profits of businessmen. Loss of confidence in the state – it was to reappear much aggravated just before and during the First World War – led businessmen and industrialists to form political parties in the post-1905 period. But their essential conservatism and narrow social basis kept them small and ineffectual. Members of the merchant-industrial class who actually sat in the Duma never made up more than 9 per cent of its total membership. They collaborated with the moderate conservatives and rightists (most of them landlords) who accepted the political changes brought about by the 1905 Revolution and now wished to strengthen the state, to resist the democratization of political institutions and the economic demands of the masses. The liberalism of the majority of the bourgeoisie went no further than the wish for an efficient government, one which was observant of legal norms and basic civil rights, strong enough to defend the interests of business at home and abroad, financially sound, and willing to listen to men of property in the elected assemblies of national and local government.

The most effective and typical organization of the Russian bourgeoisie was not, in fact, the political party but the interest or pressure group. Beginning with 1874, when southern mine-owners held their first meeting, various branches of industry met in periodic congresses and set up bureaus or councils to coordinate their activities between congresses and to represent them in St Petersburg. In the major cities there were, in addition, joint groupings of businessmen and manufacturers and, in 1896, a national Congress of Industry and Trade met in Nizhnii-Novgorod,[45] the site of a great fair visited that year by the tsar. The festivities connected with that event, the delegations of young merchants who attended the monarch dressed in the old-Russian costumes of their class, were viewed as symbols of recognition for the importance of commerce and manufactures in the life of the nations. 'We can do anything', a local newspaper, speaking for business and carried away by the occasion, proudly proclaimed,[46] but neither in social nor in political life was the undoubted significance of capital and its representatives translated into predominance or prominence.

When a permanent Council of Representatives of Industry and Trade was formed in 1906 to advocate the interests of the business class, its publications and spokesmen repeatedly demanded that the 'industrial-trading class . . . be placed in the high position that it deserves', that it 'obtain public recognition for its preeminent role in the destinies of the country'. Since the organization grouped branches of industry rather than individual firms or their owners, it was a foregone conclusion that it would show restraint and even neutrality in political matters. If it was a question of forming a united front against the workers, of agreeing, for example, not to raise wages except by common agreement, unity was not hard to achieve, but on political issues the Council spoke cautiously or not at all. The public protests of Russian business against such governmental policies as ethnic and religious discrimination (1914) or the dismissal of liberal professors (1911) came almost exclusively from Moscow, where gentry and merchantry cultivated and cherished a certain distance from bureaucratic and military St Petersburg.[47]

It was at the Moscow Stock Exchange Club in 1912 that the local industrialist, financier, and newspaper publisher P. P. Riabushinskii (who came from a family of Old Believers), responding to a speech by Kokovtsov, criticized persecution of religious dissenters and a foreign policy which was by turns bellicose and subservient to foreign interest. 'The merchant is coming,' he proclaimed, and proposed a toast 'not to the government, but to the long-suffering and patient Russian nation which is still awaiting its true liberation'.[48] He and another Moscow magnate of Old Believer background, the textile manufacturer A. I. Konovalov, were instrumental in 1912 in forming the Progressive Party whose leaders were in such despair by early 1914 over what they considered the regime's fatal policies, that they became convinced of the likelihood of another revolution and in expectation of its coming tried to build bridges to the Bolsheviks. By then that most typical representative of Moscow's monarchist *haute bourgeoisie*, Alexander Guchkov, leader of the Octobrist party that had in 1906 rallied his class to the government's side, was also in the opposition, showing how far some elements of the commercial-industrial class had moved from the shelter of the state. The bourgeois does not need the chinovnik, Riabushinskii declared, nor would he emulate the nobility or seek to join it. Such sentiments, and more particularly their expression or translation into political activism, were far from universal among his fellow-manufacturers. To say businessman or industrialist was not necessarily to say liberal bourgeois. Bourgeois liberalism recruited its forces from a variety of groups – from the gentry active in the zemstvos, from the professions, from the intelligentsia, from progressive former members of the bureaucracy and last, as well as least, from the commercial-industrial class.

Russia was not an industrial or urban or bourgeois society as she entered the twentieth century. While more of her people than ever before had been drawn into industry and commerce, the vast majority were still not engaged in either or dominated by the capitalist ethos and the values of business. 'An industrial society', the sociologist Talcott Parsons has written, 'is or has been one in which economic considerations have had a certain primacy over others.' That was true neither for the government nor for most of its subjects; and it was only partially true among the business class. Its members did not always combine a consciousness of their growing economic importance with pride. Many passed into the gentry or, leaving business pursuits behind, acquired estates, affected a noble style of life, became scholars or patrons of the arts. The case of the rich merchant who declined the opportunity of ennoblement was rare enough to provoke comment; still more unusual was the millionaire who refused to leave the merchant class for the category of 'honoured citizen' or rejected the special uniform, sword, orders of merit and titles that went with great wealth.[49]

The businessman's ambivalence about his role and worth is hardly surprising when one reads in the memoirs of its greatest champion, Witte, that the class was poorly endowed with 'the qualities of kindness and generosity of spirit which are found in many Russian noblemen' and that it had, on the contrary, an overabundance of 'all the bad qualities that come from great wealth, underestimated the labour of others and sometimes their hearts as well'.[50] To hear one of its advocates condemn the bourgeoisie for pettiness and money-grubbing in terms usually employed by its aristocratic and radical critics, throws into sharp relief the transitional nature of the age, of the class criticized, and of its critic. Public attitudes to industry and capital and their possessors were not nearly as favourable in Russia as they were in the West, and both were attacked for the harm they had already done and for the sins they had not yet had a chance to commit.

Both those who deplored and those who welcomed the factories and their armies of workers, the quickened movement of money, men, and goods, were apt to overstate what they saw. 'Look at the hideous smokestacks of the great factories that are now scattered over Russia,' the sage of Iasnaia Poliana, Lev Tolstoi, said to an American visitor in 1901. 'They disfigure God's landscape . . . It is all a mistake.'[51] Boris Pasternak, recalling the changing Moscow of his childhood, makes one forget that much of that city retained its old-fashioned aspect of narrow lanes and mews, wooden houses and gardens, for many more years. 'With the coming of the new century . . . everything changed as if by the wave of a magic wand. Moscow, like other great capital cities, was seized by the frenzy of business. Investors rushed madly to build huge apartment houses for the sake of high profits. Arising unnoticed, these brick giants reached towards the skies.'[52] Somewhat dowdy and neglected for two hundred years, Holy Moscow was turning into 'calico Moscow', a great city which was overtaking the younger northern capital in every respect. But great cities, urban bustle and an urban way of life were still atypical for the country as a whole.

European Russia (exclusive of Poland and the Baltic provinces) had in 1897 some 52 cities of which the smallest had a population of 12,500, while the largest 28 ranged from St Petersburg (1.2 million) and Moscow (1 million) to Orenburg (72,000) and the textile centre of Ivanovo-Voznesensk (54,000). There were 11 cities with more than 100,000 inhabitants: Kiev, Odessa, Kishinev, Kharkov, Kazan, Rostov-on-Don, Ekaterinoslav and Saratov, plus Baku, the oil city on the Caspian, the Georgian capital of Tbilisi, and Tashkent in Central Asia. The 1897 census also listed 6,376 'rural' settlements containing from 2,000 to 41,000 inhabitants, for a total of 23.3 million. Inclusion of at least the larger settlements in the urban column might have made a difference of as much as 5 per cent. However, these were not towns or cities in any meaningful sociological or cultural terms. They were not densely settled centres of trade or administration or municipalities with the right of self-government. Altogether, only 13.4 per cent of the population was urban, as compared with England's 72 per cent (1891), Germany's 47 per cent (1890) and America's 38 per cent (1890). If urbanization is a measure of modernity and progress, Russia was still backward and rural.

Yet changes there had been, and they cannot be gauged by the urban–rural proportion alone. They could be seen and felt in the tempo and dynamism of urban growth and life, in the absolute numbers of individuals who were undergoing urbanization, and in the disproportionately large role they played and were still to play, in the great events of the coming years.

The proportion of Russians who lived in the urban areas of the Empire (excluding Finland and Poland) increased but little between 1867 and 1897 – from 10 to 13 per cent – but their numbers doubled – from 7.3 to 14.6

million –, whereas the rural population grew by only two thirds. By 1913 the relationship between the two sectors had not changed markedly, but the number of city dwellers had grown to over 21 million. There were a hundred cities of over 50,000 on the eve of the First World War (there had been fifteen in 1870) and twenty of over 100,000. Whereas the total population had grown 3.55 times from 1811 to 1913, the urban population increased eight times. Petersburg, Moscow, Odessa, Minsk and Samara had all grown fourfold in the half century before 1913, while Kharkov, Rostov-on-Don and Kiev grew five, six, and seven times respectively. Ekaterinoslav and Tsaritsyn grew tenfold, whereas Baku, with 13,000 inhabitants in 1863, reached 232,000 in 1914. It was railroads (as at Kharkov), the exporting of grain (Odessa), the development of coal mining and of an iron and steel industry (Donets Basin), the expansion of textile production in and around Moscow, the discovery of oil at Baku that led to these high rates of urban growth, as did the services and professions the cities required and attracted.[53]

It was in the cities that the educated classes lived – more than 80 per cent of those who had received a higher education and 70 per cent of those with secondary schooling – their total number 1,384,143 according to the 1897 census. It was in the key cities that the universities (eight of them in 1900, nine in 1912) were located. Their student bodies were not in the aggregate large; there were 17,000 university students in 1900 and 38,000 in 1909, with approximately twice these numbers enrolled in higher technical and other specialized institutes – but they were large enough and unruly enough, especially in Moscow and St Petersburg, to constitute an important political force that was often in the forefront of demonstrations and disturbances. In 1897, 24.5 per cent of the rural population between the ages of 10 and 49 was literate; in the cities it was 57.5 per cent. It was in the cities that most of the nation's 11,000 lawyers were to be found, most of its 18,000 doctors and dentists, its secondary teachers, and the journalists writing for the nation's several thousand periodicals and newspapers. There were 123 of the latter in 1897, 800 in 1908, 1,158 in 1914; and over 2,100 periodicals in 1912. Petersburg and Moscow alone accounted in 1897 for 46 per cent of Russia's 3,300 scholars and writers; 31 per cent of her 18,000 musicians, artists, and actors, as well as of her 4,000 engineers and technologists.[54]

While most of these people were not members of the bourgeoisie in the sense of being directly engaged in commerce, industry, or finance, they and their professions were intimately connected with the growth and functioning of the urban and non-agricultural sector of the economy. They had first become numerous with the reforms of the judiciary and of local government, the educational system and the censorship in the 1860s, and their weight and numbers had been further enlarged by subsequent economic changes. It was they, rather than the business classes, who played the role of a classic bourgeoisie and were the main carriers of Russian liberalism in the years before and after the Revolution of 1905. By creating a quantitatively significant concentration of workers in the cities, by fostering the growth of an urban liberalism based on the professional classes, industrial capitalism and the needs it generated had introduced into Russian society the elements that were most ready and likely to challenge traditional arrangements and were, in fact, doing so. 'Russia is still a peasant country, one of the most backward in Europe,' Lenin said in March 1917.[55] Yet there was enough of progress and modernity to create an impatience for more, to intensify social tensions, political discontent, and economic dislocation.

The incompleteness of Russia's industrial advance manifested itself in a variety of ways, some of them already noted. A limited market for factory-produced consumer goods helped to keep alive an artisan and handicrafts industry which as late as 1914 employed about two thirds of the non-agricultural labour force to turn out one third of industrial output in some 150,000 establishment.[56] Productivity was low even in some of the large modern enterprises. In 1901 a Polish or Upper Silesian miner hewed nearly twice or three times as much coal as his counterpart in the Ukraine, while a Russian worker tended only one half or one quarter the number of machines looked after by his German, English or American comrades.[57] There was a marked inadequacy also of communications between the different areas of industrial development. But it was most noticeable in industry's failure to achieve what had been, explicitly or not, one of its major goals and the justification for much of the suffering it caused – to absorb the excess population of the countryside.

Relative occupational patterns were as little affected by the industrial spurt as the urban–rural distribution, with agriculture continuing to be the main source of support for the overwhelming majority. Estimates of the share of the population engaged in agriculture or rural occupations around 1900 range from 70 to 80 per cent, and those figures remained remarkably stable until 1914. Some 70 per cent of Russians have been described as 'dependent' on agriculture in 1891–96 and producing 32 per cent of national income, as compared with Britain's 10 and 8 per cent at the other end of the scale and Germany's 39 and 20 near its middle.

The shortcomings of industrial development were not alone responsible for this. It was also the extraordinary fertility of the Russian peasant. The western and central black soil provinces which were most crowded and most in need of relief were not those from which factory labour was primarily recruited, and there peasants, as before, hired out as agricultural labourers to supplement their incomes. During 1901–05 in European Russia only 1.5 per cent of the natural population increase of 7.9 million was absorbed by in-town migration and no more than 3.4 per cent by emigration beyond the Urals. That picture would improve substantially with the agrarian and resettlement politics introduced by Stolypin, when nearly half of the natural rural increase left either for the cities or for new lands between 1906 and 1913. Nevertheless, more than one half the additional 14 million peasants stayed in their villages where the area of land at their disposal during those same years increased by only 6 to 7 per cent. The 'surplus' agricultural population has been estimated by Soviet historians to be 23 million at the beginning of the twentieth century and to have risen to 32 million in 1913.[58] Definitions of surplus may vary and these estimates may be excessive; yet there is no mistaking the general trends and the difficulties they spelled.

Thus, Russia's entry into the ranks of industrial powers faced her, at one and the same time, with all the problems she had inherited from an earlier stage of her history as well as those that industrialization itself was creating.

REFERENCES

1. Roger Portal, 'The industrialization of Russia', in *The Cambridge Economic History of Europe*, vol. VI, part 2 (1966), pp. 811, 815; W. A. Cole and Phyllis Deane, 'The growth of national incomes', ibid., part 1 (1956), p. 20.
2. A. A. Polovtsov, *Dnevnik* (Moscow, 1966), I, p. 201.
3. Olga Crisp, *Studies in the Russian Economy Before 1914* (London and New York, 1976), pp. 96–110; T. H. Von Laue, *Sergei Witte and the Industrialization of Russia* (New York, 1963), pp. 138–46; Bernd Bonwetsch, 'Das ausländische Kapital in Russland', *Jahrbücher für Geschichte Osteuropas* 22 (1974), pp. 412–25; V. I. Bovykin, 'Probleme der industriellen Entwicklung Russlands', in Dietrich Geyer (ed.), *Wirtschaft und Gesellschaft im vorrevolutionären Russland* (Cologne, 1975), pp. 193–8.
4. W. L. Blackwell, *The Industrialization of Russia* (New York, 1970), p. 40.
5. B. B. Grave, 'Byla li tsarskaia Rossiia polukoloniei?', *Voprosy Istorii* 6 (June 1956), pp. 63–74; J. P. Sontag, 'Tsarist debt and tsarist foreign policy', *Slavic Review* 27 (Dec. 1968), pp. 529–41.
6. J. P. McKay, *Pioneers for Profit: Foreign Entrepreneurship and Russian Industrialization, 1885–1913* (Chicago and London, 1970), p. 368; cf. Crisp, op. cit., pp. 191–2.
7. P. R. Gregory, 'A note on Russia's merchandise balance and balance of payments during the industrialization era', *Slavic Review* 38 (Dec. 1979), pp. 655–62.
8. P. I. Liashchenko, *Istoriia narodnogo khoziaistva SSSR* (Moscow, 1948), II, pp. 124–9; Blackwell, op. cit., pp. 45–7; S. G. Strumilin, *Statistiko-ekonomicheskie ocherki* (Moscow, 1958), pp. 621–2.
9. Letter of Friedrich Engels to N. F. Danielson, 22 September 1892, in S. S. Dmitriev (comp.), *Khrestomatiia po istorii SSSR* (Moscow, 1952), III, p. 197.
10. Cole and Deane, see ref. 1, p. 21; Alexander Gerschenkron, 'The rate of industrial growth in Russia' in *The Tasks of Economic History*, Supplement VII (1947) of *Journal of Economic History*, pp. 144–56.
11. P. R. Gregory, 'Economic growth and structural change in tsarist Russia: a case of modern economic growth?', *Soviet Studies* 23 (Jan. 1972), pp. 420–3; Strumilin, op. cit., pp. 461–3; K. C. Thalheim, 'Russia's economic development' in E. Oberländer *et al.* (eds), *Russia Enters the Twentieth Century* (New York, 1971), pp. 89–98; Blackwell, op. cit., pp. 50–3; *Istoriia SSSR* VI, pp. 260–3.
12. T. H. Von Laue, 'A Secret Memorandum of Sergei Witte on the Industrialization of Russia', *Journal of Modern History* 26 (March 1954), pp. 60–74.
13. Ibid., p. 71; Jeremiah Schneiderman, *Sergei Zubatov and Revolutionary Marxism* (Ithaca, NY, and London, 1970), pp. 22–3; I. Kh. Ozerov, *Politika po rabochemu voprosu v Rossii v poslednye gody* (Moscow, 1906), p. 25; V. Ia. Laverychev, *Tsarizm i rabochii vopros v Rossii 1861–1917* (Moscow, 1972), pp. 72–3.

14. David Heer, 'The demographic transition in the Russian empire and the Soviet Union', *Journal of Social History* 1 (Spring 1968), p. 219; *Istoriia SSSR* VI, p. 318.

15. R. E. Zelnik, 'The peasant and the factory' in W. S. Vucinich (ed.), *The Peasant in Nineteenth-Century Russia* (Stanford, Cal., 1968), p. 178.

16. Schneiderman, op. cit., p. 24.

17. 'K istorii rabochego dvizheniia 80–90-kh godov', *Krasnyi Arkhiv* 91 (1938), pp. 162–3.

18. F. C. Giffin, 'The "First Russian Labor Code": the law of June 3, 1886', *Russian History* 2 (1975), pp. 83–100; and 'The formative years of the Russian factory inspectorate, 1882–1885', *Slavic Review* 25 (Dec. 1966), pp. 641–50.

19. G. V. Rimlinger, 'The management of labor protest in tsarist Russia: 1870–1905', *International Review of Social History* 5 (1960), pp. 226–48. For Kokovtsov's survey of labour legislation and policy see '9-e Ianvaria 1905 g. Doklady V. N. Kokovtsova Nikolaiu II', *Krasnyi Arkhiv* 11–12 (1925), pp. 3–23.

20. J. G. Gliksman, 'The Russian urban worker: from serf to proletarian' in C. E. Black (ed.), *Transformation of Russian Society* (Cambridge, Mass., 1960), p. 312; T. H. Von Laue, 'Russian labor between field and factory, 1892–1903', *California Slavic Studies* III (1964), pp. 33–65. Two thirds or more of the inhabitants of Moscow and Petersburg were registered as peasants at the turn of the century.

21. R. E. Johnson, *Peasant and Proletarian* (New Brunswick, NJ, 1979), pp. 155–62.

22. Diane Koenker, 'Urban families' in D. L. Ransel (ed.), *The Family in Imperial Russia* (Urbana-Chicago and London, 1978), pp. 286–7; J. H. Bater, *St Petersburg: Industrialization and Change* (London, 1976), pp. 254–8, 326–30, 342–53; S. G. Strumilin, op. cit., p. 210, and *Ocherki ekonomicheskoi istorii Rossii* (Moscow, 1960), pp. 122–3; *Istoriia SSSR* VI, pp. 321–2.

23. *Istoriia SSSR* V, pp. 339–40; VI, pp. 319–20; McKay, op. cit., p. 250, n. 29; Johnson, op. cit., pp. 35–8; A. G. Rashin, *Formirovanie rabochego klassa Rossii* (Moscow, 1958), pp. 564–76.

24. Strumilin, *Ocherki ekonomicheskoi istorii*, p. 539; L. S. Gaponenko, 'O chislennosti i kontsentratsii rabochego klassa Rossii nakanune velikoi Oktiabrskoi sotsialisticheskoi revoliutsii', *Istoricheskii Arkhiv* 1 (1960), p. 77.

25 Heer, loc. cit., p. 223; Diane Koenker, *Moscow Workers and the 1917 Revolution* (Princeton, NJ, 1981), p. 29; Jeffrey Brooks, 'Readers and reading at the end of the tsarist era' in W. M. Todd (ed.), *Literature and Society in Imperial Russia, 1800–1914,* (Stanford, Cal., 1978), p. 119; Arcadius Kahan, 'Social structure, public policy, and the development of education and the economy in czarist Russia' in C. A. Anderson and M. J. Bowman, *Education and Economic Development* (Chicago, 1965) p. 369.

26. Richard Pipes, *Russian Social Democracy and the St Petersburg Labor Movement, 1885–1897* (Cambridge, Mass., 1963); and A. K. Wildman, *The Making of a Workers' Revolution. Russian Social Democracy, 1891–1903* (Chicago and London, 1967).

27. Kokovtsov, '9-e Ianvaria 1905 g.', in *Krasnyi Arkhiv*, p. 15.

28. On Zubatov and the Zubatovshchina see Schneiderman, op. cit.

29. Walter Sablinsky, *The Road to Bloody Sunday. Father Gapon and the St Petersburg Massacre of 1905* (Princeton, NJ, 1976); G. D. Surh, 'Petersburg's first mass labor organization: the Assembly of Russian Workers and Father Gapon', *Russian Review* 40 (July 1981), pp. 241–62; and 40 (Oct. 1981), pp. 412–41.

30. H. Rogger, 'The formation of the Russian Right, 1900–1906', *California Slavic*

Studies III (1964), pp. 66–94; and 'Was there a Russian fascism? The Union of Russian People', *Journal of Modern History* 36 (Dec. 1964), pp. 398–415.

31. I. F. Gindin, 'Russkaia burzhuaziia v period kapitalizma. Ee razvitie i osobennosti', *Istoriia SSSR* 2 (March–April 1963), p. 64; J. Nötzold, *Wirtschaftspolitische Alternativen der Entwicklung Russlands in der Ära Witte und Stolypin* (Munich, 1966), p. 174. Lower figures for selected industries are given by McKay, op. cit., pp. 138–40, 156–7. A spokesman for the Association of Industry and Trade declared that in 1907/08 average net profits of joint-stock companies were only 4.4 per cent as compared with a rate of 7.01 per cent in Germany. See R. A. Roosa, 'Russian industrialists and "State Socialism", 1906–1917', *Soviet Studies* 32 (January 1972), p. 409, n. 34.

32. S. Ia. Borovoi, 'Ob ekonomicheskikh sviaziakh burzhuazhnoi verkhushki i tsarizma v period imperializma', *Istoriia SSSR* 2 (March–April, 1970), p. 107.

33. A. A. Novoselskii (ed.), *Maloissledovannye istochniki po istorii SSSR XIX–XX vv.* (Moscow, 1964), p. 97, n. 26.

34. C. A. Goldberg, 'The Association of Industry and Trade, 1906–1917: the successes and failures of Russia's organized businessmen', Ph.D. Diss., University of Michigan, 1974, pp. 198–9.

35. Borovoi, loc. cit., p. 109.

36. Witte's report to Nicholas 'On the situation of our industry' in Dmitriev, op. cit., III, pp. 222–8.

37. E. D. Chermenskii, *Burzhuaziia i tsarizm v revoliutsii 1905–1907 gg.* (Moscow-Leningrad, 1939), pp. 68ff.

38. G. V. Plekhanov, *Selected Philosophical Works* (Moscow, n.d.), p. 239.

39. George Fischer, *Russian Liberalism* (Cambridge, Mass., 1958), p. 90.

40. V. M. Chernov, *Zapiski sotsialista revoliutsionera* (Berlin, 1922), pp. 118–19.

41. R. E. Pipes, *Struve. Liberal on the Left, 1870–1905* (Cambridge, Mass., 1970), p. 195.

42. V. Ia. Laverychev, *Krupnaia burzhuaziia v poreformennoi Rossii* (Moscow, 1974), pp. 65–71, estimates the upper bourgeoisie to have numbered between 800,000 to 1 million in the 1880s. D. R. Brower, 'Urban Russia on the eve of World War I: a social profile', *Journal of Social History* 13 (Spring 1980), pp. 424–36, considers his estimate to be based as much on intuition as quantitative data. 'Russia's "merchant and industrial bourgeoisie"', Brower writes, 'were predominantly very small-scale businessmen' (p. 430).

43. Louis Menashe, 'Alexander Guchkov and the origins of the Octobrist Party: the Russian bourgeoisie in politics, 1905', Ph.D. Diss., New York University, 1965, p. 25.

44. Goldberg, op. cit., p. 26.

45. Ibid., pp. 14–16; H. Seton-Watson, *The Russian Empire, 1801–1917* (Oxford, 1967), pp. 522–3; Menashe, op. cit., pp. 43–51.

46. S. Ia. Elpatevskii, *Vospominaniia* (Leningrad, 1929), pp. 210–11.

47. Gindin, 'Russkaia burzhuaziia', *Istoriia SSSR* 3 (May–June 1963), p. 57; A. Ia. Avrekh, *Stolypin i tretia Duma* (Moscow, 1968), p. 297.

48. V. N. Kokovtsov, *Out of My Past* (Stanford, Cal., and London, 1935), p. 307.

49. V. T. Bill, *The Forgotten Class* (New York, 1959), p. 153; Gindin, 'Russkaia burzhuaziia', *Istoriia SSSR* 2 (March–April 1963), p. 75.

50. S. Iu. Vitte, *Vospominaniia* (Moscow, 1969), I, pp. 414–15.

51. A. J. Beveridge, *The Russian Advance* (New York, 1904), p. 430.

52. Boris Pasternak, *I Remember: Sketch for an Autobiography*, trans. by D. Magarshack (New York, 1959), p. 31.

53. There is considerable variation – depending on the criteria employed and the inclusion or exclusion of certain areas (such as Finland, Poland, the Baltic Provinces or Asiatic Russia) – in the figures given by different authors for the country's urban population. Some estimates range as high as 20 per cent (Brower, op. cit., p. 424). Cf. T. S. Fedor, *Patterns of Urban Growth in the Russian Empire During the Nineteenth Century* (Chicago, 1975), pp. 173–8; C. D. Harris, *Cities of the Soviet Union* (Chicago, 1970), pp. 7–8, 226, 229, 232; J. W. Leasure and R. A. Lewis, *Population Changes in Russia and the USSR* (San Diego, Cal., 1966), pp. 28–9; A. M. Anfimov, *Krupnoe pomeshchiche khoziaistvo Evropeiskoi Rossii* (Moscow, 1969), p. 371; Haiko Haumann, 'Die russische Stadt in der Geschichte', *Jahrbücher für Geschichte Osteuropas* 27 (1979), pp. 481–97; A. G. Rashin, *Naselenie Rossii za 100 let (1811–1913gg.)* (Moscow, 1956), pp. 85–93.

54. Ibid. pp. 320–46; L. K. Erman, *Intelligentsiia v pervoi russkoi revoliutsii* (Moscow, 1966), ch. 1; *Sovetskaia Istoricheskaia Entsiklopediia* VI, p. 115; Leasure and Lewis, op. cit., pp. 33–5; Kahan in Anderson and Bowman, op. cit., p. 273; T. G. Stavrou, *Russia Under the Last Tsar* (Minneapolis, Minn., 1969), pp. 92, 164.

55. V. I. Lenin, 'Farewell letter to Swiss workers' in *Collected Works* (London and Moscow, 1960–78), XXIII, p. 373.

56. Gindin, 'Russkaia burzhuaziia', *Istoriia SSSR* 3 (May–June 1963), p. 37; Alec Nove, *An Economic History of the USSR* (London, 1969), p. 17.

57. W. O. Henderson, *The Industrial Revolution in Europe* (Chicago, 1961), p. 204; Strumilin, *Statistiko-ekonomicheskie ocherki*, p. 211.

58. Anfimov, op. cit., p. 370.

CHAPTER SEVEN

Politics and revolution

Although they did not remain confined to the cities and factories, the three great unheavals that convulsed Russia in little more than a decade – one in 1905 and two in 1917 – were urban revolutions. Peasant protests and problems made major and essential contributions to their long-range causation, duration, and eventual success. But the Russian Revolution, to speak of it as a continuing process or phenomenon, was urban in its immediate origins, in the social and geographic locus of its beginnings, in its leadership, and in its political vocabulary. Theorists and practitioners of reaction, like Pobedonostsev and Pleve, had warned of the unsettling effects of the reforms which the autocracy had initiated in 1861 and of the industrialization it intermittently pursued in subsequent decades. They had suggested immunizing Russia against revolution by immobilizing her as much as possible and had proved to be more nearly correct in their fears than had Witte in his hopes that the existing political system could be preserved, indeed strengthened, by economic modernization.

Economic development had set in motion forces that threatened social and political stability, forces the autocracy could neither accommodate nor neutralize. Economic change also contributed greatly to social ferment and, after the relative quiet of the 1880s, to the revival of political debate and of the revolutionary movement in the 1890s. It did so not only by increasing the numbers of factory workers who became the vanguard of the urban revolution. An equally, possibly more important by-product and consequence of the spread of capital and industry was the intensification and extension of processes that had begun decades earlier: the appearance of spheres of activity and sources of livelihood for educated and ambitious men outside of state service. What the Great Reforms had begun, industrialization and urbanization continued by creating a diversified society with a diversity of needs, interests, viewpoints and occupations. The lawyers, doctors, journalists, managers and technicians, scientists and teachers who served business or local government enjoyed an unprecedented degree of economic independence of the state and developed a sense of their own importance to society's functioning that was reflected in growing political awareness, discontent and, ultimately, action.

And finally, the tangible and visible achievements of an industrial economy, the heightened sense of possibility that came with railroads and electric tramways, with machine production, newspapers, the telegraph and foreign travel, made all the more intolerable and shameful the contrast with the country's unreformed, unchanging political regime and its continued lagging behind the 'civilized' countries of the world. Even Lev Tolstoi, no believer in the benefits of material progress or the magic of institutional renovation, was struck by the incongruity of a retrograde government and an advancing people. 'Autocracy', he wrote in a letter to Nicholas II in 1902, 'is a superannuated form of government that may suit the needs of a Central African tribe . . . but not those of the Russian people, who are increasingly assimilating the culture of the rest of the world. That is why it is impossible to maintain this form of government . . . except by violence . . . .'[1] Vladimir Korolenko, a novelist of populist sympathies, when chided for wanting impatiently to catch up with the West in all things at once, told an English interlocutor in 1905: 'You mustn't forget that we are now in the twentieth century, and, to make a comparison, if I want to light a new town, it would be absurd to use tallow candles first and then to replace them by lamps and then employ gas until I shall finally make use of electric light. Electric light can be generated, and it is only natural that I should use it at once.'[2] Electricity stood for democracy and modernity, but the choice of the analogy was not accidental in a country which was in its material development skipping stages or shortening them.

The gap between Russian reality and Russia's potential – perceived more and more often as a function of the breach between an immobile state and a dynamic society – made for impatience in the years just before and after 1900, even among men who were not of radical or revolutionary temperament or convictions. New only in its extent, impatience had been since the early part of the nineteenth century the dominant, perhaps the defining, characteristic of the Russian revolutionary movement. While revolutionaries and their organizations had (as before) been dispersed, and disappeared from view in the aftermath of their brief success and greater failure of 1881, their movement had not died. The impatience that nourished revolutionary expectations and attitudes survived and was beginning once more to show signs of vitality, to demonstrate that there was a revolutionary tradition whose continuity had not been broken. The existence of such a tradition, which went back to the Decembrist rising of 1825, legitimated acts of rebellion against authority that might otherwise have been regarded as crimes or madness and created in key segments of society funds of sympathy (and occasionally of money) on which the revolutionaries could at critical times draw.

The impotence of the revolutionaries of the People's Will, made manifest in their inability to follow up the assassination of Alexander II by disorganizing the machinery of power or by rousing the masses, made such a development appear highly improbable. There was good reason to think that by choosing for their victim the Tsar-Liberator just as he was about to promulgate the Loris-Melikov 'Constitution', the terrorists had finally exhausted the tolerance and good will of reform-minded but respectable society. The disintegration of the People's Will under the blows of police action was taken as further proof that revolutionary energies had spent themselves. All that the disoriented survivors could for the moment do was to lie low, at best to engage in non-revolutionary, non-political, legal educational and social work on behalf of the people.

The view of the 1880s as an unheroic or fallow decade in the history of the revolutionary movement is not incorrect; it is not, however, the whole of the story. There was fatigue and fear, pessimism and the waning of great hopes, expressed in a variety of ways: a flight into aestheticism and art for art's sake; Tolstoian non-resistance to evil; a rejection of the philosophical materialism and positivism that had guided the intelligentsia in the 1860s and the 1870s. Among liberals as well as radicals the new mood expressed itself most often in a call for sober, practical, small and cautious steps for the betterment of Russia and her people, for the abandonment of great dreams and schemes. There was, then, an unmistakable ebbing of the revolutionary tide and a growth of meliorist and apolitical attitudes. Yet there was no wholesale rejection by the survivors of revolutionary populism, and still less by the generation which was coming to consciousness in the 1880s, of revolution as desirable and, indeed, necessary for the removal of an autocracy that appeared more rather than less odious and repressive.

For the time being the revolutionary disposition was just that; deeds were few and futile, but in view of the rigorous security measures taken against them, they sustained the belief in revolutionary action as moral and imperative and of its actors as heroes. The scattered, disconnected circles that carried on a precarious existence in St Petersburg and the provinces had greater psychological than practical impact. One of them, the short-lived Young People's Will of 1883, made 'propaganda by the deed' an essential part of its programme, in order by displays of revolutionary courage to gain the sympathy and admiration of society and the masses. The ill-fated, university-hatched conspiracy against the life of Alexander III, planned for the 1887 anniversary of his father's death, was an almost literal carrying out of the injunction which one of the founders of Young People's Will had given to his generation.

What is important is not living individuals, not material strength, but principles, ideas. These . . . will be incomparably more vital, vibrant, powerful and widespread, if they are proclaimed not by the mouths of separate, verbalizing individuals but by the thunder of heroic facts, stunning the mind and fantasy with the brilliance of sacrifice, the brilliance of struggle, and the power of our faith in the justice of our cause.[3]

The author of these lines, a young poet by the name of Petr Iakubovich, was a descendant of the Decembrist Alexander Iakubovich. The most famous of the student conspirators of 1887 was Alexander Ulianov, older brother of Vladimir, the future Lenin, leader of Social Democracy and one of the editors of the Marxist journal *Iskra* ('The Spark') which carried as its motto the line addressed by one of the Decembrists to Pushkin: 'From the spark shall grow the flame.'

The case of Alexandr Ulianov, who came to the university determined to pursue his scientific interests, and in the very midst of the 'quiet period' was made to feel guilty about his detachment from student politics, is the best example of the lasting power of the revolutionary mood and example. It mattered less to him and his comrades which road to revolution a man chose than that the choice be made. Not long before he was apprehended and executed he wrote: 'Our disagreements [with the Marxists] seem to be very insignificant and only theoretical.'[4] His brother Vladimir would have been shocked by this denigration of theory, yet he admired the revolutionary dedication of the men and women of People's Will and, in a superbly controlled way, shared their eagerness for action. Individual terror, although he like all Marxists rejected it, was only the most obvious expression of this eagerness. Another was Lenin's own hectoring of his party in October 1917 to seize power, not to delay, not to spoil chances for a perfectly good revolution by waiting for majority backing from a Congress of Soviets or Constituent Assembly.

A revolutionary outlook and commitment, whether its sources were emotional or intellectual, did not, as the future history of the revolutionary movement would show, ensure unanimity about the nature of the coming revolution, who should lead it, or what its goals should be once the incubus of absolutism had been lifted. The disorientation in radical ranks which followed 1881 was not only organizational; it was psychological and theoretical as well, and for some of those who kept reaffirming the revolutionary creed in words and deeds, reaffirmation had the purpose of stilling doubts. Doubt had made its appearance even before 1881; the shattering blows of that and later years deepened it and led many revolutionary Populists, condemned to inactivity or exile, to re-examine the basic tenets by which they had lived and fought.

Populism – the term gained currency only in the 1870s – was from its very origins in the 1860s more an amalgam of emotions and the diverse, even conflicting, ideas of many minds than a complete, unified body of political or social doctrine. It was always particularly susceptible to organizational and intellectual disintegration. The source of its strength and appeal – devotion to and faith in the people – *narod*, from which came the movement's Russian name, *narodnichestvo* – was also the source of its greatest weakness. For all practical purposes, people meant peasants, and Russia's peasants repeatedly refused to behave as their revolutionary (or, for that matter, conservative) mentors, admirers, and tribunes predicted and expected.

The most unsettling disenchantment with the people occurred in the 'mad summer' of 1874, when as many as 2,500 to 3,000 young people left university lecture halls or the comfortable homes of their parents to 'go to the people'. Some of them (followers of the anarchist Mikhail Bakunin) went to unleash the rebellious instincts of the peasants; others (the disciples of Petr Lavrov) to prepare them for the coming revolution by teaching them socialist principles and to make them realize who their oppressors and exploiters were. They combined their agitational or propagandist activities with service as village teachers, medical assistants, or simple labourers, in discharge of the debt which they and their ancestors had accumulated over the centuries. The peasants whose friendship the young radicals were seeking met them with incomprehension or hostility. The majority were rounded up by police or gendarmes, with occasional help from a muzhik who suspected the altruism of people who came from the other side of the class barrier to share his misery by choice rather than necessity.

The peasants turned out to be neither the inflammable material that the insurrectionary agitation of the Bakuninists wanted to ignite, nor the receptive soil on which the anti-tsarist and socialist propaganda of the Lavrovists would flourish. The most disheartening evidence brought to light by the 'Going to the People' movement in its last phase was the continued trust of the rural masses in the ruler as their benefactor and protector. In the only instance in which peasants joined their youthful liberators, they were persuaded to do so by a spurious tsarist charter which granted them the land which greedy land-lords and corrupt officials had supposedly kept from them at emancipation. This was hardly a firm basis for building a revolutionary movement or pro-voking a rising of the people whose anger would cleanse Russia of despotism, allow her to bypass capitalism and bourgeois rule, and usher in liberty and equality under a socialist republic of self-governing associations of rural and urban producers. The revolutionary impatience felt by the educated urban rad-icals, the intelligentsia, and projected by them onto the people was not present among the latter, and neither was the innate socialism which the commune and the artisan cooperative (artel) had supposedly fostered and kept alive. These sobering facts the revolutionary populists were psychologically incapable of fully admitting or explicitly incorporating into their world view; they influenced the movement's future character and conduct none the less and made revolution less exclusively a task to be achieved by the masses for themselves.

With the foundation in 1876 of a revolutionary party of more than ephem-eral duration (it took the name Land and Liberty in 1878), there began a subtle shift in populism from the narod to the intelligentsia, from following the masses to guiding them, from mass agitation to more selective indoctrination. None of the old positions was repudiated, but the party's centralization of authority and structure (although intended merely as defensive measures against police penetration) was bound to limit the weight any potential mass membership might have in its councils.

The use of terror to disorganize the governmental apparatus was a further step away from revolutionary action defined and carried out by the masses, even if its purpose was ultimately to facilitate such action. In face of the peasants' continued failure to respond to the appeals of Land and Liberty, assassin-ating officials and finally the Tsar himself became a dominant rather than auxiliary part of the party's programme and led to a split in its ranks in 1879. One branch, calling itself the People's Will (Narodnaia Volia), retained and refined violence and conspiracy, either to frighten tsarism into granting a con-stitution – which would make open agitation possible – or to seize power. Another, Black Partition (Chernyi Peredel), meaning the transfer of all lands to the peasants, led by Georgii Plekhanov and Pavel Akselrod, disavowed terror and the merely political overturn that was at best all a minority conspiracy could achieve and that most probably would end in reaction. A genuine revolution required the longer road of mass action by workers and peasants seizing lands and factories and developing a socialist consciousness in the process. Only then could liberty and socialism strike roots and survive. For a few intellectuals to seize power and expect that a backward people would follow their prescriptions for the nation's political and economic organization was, Plekhanov warned, to ignore the lessons of the last few years.

The silence with which the villages greeted the news of the regicide of 1 March 1881 proved him right, yet this was little comfort to the adherents of Black Partition. Their more deliberate and long-range efforts to cultivate a revolutionary readiness among the peasants were no more successful than the bold strokes of People's Will. Black Partition soon faded from the scene, while People's Will could only follow up its 'victory' by asking the new Tsar for a political amnesty and a popularly elected constituent assembly as the price for ending an assault which it was powerless to mount.

The futile demand for political liberty made by People's Will – which critics saw as the predictable outcome of its turn to terror – marked more than the decline of organized revolutionary populism. It signified a turning-point for the revolutionary movement as a whole and highlighted the unsolved questions which populism left to its successors. The most troubling of these was the nature of the relationship between the revolutionaries and the people to whom they were dedicated. In classic populism, dedication was synonymous with carrying out the people's will, with doing no more than clearing away the obstacles which kept the narod from expressing its moral excellence, its yearning for equality and social justice. Belief in popular virtue and good sense made it unnecessary for the populists to describe in detail the future political order; the example of Western Europe, where liberalism and parliaments had replaced the rule of old regimes with that of a grasping bourgeoisie, made it undesirable. The strong anarchist strand in populism filled its adherents with an abhorrence of politics and liberal reforms, with a distrust of merely political or institutional changes, and a disinterest in political power. The goal was the abolition of state power, the social revolution made by and for the masses.

When the latter did not rise and the state successfully resisted the onslaughts of the shock troops of People's Will, the revolutionary potential of the masses and the utility of terror were both called into doubt. So was the right and the ability of an elite (for that is what the revolutionaries were, by class origin or education) to speak or act for 'the people'. And if that right was denied, were they condemned to inactivity as long as autocracy kept the slumbering giant, the narod, in ignorance and captivity? Were impotence or elitist conspiracies the only choices? The question was rarely posed in such simple terms, but it plagued the revolutionaries until 1917 and beyond. 'Whence to draw strength for the struggle with tsarism?'[5] was how Plekhanov formulated the quandary of the relationship of a radical elite that was insufficiently numerous to a people that was insufficiently revolutionary.

In the late 1870s there first emerged a modification of populist strategy that was to gain ground and favour in the years after 1881: a joining of all oppositionist forces that were prepared to fight autocracy for political and civil rights. Since this meant collaborating with liberals, and an at least temporary retreat from preoccupation with the concrete interests of peasants and workers, it was not a position widely adopted by the activists of People's Will. But there was the adumbration of a 'liberal' and, in Black Partition, of a political populism that foreshadowed the importance assigned to the struggle for political freedom and democracy by Marxism and, in fact, by all the revolutionary parties of the 1890s and after. Whether they viewed the achievement of constitutional safeguards as primary or not, all saw it as desirable and some as essential, an intermediate step to socialism. A period of basic freedoms and security would allow the masses to achieve political maturity and revolutionary consciousness to match their anger and egalitarian instincts.

To countenance the possibility of a qualified and, it was hoped, temporary participation in the fight for a liberalized political order was for populists more than a change of strategy. It was an admission of doubt in one of the central beliefs that had sustained them for two decades: that Russia was favoured by having only a rudimentary capitalism and middle class; that this would allow her to bypass the stage of a liberal (and inevitably capitalist) political and economic system and to advance directly to socialism for which the building blocks were present in the village commune and the craft artel. The aim had always been that of all European socialists, but the road was to be a Russian one.

Before as well as after 1881 some populists simply ignored the evidence of the inroads that capitalism was making in town and country; others intensified their attack on the state as the main source of the evil and saw its overthrow as a pre-emptive measure against the further spread of capitalism; still others, frustrated in the villages, looked to the workers, yesterday's peasants, as the most promising striking force of the revolution, and to the liberals as possible allies. None could avoid wondering and worrying what an industrial capitalism fostered by the state would do to their version of Russia's fate and future, whether it could or would take permanent root and give birth to a viable middle class. And if the answers could be found, what would they mean for populism? How was the timetable for revolution to be fixed, what was its first target to be, where were its armies to be recruited?

What has been called 'the crisis of Russian populism' was deep and real, and since populism was to all intents and purposes synonymous with the revolutionary movement, its activists and sympathizers were equally afflicted by it. Because the latter were more numerous than the former and not caught up in the heady atmosphere of conspiracy which left little time for reflection or study, they were naturally the first to conduct a sustained review of populist positions. Since their writings were academic in tone, eschewed revolutionary aims and phrases, and understated or concealed socialist goals, they could be published openly. Theirs became known as 'legal' populism, a position of moderation to which conviction as well as caution had brought them. Their studies of *The Fate of Capitalism in Russia* – a book by that title was published in 1882 by the chief representative of the trend, V. P. Vorontsov ('V.V.') – led the legal populists to an 'optimistic' conclusion. Industrial capitalism, wealth for the few and misery for the many, could indeed be avoided in Russia and popular and cooperative production (i.e., socialism) attained without it. Whatever the state might do, it was too late for a backward country to imitate the capitalist road to progress and power taken by the Western nations. These had already carved up the world's markets among themselves; their technological superiority made competition hopeless; while an agricultural people which a harsh climate condemned to low living standards and which was being further impoverished to pay for the development of industry, could never create the domestic markets to sustain it. That being so, Russian capitalism, like the Russian bourgeoisie, was stillborn, a creature which no amount of artificial stimulation could keep alive.

Vorontsov's findings were anti-revolutionary and anti-insurrectionist. If there was no chance of implanting capitalism, there was no need for a frontal attack on the state which sheltered it. The principal objects of the moment, therefore, should be the intellectual advancement of the masses, the strengthening of communal agriculture and cooperative production. This required that the intelligentsia work at practical tasks and seek help from any source – liberals or bureaucrats – to get lower taxes, cheap credit, better tools and techniques, more land and schools for the betterment of the people. As it had once been made to see the necessity and advantages of emancipation the state would see the benefits of these measures – the more so since the capitalism it had fostered would surely founder – and support both the nationalization of large-scale industry and the gradual growth of cooperative small-scale enterprises in town and country. The ultimate goal was 'socialized forms of production' in both.

Another influential legal populist, who had translated volume one of *Das Kapital* into Russian in 1872 and considered himself a follower of Marx, arrived at similar conclusions. But writing about a decade after Vorontsov under the pen-name Nikolai-on, N. F. Danielson stressed not the impossibility of a Russian capitalism but the catastrophic impact its artificial spread was having on all sectors of the national economy, the ruin to which it was inevitably leading. Danielson did not share Vorontsov's faith in the viability of commune or artel in their present forms, however great their moral and social virtues. Their resistance to capitalist differentiation and competition was low, as was the ability of such small production units to meet the needs of an expanding population. He did not believe that the gradualist, meliorist approach of Vorontsov would work, even if it were limited to the attainment of a modest livelihood for the immediate producers. To improve the 'national' economy – for Russia was no longer a country of self-sufficient economic units – required a national plan, state intervention and sponsorship of technological innovation to increase industrial and agricultural productivity. Only an efficient, modern, large-scale economy could assure the surpluses necessary for the nation's progress and its people's welfare. The massive economic reorganization which Danielson envisaged was, of course, to be carried out under public auspices, without passing through the stage of capitalist property and profit with its horrendous social dislocations and injustices, and it had to be done quickly, before what was left of communal production was destroyed.

We must graft scientific agriculture and modern large-scale industry onto the commune, and at the same time give the commune a form that will make it an effective tool for the organization of large-scale industry and the transformation of the form of that industry from a capitalist to a public one. There is no other way for the organization of the economy: either growth, or deterioration and death.[6]

Danielson also realized that Russia's growing involvement with foreign trade, finance and technology created the danger of dependence on the suppliers of technique and capital. His question – 'how to prevent Russia from becoming a tributary of more advanced countries' – was echoed by other legal populists, including Voronstov, who came to accept the need for modern factory production and comprehensive non-capitalist planning. He too saw the country's economic problems with ever greater urgency and as transcending the traditional needs of her primary producers. After the Japanese war, which had 'shown with painful clarity to what dangers our nation is subject if it fails to adopt not only modern military techniques but Western culture in general', Vorontsov said that Russians wanted to live as did the people of modern, not medieval Europe.[7]

Inexorably the legal populists came face to face with the political reality which they had neglected or ignored: how could a backward state become the engine of an accelerated economic advance that would lead to popular welfare as well as national greatness? The constitutional road was slow and, since liberalism was weak, was likely to be ineffective. Liberals could not, in any case, be trusted to work for the people's well-being once their own goals had been attained. Since it was hardly conducive to orderly planning and might destroy the cultural achievements of the past, a rising of the peasant masses was undesirable, as was a minority seizure of power such as the revolutionary populists had envisaged. The Marxist formula of welcoming capitalism and the proletariat that would eventually destroy it was equally unacceptable, so there was little choice, in effect, but to look to the government, to convince it by force of argument and proof of self-interest to choose the right (i.e. non-capitalist) policies of economic development.

The legal populists made valuable contributions to the debate over Russia's industrialization, demanding that its costs to the masses be minimized and suggesting ways of doing so. But their theories could not for long fill the moral and psychological void felt by the defeated revolutionaries or answer the questions which tormented them. The legal populists were still an elite prescribing for the people rather than working with them for their emancipation. In recognizing the need for a speedier catching up with Europe, they displayed the impatience of revolutionaries who rejected revolutionary conclusions. They wanted Russia to live in the modern world, but thought that modern technology, mass production, and social welfare could be had without 'bourgeois' constitutions or revolutionary politics. Their humanitarianism, their economic insights, their political moderation did not spare them isolation from the masses, the radical intelligentsia, or the government – that is, from any force that could conceivably have adopted and realized their ideas. Legal populism was not a party or a movement; it furnished the opponents of the government's economic policies with intellectual ammunition, but did not supply a structure or rationale for action when revolutionary energies revived after a decade of desperate gestures, small deeds, or passivity.

No small part in that revival was played by the famine and cholera epidemic of 1891/92 and the bureaucracy's seeming inability to deal with it unaided. Among moderates and liberals the experience of the famine gave renewed impetus to thoughts of political reform. Populists saw the catastrophe as confirmation of their dire predictions of failure for the hothouse capitalism fostered by the state with its undermining of 'popular' production in town and country. To the Marxists it proved the opposite, that cooperative craft industries and communal peasant agriculture were incapable of resisting the advance of capitalist forms of production and ownership. The cause of the crisis was too little rather than too much capitalism – in short, backwardness, the result of antiquated, artificially maintained property and production relations. In the years following the famine the Marxist case gained a wide and sympathetic hearing. Put largely in academic terms by Peter Struve in his *Critical Remarks on the Question of Russia's Economic Development* (1894), its plotting of the inevitable replacement of a natural by an exchange economy and by large-scale, centralized commodity production was considered sufficiently safe or abstract to pass the censorship. There was now a 'legal' Marxism to contest populism's intellectual and moral authority with the educated public. Its appeal lay in the certainty that capitalism, for all its horrors, brought advances in every sphere of life, that it was the precondition for progress and culture in the broadest sense. *Laissez-faire* liberals, Westernizers, modernizers of all kinds could welcome Marxism's application of universal laws to Russia while rejecting or ignoring its revolutionary implications. These were in any case stated with such restraint that Lenin complained of Struve's glossing over the social antagonisms that accompanied the growth of capitalism.[8]

Lenin's fears that Struve's stress on the objective, determinist aspects of Marx's teaching would disarm it as a revolutionary doctrine were justified but premature. Struve and other legal Marxists did not join the liberal camp for several years, and in Russia even liberalism had its radical and revolutionary sides. But ever since there had been Marxists in Russia, they had debated whether to wait for the ineluctable forces of history to do the job of destroying autocracy and 'feudalism' or whether to hurry history along by the wilful intervention of the revolutionaries. Indeed, what made Marxism so attractive in the 1890s – the assurance it offered in a period of political depression that change would come no matter what the government or its opponents might do – had in the 1870s led to its rejection by populist youth. They had thought Marx a very learned man, but not really a revolutionary.

The populists were neither unfamiliar with Marx nor uninfluenced by him

141

and held him in high esteem as a critic and analyst of capitalist economics and bourgeois politics. But they rejected those consequences of his doctrine that sentenced Russia to follow the capitalist path, its peasants to become factory hands or rural proletarians, and the radical intelligentsia to stand by with folded arms as all this happened or even help it to happen as Struve suggested. They were voluntarists, not determinists, and believed that the critically thinking individual and his conscience could and should play a decisive role in history. They were revolutionaries and not, as they accused the Marxists of being, sociologists.[9]

If Russian Marxism none the less won to its side a significant number of radical youth it did so by appealing to their will to action, by constituting itself into a force for revolutionary combat, by meeting some of the same psychological needs and emotional drives its great ideological rival, populism, had sought to satisfy. That Marxism also produced an intellectually satisfying and coherent view of politics and history, a view that promised success as well as struggle, was an added advantage and one that it owed in greatest measure to Plekhanov as it owed its activist appeal mainly to Lenin.

Plekhanov's break with Land and Liberty in 1879 was the first step of his abandonment of populism and of his conversion to Marxism. The issue of terror had precipitated the break, but it stood for other grave shortcomings of the revolutionary party that his powerful intellect could no longer tolerate. Terror was by its very nature directed against isolated targets by isolated individuals; it openly advertised their isolation and was a poor substitute for mass action. Terror, therefore, condemned revolutionary deeds to remain without resonance and its practitioners to remain separated from the people and ignored by the rulers. Terror was the assertion of minority will over majority needs and unreadiness, it was politics divorced from objective historical and social reality. That, and the fear that tsarism would quickly be replaced by a narrow upper-class regime, was the burden of Plekhanov's opposition to politics as practised by People's Will, an opposition which he abandoned to call in 1883 for a broad-based political struggle that was his and Marxism's original and significant contribution to the strategy of the Russian Revolution. Its primary goal remained the removal of autocracy, the conquest of political freedom and a 'significant interval' of bourgeois democracy which would allow the labour movement to grow and prepare for the next, the socialist, revolution which would achieve land *and* liberty, social justice *and* political freedom, socialism *and* democracy. For Russian Social Democracy, which is what the Marxists called their movement, there need be no contradiction between politics and revolution.

From 1880 until 1917 Plekhanov lived in Geneva where he and other Black Partitionists founded the first organization of Russian Marxists in 1883, the Liberation of Labour Group. There too he wrote *Socialism and Political Struggle* (1883), *Our Differences* (1885), *On the Question of the Development of the Monistic Conception of History* (1894) and other works in which he critized the central assumptions of populism and applied the Marxist formula to Russia.

For the intelligentsia to cut itself off from the masses was wrong, but so was its reliance on the peasantry, on its supposedly radical instincts and communal institutions. The peasant who demanded or seized gentry land was at heart a conservative who protected the agrarian base on which the whole social and political structure of Russia rested. And the village commune was very far from being the nucleus of a future communism. A purely juridical form of joint property in land which was common in natural economies, it had not led to the collective working of the land or the sharing of its products, and had been maintained long beyond its natural life for the administrative and fiscal convenience of the state. That convenience had also irrevocably drawn the commune into the money economy, into production for the market in which the peasant had to sell his grain to pay taxes and redemption dues. The end result of that process – already far advanced – was the destruction of the commune, the rise of a class of well-to-do farmers, the proletarianization of the rest, and the triumph of capitalism. For Russian socialists it was foolish to try to prevent the coming of capitalism; it had arrived in town and country, its further spread was certain and, indeed, to be welcomed as a higher socio-economic stage.

But did this require the silent acquiescence of the revolutionaries? Could they not shorten the 'significant' interval or did they have to wait patiently for a century or more until capitalism, as in the West, had matured and was ready to be replaced? Were they to accept as historically determined all the misery and indignity associated with the rule of money and the moneyed classes? Plekhanov knew only too well that so rigid a scheme of history would be rejected by his radical countrymen as inhuman. Fortunately, the acceptance of historical inevitability did not require the abandonment of revolutionary action; it could and should reduce the labours of society which need not be as long and painful in Russia as elsewhere. There were unique forces and factors, domestic as well as international, that could hasten capitalism's coming and fading. There was the possibility of importing advanced technology and advanced social theory (i.e., Marxism); there was the strength of the intelligentsia's revolutionary commitment and the relative weakness of a bourgeoisie which had still to fight a backward state and remnants of the feudal order and was unable, therefore, to establish its intellectual and political dominance over the masses.

These special circumstances dictated to revolutionary socialists collaboration with all opponents of autocracy for the winning of general political and civil liberties. Such collaboration was necessary in order to create favourable conditions for open political combat and possible because of the weakness of bourgeois liberals. It should not, however, lead to fusion with them or to acceptance of their hegemony in the struggle against autocracy. Plekhanov was as convinced as any populist that the exploiting classes would betray their radical allies and the masses once they had wrested a constitution from the tsar. But he saw contradictions among the exploiters which the socialists could turn to their advantage as long as they realized the tactical and temporary nature of the alliance and used it to organize their own party which would, in a second revolution, wrest power from the new ruling classes to establish democratic socialism.

The instrument of that final transformation was to be the industrial working class, the proletariat, which capitalism was steadily increasing in numbers and training in revolutionary consciousness. Here, Plekhanov told the *intelligenty*, was the narod which they needed and which needed them, the class which would not disappoint them as the peasants had done and the satisfaction of whose desires did not conflict with the march of social and economic progress. 'Once they have understood these simple truths, the Russian socialists "from the privileged sections" will put aside all thoughts of seizing power, leaving that to our workers' socialist party of the future. Then their efforts will be directed only towards the creation of such a party and the removal of all conditions which are unfavourable to its growth . . . .'[10]

Like all of Marxism, Plekhanov's Russian version was not seamless, did not fully reconcile the call for submission to historical necessity with that for resistance to its concrete forms. It could be and was used, by Plekhanov himself at different times, as a warrant for gradualism, for letting history take its course as well as for anticipating it and speeding it up. It helped to renew hopes for fruitful activity on the part of the radicals because it influenced all of them, including the non-Marxists, to see political action as important and capitalism and the working class as making it possible. It persuaded many Russians of the futility of thinking that their country was exempt from the laws of progress and its social order as superior. Marxism's belief in the inevitability and universality of history's forward march strengthened all who opposed autocracy and welcomed economic modernization as a necessary step to Russia's cultural and political westernization. Through reading Plekhanov, Angelica Balabanoff discovered Marxism as she recalled many years later. 'I found in it exactly what I needed at the time, a philosophy of method that gave continuity and logic to the processes of history and that endowed my own ethical aspirations, as well as the revolutionary movement itself, with the force and dignity of an historical imperative.'[11]

Yet even for the Marxist segment of the revolutionary movement, Plekhanov did not solve with finality the problem of the intelligentsia's relationship to the masses. In the abstract he viewed the working class, made socialist and revolutionary by the experience of capitalist exploitation, as taking the initiative in fighting for its own and the nation's liberation; in practical terms he had to recognize that for untutored workers under the limiting conditions imposed by tsarism, it would be difficult to develop a revolutionary consciousness and even more to form an effective striking force. Creating a working-class party, therefore, would unavoidably be the task of men from 'the privileged sections' who had the requisite resources and leisure and who were bound, as a result, to play a guiding role in what they had created. And in determining when the workers, the country, and historical circumstances were ripe for making the revolution, their voice would be decisive. Plekhanov foresaw such a possibility and warned of the dangers of rushing ahead of the masses and of history: the workers themselves must develop the programme of their party and determine its policies. Still, there was need for the intelligentsia to keep the workers' eyes fixed firmly on the distant socialist future, to make them see that the satisfaction of their immediate demands for better wages and hours must not deflect them from the goal of revolution.

As long as the proletariat was still a disembodied concept, it was easy for the few Marxists inside Russia who read Plekhanov's pamphlets and books to disregard the contradictions inherent in his harmonizing of the workers' short-range interests and the Marxists' own long-range goals. It was also vital, for the proletariat was 'the people' which was to justify their beliefs and their existence, the historical force which promised to deliver them from isolation and from history itself, and they waited for it to appear, as Plekhanov said, as for the coming of the Messiah.[12] When in the 1890s the Marxists came face to face not with a concept but with living human beings, they realized that the relationship would not be automatically harmonious. The strikes and embryonic workers' circles of the decade had mostly been without benefit of guidance from Social Democratic intellectuals who now thought it best to shift from the propaganda of Marxist revolutionary theories to agitation on the basis of the workers' day-to-day grievances. It was this viewpoint, advocated by Iulii Martov, a future leader of the Menshevik wing of Social Democracy, that was dominant at the founding of the St Petersburg Union of Struggle for the Liberation of the Working Class in 1895.

For Martov, as for the other founders of the Union, there was no conflict between widening the worker's horizon to broader socialist perspectives and giving priority to his struggle against the bosses. By joining that struggle, by deepening and expanding it, the Social Democrats could best make the workers aware of its larger implications, get close to them, awaken their political consciousness and arrive, in the end, at a truly Marxist, truly revolutionary party of the working class. For another of the Union's founders such an outcome was far from certain. He thought it essential to break out of the circles in which a few intellectuals had preached to even fewer workers and to meet the masses on their own ground. But Lenin did not believe that the workers could achieve political consciousness as a natural outgrowth of their fight over bread-and-butter issues. Much less did he expect that such a fight would lead to the formation of a viable party unless it were led and its aims defined by the Social Democrats.

The break between Martov and Lenin, in which both men could hark back to different aspects of Plekhanov's compromise between an autonomous workers' movement and one guided by a theoretically sophisticated leadership, with the master uneasily shifting back and forth between them, did not come until 1903. It was postponed by their arrests in late 1895 and early 1896 and by their joint battle, carried on mainly by the written and printed word from Siberian exile and, after 1900, from Western Europe, against the heresies of Revisionism and Economism.

The originator of the former, the German Social Democrat Eduard Bernstein, denied Marx's prediction of the inevitable pauperization of the proletariat, of the intensification of the class struggle, and of the revolution that was sure to follow it. Socialism could be attained peacefully and gradually, by using and transforming rather than overthrowing the existing political system. This, most practising Russian Marxists feared, would not only blunt the attack on tsarism; it also bore the danger of reformism, of limited economic and social improvements that would rob mass discontent of its revolutionary sting. That danger was increased by Economism's stress on the workers' economic struggle as the basis for a Marxist movement which should, moreover, participate fully in the general opposition of society to absolutism. These seemingly scholastic quarrels were made real and urgent by what was happening among the workers.

The spread of proletarian militancy had not been stopped by the arrest of most of the leaders of the Union of Struggle. The strike movement continued, and it impressed particularly those Marxists who were still at liberty by its determination and independence. The workers were in effect declaring that they could carry on without them, that they were perfectly capable of deciding for themselves what they did and did not want. They did not want to fight others' battles for the dubious blessings of political liberty. They wanted immediate and concrete benefits for themselves and their children, not the glories of a future Utopia. They began to suspect their intellectual allies of pursuing aims of their own or even viewed them as belonging to the world of privilege arrayed against them. *Rabochaia Mysl* ('Workers' Thought'), a journal written mostly by educated radicals who identified with their readers, expressed the workers' distrust of their mentors in October 1898:

They say we are 'against the intelligentsia'. To a great extent that is true . . . . These Russian intelligenty by some sad (or laughable) misunderstanding regard themselves as born revolutionaries . . . . It is well to remember that today's revolutionaries are tomorrow's prosecutors, judges, engineers, factory inspectors, in a word, chinovniki of the Russian government. We are happy to accept their services, as well as the services of all who wish us well, intelligenty and non-intelligenty. But any interference on their part in our affairs which goes further than just those services we regard as out of place. In this sense we are against the intelligentsia. [13]

That untutored workers should think so was regrettable, but understandable; for sophisticated Marxists it was unforgivable. Plekhanov, Martov, and Lenin watched anxiously but impotently, restricted as they were to smuggled letters and the illegal press. They warned that the way things were going, there would be no revolutionary movement, only trade unions with the Social Democrats becoming their secretaries and the unions themselves becoming appendages of the liberal opposition, eventually to be swallowed up by it. They therefore welcomed the foundation of the Russian Social Democratic Workers' Party (RSDWP or SDs) by their still active comrades in 1898 as an attempt to consolidate the surviving groups into a party with a binding programme and reliable leaders. The police soon foiled the attempt and it was not repeated for another five years.

Lenin, in the meantime, tried to fill the gap by rallying the scattered and doctrinally confused elements of Social Democracy around the journal *Iskra*, to reassert Marxist orthodoxy and to make the paper the ideological headquarters linking all revolutionary Marxists. In its very first issue of December 1900 he revealed his abiding concerns: to instil the proletarian masses with Social Democratic ideas and consciousness, to organize a strong and disciplined party of full-time revolutionaries, and through them to forge firm links with the spontaneous labour movement. This, he felt, was the way to keep the workers from drifting into reformism and the intelligentsia from remaining mere debaters of doctrine.

Lenin's comrades on the editorial board of *Iskra*, Martov and Plekhanov among them, did not yet discern the lengths to which his emphases would carry him; they became quite clear in the following years. Lenin had won his theoretical spurs with a polemical work against populist ideology (*Who are the 'Friends of the People' and How Do They Fight Against the Social Democrats?* 1894) and by publishing a substantial work on *The Development of Capitalism in Russia* in 1899. But he was a revolutionary before he was a Marxist, in point of time as well as by temperament, and made his most lasting contribution as leader of a fighting political movement and author of its organizational and operative principles. Stated first in *Iskra*, these were elaborated in *What Is To Be Done?* (1902) and their meaning made more explicit during and after what was nominally the Second Congress of the RSDWP which met in Brussels and London in 1903.

We now know that the 1902 pamphlet signalled the birth of Leninism which, for all its originator's genuine and lasting commitment to the teachings of Marx and Engels, was as decided a novelty as the Revisionism and Economism he had attacked in the name of orthodoxy. Lenin's comrades, however, were not at first shocked by his conception of the centralized, conspiratorial party of professional revolutionaries, so reminiscent of the People's Will. Nor were they yet sensitive to its elitist potential, its certainty that the ordinary workingman could develop only a trade union consciousness in the conditions governing his life, or startled by the call for Marxist *intelligenty* to bring revolutionary consciousness to the proletariat from 'without'. Plekhanov, Martov, and their adherents had, after all, seemed to be saying much the same things: that they themselves, sons of the privileged classes, had to help the workers to attain political maturity, that they must be the catalysts of history and hurry along the proletariat's readiness to play the role history had assigned to it. They also agreed that police harassment made an open, democratically run movement a luxury. But Plekhanov and Martov had never thought of themselves as independent agents of history, only as its interpreters and helpers. They now began to fear that Lenin's views might lead to the party becoming a historical force in its own right, a small group acting in the name of the working class and on its behalf, a caricature of the tsarist bureaucracy. Sooner or later all the most distinguished and devoted Marxists of Lenin's generation recoiled from what they saw and parted company with him.

The schism in Russian Social Democracy began at the 1903 Congress which had been called to unite it. It came, improbably, over the definition of party membership and despite the fact that a solid majority of the fifty-seven delegates – only four of them workers – backed most of the party rules and programme that Lenin had drafted and presented to them on behalf of the *Iskra* editorial board. In the course of the debates, some disturbing questions were raised – over the extent of control the party's central organs would exercise over local committees and members, for example – and these contributed to the unease aroused by Lenin's insistence on having his way and the blunt tactics he employed to get it. That he should be so determined to have the Congress accept his version of Point One of the rules – criteria of party membership – when it was so little different from that of his ally Martov, alerted the delegates to its importance, as did the fact of Martov's opposition.

Lenin's draft of the statutes declared that a member of the party was anyone who accepted its programme, who gave material support to it and who also participated in one of its organizations. Martov's definition was nearly identical, except that for 'personal participation in one of the party's organizations' he substituted 'and by regular personal support under the guidance of one of its organizations'. The discussion which ensued on this and other issues forced Lenin's opponents at last to articulate their suspicions. They wanted a more open party, one which, although it would necessarily have a clandestine centre, would be linked in various ways and through all kinds of individuals to the proletarian masses, a party not so completely dominated by its hierarchy that it would lose touch with the workers and out of a fearful concern for doctrinal purity close itself off from the organizations the working class was creating. The RSDWP should be a mass party which helped the workers, not a group of plotters deciding for them.

Lenin was now accused, by L. D. Trotskii, among others, of excessive centralism, of wanting a staff without an army, of Bonapartism and Jacobinism. He in turn charged his opponents with anarchism and 'democratism'; their flabby unwillingness to draw a line between chatterboxes and doers would cause the movement's course to be set by adherents who were not subject to its discipline. Lenin was defeated on Point One by a vote of twenty-eight to twenty-one. Defeat turned into victory when a handful of Economists and Bund delegates withdrew, the latter because the Congress refused to recognize the Bund as the sole party representative of the Jewish workers it had been organizing with success in Western Russia, Poland, and Lithuania since 1897. Lenin prevailed when the make-up of the Central Committee and the new editorial board of *Iskra* were determined. On the slender basis of twenty ayes, two blank ballots, and twenty abstentions by Martov's faction, the Leninists now called themselves 'Bolsheviki', those of the majority, while their opponents were forever after to be known as the minority, 'Mensheviki'.

'Give us an organization of revolutionists,' Lenin had asked, 'and we shall overturn Russia'.[14] As a result of his victory he now had such an organization, on paper for the most part, for in achieving it he had also divided the forces and energies of Russian Social Democracy. The depth and permanence of the split would not be apparent for some time to come. The Congress had managed to adopt a common programme containing the party's 'minimum' demands. Their realization through the bourgeois revolution would bring about the end of autocracy and its replacement by a democratic republic; a unicameral legislature to which elections would be universal, equal, direct, and secret; extensive local autonomy; full civil and minority rights (including self-determination); a people's militia instead of a regular army; separation of church and state; free compulsory education to the age of sixteen; and in place of indirect taxes, progressive income and inheritance taxes. There was to be an eight-hour day for workers, as well as extensive social insurance, and for peasants an end to the legal disabilities from which they still suffered and the return of the cut-offs (otrezki), the lands they had tilled and lost at the time of emancipation. The programme stopped short of asking for the transfer to them of all gentry lands.

It was a radical and a revolutionary programme, but it was not a socialist one. It was designed to ensure that in the coming political battles Social Democracy would not be isolated. To proclaim too openly or too belligerently the ultimate goal of the proletarian revolution would only endanger cooperation with other classes, frighten and alienate them, weaken their determination and risk their seeking an accommodation with tsarism on the basis of limited concessions. Lenin was as orthodox as any of his party comrades in accepting the necessity for a transitional bourgeois-capitalist stage and in viewing its successful achievement as depending on a strong alignment of oppositionist forces, including peasants, liberal gentry, and bourgeois. But his distaste for collaboration with the liberals was greater than theirs – 'You turn your back to the liberals while we turn our faces to them,' Plekhanov once told him[15] – as was his revolutionary impatience or what has been called his 'fighting pessimism'.[16] The 1905 Revolution and the years following it confirmed Lenin's fears of a liberal betrayal and made him think that in Russia an uncompromisingly radical proletariat must take the bourgeoisie's role and hour on the historical stage and make the bourgeois revolution. It was then that the implications and possibilities of his organizational model became fully visible in the doctrinal and tactical flexibility it gave to Bolshevism.

The immediate effect of the birth of the Leninist party seemed to be, as some had predicted, its separation from the masses it wanted to attract and serve. Two years of strikes and demonstrations. Culminating in Bloody Sunday of 1905, were not caused and little utilized by Mensheviks or Bolsheviks. Both factions were so preoccupied with intra-party squabbles, so intent on winning over local committees in various parts of the country, that their efforts to contact and win the workers suffered as a result. This failure of the advance guard, the party, to establish close links with the main force of the proletariat cannot be blamed on Lenin's intransigence. The membership of both factions came disproportionately from the privileged strata of society, while most of the rank-and-file were of the urban and rural lower classes and included a high representation of industrial workers. And it was the Mensheviks, ironically, who had the more 'elitist', more educated and urban following – professionals and skilled workers – while Bolshevik recruiters were more successful among the younger, less qualified and less literate factory hands and peasants.

Exactly how many workers there were among the 12,000 active Social Democrats on the eve of the 1905 Revolution is a matter of some dispute – a majority according to a recent estimate – as is their factional distribution. There is no doubt, however, that Mensheviks and Bolsheviks alike were at this point led by *intelligenty* of upper- or middle-class background. The Bolsheviks soon acquired a junior or second level of leadership in which there were men, like the peasant's son and future head of state M. I. Kalinin and the Georgian cobbler's son I. V. Stalin, who came from the lower orders and whose contribution to the party was practical rather than theoretical. In their social composition it was the Bolsheviks who turned out to be the less elitist, more 'democratic' group, whereas Menshevism was structurally more open, intellectually more tolerant, and nationally more inclusive – less 'Russian' than its rival – because of the greater proportion of Jews and Georgians in its ranks. [17]

Thus Lenin's centralism was not directed against workers *qua* workers. It was to keep the party from losing sight of the Marxist vision of the future while it was engaged in the battles of the present. For the time being the intelligentsia embodied that vision, but workers too could rise to it and share in the leadership of Social Democracy. Lenin had no automatic preference for intellectuals. Indeed, the discipline and authority he so valued were as much designed to keep independent-minded and argumentative intellectuals in line as to prevent less discerning proletarians from falling into heresy or being seduced by a Zubatov or Gapon. The wide powers of the party's leading organs and narrow basis on which they rested, were to make possible a mass membership of differing levels of political maturity and to 'merge into a single whole the elemental destructive force of the masses with the conscious destructive force of the organization of revolutionaries'. [18] The wider the party opened its gates to a diverse membership, the greater was the need for firm and constant control from the centre.

The need had been demonstrated for Lenin by the tendency of the students, zemstvo employees, returned political exiles and advanced workers who had gravitated to Social Democracy after the turn of the century, to decide for themselves or their local committees what stand to take in relation to the growing movement of opposition in the country. The workers were no longer the only force that had openly taken the field against the government. There were others now, equally vocal and determined and more readily accessible. There was student unrest in the universities and secondary schools that found a wide echo in society and claimed its attention and support after clumsy efforts at repression. There was a renovated revolutionary populism which once again provided examples of heroic deeds that were more appealing and effective than the dry-as-dust debates of Marxist scholastics. Finally, there was the emergence of an overtly political liberalism whose determination and resources invited collaboration and even defection from Social Democrats. Protest and opposition to tsarism had become accepted and widely practised activities and revolution their entirely conceivable outcome. In this atmosphere of shared and realizable hopes, Lenin was doubly intent on marking his party off from others in order to preserve its separate identity and sense of special mission.

In the competition for the allegiance of radical-minded Russians, the Party of Socialist-Revolutionaries (SRs), founded in late 1901, was the most serious rival of Social Democracy. It represented the striving for unity and a common platform of the surviving veterans of Land and Liberty, of People's Will, and of younger admirers of the heroic tradition of populism. The latter in particular recognized that the tradition had to be refurbished so that it could respond to the changed needs and opportunities of the moment and stand comparison with the greater intellectual prestige and sophistication of the Marxists.

That task was not nearly as difficult as the continuing debates between the two camps made it appear, for revolutionary populism had no great amount of theoretical baggage to shed. Nor had its reliance on the peasantry, a chief point of difference with the Marxists, ever prevented populist propagandists and organizers from recognizing the importance of the workers and their revolutionary potential. Workers also belonged to the narod, and in the heyday of *narodnichestvo* most of them were still peasants or regarded themselves as such. Moreover, the greater likelihood of detection in the countryside and the experience of their rejection by the peasants in 1874, had made many narodniks turn to the factories as a more accessible and fruitful sphere of action. The first workers' 'Unions' were, in fact, organized by populists – a South-Russian one at Odessa (1872–75) and and a Northern Union at St Petersburg (1878–81). The 1879 programme of People's Will spoke of the urban workers' special importance to the success of the revolution and in 1897 the Saratov Union of Socialist Revolutionaries (one of the main components of the SR party) described the industrial proletariat as the advance guard of a working class which also included the peasants and the working intelligentsia, indeed all those who toiled and did not exploit the labour of others.

So elastic a definition of class had great advantages. It permitted the SRs to say that they did not, like the SDs, represent only wage labour and to seek a coalition of revolutionary forces to which a broad spectrum of individuals and social groups could be admitted on equal terms. This absence of doctrinal rigidity was also reflected in the party's internal structure. Loose and fairly informal, it left considerable autonomy of the Central Committee to local sections and complete tactical independence to the 'Combat Organization' which carried out the political murders of a Grand Duke, two interior ministers, and some 139 other officials. Terror, that legacy of the People's Will, was no longer expected to disorganize the government, force it into concessions, or serve as a substitute for the struggle of armed masses against police and troops. Yet it was accepted even by those SRs who disapproved of it as a useful and necessary, if auxiliary, weapon in the opening skirmishes against tsarism. Before the Revolution of 1905 it was successful beyond all expectations. A few SD groups were converted to terror and in 1902 Struve, by now a liberal, asked fellow-liberals to understand it as a 'historically inevitable and morally justifiable' response to the terror practiced by the state.[19] The assassination of Pleve in 1904 achieved what the killing of Alexander II had not: disorientation in the ranks of government and a change of course. It could not, however, satisfy or unify the revolutionaries.

Mensheviks and Bolsheviks alike were repeatedly warned by their leaders not to admire or imitate what Lenin called these 'revolutionary pyrotechnics'.[20] To him they were evidence that the Socialist-Revolutionaries, like their populist predecessors, had failed to understand the objective forces operative in society and to work with and through them. Terror absorbed too many energies and resources and betrayed a belief that individuals could determine the course of history or force its pace. If the neo-populists admitted that capitalism (and the working class) had become a fact of Russian life – and it would have been quixotic for them to try to deny it – they had yet to draw the correct conclusions from this.

Primarily the work of Victor Chernov, the outstanding leader and thinker of the SRs, neo-populist ideology was and remained an eclectic set of assumptions which never hardened into doctrine. It reflected the breadth of view and humanity of its author and like his party tried to reconcile differences and even to accommodate contradictions. Both ideology and party were eventually to disintegrate because of this, but the many sympathizers they attracted seemed to make up for the absence of discipline and cohesion. The 50,000 men and women who were formally members of the Socialist Revolutionary Party in autumn 1906 were only one third the number the Social Democrats could boast in early 1907. But the SRs had some 350,000 followers who collaborated with their organizations or were said to be 'under constant party influence'. Moreover, the figure of 150,000 SDs for May 1907 includes, besides 38,000 Mensheviks and 46,000 Bolsheviks, members of the Bund as well as of the Polish and Latvian Social Democrats.[21] In 1917 the SRs became the country's most popular party, but numbers did not assure victory – which went to the Bolsheviks. The fate of the SRs might have served Lenin as a text for his preachments on discipline, firm leadership, and binding doctrine; not until 1906 did they hold their first congress and adopt a party programme.

What any Marxist was bound to find most disturbing and challenging to his beliefs and tactics in the programme which Chernov constructed was the importance assigned to the peasants. Chernov himself had never written them off, had conducted propaganda among them in his youth and in the late 1890s had organized the first peasant 'brotherhood' or union in the area of Tambov. It became a model for others, some of them closely linked to his party, others, like the all-Russian Peasants' Union (founded in August 1905) quite independent of it. The outbreak of massive agrarian disorders in Poltava and Kharkov provinces in the spring of 1902 reminded even those few SRs who had forgotten it of their populist heritage and of the fact that they had turned from the villages to the cities by necessity rather than choice. It seemed to them that the rebellious countryside opened up greater opportunities than the factories offered. Besides, they now found the peasants less naive, less suspicious of town-bred *intelligenty* (whom they had met in larger numbers as zemstvo specialists) and less trusting of the benevolence of the tsar.

All this confirmed Chernov in his conviction that the toiling peasants – the vast majority of the class – could also be brought into the revolutionary camp to become its main army and, what is more, won over to socialism. The SRs would not, like the Marxists, look upon peasants as backward, a petty bourgeoisie condemned to disappear; nor would they set the poorest among them against the rest. That would only drive the bulk of the class into the arms of reaction. Instead the peasants should be shown where their true interests lay: in the solidarity of all toilers of town and country. The real conflict was between those who lived by the labour of their fellow-men and those who did not. Into the concept of class war there was thus introduced a moral note which was as characteristic of SRs and populists as their common belief in the value of the human personality and the power of the human will. This is why they valued political activism, personal commitment and sacrifice more highly than ideology. Marxist determinism was as little to their liking as Marxist neglect and suspicion of the peasants as petty bourgeois. It was in the traditional areas of peasant poverty and rebelliousness, in the black soil districts from Kharkov to Samara and across the Volga to Perm and Viatka, that the party's speakers and agitators found receptive audiences and also the votes that were to give them a majority in the elections to the Constituent Assembly in December 1917. The steadiest and most reliable contingents of the party's members (as distinct from voters) were, however, furnished by the cities – by the intelligentsia, by urban craftsmen, clerks and employees as well as by industrial workers. In 1905 workers and artisans accounted for nearly half the active membership. Thus the Socialist-Revolutionaries were, after all, a party for rather than of the peasants whose widely scattered numbers and sporadic outbursts so loosely jointed an organization could translate into power only through the promise of land and the ballot box. When the victorious Bolsheviks enacted the land programme of the SRs and denied them the ballot box, they also closed off their road to power.

Power – the ability and willingness to impose their socialist vision – was not, as time would show, the first priority of the SRs. It was the democratic revolution, the end of autocracy, the democratic (possibly federal) republic, local autonomy, self-determination for national minorities, the universal franchise, the referendum and initiative, the eight-hour day, social security, a voice in management for the workers. All land was to be 'socialized' and turned over to peasant communes or associations for apportionment on an egalitarian basis to those who worked it. The immediate goal was the clearing away of the obstacles which had blocked the free expression of the popular will which would undoubtedly be in favour of socialism. Its advantages would become evident to peasants and workers, aided by the intelligentsia, once the old regime, the main prop of capitalism, of inequality and selfishness was removed. Then there would be a transition period in which capitalism would be gradually restricted and the foundations of a socialist order laid. Then too the socialization of industry would begin and the peasants change voluntarily to full agrarian socialism, from the collective ownership of the soil to its collective cultivation. No compulsion would be employed and none, the SRs were confident, was needed. The increasing weight and attractiveness of the socialist sector would guarantee the coming of socialism.

There was much in this programme that liberals and Marxists could accept, with the latter sharing hopes for the eventual transformation of the political into a social revolution. The Social Democrats could not, however, simply promise ownership of the land to the peasants; that would be a backward step away from socialism. The precondition of socialism in agriculture, as in industry, was the development of capitalism, the dissolution of the commune, the growth of large-scale farming, and the transformation of the dispossessed peasants into rural and urban proletarians. The Marxists thought it romantic nonsense to look upon communal traditions, in agriculture or craft industries, as favouring the coming of socialism. Distributing land to the peasants for their individual use would only prolong their attachment to it and preserve an inefficient agriculture. The SDs were limited, therefore, to an embarrassingly modest agrarian platform in their 1903 programme, the return of the cut-offs. They also criticized their socialist rivals for planning to inhibit capitalism in the transition period, for thinking that socialist construction could begin before capitalism had run its course and done its work of economic modernization. The populists were once again asserting an unscientific voluntarism which would frighten the bourgeoisie and weaken its resolve to fight tsarism. Their revolutionism wasn't socialist and their socialism wasn't revolutionary, *Iskra* taunted the SRs.[22]

Iskra was right in discerning that the SRs might lack the will to make the socialist revolution once the political one had been achieved. They wanted socialism, but they were reluctant to force it upon an unwilling or unready people. The Mensheviks in 1917 shared that reluctance, while Lenin's Bolsheviks, in a curious reversal of previous positions, embraced the maximum goals of the SRs as realizable, pushed for the proletarian *and peasant* revolution within weeks of tsarism's fall and, abandoning their own revised agrarian programme, adopted that of the Socialist-Revolutionaries. By Lenin's own admission it was the basis of the Bolsheviks' success in October 1917.

In Lenin's eyes the great threat the SRs posed to the unity of the socialist camp was their contradictory and vacillating conduct towards the political forces of the bourgeoisie. Other Marxists joined him in laying bare the theoretical confusions of neo-populism, but none was as vociferous as he in denouncing their blurring of sharp class lines – in building their heterogenous movement and in its ambivalent relations with the liberals. SRs, Mensheviks, and Bolsheviks had all embraced the formula of striking together and marching separately against absolutism. He was merely more fearful than most that entering a tactical coalition with the liberals would lead to their dominating the opposition. His fears were deepened when some SRs attended a conference of opposition parties in Paris in October 1904. The Social Democrats revealed their own uncertainties by first expressing an interest in the meeting, then boycotting and attacking it as a bourgeois affair. The Bolsheviks explained that they did not wish to give the appearance of fusing with other parties, yet offered their support on certain minimal conditions.

The emergence of a vigorous, organized political liberalism in the years after 1900 was truly a problem for all socialists. Viewed as the political arm of the bourgeoisie, liberalism was no longer an abstration taken from Marxist texts or the experience of the West. It was now a fact and a force – with prominent and respected leaders, with legal as well as illegal newspapers, with links to society and roots in local government, the universities and professions, with financial resources and wide sympathies the parties of the Left could not hope to match. Would entering a coalition with such allies not strengthen the bourgeoisie to the point where it could swallow its lesser partners? On the other hand, would fighting instead of supporting the bourgeoisie not frighten it and cause it to recoil from carrying out its historically assigned task? There could be no truly satisfactory resolution of such a dilemma as long as liberalism was thought to be an effective social and political force, or as long as the socialists were unsure that they could rally the inchoate masses to their banners and point them in a desired political direction. Suspended between the unguided rebelliousness of the masses and a purposeful, fast-growing liberation movement of the middle and upper class, the Left turned its attention and energies now to one, now to the other. As a result it did less than either to bring about the Revolution of 1905.

The socialists' disagreements over how to deal with the liberals reflected differing appraisals of liberal strength and determination and of their own prospects for building a mass movement. Lenin, perhaps, lacked confidence that the small Bolshevik faction would soon be able to hold its own in a coalition, whereas the SRs were optimistic that they could attract peasants as well as educated men to their ranks. Equally important were divergent interpretations of the character of Russian liberalism. It was a more complex phenomenon than Marx had described and consisted largely of elements – landowners, intellectuals, professionals – which it was hard to subsume under the general heading of bourgeoisie or capitalist business class. For those socialists (mainly the SRs) whose Marxism informed but did not determine their view of the world, this made possible a range of positions, from strict separatism to close cooperation. For the liberals themselves it meant an independence of class interests and a non-class appeal, as well as a degree of political radicalism and social reformism, that classical liberalism in the West had rarely displayed. The willingness to countenance revolution and the commitment to social justice were less the outcome of the liberals' imitative Westernism (as some of their critics charged) than of autocracy's deafness to pleas for change. Russian liberalism was moderate at its origins, and significant segments always remained so, hopeful of persuading the monarchy and of cooperating with it. If most liberals found themselves in revolutionary opposition in 1905, it was tsarism's intransigence that had driven them there.

As early as 1879 Ivan Petrunkevich, the zemstvo leader from Chernigov, had rejected the idea of a liberalized autocracy and had spoken out for an elected constituent assembly to determine the nature of Russia's government. Such revolutionary notes were rarely sounded by liberals before the twentieth century, however. The enlightened members of the gentry who used the zemstvos as the main forum for voicing their political aspirations were very much more restrained. In the 1860s they petitioned for a national zemstvo, for 'crowning the edifice' of local self-government by an elected national representation; more often they asked that delegates of the zemstvos be allowed to meet for the discussion of common concerns, or protested against administrative restrictions of zemstvo rights and functions. They were severely chastised and their more vocal spokesmen arrested or banished to their estates. The liberals subsided and kept their peace until the late 1870s.

The Russo-Turkish War of 1877–78 and acts of revolutionary terror revived hopes that a beleaguered government might see the utility of concessions and an accommodation. The bureaucracy nourished these hopes by tolerating the renewed expression of demands for political reform and by quietly allowing the chairmen of four provincial zemstvos to meet in 1879 and form a Zemstvo Union. But as the constitutionalist goals of the movement became clearer and its pleas for 'true self-government, the inviolability of the individual, the independence of the courts and freedom of the press' grew more insistent, further meetings at the national or local level were prohibited. They continued, none the less, with the Union financing publication of a newspaper abroad, *Volnoe Slovo* ('Free Word'), and two of its leaders (F. I. Rodichev and Petrunkevich) negotiating unsuccessfully with People's Will for an end to assassinations and a common struggle for political liberty. Russian liberalism had made its first, if abortive, opening to the Left.

The constitutional rights and liberties which Alexander II had granted the Bulgarians after their liberation from the Turks he thought inappropriate or premature for his Russian subjects. He was prepared only to concede a consultative voice to a few appointed experts and elected representatives of town councils and zemstvos. His successor would not go so far as that and kept even the most loyal and educated Russians from any share or say in the making of domestic or foreign policy. The first of March 1881 and the reaction following it divided and discouraged the liberals. The more timid agreed with Chicherin when he told Pobedonostsev that a limited monarchy and political liberty were ideals for a remote future, that state and society must now join to combat the forces of destruction, and that the goal of unity and order would be furthered by including nobility and zemstvo delegates in the Council of State. That advice too was ignored. Even the boldest of the constitutionalists were soon forced to admit that liberalism could not survive as an organized movement. By 1883 'Free Word' closed down for lack of funds and their source, the Zemstvo Union, expired a year later.

The dream of a constitution was laid to rest or deferred; 'small deeds' of public service of a non-political kind and cautiously expressed hopes for improved social and economic policies replaced it. The retreat from politics did not in these dark days cause liberals to abandon the call for social justice they had sounded in the past and would continue to sound in the future. Russian liberalism, one of its chief organs, the monthly 'Messenger of Europe', protested in November 1884, is not merely a copy of the selfish bourgeois liberalism of the West with which radicals and conservatives try to identify it. It is not the *laisser-faire* liberalism of the capitalist class, nor an attempt by the gentry to seek political power in compensation for the loss of serfs and land.

Where are the speeches or articles defending property qualifications for voting, the unrestricted rights of capital or landed property, the strict indifference of the state to economic questions, the favouring of the interests of the minority in industry, agriculture, finance or local self-government? [Liberalism] stands for the Peasant Land Bank, for inheritance duties, for a surcharge on the profits of big industry and trade, for the earliest possible adoption of the progressive income tax, for a radical reform of factory legislation in favour of the workers, for organizing local government in such a way that it will not be the monopoly of one class or controlled by powerful land-owners; it is for extensive state control of corporations, for the legal regulation of banks and railroads, and for the limitation of private property rights on behalf of the public interest.[23]

The political and social ideals and sentiments which had given birth to liberalism did not disappear. Liberals might no longer agree on the need or desirability of a constitution; not all of them shared the social concerns voiced by the 'Messenger of Europe'. But they were all offended by the 'counter-reforms' of the 1880s, by attacks on the press and the courts, and especially by what looked like a concerted drive against the very existence of local self-govern-ment. If even that arena, to which moderates were now willing to confine their activities, was going to be denied to them, there was little prospect of count-ering the arguments of constitutionalists and radicals for a frontal attack on autocracy.

The moderate case – a variety of liberal Slavophilism – was made more difficult by the arbitrary conduct of bureaucracy and police. Could they really be curbed and made to observe legal norms if the autocrat in whose name they acted remained unchecked? In the reign of Alexander III it was hard to see the monarchy as the guarantor of legality or as the defender of the people from the transgressions of his officials. It was he who had sanctioned the expansion of their powers, sometimes by decree rather than by legal enactment of the State Council, sometimes by going against the majority of its senior bureaucrats.

This had happened, for example, when elected justices of the peace were replaced by appointed land-captains and when a new University Statute (1884) subjected students, faculties, and curricula to administrative control and ended university autonomy. There were student disorders in 1884 and 1887; in Moscow they became almost an annual occurrence. The expulsions and arrests to which they led radicalized many young people, angered professors and par-ents, and made the universities a recruiting ground for a revived constitutional movement. Its ranks were filled with university graduates who had gone to take up service in the zemstvos either as elected deputies or, more often, as professional employees. They helped greatly to broaden the social base and the intellectual horizon of liberalism and to return it to politics.

It was the government which gave the chief impetus to the renewal of lib-eral activism. In the wake of the 1891 famine zemstvo men tried again to form a common organization and were strengthened in their determination by the rude rebuff Nicholas handed them in his 'senseless dreams' speech of January

1895. They had asked very little and had done so in the most loyal tones: that there might be unity between society and the throne and that the voice of the zemstvos and town councils be heard when they spoke of the nation's needs. When the formation of a new Zemstvo Union was prohibited, its guiding spirits met in regular private conferences. In 1899 essentially the same people established *Beseda* ('Symposium'), a society of elected zemstvo deputies which included a determined minority of constitutionalists. The most prominent member of both groups was D. N. Shipov, chairman of the Moscow province zemstvo, who still harboured hopes that the tsar could be persuaded by legal means to resume the path of reform and the constitutionalists dissuaded from asking for formal limits on his powers. The vision of a benevolent monarch, of a tamed bureaucracy which respected the law, and of strengthened self-government whose representatives would give their views on pending legislation seemed to Shipov attainable; it was in keeping with Russian traditions and preferable to the strife of parliaments and parties.

In 1900 and 1901 when Shipov put forth his programme, it was probably already too late to command enough support to force governmental acceptance. Moreover, the authorities appeared bent on doing all they could to undercut Shipov's moderate position. New restrictions and punishments rained down on individuals as well as private and public bodies during 1899 and 1900. Limits were placed on the taxing powers and competence of the zemstvos; the independence of the Moscow Law Society was curbed; the Imperial Economic Society was closed down for five years; student demonstrators were drafted and the autonomy of Finland, which Russia's monarchs had until then respected, was curtailed.

In November 1904 a conference of zemstvo leaders defeated Shipov's views by 71 votes to 27. The majority pronounced in favour of a constitution and for a freely elected assembly that would not merely advise the monarch but make laws and control the state and the actions of its officials. The minority had become the majority. The way was open for the anti-autocratic coalition that was both feared and wished for among the socialists and that Shipov had tried to forestall. He continued to be admired, respected, and active, but events had overtaken the liberalism of conscience and conciliation he represented.

The leftward evolution of Russian liberalism which carried along the zemstvo constitutionalists was neither initiated nor, in all cases, completed by them. Its chief advocates and tacticians were urban intellectuals, like the historian Pavel Miliukov and the erstwhile Social Democrat Petr Struve. The latter's progression from Marxism to liberalism by way of Revisionism was not, he himself insisted, a sudden conversion; it followed from the realization that no single class could be the carrier of the ethical ideas underlying freedom or the instrument of its achievement. He had been a liberal first, and it was only the earlier weakness and the apoliticism of the liberals, Struve's biographer R. E. Pipes has shown, that accounted for his joining the Social Democrats. The signs of vigour, therefore, which liberalism displayed after the beginning of the new century led Struve and other ex-Marxists (including the philosopher Nikolai Berdiaev) to think that the creation of a broadly based liberal party was possible and that it offered the best chance for reaching the goal of political freedom that Marxists and populists also shared. With funds raised largely in zemstvo circles, Struve began in June 1902 to publish *Osvobozhdenie* ('Liberation') in Germany. A Union of Liberation was founded in September 1903 and formally established in January 1904. Like the Marxists and the Socialist-Revolutionaries, the liberals now had an illegal organization and a journal which was smuggled into Russia and served to link the Union's affiliates and to define their common aims.

In the very first issue of 'Liberation' Struve had written that the political and cultural liberation of Russia could not be the task of only one class, one party, or one doctrine, but that it must become the cause of the nation as a whole.[24] His conviction that liberalism could and should be independent of any one social group and not identify itself with the economic interests of the propertied classes was reflected, after a period of initial moderation, in the pages of the journal. With the help of Miliukov, it found its way into the programme adopted by the Union of Liberation in October 1904. Its demands for an eight-hour day for workers and for the compulsory (if compensated) expropriation of private lands for the peasants were radical, indeed, while the call for a Constituent Assembly (to be elected by universal franchise) was nothing short of revolutionary, for it challenged the very basis of the emperor's authority and the monarchy itself. The Union also resolved to cooperate with the parties of the Left and to work out a programme of common action with them. Within weeks Liberationists, SRs, and representatives of revolutionary or radical groups from Finland, Poland, Georgia, Armenia and Latvia had met in Paris. To energize the groups to its right, the Union urged the zemstvos to call for a constitution, arranged for a campaign of political banquets and began to organize unions of the professions (doctors, lawyers, teachers, etc.).

There were liberals who recoiled from what they considered the extremism of the Liberationists, but their position was once again undermined by the stubbornness of the tsar. The mounting chorus of protest and agitation which the Union had helped to orchestrate, and the arguments of his minister of the interior, Sviatopolk-Mirskii, finally persuaded Nicholas to permit the discussion of governmental reforms by his advisers. A decree of 12 December 1904 promised a measure of religious toleration, relaxation of the censorship, and an improvement in the zemstvo law. But there was no mention of any role, not even a purely consultative one, for representatives of the public. Mirskii had proposed adding individuals elected by the zemstvos and other bodies to the Council of State, but Nicholas vetoed his suggestion.

It is doubtful that even Mirskii understood how far matters had gone, how little prospect there was of pacifying the majority of the liberals (much less the country) by the modest concessions he had wished to offer. On 30 October 1904 Mirskii's wife recorded in her diary the visit Shipov and another zemstvo leader had paid the minister . Echoing her husband's reactions, she complained of his callers' urgency, of their inability to understand that it was impossible to correct in two months all the mistakes made in the course of ten or even forty-five years.[25] If even Shipov could be thought impatient by the man who was considered the liberal among the tsar's ministers, the gulf between society and state was deep indeed and the thought of accommodation utopian.

The Union of Liberation had come to dominate liberalism and through it liberalism came to accept revolution and began to develop a mass appeal. The Union of Liberation had also enabled liberalism to unify under its wing a broader spectrum of society and opinion than had ever before joined for common action in Russia. That unity, short-lived and fragile as it was, would be a decisive factor in the defeat inflicted on autocracy in October 1905.

REFERENCES

1. Henri Troyat, *Tolstoy* (Garden City, NY, 1967), p. 567.
2. Lionel Decle, *The New Russia* (London, 1906), p. 161.
3. R. Wortman, *The Crisis of Russian Populism* (Cambridge, 1967), p. 187.
4. Alexander Ulianov quoted by Leonard Schapiro, *Rationalism and Nationalism in Russian Nineteenth-Century Thought* (New Haven, Conn., and London, 1967), p. 129.
5. A. K. Wildman, *The Making of a Workers' Revolution* (Chicago, 1967), p. 145.
6. S. M. Schwarz, 'Populism and early Russian Marxism on ways of economic development of Russia: the 1880s and 1890s' in E. J. Simmons (ed.), *Continuity and Change in Russian and Soviet Thought* (Cambridge, Mass., 1955), p. 47.
7. A. P. Mendel, *Dilemmas of Progress in Tsarist Russia* (Cambridge, Mass, 1961), p. 59.
8. L. H. Haimson, *The Russian Marxists and the Origins of Bolshevism* (Cambridge, Mass., 1955), p. 105.
9. S. H. Baron, *Plekhanov: The Father of Russian Marxism* (Stanford, Cal., 1963), p. 122.
10. G. V. Plekhanov, 'Our differences' in *Selected Philosophical Works*, English edn (Moscow and London, 1961–81), I, pp. 373–4.
11. Angelica Balabanoff, *My Life as a Rebel* (New York, 1938), p. 18.
12. J. L. H. Keep, *The Rise of Social Democracy in Russia* (Oxford, 1963), p. 20.
13. Wildman, op. cit., p. 137.
14. V. I. Lenin, 'What is to be done? Burning questions of our movement' in R. C. Tucker (ed.), *The Lenin Anthology* (New York, 1975), p. 79.
15. Haimson, op. cit., p. 107.
16. A. G. Meyer, *Leninism* (Cambridge, Mass. 1957), p. 84.
17. David Lane, *The Roots of Russian Communism* (London and University Park, Pa., 1975), pp. 11–58; W. E. Mosse, 'Makers of the Soviet Union', *Slavonic and East European Review* 46 (Jan. 1968), pp. 141–64.
18. Tucker, op. cit., p. 108.
19. R. E. Pipes, *Struve. Liberal on the Left, 1870–1905* (Cambridge, Mass., 1970), p. 322.
20. Haimson, op. cit., p. 151.
21. Lane, op. cit., p. 13; O. H. Radkey, *The Agrarian Foes of Bolshevism* (New York, 1953), p. 63.

22. B. Nikolaevskii, preface to V. M. Chernov, *Pered burei* (New York, 1953), p. 14.
23. From K. K. Arsenev, *Za chetvert veka* (Petrograd, 1915), p. 151.
24. Pipes, op. cit., p. 319.
25. 'Dnevnik Kn. E. A. Sviatopolk-Mirskoi, 1904–1905'. *Istoricheskie zapiski* 77 (1965), p. 251.

CHAPTER EIGHT

Empire abroad: foreign policy till 1905

If, as Witte charged in his memoirs, Viacheslav Pleve really wished and worked in 1903 for 'a small, victorious war' against Japan in order to stifle domestic discontent and disturbances, he was in a minority among Russian statesmen.[1] Almost without exception they urged caution and restraint in foreign affairs after the loss of the Crimean War (1853–56). The shame and trauma of that defeat at the hands of England, France, and Turkey were only partially redeemed by victory over the latter in 1877–78. The Balkan campaign against a presumed inferior Ottoman Empire had been unexpectedly costly and difficult. The post-Crimean reforms were far from having cured the nation's grave deficiencies in supply and transport, in army organization and command. Russia's continued economic and military weakness, moreover, contributed to her diplomatic defeat when, after reaching the outskirts of Constantinople and imposing the victor's Treaty of San Stefano (March 1878), she was compelled by a congress of powers held in Berlin (June–July 1878) to surrender a portion of her hardwon gains.

Turkey's territorial losses in Europe were cut back and the gains of Russia's allies and clients, the Christian peoples on whose behalf she had fought the Turks – Roumanians, Serbians, Montenegrins, and Bulgarians – were considerably reduced; so were the Russian government's influence in the Balkans and its prestige at home. Troubled by the exhaustion of his treasury, his armies, and the rise of revolutionary terror, Alexander II was forced to consent to the Treaty of Berlin. It marked the humiliating outcome of a war which he had entered reluctantly, a war which his chief ministers had opposed or tried to avoid by seeking agreement with the European powers for common pressure on Turkey to secure the religious and national rights of the Sultan's rebellious Slavic subjects in the Balkans. Only when that effort failed, because of Turkish recalcitrance and British reluctance, had Alexander felt compelled to declare war in April 1877.

The waverings and misgivings which preceded and accompanied the tsar's decision reveal certain constants of Russian conduct in the international arena. There was, to begin with, a too painful awareness of Russia's lack of money, railways, and industrial capacity to allow recourse to arms if that meant risking a major or prolonged war. Not only was success unlikely in such a conflict; failure would undo what progress had already been made in building military strength and undermine the economic improvements that were essential for its achievement and for the maintenance of domestic tranquillity. And any unilateral attempt to meet the country's foreign needs and goals by force would inevitably and almost everywhere meet with the determined opposition of the European powers. This was particularly true of Russia's neighbours Germany and Austria in areas (notably the Balkans) where one or both claimed influence or interests, and of Great Britain when it came to the question of Turkey, the Turkish Straits (Dardanelles and Bosphorus), and Russia's rights and role in both.

Recognizing these harsh facts of national and international life, the makers of Russian policy throughout the nineteenth century were concerned to let their counterparts know that they were striving not for hegemony in Europe but only for what they considered to be their vital interests and historic rights and that they meant to achieve these by negotiation and agreement. This Nicholas I had sought in 1853 from the British, whom he assured that he had no intention of taking Constantinople, but would not allow any other power to do so. The Russian war plan of 1877 made it clear that occupation of the Turkish capital (not, in the event, carried out) would be a purely military and temporary measure and that there was no thought of making a permanent conquest of it or of the Bosphorus.

In 1896 Nicholas II and his advisers once again weighed seizure of the Straits because of their great strategic and economic importance to Russia, but rejected it as not feasible on military and political grounds. It was thought better to try to secure international consent for a revision of the Convention of 1841 which closed the Straits to all foreign warships and thus barred Russian egress from the Black Sea. Even in an area so close to home and supposedly the age-old object of their dreams and power, the Russians moved with care and circumspection. It was the view of N. K. Giers, the foreign minister of Alexander III, that Russian hopes for acquisition of the Straits were utopian and impossible of realization for generations to come.[2] It would have astounded and amused him and his master to learn that in 1867 – the very year Alaska was sold to the United States – Karl Marx had declared world domination to be the changeless goal of Russian policy.[3]

The country's leaders were not so desperate or confident as to contemplate going it alone and upsetting a balance of power which they had themselves helped to establish and preserve. They were traditional statesmen and calculating diplomats who thought of themselves and their fatherland as part of an international community of states whose members competed fiercely but who also observed certain limits which it was dangerous to cross. They were neither world conquerors for the sake of gain or glory nor were they driven by a heady sense of mission in the name of Orthodox Christianity or Slavic brotherhood. Panslavism, they believed, might be good poetry, but it made for bad politics; like all nationalistic and messianic doctrines it had a popular and democratic component whose dynamism was unpredictable and conflicted with the conservative and dynastic principles on which the monarchy rested. The tsars could not place themselves squarely at the head of a crusade for Slavic unity and liberation from Ottoman and Austrian rule because they realized that in their own multi-national empire the call for national liberation would find an explosive echo.

Caution and conservatism, restraint and rationality, did not, however, mean passivity or withdrawal. Isolationism, although it might have served the country well at times, was never considered a serious option. Alexander III and Nicholas II could not conceive of surrendering the great power position to which they believed their nation was entitled by history and destiny, by its human and material potential. They would not have agreed with Marx and others who saw as an eternal imperative of the Russian state the constant process of growth and conquest that had by 1914 transformed the principality of Muscovy, with an area of 15,000 square miles in 1462, into a continental empire of 8.6 million square miles reaching from the Carpathians to the Pacific, from the Arctic to the borders of Persia, Afghanistan, and China.

But neither did Russia's rulers ignore the legacy their ancestors had bequeathed to them or resign from the burdens of empire for fear of its disintegration or the loss of their throne. Ever since Peter the Great, the first Emperor (*Imperator*), had founded and named the Russian Empire (*Rossiiskaia Imperiia*) to mark his victory over the Swedes, its greatness was closely linked with the fate and fortunes of the Romanov dynasty. Empire need not and did not imply universal ambitions or dominion; its proclamation by Peter had been no more than a demand for recognition, for equal status among the kingdoms and empires of Europe, a declaration of political maturity and independence. Yet for the country's elite certainly, and for many of its subjects probably, the maintenance of the empire's power and honour was the first duty of the ruler: how he performed it was a measure of his ability and their respect. Both the empire and the dynasty came to an end when Nicholas II failed them as a leader during the test of the greatest war Russia had ever had to fight.

After the Napoleonic Wars and the annexation of Poland, Finland, Bessarabia (and much of the Caucasus), there was no further extension of Russian settlement and sovereignty to the west, and the empire could be considered a conservative power in territorial as well as political terms. Yet there were still acquisitions: from 1858 to 1860 in the Far East, along the Amur and the Pacific (where Vladivostok, 'Ruler of the East', was founded) as well as in Central Asia from 1864 to 1885. The empire's security and the monarchy's prestige could on occasion and in selected areas be interpreted to require expansion or a forward policy. Perhaps precisely because in Europe Russia was checked and contained in the nineteenth century by powerful neighbours, energies turned towards Asia. Russia, as Foreign Minister Prince Gorchakov had declared in a circular note of 1864, was in its Central Asian advance only following the example of the United States in America, of France in Africa, and of Britain in India: concern for the safety of their settlements and the interests of trade had compelled these states to seize control of neighbouring territories occupied by warlike tribes.[4]

Gorchakov's insistence that Russia was behaving no differently from other colonizers, that, like them, she was acting out of necessity and bringing the blessings of civilization to 'primitive' peoples, was difficult to refute. He might have made a still better argument for Russian expansion by pointing out that it took place in territories contiguous to the homeland and that Russia, unlike the Western colonial powers, had not crossed the seas to conquer distant and alien lands which could not possibly pose a threat to the mother country. There was, indeed, something natural, almost elemental and irresistible, about the long course of Russian colonization and migration. In two and a half centuries, and sometimes without the sponsorship of the state, it had taken millions of peasants beyond its frontiers to the southern steppes and Siberia in search of land and freedom. The state soon followed them, however, and by imposing serfdom (in the south) or its own authority (in Siberia) it restricted freedom and mobility.

During the nineteenth and early twentieth centuries such migration as was allowed had to take place within the boundaries of the empire; not until the end of the period was it officially encouraged and supported to relieve overcrowding at home. Arid, remote, and turbulent Central Asia held few rewards for Russian traders, manufacturers, or agriculturalists until, many years and many millions of rubles later, railroads, pacification, and irrigation made it truly a part of the empire and began to redeem the promises of its conquerors.[5]

Military men for the most part, these conquerors had seized the chance, offered by fluid frontiers which they had been sent to stabilize, of gaining fame for themselves and demonstrating to the world that in spite of defeat in the Crimea and retreat at Berlin, their nation was still to be reckoned a formidable power. Although official St Petersburg, fearing complications with the British in India, had initially hesitated to support the actions of local commanders who at times exceeded their orders, it too took pride in the successes of Russian arms; so did important segments of public opinion. For many who had been disheartened by their country's poor showing in war and diplomacy, victory — even victory over the weak native rulers of Kokand, Bokhara, Khiva and their Turkoman warriors — was a reaffirmation of the nation's will and vitality. 'With an aspiration for Asia, our spirit and forces will be regenerated,' Dostoevskii wrote.[6] Generals M. G. Cherniaev, the conqueror of Tashkent (1865), and D. M. Skobelev, whose victory at Geok Tepe (1881) all but completed the conquest of Central Asia, became national heroes who were celebrated by press and public.[7]

Turkestan, besides buoying the self-esteem and confidence of the military and the government, also brought more tangible benefits. Through the possibility of pressure on the British in India, it offered a means of asserting Russia's European presence and aims which the English and Austrians often blocked. And Europe was and remained for the governmental and social elites the decisive testing-ground, the real yardstick of advance or retreat. 'Our future lies in Europe, not in Asia,' Katkov had written in his *Moskovskie Vedomosti*: ('Moscow Gazette').[8] Asia could momentarily compensate for disappointments elsewhere, but in so far as there was a public which took an interest in foreign affairs and could make this interest known, it cared less for the acquisition of huge tracts of land beyond the Caspian than for influence and respect along the Black Sea and the Danube.

That fact was forcefully impressed upon Alexander II at the time of the Turkish War of 1877/78 and of the anti-Turkish risings in Serbia, Montenegro and Bulgaria which preceded it. Much as the tsar and his advisers distrusted the enthusiastic clamour for Russian intervention that was voiced in newspapers and meetings of the Slavic Benevolent Committees, they were yet mindful of the echo it had found in much of educated society, among the military, in the government and in the imperial family itself. It was impossible to remain aloof without appearing to concede the charge of Panslavists like Ivan Aksakov and strident patriots like Katkov that the monarchy and the bureaucracy were deficient in national feeling and decisiveness. That Alexander yielded in the end to the agitation he had earlier ignored and at times silenced, underlines the way in which his liberalizing reforms made it necessary to take some account of public opinion on questions of foreign policy. 'Either the government takes this popular movement in hand and guides it,' Pobedonostsev had warned in June 1876, 'or it will grow wider and wilder . . . and may even turn against the government with feelings of suspicion and hostility.'[9]

Opposed to unauthorized and uncontrolled expressions of popular sentiment, even when they came from the most loyal and conservative strata of society, Pobedonostsev worried that nationalist fervour, if not vented abroad, might turn inward and open a gulf betwen state and nation 'deeper than any our history has known'. Always the pessimist, he exaggerated the dangers threatening the regime, for liberals and radicals, whom he feared most, were to an unusual degree preoccupied with home affairs. They either viewed calls to imperial greatness as distractions from pressing social and economic problems, or they saw foreign entanglements as offering opportunities for exacting concessions from the government and, perhaps, for weakening it.

The experience of the war of 1877–78 none the less created both inside and outside the government a heightened awareness of the domestic dimensions of foreign affairs. Foreign policy remained before as well as after the constitutional changes of 1905 the exclusive prerogative of the monarch and a small circle of advisers who were the executors of his will rather than independent agents. But relations with the rest of the world could no longer be insulated from broader interests, pressures and emotions.

This was pre-eminently true of relations with Austria-Hungary and Prussia-Germany, and most especially the latter. The bonds, though often strained, which for a century had linked the two monarchies were forged by their shared conservatism and resistance to revolutionary nationalism in divided Poland; by the family connections of their ruling houses; by the great role German markets, capital, and industry had come to play in the Russian economy in the 1860s and 1870s; and by Russia's need of friends and allies in her post-Crimean isolation. That very need, born of weakness, also bred powerful feelings of resentment. They were to grow, when Prussia, aided by Russia's benevolent neutrality, defeated Austria (in 1866) and France (in 1871) to assume leadership of a united German Empire, now the continent's dominant state.

Determined to safeguard his creation from any efforts an embittered France might make to recover the position and territories she lost in 1871,Otto von Bismarck, the Imperial Chancellor, extended the hand of reconciliation to Austria. When the rulers of the two Germanic empires met in Berlin in 1872, Alexander II, fearful lest his imperial cousins become too intimate, asked to join them. Their separate and collective anxieties led to diplomatic and military agreements designed to preserve the status quo in the Balkans and Central Europe and culminated in 1873 in the Three Emperors' League. Less a formal alliance than a declaration of monarchial solidarity against subversive movements, the League also gave Germany the assurance of support or non-interference should there be trouble with France.

But none of the partners could long forget their underlying incompatibilities. There was a friction in south-eastern Europe, where Austria's restive Slavic subjects and neighbours sought, and on occasion found, Russian backing; tension between Russia and Germany over the latter's threat of preventive war against France; and anger at Bismarck for his role of 'honest broker' at the Congress of Berlin which many Russians saw as a betrayal. The close alliance concluded between Germany and Austria in 1879 which lasted until 1918 (and was joined by Italy in 1882) was inspired by Bismarck's fears of Russia drifting out of his orbit and designed to impress upon her the costs of isolation. It showed how much juggling and bullying the master diplomatist had to do to keep his 'system' from falling apart and creating the very instability it was meant to avoid.

When to the uncertainties of shifting international alignments there were added the domestic complications of German agrarians and Russian manufacturers demanding to be protected from their competitors in the other country, the pro-German orientation of Russian diplomacy was placed under a heavy burden. The Prussophile Alexander II began to wonder whether his nationalist critics might not be right when they preached that friendship with republican France would serve Russia and the cause of the Slavs better than the crushing embrace of a Germany which was bound to give aid and comfort to its Austrian ally.

Alexander's and Russia's options were too limited, however, to enable them to act upon that recognition. For the time being Bismarck's gamble paid off. Alexander proved receptive to his overtures for a transformation of the defunct league of the emperors into a formal treaty of alliance. Negotiated for a term of three years and renewed for another three in 1884, the treaty committed its signatories to benevolent neutrality if one of them should be at war with a fourth great power; it provided for prior agreement among them on territorial changes in Turkey's possessions which might result from a conflict with one of the partners; it reaffirmed the principle of the closure of the Straits and the Turks' obligation to enforce it; gave Austria the right to annex Bosnia and Hercegovina (nominally Turkish but under Austrian administration since the

Congress of Berlin) when she saw fit to do so; and allowed for the eventual union of Bulgaria and Eastern Roumelia, the southern province which had at Berlin been placed under the Ottoman government to prevent the emergence of a great Bulgarian state under Russian aegis. In this way, it was hoped, both Russia's and Austria's interests would be satisfied and reconciled.

Fervent nationalist though he was, and very much more receptive as Crown Prince than Alexander II to the ambitious dreams of Panslavism, the new tsar, after a delay caused by the assassination of his father, none the less signed the Alliance of the Three Emperors in June 1881. Uncertain how widespread was the revolutionary conspiracy which had brought him to the throne on 1 March, Alexander III shied away from risky initiatives in foreign affairs and put aside his distaste for the German connection that many of his subjects shared. His adherence to it was made easier by the secrecy in which it was kept (even from his generals) and by the country's desperate need for quiet.

A circular dispatch to the powers of 4 March assured the world that the tsar would concentrate his attention on the nation's internal development, that his foreign policy would be peaceful, and that 'Russia will be concerned above all with herself. Only the duty to defend her honour or safety can deflect her from her internal labours.'[10] Although there was high tension in the Balkans – where Bulgaria's Russian-backed ruler defied his sponsors, only to be replaced by an Austrian protégé (1885–87) – and an acute crisis with Britain over Russian moves in the direction of Afghanistan and, London feared, India (1885), caution and compromise remained the watchwords, indeed a necessity, of Russian conduct.

Otherwise the reduction of the military budget by 25 per cent, imposed in 1882, would have been unthinkable. It meant a lowering of troop strength by about 10 per cent and a scaling down or stretching out of plans for modernizing the army's equipment and weapons, for building strategic railroads, fortresses, and ships. Military expenditures were not again to reach the level of 1881 until ten years later; even then, the Black Sea fleet was no match for Turkey's and the Baltic one incapable of preventing a British landing. The navy minister, Admiral I. A. Shestakov, whose 1882 proposals for expansion had remained on paper, warned in 1885 that the country was quite unprepared for a major conflict and expressed the worry that was never far from the minds of Russian statesmen – that war abroad could lead to revolution at home. His concern was echoed by Foreign Minister Giers who told the emperor in 1887 that Russia had to fear war less than its consequences. It was a theme restated frequently by many senior bureaucrats in the years before the First World War.[11]

Apprehensions of domestic turmoil and the ever-present reality of financial embarrassment went together with the unhappy knowledge of industrial and technological backwardness. 'Russia needs roads and schools, not victories or honour,' State Secretary A. A. Polovtsov said to the minister of war, General Vannovskii, in 1885, 'or else we'll become a Lapland.'[12] In 1892 Count Vladimir Lamzdorf, director of chancellery in the Foreign Ministry and minister from 1900 to 1906, observed that the famine had revealed Russia's weakness for all the world to see; the inadequacy of her transport and communications had advertised to potential enemies the difficulties that would attend the mobilization of her forces.[13] All the advances made in their size and efficiency, Vannovskii's successor, General A. N. Kuropatkin, noted in a report of 1900, had only brought them to a point where their concentration at the frontiers would take twice the time required by Russia's neighbours. And neighbours meant not a weak China or a declining Turkey, but Austria and Germany. An analysis of their strength and resources, Kuropatkin told Nicholas II, forced upon him the conclusion that the western frontiers had never in the whole history of Russia been so vulnerable: '. . . accordingly, the attention of the Ministry of War in the first years of the present century should be confined to strengthening our position on that side, and not be diverted to aggressive enterprises elsewhere'.[14]

This was said in a year when ordinary budget expenditures for the army were ten times greater than for education and the navy received more money than the Ministries of Justice and Agriculture combined.[15] Kuropatkin was also conscious of the political situation at home and complained that in the closing years of the nineteenth century his troops had been too frequently employed for the suppression of civil disorders. Discontent and revolutionary propaganda were certain to continue, making it all the more necessary that the army keep to a defensive role.[16]

Given these constraints, it was left to diplomacy to defend the country's interests as best it could. In the Bulgarian imbroglio it proved itself unequal to the task. The monopoly of policy formulation and execution vested in the autocrat and his foreign minister was unable either to impose unity of purpose and action on their agents or to endow them with enough skill and tact to preserve Russia's position of dominance in the one Balkan (and Slav) state where it seemed secure. Serbia in 1881 and Roumania in 1883, feeling aggrieved and abandoned by Russia, had moved close to Austria. The Bulgarians, who owed their liberation from the Turks and the very existence of their state to Russian arms and to whom Alexander II had granted a constitution and a national assembly – which elected his favourite nephew, Prince Alexander of Battenberg, as their ruler – were expected to be grateful and pliant. Instead, they disappointed their benefactors who all too often behaved like conquerors rather than elder brothers.

Given a mandate by the Congress of Berlin to organize Bulgaria's government, administration, and army – all officers above the rank of captain were Russians – the tsar's representatives, working at cross-purposes, interfered in the principality's affairs with a heavy hand. The military men tended to support the Liberals; the diplomats favoured the prince, who had changed the constitution in 1881 to give himself greater power; and Russian business interests alienated their natural allies, the Conservatives, by trying to gain exclusive railroad and other concessions and prevent western (especially Austrian) economic penetration. 'By September 1883, the three naturally rival forces had been united by repeated Russian tactlessness in common opposition to Russian policy.'[17]

Alexander III had at first approved of his cousin's setting aside the constitution and naming the Russian general who had been Bulgarian minister of war as head of his government. But it soon became obvious that the prince could not keep his throne as well as Russia's friendship. His restoration of the constitution in 1883 in order to win the backing of the Liberals enraged St Petersburg which correctly saw Bulgaria and the Prince escaping from Russian control with the help of nationalist and liberal sentiment and the sympathy of Austria and Britain. When in September 1885 an anti-Turkish revolt, of which the Prince knew in advance, broke out in Eastern Roumelia, the rebels offered him the headship of a united Bulgaria. Battenberg, ignoring the most dire warnings of the Russians, accepted, and so confirmed their worst fears.

The petty German princeling of a minor Balkan state had managed to defy the mighty Russian Empire and its tsar in their own backyard, and brought about the union of the two Bulgarian provinces which neither Russian troops nor diplomats had been able to achieve in the face of European opposition. To compound the indignity, the powers in 1886 allowed Alexander of Battenberg to do what they had denied to Alexander of Russia in 1879. Although the letter of the Treaty of Berlin was observed by keeping Roumelia a province of the Ottoman Empire, its spirit was violated by having the Sultan appoint as its governor the Prince of Bulgaria (to spare Russian sensibilities, no name was mentioned) who, in short order, joined the two provinces.

Alexander III took the Bulgarian events and his cousin's role in them as a personal and national affront. Yet for all his bitterness and anger there was little he could do. He lent his support to an officers' conspiracy which spirited Battenberg out of the country and, after the prince's brief recall by nationalist forces, the tsar could take some solace in his final abdication. But he could not assure the success of renewed Russian interference in Bulgarian affairs. It merely aggravated anti-Russian feeling, caused a rupture of relations, made impossible the election of a Russian candidate to the throne, and assured the election of Prince Ferdinand of Coburg, an Austrian subject, whom Russia refused to recognize for ten years. The tsar dismissed the idea of a military occupation of Bulgaria and declared that going to war with Turkey and risking a wider conflict with Europe would be unpardonable and, with respect to Russia, criminal. His ministers of foreign affairs and finance agreed, so did his chief of staff.[18]

In spite of its musical comedy aspects, the Bulgarian crisis had the most serious, profound, and lasting consequences for Russian policy and, ultimately, for the peace of Europe. The Russians had once again been given a demonstration of the inadequacy of their own resources and of how little trust they could place in the Alliance of the Three Emperors either to safeguard their primacy in the eastern Balkans or to realize the more distant aim of controlling the Straits. Austria was the proximate source of their troubles, but it was Germany they made the target of their frustration. Bismarck had been unable or unwilling to force the Austrians to compose their differences with Russia and agree to a delimitation of their respective spheres of influence in south-eastern Europe. A vehement Russian press campaign, led by Katkov, which denounced the German role in the Bulgarian crisis, was seen, correctly, to reflect official sentiment. That impression was confirmed in March 1887 when Katkov's revelation of details of the Three Emperors' Alliance went publicly unpunished, although the tsar, infuriated by the journalist's indiscretions, had privately rebuked him.

The Germans had already been given to understand at the end of 1886 that Russia was unwilling to renew the Three Emperors' Alliance upon its expiration in 1887. But Alexander, and Giers even less than his master, was not yet ready to head the rising public chorus of demands that he cut the German tie and restore Russia's freedom of action by a rapprochement with France. Continued distrust of the Third Republic's internal instability, the dread of being dragged by its revanchist politicians into a war for the recovery of Alsace and Lorraine, and the absence of a strong community of interests in areas of primary importance to Russia, still precluded the taking up of the French option.

Franco-Russian diplomatic collaboration against English policy in Egypt in early 1887 may have been a portent of things to come and served as a warning to Bismarck; but it was the latter who could offer the greater benefits to Russia as Germany was also her greatest danger. After difficult negotiations a secret Russian-German agreement, the so-called Reinsurance Treaty, was signed in June 1887 in which the two powers promised to remain neutral in case either became involved in a defensive war with a third power. The likelihood of German aggression against France or of a Russian attack upon Austria was thus reduced; Russia's preponderant influence in Bulgaria was recognized; Bismarck agreed to work with her for the status quo in the Balkans and to give moral and diplomatic support to such measures as the tsar might take 'to control the key of his empire', the entrance to the Black Sea.[19]

The Reinsurance Treaty, Bismarck's last great balancing act to keep his system from destroying itself, did not live up to its name. The concession of Russian pre-eminence in Bulgaria came late in the day and did nothing to prevent the election of Prince Ferdinand just three weeks after the treaty's signing. The promise of German assistance in the Near East cost Bismarck nothing, for he knew that Britain and Austria (particularly after their Mediterranean Agreement with Italy of December 1887) would make it unnecessary for him to keep it. And the virtual closing of German financial markets to Russia from midsummer 1887 on was anything but a gesture of friendship or reassurance towards a country starved of capital. Bismarck's order to the Reichsbank to stop accepting Russian securities as collateral for loans (the *Lombardverbot*) was issued in November, only weeks before Alexander III was to visit Berlin.

Why Bismarck took these offensive steps remains a matter of some doubt. He may have been genuinely concerned that too much Russian paper was being held in Germany; he may have retaliated for new Russian tariffs which cut deep into German industrial exports, or for a law which forbade foreigners (mainly Germans) from acquiring land in Russia's western provinces. Most probably he wanted in his usual blunt fashion to remind the Russians of their need of Germany and what the costs would be if they abandoned her for France. To that end he also revealed to them, as well as to the French, the existence of the Dual Alliance with Austria and the main terms of the Mediterranean Agreement and the Triple Alliance of 1882 (Germany, Austria, and Italy). There were also domestic opponents to fend off who thought his policy too friendly to Russia; they included the young Emperor William II, agrarians who agitated for further restrictions on Russian imports of grain and cattle, as well as military men who not only decried the building of Russia's military strength with the help of German bankers, but went so far as to join their Austrian colleagues in calling for a 'prophylactic' war against her.

Although he was able to thwart their plans, Bismarck was clearly losing ground. The vain and ambitious William II, eager to emerge from the shadow cast by the towering figure of the Iron Chancellor, dismissed him in March 1890. The Reinsurance Treaty was allowed to lapse in June. About a year later Alexander III stood at attention when the forbidden revolutionary hymn, the *Marseillaise*, was played to honour a visiting French naval squadron.

The 1894 alliance with France became the cornerstone of Russia's military and foreign policy and saved her from isolation. Historians disagree as to whether it was the avoidable outcome of Germany's brusque rejection or whether the divergence of interests between the two empires would not, in time, have had the same result of driving Russia into the open arms of France. The Franco-Russian Alliance was indeed a response, if a reluctant and slow one, to the deteriorating relationship with Germany and the challenge of the Triple Alliance. It foreshadowed the line-up of powers that would enter the First World War in 1914, even if it was not a sufficient cause for the coming of that conflict and in its initial stages served to check rather than inflame French militancy. On the Russian side the agreement was conceived as a purely defensive instrument which did not preclude efforts at restoring cordial relations with both Germany and Austria. A tariff treaty concluded with the former in 1894 ended a long and bitter customs war and an accord reached with the latter in 1897 removed the Balkan questions from contention for a decade. Nor did the Germans view their actions of 1887 and 1890 as the final slamming of a door. The *Lombardverbot* was lifted and by 1902 Germany received 41 per cent of Russia's exports and supplied 35 per cent of her imports – vastly more than France.[20]

Nevertheless, the delicately tuned balance of the European powers was disturbed by the shocks which Bismarck and his successors had administered to it and which sensitive St Petersburg registered as being greater than in fact they were. The toast which the tsar in 1889 offered to his guest, King Nicholas of Montenegro, as Russia's only true friend, was the hyperbolic expression of that sensitivity.[21] German failure to renew the Reinsurance Treaty undercut the position of men like Giers and Lamzdorf who warned against creating an irreparable division of the continent into two armed camps by moving too close to France and who thought Russia powerful enough to make this unnecessary; it strengthened the hand of nationalists and strategic planners, all those who held Germany responsible for frustrating Russian aspirations in the Balkans and at the Straits or feared that Russia was too weak to withstand the onslaught of her western neighbours alone.

In both countries it was, in fact, the general staffs who took the lead in converting the loose Franco-Russian agreement of August 1891 – which provided for mutual consultation in case the security of either country was threatened – into the detailed and binding military-political alliance of January 1894. Designed to last as long as the Triple Alliance (and after its extension in 1899 until either side should withdraw from it) the Franco-Russian entente obligated Russia to launch all her available troops against Germany's eastern frontier if the latter should attack France or support an Italian attack on France. If Russia were attacked by Germany, or by Austria with German backing, the French would immediately commit all their available forces against Germany. To make entirely certain that Germany would have to fight on two fronts and that the Russians would not concentrate the bulk of their armies against Austria alone, it was stipulated that 1.3 million French soldiers and 700,000 to 800,000 Russians would take the field against the common enemy. Mobilization by any member of the Triple Alliance, it was agreed, would immediately be answered by mobilization in Russia and France.

The Franco-Russian alliance was the achievement of what Katkov had preached until his death in 1887. The conversion of Alexander III to his views (and their acceptance by Giers, who died in 1895), was facilitated by the realization that however much matters and manners between them might improve, in any relationship with Germany Russia would for the predictable future be the junior partner and in most respects a petitioner. In the case of France it was the Russians who were sought after and needed and consequently allowed a greater measure of freedom and flexibility. That was so even though the financial ties that developed between the two allies put Russia more deeply in debt to France than she had ever been to Germany. While the Reich remained Russia's best customer, France and French investors became her chief creditors. By 1895 more than half of all publicly traded Russian securities were in French hands, and by the turn of the century about a quarter of all French investments abroad were in Russian public or corporate obligations and shares.[22]

The political implications of this financial burden for the debtor have been the subject of much dispute. There is no doubt that it gave to French diplomats, generals, and bankers a means of pressure which could neither be ignored nor always resisted. In one instance, the granting of new credits was made conditional upon Russian agreement to build a strategic but unprofitable railway. In another, Witte, in order to obtain a loan, had to consent to a three-year moratorium on the placement of new Russian issues in France. Other military and economic concessions were exacted. The burdens and obligations did not, however, rest only on one side. But to the Russian public they were more acceptable than the smaller indebtedness to Germany, for they preserved the appearance and to a considerable degree the reality of Russia as an autonomous actor on the international stage. To the government the French alternative and support gave the possibility of dealing from strength with the

Germans (when seeking funds or better terms of trade) or with its own people. In 1905–06 tsarism was able to withstand the onslaught of revolution in large part because of French financial aid. No lender can afford to be indifferent to the fate of a borrower, particularly one who is also an ally and comrade-in-arms. If Russia was a semi-colony of the West, as many Soviet and Western historians have considered her, she was a unique colony indeed.[23]

That the link with France could both hobble and enhance Russian freedom of action was amply illustrated in the diplomatic history of the decade that followed its formation – most clearly in the Far East. The alliance kept the empire from sinking to the level of Turkey and China and helped it to continue playing the part of a power of the first rank in international affairs. Massive infusions of French money were incapable, however, of solving the domestic problems which called into question Russia's status as a great power.

The resumption of military reforms and growth was made more difficult by the financial requirements of the Witte system. The first substantial increase in army allotments in ten years took place in 1894, and in 1897 a naval construction programme was adopted. However much a military buildup may have been dictated by the technological superiority of potential enemies and by the obligations to the alliance, they were too great a tax on the country's strength. As early as 1891 Lamzdorf had thought that Russia should put forward a proposal for general European disarmament. In 1898, most probably at Witte's suggestion and certainly with his support, foreign minister M. N. Muravev launched the idea of an international convention for the reduction of armaments. Embarked on a costly infantry modernization programme, Russia could not afford to meet the challenge posed by the introduction of rapid-fire artillery and other improvements in the German and Austrian armies and also continue her industrial development.[24]

Nicholas II, perhaps attracted by the prominent role he would play on the world scene, yielded to Witte's urging and issued a call for universal peace and a reduction of the excessive arms burden through international agreements. His appeal resulted in the convocation of the first Peace Conference at The Hague (1899). Because of French resistance, and that of other states, neither the first nor the second Peace Conference (1907) accomplished more than the adoption of rules to humanize the conduct of war and the setting up of an international court of arbitration. The armaments race went on and faced Witte and his successors with continuing and conflicting demands to meet military, social, and industrial needs. The finance ministry's traditional reluctance or inability to meet the requests of the armed services remained a source of conflict in the top levels of government and contributed to Witte's downfall in 1903.

Another of its causes was friction with a group of the tsar's advisers and favourites whose ineptness Witte justly blamed for the naval attack on Port Arthur of early 1904 and the war with Japan; its long-range causes must, however, be sought in Witte's own inflated visions and projects. These aimed at nothing less than the assumption by Russia of an imperial mission in the Far East which would make her unassailable in Europe and secure material benefits to speed up her transformation into a great industrial and commercial empire. Witte was confident that his plans for the peaceful, gradual, and largely economic penetration of China could be accomplished without clashing with the other states that were scrambling for concessions or spheres of influence in the enfeebled Manchu Empire. To establish a dominant Russian presence in its northern portions (Manchuria); to acquire markets, warm-water ports, sources of raw material, and a field for lucrative investments; to secure rail communications with Russia's Pacific provinces and make them, instead of the Suez Canal, the profitable carrier of the West's trade with Asia – these were goals which Witte considered both possible and desirable and for which he found much sympathy in business and government.

The building of the Trans-Siberian Railway, begun in 1891, became Witte's chief instrument for the realization of the grand design he sketched for a receptive Alexander III in 1892. His confidence was boosted and the Trans-Siberian advanced by the availability of French funds. These were far from adequate, however, to defray the costs of an enterprise which not only failed to yield the expected profits but saddled the exchequer with unanticipated expenses it could ill afford at the very onset of a world-wide depression towards the end of the decade. All that Witte's plans had helped to stimulate or justify combined in the end to defeat him and to check Russia in the Far East as she had already been checked in the West: the ambitions of Nicholas and some of his courtiers; the greed of concessionaires; the designs and requirements of the military; the anti-foreign rising of the Chinese Boxers (1900) which necessitated the dispatch of 170,000 troops to protect Russia's interests in Manchuria; the growing suspicion on the part of the other powers of Russian moves and motives, particularly in Korea, which was a tributary of China and an object of Japanese expansionism.

Although they had reached the shores of the Pacific as early as 1639, and soon clashed, traded and treated with the Chinese, the Russians were too thinly stretched over the vast expanse of Siberia to follow up the probes of Cossacks, explorers, adventurers and trappers in any systematic way. Even when a China distracted by rebellion and foreign intrusions had to cede the left bank of the Amur River and the region of the Ussuri (1858–60) – territories that were to form Russia's Maritime Province on the Sea of Japan – Russia's preoccupation in the Balkans and Central Asia kept the tsars from exploiting China's weakness or blocking the Japanese drive. Not until the 1890s and the building of the Trans-Siberian did the Russians give much attention to their Far Eastern possessions and discover the dangers to which they, and the railroad that was to make them part of the empire, might be exposed. Only then did St Petersburg begin to think of these possessions as forward bases in a push towards northern China and Korea which would secure valuable strategic and economic benefits.

The Sino-Japanese War of 1894–95, the outcome of a decade of rivalry between the two Asian states, and the Treaty of Shimonoseki which concluded it, fully brought home to the Russians the risks and opportunities facing them. The Japanese victory exacted from the Chinese Formosa (Taiwan), the

Pescadores Islands, a large indemnity and, most important from the Russian point of view, the independence of Korea and the cession of the Liaotung peninsula. Jutting out from southern Manchuria between the Chinese mainland and Korea, the peninsula, with Port Arthur at its southern tip, put the Japanese within easy reach of northern Manchuria and brought them uncomfortably close, as would their presence in Korea, to the railway and its eastern terminal at Vladivostok.

Witte saw his entire conception set at hazard by the Japanese thrust; its real target, he insisted, was Russia. Against the foreign office and the service chiefs, who were ready to come to terms with Japan and seek territorial compensation and an ice-free port in Korea, he argued that the Japanese had to be removed from the peninsula altogether, lest all of southern Manchuria and eventually Korea become their exclusive and permanent preserve. They were to be allowed no foothold on the mainland, no special rights in China, which Russia would from now on take under her wing and protect against further Japanese incursions. He prevailed, and with German and French support was able to make Japan surrender the Liaotung peninsula in return for an increased Chinese indemnity which a Russian loan, provided by French banks, helped the Chinese government to pay.

In June 1896 Russia garnered the fruits of her intervention. In the secret Li-Lobanov treaty, a defensive alliance concluded for fifteen years, she pledged herself to the preservation of China's territorial integrity and then infringed it by receiving permission to build the Chinese Eastern Railway – financed by the Russo-Chinese Bank and, once again, French capital – across Manchuria to Vladivostok. The route of the Trans-Siberian was thus shortened by 450 miles and a Russian enclave with armed railway guards and administrators established on Chinese soil. In Korea, Russian attempts to supplant or restrain the Japanese by agreement were only temporarily successful; constant friction led to growing irritation on the part of Japan and, ultimately, a determination to exclude the Russians from Korea.

Only two years after becoming China's ally and protector, Russia did what other powers were doing and what she had denied Japan. She exacted a lease to the Liaotung peninsula, permission to build a naval base at Port Arthur as well as a commercial port at Dalnii (Dairen), and a concession for the South Manchurian Railway which would connect Kharbin, on the Chinese Eastern Railway, with Port Arthur to the south. This time Witte objected strenuously: Russia would be overextended, Britain alarmed, France worried, China antagonized by a protector who behaved like an aggressor, and Japan mortally affronted by Russian duplicity. Only Germany was glad to see her neighbour become embroiled in distant Asia.

Events proved Witte right, yet he was not averse to using them in an attempt to strengthen his own position in St Petersburg and Russia's *vis-à-vis* China. By promising the phased withdrawal of the troops introduced into Manchuria at the time of the Boxer rising, he and the ministers of war and foreign affairs (Kuropatkin and Lamzdorf) tried to persuade the Chinese to restore their special relationship with Russia and to grant further and exclusive mining and railway rights – not only in Manchuria, but in Mongolia and Sinkiang. The failure of these negotiations, which the Chinese caused to become known, and the simultaneous failure to reach an accommodation in Korea with Japan, led the latter into a defensive alliance with Britain in January 1902. The Russians were forced in April 1902 to agree to withdraw their troops from Manchuria by October 1903 without having obtained those economic or political concessions which would, they believed, have pre-empted challenges to their position or allowed more time for strengthening it.

The advocates of a policy of 'peaceful penetration' (Witte), of patient diplomacy (Lamzdorf), and of limiting Russia's territorial goals to defensible dimensions (Kuropatkin) were discredited in the eyes of the tsar and increasingly shunted aside. Their warnings of Japanese strength and Russia's danger were ignored by the men who replaced them in the tsar's favour and in the management of the country's Far Eastern policy. Yet they were kept in office – Witte until August 1903 – and in the case of Kuropatkin and Lamzdorf left to execute policies they disapproved. Nor did they resign in protest. They neither would nor could have taken their case to the public, for their power and position derived from the sovereign, not the nation. When he was criticized for remaining in office, Lamzdorf explained that in Russia a minister could not quit his post unless discharged; his sole function was to study the questions pertaining to the empire's foreign relations and to present his conclusions to the sovereign who alone decided on a course of action that would be binding on the foreign minister.[25]

The appeal of Russia's 'Oriental Mission' may have been enhanced for Nicholas by the prospect of finding in Asia a field of action where his authority would not be challenged by argumentative ministers or checked, as at home, by intractable problems. He was encouraged by William II of Germany, by his friend Prince Esper Ukhtomskii (first chairman of the Russo-Chinese Bank and a director of the Chinese Eastern Railway), by the so-called Bezobrazov clique, by some of the naval leaders, and by his own misplaced confidence in himself and his power to control events. 'There will be no war,' he wrote to William, 'because I do not wish it.'[26]

The steps Nicholas took to enforce that wish had the opposite effect; they diluted his authority and instead of concentrating and coordinating Far Eastern policy in fewer hands, they made a shambles of it. Shortly after Witte's dismissal, the tsar set up a vice-royalty for the entire region east of Lake Baikal under Admiral E. I. Alekseev. With his headquarters at Port Arthur, the admiral was placed in charge of relations with China, Korea, and Japan and reported directly to the emperor. The creation, a month later, of a Far Eastern Committee in the capital added to the confusion and disunity of Russian purpose.

The St Petersburg Committee was directed by A. M. Abaza, a naval captain who was a cousin of the retired guards captain A. M. Bezobrazov. Bezobrazov had in 1897 acquired a timber concession on the Yalu River on the border between Korea and Manchuria. In 1899, together with other aristocratic entrepreneurs, he had formed the East Asian Development Company in which the tsar became a shareholder. Although these plans came to naught, and the activities of Bezobrazov and his friends have figured too large in accounts of the pre-history of the Russian débâcle in Asia, [27] they exasperated the Japanese. Their suspicions were deepened when in June 1903 the Yalu concession and a company to exploit it were revived. This followed hard on the heels of the Russians stalling the evacuation of their troops from Manchuria and presenting new demands to the Chinese.

These developments cast a pall over the Russo-Japanese negotiations that went on from August 1903 to February 1904. There was little inclination on either side now to reach the sort of compromise that might have prevented war: a clear delimitation of exclusive spheres of influence in Korea and Manchuria respectively. The Japanese, assured of the diplomatic backing of Britain and the United States, became convinced that they would have to fight. The Russians thought they could avoid doing so. They underestimated their opponents' readiness and determination and responded slowly and uncertainly to Japanese proposals. The last Russian communication did not reach Tokyo until after the beginning of hostilities.

Nicholas was genuine in his desire to evade a conflict of whose consequences even Pleve was afraid and which, according to the Austrian ambassador, Pleve too did not want. But Nicholas did not himself follow the instructions he had telegraphed to Alekseev, to 'take all measures so that war will not occur'.[28] When it did, the tsar remained light-hearted; he dismissed as a flea-bite[29] the surprise naval attack on Port Arthur (27 January/9 February 1904) which gave the Japanese command of the seas and safety to their troop convoys. The reports of patriotic manifestations the tsar received made him confident of the outcome of the war and of the country's loyalty – here was the nation's true voice – but enthusiasm, even where it was genuine, was neither deep nor lasting. It did not survive the reverses suffered by Russian arms. Nor did the cause of empire in Asia find such an echo in Russian hearts and minds as did the fate of the Slavs, vital commercial and strategic interests at the Straits, or the security of the Western frontier. To the political protests of the educated and the discontent of peasants and workers, there was now added the disenchantment of patriots with a government that was incapable of carrying out its most basic mission: the defence of the national interest and honour against foreign foes.

Lack of leadership and of tactical arms, poor training and battlefield communications, ignorance of the enemy and contempt for his capabilities, together with the enormous logistical problem of assembling and supplying an army over the single-tracked Trans-Siberian, helped to defeat Russia on land and sea. During the 1890s the infantry had been outfitted with the Mosin rifle, as good as any to be found in Europe at the time. Rapid-fire field guns were introduced at the turn of the century. But the country's industry (or treasury) had been able to re-equip only one third of the field artillery with the new weapons by 1904. Machine-guns began to appear in 1902, when the licence to manufacture them in Russian plants was acquired from Vickers, a British firm. At the outbreak of war the 125,000 Russian soldiers and border guards stationed in the Far East had at their disposal approximately 175 field pieces and 8 machine-guns. Telephones and telegraphs had to be imported, and many Russian units were without them. There was a shortage of binoculars, telescopes, and range finders.[30]

Technological inferiority was not simply the exclusive or fated consequence of industrial backwardness; it was the result also of military and political institutions and conceptions that were rooted in traditional assumptions about the intrinsic superiority of the Russian way of life, the hardiness and loyalty of the peasant soldier, and the exemplary qualities of his officers. In addition to an ideologically dictated distrust of 'foreign' innovations, there was bureaucratic inertia and an inordinate regard for the rights of seniority. Some of the older officers – including two commanders of the General Staff Academy – had belittled or resisted machine-guns, rapid fire artillery, the magazine loading rifle, and protective shields for cannon as either blindly imitative of Western models or as undermining the offensive spirit of the troops. Respect for the doctrine of the eighteenth-century General A. V. Suvorov, that the sturdy Russian soldier had no equal in the use of the bayonet, led to an excessive reliance on that weapon, to costly frontal assaults, and to belated modernization and technological innovation. Military reform was inhibited also by the fact that few general officers had seen combat since the Russo-Turkish War. Their average age was seventy; 50 per cent of corps commanders were between the ages of sixty-one and sixty-five.[31]

Confidence that Russia would prevail over the enemy was based on the not unreasonable calculation that greater numbers – once they could be transported to the distant battlefield – would prove decisive. Pleve told a colleague that 150 million was three times 50 million: it was as simple as that.[32] After a year of reverses, Nicholas spoke of the hour of victory as approaching. By June 1905, after sixteen months of war, and a very impressive improvement in the capacity of the Trans-Siberian, Russian numerical superiority on land did, in fact, begin to tell and the Japanese were discovering that their successes were more costly and difficult than anticipated. Russia's defeats on the other hand – the fall of Port Arthur in December 1904; the battle of Mukden the following February; and the annihilation of the Baltic Fleet in the Straits of Tsushima in May 1905 – exasperated a public which was no longer willing to extend time or credit to the government. The growing strength of the Russian land forces at the front came too late to achieve victory, although it helped Witte to negotiate the compromise peace with Japan (Treaty of Portsmouth, 25 August/5 September 1905) that the threat of revolution and the denial of further French loans had made imperative.

Russia's experiment in imperialism, the abandonment by her leaders of the moderation they had shown in foreign affairs for so long, was ended just in time to contain upheavals at home and limit losses abroad. Through the mediation of President Theodore Roosevelt of the United States, the Russians were spared having to pay the indemnity on which Japan had initially insisted. But they did have to yield rights and territories on which they had counted as sources of future wealth and greatness. Manchuria, to be evacuated by both powers, was restored to China. Russia surrendered to Japan the southern half of the island of Sakhalin, the lease of the Liaotung peninsula with its ports, and the South Manchurian Railway. Korea was declared to be independent and within the Japanese orbit. The restraint that both sides showed at the Portsmouth (New Hampshire) peace conference in 1905 allowed them to come to the kind of agreement for the despoliation of China that would, a few years earlier, have kept them from coming to blows. With their control of northern Manchuria and Mongolia recognized by the Japanese in 1907, 1910 and 1912, the Russians could once again turn their attention to Europe and try to master the lessons of their defeat at the hands of an 'inferior' Asian people.

REFERENCES

1. S. Iu. Vitte, *Vospominaniia* (Moscow, 1969), II, p. 291. There is reason to think that Pleve, like other ministers, was aware that war abroad could weaken rather than strengthen internal security. See R. E. Pipes, 'Domestic politics and foreign affairs' in Ivo Lederer (ed.), *Russian Foreign Policy* (New Haven, Conn., and London, 1962), p. 156; and B. V. Ananich and R. M. Ganelin, 'Opyt kritiki memuarov Vitte' in *Voprosy istoriografii i istochnikovedeniia istorii SSSR* (Moscow-Leningrad, 1963), p. 340.
2. Reinhard Wittram, 'Das russische Imperium und sein Gestaltwandel', *Historische Zeitschrift* 187 (June 1959), p. 589.
3. Karl Marx and Friedrich Engels, *Werke* XVI (Berlin, 1962), p. 202.
4. G. Vernadsky *et al.* (eds.), *A Source Book for Russian History* (New Haven, Conn., and London, 1972), III, p. 610.
5. See David MacKenzie, 'Turkestan's significance to Russia (1950–1917)', *Russian Review* 33 (April 1974), pp. 167–88.
6. F. M. Dostoevskii, 'Geok-Tepe. What is Asia to us?' in *The Diary of a Writer*, trans. by B. Brasol (New York, 1954), p. 1048.
7. David MacKenzie, *The Lion of Tashkent: The Career of General M. G. Cherniaev* (Athens, Ga., 1974); and Hans Rogger, 'D. M. Skobelev: the hero and his worship', *Oxford Slavonic Papers* 9 (1976), pp. 46–78.
8. Dietrich Geyer, *Der russische Imperialismus* (Göttingen, 1977), p. 77.
9. Ibid., p. 65; H. Rogger, 'Nationalism and the State: A Russian Dilemma', *Comparative Studies in Society and History*, 4 (April 1962), pp. 253–264.
10. From K. K. Arsenev, *Za chetvert veka* (Petrograd, 1915), p. 53.
11. Geyer, op. cit., pp. 91–2; M. T. Florinsky, *Russia* (New York, 1953), II, p. 1125; V. N. Lamzdorf, *Dnevnik, 1886–1890* (Moscow, 1926), p. iv; A. A. Polovtsov, *Dnevnik* (Moscow, 1966), II, p. 134.
12. Polovtsov, *Dnevnik*, I, pp. 320–1.
13. V. N. Lamzdorf, *Dnevnik 1891–1892* (Moscow, 1934), p. 255.
14. A. N. Kuropatkin, *The Russian Army and the Japanese War* (New York, 1909), I, 77.
15. Vernadsky, op. cit., pp. 822–4.
16. Kuropatkin, op. cit., pp. 102–3.
17. H. Seton-Watson, *The Russian Empire, 1801–1917* (Oxford, 1967), p. 568.

18. Charles Jelavich, *Tsarist Russia and Balkan Nationalism* (Berkeley and Los Angeles, Cal., 1962), p. 256; Geyer, op. cit., p. 95.

19. V. M. Khvostov, *Diplomatiia v novoe vremia, 1871–1914* (Moscow, 1963), p. 257: vol. II of *Istoriia Diplomatii*, eds. V. A. Zorin *et al.*

20. Geyer, op. cit., p. 127.

21. G. F. Kennan, *The Decline of Bismarck's European Order* (Princeton, NJ, 1979), p. 398. There is an apocryphal story that when journalists asked King Nicholas how strong was his army, he replied: 'Together with our great Russian ally we are a million strong.' Pressed to indicate his army's size if the Russian one were subtracted, he declared: 'Montenegro will never abandon her friends.'

22. Geyer, op. cit., pp. 133, 143.

23. See pp. 103–5 above.

24. Dominic Lieven, 'Pro-Germans and Russian foreign policy 1890–1914', *International History Review* 2 (Jan. 1980), p. 35; D. L. Morrill, 'Nicholas II and the call for the first Hague Peace Conference', *Journal of Modern History* 46 (June 1974), pp. 296–313; V. M. Khvostov, op. cit., pp. 457–562.

25. A. P. Izvolskii, *Recollections of a Foreign Minister* (Garden City, NY, and Toronto, 1921), pp. 122–3.

26. Nicholas quote from David MacKenzie and M. W. Curran, *A History of Russia and the Soviet Union* (Homewood, Ill., 1967), p. 369.

27. For a challenge to the conventional view, see Bernard Brodie, *War and Politics* (New York and London, 1973), p. 286.

28. Andrew Malozemoff, *Russian Far Eastern Policy, 1881–1904* (Berkeley and Los Angeles, Cal., 1958), p. 243.

29. S. D. Urusov, *Memoirs of a Russian Governor* (London and New York, 1908), p. 177.

30. Sterling Hart, "The Russo-Japanese War, 1904–1905', *Strategy and Tactics* 59 (Nov.–Dec. 1976), pp. 28–43.

31. A. K. Wildman, *The End of the Russian Imperial Army* (Princeton, NJ, 1979), pp. 17–18, 46; Rogger, 'Skobelev' p. 73; Peter Kenez, 'A profile of the pre-revolutionary officer corps', *California Slavic Studies* 7 (1973), pp. 121–57; N. A. McCully, *The McCully Report: The Russo-Japanese War* (Annapolis, Md., 1977); John Bushnell, 'The tsarist officer corps, 1881–1914: customs, duties, inefficiency', *American Historical Review* 86 (Oct. 1981), pp. 753–80; I. I. Rostunov (ed.), *Istoriia russko-iaponskoi voiny* (Moscow, 1977), pp. 66–84.

32. Urusov, op. cit., p. 178.

CHAPTER NINE

Empire at home: the non-Russians

One need not accept Lenin's description of Imperial Russia as a 'prison of peoples'[1] to concede that the acquisition of alien populations and territories would lead to friction between conquerors and 'natives'. Even where the imposition of Russian rule had been welcomed, ethnic and political tensions, religious and economic conflicts were bound to arise. The most neutral definition of empire suggests the existence of a problem: 'an extended territory usually comprising a group of nations, states, or peoples under the control or domination of a single sovereign power'.[2]

The tendency of that power to view a conglomerate of over 100 ethnic groups, cultures, creeds, and tongues as an undifferentiated mass of subjects in practice yielded to the reality of diversity. Yet the search for legal-administrative uniformity and order and the principle that the empire was a unitary Russian rather than a multi-national (and much less a federal) state were never abandoned. Indeed, the more the principle was challenged by facts and by demands for autonomy, the more vigorously was it asserted. As the Great Russians became in the late nineteenth century a minority of its population, the empire they had formed and still dominated compensated for their decline by trying to strengthen their position of dominance. Much of the treatment of non-Russians in the years after 1881 may be seen in the light of what can only be called a demographic fear, a fear more easily understood by considering the results of the census of 1897.

Making language the test of ethnicity or nationality, it showed non-Russians to be a majority (55.7 per cent) of the country's 122.6 million people. Soviet demographers have given the still higher estimate of 59.2 per cent.[3] Some comfort could be drawn from the preponderance of the Slavic element, for together Great Russians (44.3 per cent), Ukrainians (17.81 per cent), Poles (6.31 per cent), and Belorussians (4.68 per cent) accounted for almost three quarters (73.12 per cent) of the total. But comfort had to be tempered by the admission that the Catholic Poles cherished their nationhood and religion more than the bond of Slavdom and that many Ukrainians, though they were of the Orthodox faith, cared less for the ties of religion and the memory of a common origin than for the cultivation of their own identity.

The census also counted (or more likely undercounted) over 13 million Turkic people (10.82 per cent) – Tatars, Azerbaijanis, Uzbeks, Bashkirs, Kazakhs, Kirghiz, and Turkmens – whose Muslim faith and Turkic languages facilitated a cultural awakening in the late nineteenth century and the appearance of political movements in the twentieth; about 5 million Jews; 3 million Finnic peoples (not including 2.5 million inhabitants of the Grand Duchy of Finland); 1.7 million Germans; 1.6 million ethnically diverse Caucasian mountain peoples; 1.3 million Georgians; 1.4 million Latvians; 1.2 million Lithuanians; 1.1 million Armenians, as well as a variety of smaller groups, from Iranians and Mongolians to Samoeds and Eskimos.[4]

Located for the most part in strategically sensitive border areas, these peoples could not possibly be dealt with as the official theory of a 'one and indivisible Russia' implied. They had come under Russian authority at different times and on dissimilar terms and varied widely in numbers and social structure, in material development and national consciousness. Nor would it be correct to see all of them as victims of repressive policies which aimed single-mindedly and relentlessly at the levelling of differences and the forcible assimilation to the Russian norm. The old regime had neither the means nor the ruthless consistency to achieve what it thought desirable. When it proceeded rigorously against the subject nationalities, it did so more because it perceived (or misperceived) a threat to its security and integrity, a challenge to its interests or institutions, than in determined pursuit of an ideal of uniformity which most of its advocates knew to be unattainable by force, if at all. There was inconsistency even towards the Jews, whose treatment came closest to what is today called racism and who were subjected to greater disabilities than any other non-Russians. Jewish policy wavered between encouraging assimilation by selective concessions (under Alexander I and Alexander II), enforcing it by coercion (under Nicholas I), and preventing it in our period in order, it was explained, to protect the nation from Jewish exploitation and intrigue.

The policy of administrative integration and uniformity was far from the genocidal madness of the twentieth century and in many respects beneficial to the subject peoples. Yet it was often insensitive and, at its worst, harsh and heavy-handed. Its failures and clumsiness can be seen even in the case of the Ukrainians who were not greatly disadvantaged, who need not have been part of the nationalities problem, and who could with tact and patience have been won over to help the regime deal with the genuine and deep-seated difficulties posed by more alien and alienated groups.

The tsarist authorities could claim a measure of historical justification for their refusal to grant that the 22 to 25 million Ukrainians who lived in the empire in 1897 were a distinct nationality. Ancient or Kievan Russia knew no distinctions among its population of Eastern Slavs. Only after Kiev fell to the Mongols in 1240 and its territory was divided among Lithuanians and Poles to the west and the Grand Prince of Muscovy to the north-east, did different political loyalties and institutions, religious and cultural influences, give rise to the division of the Eastern Slavs into Great Russians, Belorussians, and Ukrainians. The latter, during their four hundred years of separation from their Great Russian brethren, developed peculiarities of speech, folkways, and socio-economic formation – such as the fiercely independent communities of peasant-warriors, the Cossacks – which Ukrainian nationalists invoked on behalf of their people's special character and needs.

Kiev and the eastern Ukraine came to Russia after the Cossack hetman, Bogdan Khmelnitskii, hard pressed by the Poles, placed himself under Moscow's protection in 1654. The absorption of the western Ukraine was completed with the partitions of Poland in the reign of Catherine II (1762–96). What was left of local and Cossack autonomy ended with the integration of the region into the empire's fiscal, administrative, and ecclesiastical system. The empress made generous gifts of Ukrainian lands to Russian nobles who worked their estates with Russian serfs. The Cossack horsemen were formed into units of the Russian army, while their officers acquired the status and privileges of Russian nobles. This diminished or removed the hostility of the Cossack elite for its new masters with whom it identified, intermingled, and served. An articulate Ukrainian nationalism, therefore, was the creation of intellectuals of lower and middle-class background who combined the search for a national identity with the quest for democracy and social justice for the predominantly rural masses.

There was no thought at first of an independent Ukrainian state. Before 1917 separatism, or the dream of a greater Ukraine which would include Austrian Galicia, was confined to a few extremists and irredentists. When the cultural nationalism that appeared in the 1820s went beyond language and literature and resulted in the formation of the secret Society of Saints Cyril and Methodius in 1846, the authorities were alarmed. That the radicalism of the Society's membership of students, historians, and writers did not go beyond hopes and talk was less important than that they talked of a federal republic of Slavs and education for all, of an end to serfdom and class privilege. The Society was suppressed in 1847; its members were imprisoned or exiled. The revolutions that swept the rest of Europe in 1848 confirmed for Nicholas I the need for vigilance.

After his death, the authorities for a time took a more lenient view of activities devoted to the study of the Ukrainian past and present. There was never any disposition, however, on the government's part – and little on the part of Russian society, whether liberal or conservative – to concede the uniqueness of the Ukrainian national experience and consciousness. The very word Ukraine was unknown to Russian law and shunned in official usage. A minister of Alexander II declared that there was not and never had been a 'Little Russian' language and not until 1905 did members of the Russian Academy recommend, by a majority of one, that Ukrainian be accepted as a language in its own right rather than merely a dialect of Russian.[5]

Although Ukrainian nationalists had not risen when Polish rebels did in 1863, the possibility that they might do so at another favourable moment or join forces with Russian revolutionaries, caused a hardening of policy in the next decade. The historian M. P. Dragomanov, who had aspired to no more than regional autonomy, was dismissed from the University of Kiev in 1875 and emigrated to Austria. A year later a prohibition was placed on the importation of books in the Ukrainian language and on its use in schools, lectures, recitals, and theatrical performances. The publication of Ukrainian works was virtually restricted to historical documents.

The situation in the Austro-Hungarian empire was markedly different. Across the border from Ukraine, in Galicia, Poles and Ukrainians enjoyed a limited measure of self-rule and a large measure of civil liberty. Austrian and émigré Ukrainians made use of these to continue and broaden acitivities proscribed in Russia. Galicia now became the base and centre of Ukrainian nationalism. Its temporary decline in Russia was not the result of tsarist repression alone. The movement was weakened also by economic changes which created new opportunities and preoccupations and tied the Ukraine more closely to the rest of the country. Large numbers of Great Russians moved to the rapidly growing towns and industries of the eastern Ukraine and peasants from its western parts migrated to Siberia, the Far East, and Central Asia.

With the onset of a depression and the revival of opposition and protest, Ukrainian nationalism revived as well and turned from quiet cultural to illegal political action and organizations. The first of these, the Revolutionary Ukrainian Party (RUP), was founded in Kharkov in 1900, made Kiev its headquarters, and fully lived up to its name. Through printed propaganda (produced mainly in Galicia) and direct agitation in town and country, it helped to stimulate the agrarian disorders of 1902–03 and to spread the idea of an independent greater Ukraine contained in the party's first programme. But its combination of social and national radicalism proved too much for some of its adherents, and although the call for separation from Russia was replaced with the more moderate one for autonomy, the RUP soon disintegrated.

The Ukrainian National Party (1902), attracted those in the RUP's right wing who thought socialism insufficiently national and inimical to specifically Ukrainian interests. They were proved correct when the RUP's extreme leftists joined the Russian Social Democrats. Another leftist splinter of the RUP, while it collaborated closely with the Russian Marxists and adopted their programme, maintained a separate identity as the Ukrainian Social Democratic Labour Party which demanded autonomy and a legislative assembly for the Ukraine. Ukrainian liberals, the last to organize, shared these goals; their Ukrainian Democratic Party resembled the Russian Constitutional Democrats (Kadets) whom they supported or joined for common action during the Revolution of 1905.

For all that the Ukrainian parties contributed to the opposition – they sent some forty deputies to the Duma in 1906 – they never developed the strength to survive the renewed governmental suppression which befell them as well as Ukrainian cultural pursuits in the aftermath of the revolution. In spite of some successes in rural cooperatives, nationalism in the Ukraine lacked a mass following in the years before the First World War, as well as Russian allies and internal unity. Advocates of the Ukrainian cause had always to be mindful of the fact, especially in the relatively prosperous years between 1909 and

1914, that inclusion in the empire offered distinct material benefits to their people and that independence would create economic as well as political difficulties. Not the least of these was the troubled relationship with the Polish element in the Ukraine and even more so in Galicia. Some Ukrainian nationalists considered the Poles a greater threat than the Russians and looked upon the latter as their protectors. Others saw Germany and Austria as allies against both Poles and Russians. The pro-German orientation in Ukrainian nationalism was strengthened by the brief wartime occupation of Galicia by the Russians who proceeded more ruthlessly against the Ukrainians there than they had done at home. The persecution of Ukrainian schools, press, and Uniate churches (which recognized the authority of the papacy while retaining Orthodox rites and liturgy) created great bitterness on both sides of the frontier. The Russians' behaviour in Galicia was viewed as the ultimate proof of their intolerance and was the prelude to Ukrainian independence. Achieved with the help of the German army in January 1918, it was lost to the Bolsheviks in 1920.

Unlike the Ukrainians, the Poles had a long history of a once powerful state whose very existence Russia had terminated between 1772 and 1795 with Prussian and Austrian connivance. They also had an unbroken tradition and community of culture, language, and religion whose distinctness and vitality the Russians recognized but regarded as irritants and sources of hostility. And to make matters worse, the Poles, perhaps by way of compensating for lost glories, cherished a sense of superiority over their conquerors that was grounded in their membership in the feudal, aristocratic, Latin, and Catholic world of medieval Europe. Their feeling of kinship with the West survived into the nineteenth and twentieth centuries. It took the form of liberal or romantic nationalism, of national or international socialism, or simply of the wish that the West, and France in particular, would come to their aid and resurrect a Polish state as Napoleon I had done when he created the Grand Duchy of Warsaw in 1807.

Alexander I had agreed to this partial restoration of Poland as a buffer state. After defeating Napoleon, he went further. In a tacit admission of the injustice committed in the partitions of Poland and of its greater readiness for self-government, he granted what he denied his own people: a kingdom of which the Emperor of Russia was the constitutional monarch. The Polish constitution was one of the most liberal in Europe. It granted the franchise to some 100,000 citizens; a separate army and a bicameral legislature (the Sejm); the use of Polish as the official language; freedom of person, press, and the inviolability of property. What it did not grant was genuine independence, since the emperor-king had full executive power, the exclusive right of legislative initiative, and an absolute veto. He appointed the viceroy and the head of the Polish army. Especially galling to patriots was Russia's retention of the Lithuanian, Belorussian, and Ukrainian lands that had been part of pre-partition Poland and became the western provinces of the empire.

The integrity of the Polish state and constitution was violated when Russian interests demanded it. There were political arrests, censorship, failure for several years to appoint a viceroy or summon the Sejm. What followed was predictable: protests, secret societies, and military conspiracies. In 1830 a full-fledged insurrection broke out and Nicholas I was deposed as Polish king. An invading Russian army occupied Warsaw and by September 1831 ended Polish resistance. The constitution was abrogated, and although Poland retained a separate administration, its upper levels were staffed by Russians. The army was disbanded and education, finance, and the courts were placed under more direct Russian control. Thousands of Polish patriots emigrated; many others were exiled, had their estates confiscated, or both. In the nine western provinces the repression of Polish influence was even more severe.

That these measures had only limited success soon became obvious even to those who had imposed them. At an imperial council which advised Alexander II in December 1855 to seek an end to the Crimean War, a minister pressed for immediate negotiations by pointing to the potential for unrest in the western borderlands. There were Swedish sympathies in Finland, discontent in the provinces annexed from Poland, and the eagerness of the Poles to rise 'as one man' the moment an opportunity presented itself.[6] They did rise, if not as one man, in 1863, and in spite of efforts at conciliation by Alexander II. These had divided Polish nationalists into moderates and radicals – the former willing to collaborate with the Russians up to a point, yet afraid of being thought unpatriotic; the latter demanding broad social and political reforms and the return of Lithuania to the kingdom. The absence of Polish unity and an army made putting down the insurrection easier than it had been in 1830–31. Still, the guerrilla war lasted more than a year. It was followed by forty years of russification.

The kingdom of Poland, which was now officially called the Vistula region, became in all important respects an integral part of the empire. Its ten provinces received Russian governors and were administered from St Petersburg. A Russian university was established in Warsaw; in 1866 Russian became the language of instruction in secondary schools and in 1885 in primary schools as well. The property of the Catholic Church was secularized, the Uniate Church abolished, and its flock converted to Orthodoxy. Poles had to conduct their business in courts and government offices in the language of the conqueror and were constantly reminded of his presence by the erection (begun in 1894) of an Orthodox cathedral in the centre of their capital city.

The economic advantages of Poland's integration into the empire – customs barriers had been removed as early as 1850 – made themselves felt in the last third of the century. The development of manufactures, mining, and commerce in the kingdom offered new outlets for Polish energies and an interest in what was called 'realism' and 'organic work'. This meant acceptance of the fact of foreign rule, of the futility of challenging it, and concentration on building the nation's prosperity and strength through peaceful labour. 'Realism' was found most often in the middle and professional classes and, after 1897, in the National Democratic Party of Roman Dmowski, successor of the more radical Polish and National Leagues of 1887 and 1893.

The renunciation by Dmowski's National Democrats of insurrection and independence in favour of legal and loyal work did not, however, mean acquiescence in the status quo. Continued pressure was to be brought on the Russian authorities to restore to the Polish people their autonomy, their language, their political and civil liberties. In 1905, when the Polish provinces too were gripped by strikes and violence, the National Democrats saw their chance of realizing these aims in collaboration with the forces of Russian constitutionalism. They were disappointed both in the few concessions the government made and in their allies. Permission for the limited use of Polish in schools and in communal government and an edict of toleration which allowed converted Uniates to return to their faith fell far short of what had been expected. So did liberal sympathy for a project for Polish autonomy which forty-six Polish members of the Second Duma introduced in April 1907. It was rejected as going too far by Kadets as well as by Octobrists and withdrawn by its sponsors. All prospects for its passage disappeared with the new electoral law Stolypin imposed in June. His purpose was to create a more manageable and conservative Duma, one which would be 'Russian in spirit' and deny to non-Russians the possibility 'of being the controllers of purely Russian issues'.[7]

There were only eighteen Polish delegates in the Third Duma. Fearful of domestic strife and international complications, both government and public became less willing after 1907 to extend to the borderlands rights which might endanger Russian strength and unity. The detachment in 1909 of the district of Kholm (Chelm) from Poland, the introduction in 1910 of laws to assure the predominance of the Russian minority in the zemstvos of the western provinces and in the municipal councils of Poland, were only the most important of a series of measures designed to deprive Polish nationalism of institutional bases. In Polish eyes, they were offensive and ominous.

In spite of all the rebuffs they were dealt, Dmowski and his National Democrats continued to see in collaboration with Russia the best hope for their country's future. Their increasing caution and conservatism, which in effect meant an indefinite postponement of Polish unity and independence, are attributable to two factors: their view of Germany as the greatest threat to Polish survival and the challenge from the Left. Neither the nationalist nor the internationalist wing of Polish socialism shared the confidence of the National Democrats' middle-class following in the benefits ultimately to be derived from the empire's economic and political progress under capitalist and bourgeois auspices.

The Polish Socialist Party (PPS), whose most prominent member, Jozef Pilsudski, would proclaim and head an independent Polish republic in 1918 was organized in 1893. Its founders believed that they could not entrust the fate of their people to Russian liberals or socialists, that even Russian revolutionaries could not fully understand how great was the need of Poland's workers for a state of their own. They suffered not only as proletarians from the low wages and high prices that were caused by discriminatory Russian taxes upon their employers; they were also disadvantaged as Poles in Russian courts and administrative offices and because their children, taught in an alien language, lacked opportunities for education and social advancement.

Unlike Dmowski, Pilsudski thought it no boon for Poland to remain part of a backward Russia; only a social *and* national revolution, leading to the establishment of a republic, could solve the Polish question. In Pilsudski's socialism the national element had always been stronger than the Marxist one, and it grew stronger still in the years after 1905. 'The historical role of socialism in Poland', he wrote, 'is the role of a defender of the West against reactionary tsardom.'[8] That position had led him to seek Japanese aid and arms in 1904. In 1914, when Dmowski and the sixteen Polish members of the Duma proclaimed their loyalty to Russia in its hour of trial, Pilsudski led a Polish legion, raised in Galicia, to fight against the armies of the tsar.

Polish Marxists found it more difficult than their rivals of the PPS to attract a mass following. The unbending internationalism which had characterized the Social Democratic Party of the Kingdom of Poland (SDKP) since its founding in 1894 – 'and Lithuania' (SDKPiL) was added in 1900 – made it, in effect, a subsidiary of Russian Social Democracy. The arguments of Polish Marxism's chief theoretician, Rosa Luxemburg, that for the proletariat to struggle for an independent Poland was an abandonment of its true interests which lay in the achievement of socialism in all the partitioning states and their eventual fusion, were too abstract for the mass of Polish workers. In the universal assault upon tsarism that took place in 1905 the SDKPiL was able to enrol nearly as many members (40,000) as the PPS (55,000) which it joined in January in calling a massive general strike. But when, beginning in 1906–7, revolutionary socialism throughout the empire was forced into retreat, the SDKPiL lost ground to the PPS and to the National Workers' Union, an ally of the National Democrats. In 1912 Polish Marxism was further shaken by a split, and the party ceased to play an effective role in Polish politics or, for that matter, in Lithuania, where it lost out to a national movement organized by Catholics. The SDKPiL had been weakened by that very nationalism which both Pilsudski and Lenin, pursuing different goals, recognized and used and which made such a powerful contribution to the disintegration of the Russian state in the revolutions of 1917.

Finland, taken from Sweden in the war of 1808–09, declared her independence in December 1917, although it required months of fighting between pro-Soviet Red Guards and nationalist White Guards to secure it. Confirmed by Alexander I in the rights and privileges they had been granted by Sweden, the Finns (i.e., the Finnish and Swedish citizens of the Grand Duchy) enjoyed a degree of self-rule and freedom unmatched in any other part of the empire. Finland's autonomy in domestic affairs was extensive and it was further enlarged by Alexander II in the 1860s. There were separate laws, a separate administration staffed by Finns and headed by the Senate, an elected legislature (the Diet), a small army and police force, separate railways and tariffs, postal, monetary, and educational systems. These gave the Finns a highly developed national consciousness which was buttressed and deepened by their liberties and economic progress. Their well-being made them even more jealous of their independence and resistant to Russian demands in the 1890s for closer control over Finnish affairs by the authorities at St Petersburg – that is, by the minister state secretary for Finland and the governor-general of the Grand Duchy as the tsar's representative.

Such demands were motivated by the military's concern for the security of the capital in case of a German and/or Swedish attack through Finland; by bureaucratic distaste for Finnish 'separatism' and the wish to align the Grand Duchy's administration and laws more closely with those of the rest of the empire; by resentment over the Finns' very small contribution in men and money to imperial defence; and by nationalist pressures for centralization and russification as bulwarks against internal subversion, external threats, or a combination of both.

The very first measures taken were both mild and of little consequence in themselves. The appointment in 1890 of a committee to review the Finnish criminal code and bring it into conformity with Russian law led to only minor revisions acceptable to both sides. The Postal Manifesto of the same year, which unified the postal systems of the two countries, was also agreed to by the Finns and brought no significant change. Yet there were protests in both instances that a principle had been breached because there had not been prior consultation or consent of the Diet and that this posed a threat to Finland's autonomy. These apprehensions were well founded, for during the coming years Russian legal and military officials proposed that laws affecting both countries be examined in the Council of State and that the integration of Finish units into the Russian army be considered.

In 1899 these proposals passed from the stage of discussion to that of decisive action. They found a willing executor in the newly appointed governor-general, N. I. Bobrikov, former chief of staff of the Petersburg military district and a man with little sympathy for Finnish particularism. His tactlessness and severity contributed greatly to the troubles that ensued when the Diet was summoned for January 1899 to receive a new military service law. Prepared by minister of war Kuropatkin who insisted that it might be discussed but not altered, the law provided for lengthened terms of service, a larger number of conscripts, and their employment outside the Grand Duchy.

Before the Diet could even voice the expected objections, an imperial manifesto of 3 February declared that in all legislation deemed by the emperor or his ministers to be of 'general imperial concern', the Diet had only the right of opinion. A 'Great Address' to the tsar, bearing the signature of 500,000 Finns, brought no change in the Russian position and what hopes remained for an accommodation disappeared with the issuance of the Language Manifesto of 1900 and the conscription law of 1901. The former made Russian the language of official business, with the clear intention of making it eventually Finland's official language; the latter all but dissolved the Finnish army as a separate entity, subjected it to Russian command, and made every Finn liable to serve in the Russian forces or under Russian officers.

Passive resistance, demonstrations, and refusals to obey the conscription law led to the adoption of ever more stringent measures and to the suspension, by 1903 – when Bobrikov was given dictatorial powers for three years –, of Finland's remaining rights. Opposition was no longer limited to petitions, sermons, refusals to proclaim, enforce, or obey the Russian laws. It now took the form also of political action, organization (Young Finns, Social Democrats, Party of Active Resistance) and armed struggle. In June 1904 Bobrikov was assassinated by a Finnish student.

The militancy of the Finns and their cooperation with the nation-wide front of liberals and socialists against the autocracy, caused the latter to soften its policies. The dictatorial powers of the governor-general and the conscription law were revoked in October 1905 and in 1906 Nicholas agreed to a reform of the Diet which made it a single-chamber legislature elected by all citizens over the age of twenty-four. This tenfold extension of the franchise gave the vote to women before they acquired it in most countries; it was also an improvement over what had been granted to men in Russia and it gave the Diet of 200 members an anti-Russian majority, including 80 Social Democrats. Proving recalcitrant to renewed attacks on its rights and Finnish autonomy, the Diet was dissolved four times between 1907 and 1911 and ceased to meet.

As the government of St Petersburg recovered its nerve under the leadership of Stolypin, it decided that Finland's special status was incompatible with the new constitutional order. The Fundamental Laws of 1906, it was argued, were applicable throughout the empire and made the State Council and Duma, not the Finnish Diet, the source of all laws of imperial concern. For Stolypin and other Russian nationalists, Finnish particularism was more than an incongruity. It was a constant provocation which was heightened by the shelter and assistance Russian revolutionaries found in Finland and by the German sympathies of many Finns. Stolypin found support for his views in the conservative Third Duma. In 1910 it passed a bill which specified what matters were to be removed from the competence of the Diet and determined by Russian legislation: taxes and tariffs; military service and the rights of Russians residing in Finland; the management of courts and schools, of posts, railways, and the currency; questions of language, public order, and much else. That Finns could elect deputies to the Duma and State Council was no consolation to them and they refused to make use of that right. Little of Stolypin's programme was put into effect before war broke out in 1914 and Finland was placed under martial law. The jubilant exclamation with which the right-wing Duma deputy Purishkevich had greeted the passage of the government's bill – *Finis Finlandiae* – soon proved to have been premature.[9]

The three Baltic provinces of Estland, Livland, and Kurland which crusading German knights had in the Middle Ages subjected to their swords and Christianity had been annexed by Russia at the end of the Northern War with Sweden (1721) and, in the case of Kurland, at the time of the Third Partition of Poland (1795). Like the Swedish and Polish kings who had exercised a loose authority over these lands, Peter I and Catherine II allowed the German nobles in the countryside and the German burghers in the cities to retain their corporate rights and institutions, their Lutheran churches, their language, schools, and courts and their virtually unchecked domination of the native lower classes of town and country.

In these provinces of the Russian Empire a minority of non-Russians in effect ruled an indigenous, largely peasant population of Estonian and Latvian serfs who worked the estates of the German barons, prayed in their churches, and were judged in their courts. Even after their emancipation without land (1816–19) the peasants owed labours dues to their masters for another fifty years and had no share in the political power which the latter exercised through their provincial assemblies. The emancipated peasants did, however, become members of self-governing rural communities which elected their own officers and maintained rural elementary schools where instruction was conducted in the native tongue; some of them began to acquire land in the second half of the century and those who migrated to the towns could vote in municipal elections after 1877.

The German nobles repaid the generosity of their Russian sovereigns with devotion and loyalty. They occupied important posts in the empire's military and civil services and were much valued for their knowledge and reliability. At the same time Russian colleagues often envied them for the special favours and preferment they received from the monarch while ordinary citizens resented them both as agents of the autocracy and for their alien ways. The methodical German who lacked the Russian's generosity and expansiveness was a stock figure of literature and popular speech. Conservative and liberal nationalists alike questioned the depth of the Baltic Germans' attachment to Russia. Doubts about their loyalty grew with the rising might of Prussia and their determination to assert their social and national privileges against all challenges.

These came from a disenfranchised peasantry; from educated Latvians and Estonians who echoed the distress of the lower classes and rose to the defence of their native languages and traditions against German cultural dominance; and from Russian publicists, like the Slavophile Iurii Samarin, who berated their own officials for abandoning an entire region to alien and selfish masters. In the reign of Alexander II these critics began to ask that a small group of aristocrats not be allowed to bar the introduction to the Baltic of the reformed courts and local governments that Russia had adopted for her own renewal. Samarin, who had served in the Baltic and had been one of the prime movers of the peasant emancipation of 1861, warned that unless Russia took the native Balts under her wing, they would become the instrument of the 'germanizing tendencies' of their lords. No more than the British or French should Russians permit anyone but themselves to control the destinies of any part of their state. To do so would invite disunity and dissolution.[10]

Attempts to strengthen the Russian presence in the provinces began with the establishment of an Orthodox bishopric at Riga in 1836. A decade later 75,000 or more Latvians and Estonians were converted to the state church, in part because it had shown some sympathy for their economic plight. In the next reign too, the nascent national consciousness of the Balts was nourished by anti-German sentiments and expectations of Russian aid and friendship. But the tsars were quite opposed to any movement, however pro-Russian or anti-German it might be, in which social protest and national yearnings were so closely and dangerously intertwined. Conversions were stopped in 1848 and

Samarin was rebuked for his attacks on the Baltic Germans by Nicholas I as well as by his son Alexander II. The latter did, however, agree that the use of Russian should become obligatory in provincial agencies of the imperial government and that the municipal institutions of 1870 should be extended to the Baltic towns.

Conversionist efforts were resumed in the reign of Alexander III, together with other measures of administrative and cultural russification. The introduction in 1889 of the reformed Russian legal system (but without the right of trial by jury) was, from the Estonians' and Latvians' point of view, an improvement over the justice dispensed in German courts and enforced by manorial police. The same could not be said of the imposition of the Russian language at all but the lowest levels of government and education and its compulsory teaching in elementary schools; of the closing of the German University of Dorpat – which did not, on reopening in 1894, become the Estonian University of Tartu but the Russian University of Iurev; or of the restrictions placed on Lutheran churches and their ministers. The Russian government and its officials generously supported the missionary activities of the Orthodox Church. Yet the results were negligible because the methods were crude – Lutheran pastors, for example, were liable to prosecution for allowing converts to Orthodoxy to return to Lutheranism – and because neither conversion nor russification could meet the economic needs of workers and peasants or the demands of middle-class liberals and radicals for the national and political rights that Russians and Germans alike withheld from them.

Ironically, it was through the University of Iurev, as well as that of St Petersburg, that young Estonians and Latvians were exposed to radical ideas, and through the region's closer economic links with Russia that the ground was prepared for their reception. The building of railroads, ports, and ship-yards; the growth of light industries, of trade, and towns, created a native bourgeoisie and intelligentsia and a working class whose members were less submissive to the Germans than their peasant ancestors had been. In the Revolution of 1905 the Baltic provinces – and above all the industrial strongholds of Social Democracy in Latvia – were the scenes of bloody clashes in which peasants and workers were ranged against German landlords and Russian soldiers.

The experience of that year caused the Russian authorities to close ranks once again with the Baltic Germans and to abandon the measures of russification directed against them. But neither their cooperation nor the adherence of Estonian and Latvian Marxists to Russian Social Democracy prevented the persistence of a nationalism which, after the fall of the tsar, reasserted itself against the Provisional and Soviet governments of Russia, against local Germans and those from the Reich who came to their aid in the civil war of 1917–18. The republics of Estonia and Latvia, proclaimed in 1918, expelled German volunteers and Soviet troops and were recognized by the Soviet Union in 1920. Like neighbouring Lithuania, which also gained its independence in 1918, they were occupied by the Red Army in 1940 and became constituent republics of the USSR.

In Transcaucasia – the area south of the Caucasus Mountains that stretch for 600 miles from north-west to south-east between the Black and Caspian Seas – the three independent republics which emerged in 1918 from the turmoil of revolution and civil war survived for only two years before they were retaken by Soviet troops. The Georgians, Armenians, and Azerbaijanis who created these states and their short-lived federation had neither resisted Russian conquest in the early part of the nineteenth century nor had they subsequently developed separatist aspirations. Statehood was almost thrust upon them by the collapse of imperial authority and by their distrust of its Bolshevik heirs.

The Georgians and Armenians had a highly developed sense of national identity. It was sustained by their Georgian Orthodox and Armenian Apostolic (Gregorian) Churches, by their own languages and literatures, and by the past glories of their kingdoms, warriors and poets. Yet they had welcomed or sought tsarist rule as a protection from the Muslim peoples and powers (Persia and Turkey) who surrounded them and who threatened their very existence. The Armenians especially, since there were nearly twice as many of them in the Ottoman Empire as in Russia, looked to her as a shield and refuge from Turkish persecution. Ethnic and social tensions, exacerbated by Russian slights to national and religious sensibilities, none the less made Transcaucasia an arena of struggle against the autocracy which gave to the revolutionary movement some of its most prominent and determined members. One of these was the future Bolshevik Joseph Stalin (born Djugashvili) who had in 1899 been expelled from the Tiflis Theological Seminary – a breeding-ground of opposition to Russian rule – where Georgian had been banned as a language of instruction in 1872 and where another expelled Georgian student had assassinated the Russian rector in 1886.

Georgian patriotism was strong and it found eloquent spokesmen, like the liberal writer Ilia Chavchavadze, in the 1870s. It was always subordinate, however, to the populist or Marxist socialism that young Georgians imbibed in Russia or the West. By the early 1900s Marxism had become the dominant force among Georgian intellectuals and began to win a following among the workers of all nationalities, including Russians, who were manning railroads and factories, mines and oilfields throughout Transcaucasia. Organized in 1901 as a branch of the Russian Social Democratic Workers' Party, Georgian Marxism, in both its Menshevik and Bolshevik variants, disavowed purely national aims. Its theoreticians insisted that the needs of all the empire's minorities could only be met by a revolution that would transform Russia into a socialist and democratic state in which there would be neither cause nor wish for ethnic or national discrimination. In a population as thoroughly mixed as that of Transcaucasia, where the influx of Russians, Ukrainians and Belorussians was constantly adding to the diversity of races and languages, it would be absurd for the Georgian working class to seek territorial or national solutions on its own. Only the Mensheviks modified this orthodox interpretation of proletarian internationalism in 1910 to allow for extraterritorial cultural autonomy for Georgia. And it was they who in 1918 reluctantly formed and led the Georgian Republic.

For the Armenians, scattered throughout Transcaucasia and a majority in only one of its six provinces (Erevan), national autonomy within the empire was still more problematical than it was for the Georgians who were concentrated in the provinces of Kutais and Tiflis. It is not surprising, therefore, that the Armenian national renaissance should seek only to preserve or, at best, to widen the considerable cultural, religious, and economic opportunities they enjoyed in Russia. The first Armenian political movement, the Marxist *Hnchak* (Clarion) which was organized in Geneva in 1887 and advocated separation from the Ottoman Empire, had little influence in Transcaucasia. None of the other Marxist groups that were subsequently active among the Armenians of Russia was much more successful. This was as true of the orthodox Social Democrats, who gave priority to the nation-wide class struggle, as of the 'specifists' of the Social Democratic Workers' Armenian Organization, who conceded that the situation of the Armenian proletariat required special attention and specific solutions. It was the Armenian Revolutionary Federation (*Dashnaktsutiun* or Federation, for short) that became almost from its inception in 1890 the most popular and powerful of the Armenian national parties.

The Dashnaks initially devoted their efforts to winning administrative and economic freedom for Turkish Armenia and to the defence of its people from Turkish depredations, if necessary by force of arms or acts of terror. The Russian authorities of Transcaucasia, although their treatment of the increasingly restive Armenian minority was less benevolent in the 1880s and 1890s than it had been earlier, did not become a target for the Dashnaks until 1903. In that year official moves, begun in 1885 to strengthen Russian influence by closing Armenian schools or changing their curricula, culminated in the confiscation of Armenian Church properties. They were to be used to pay for the new state schools that would be free of nationalist and revolutionary influence and facilitate the process of russification.

Armenian reaction was furious and virtually unanimous. The attack on their Church and schools rallied Armenian communities throughout the empire as nothing else could have done and made attacks on Russian as well as Turkish officials acceptable. Passive resistance and a boycott of Russian schools, courts, and other agencies were so effective as to bring about the recall of the governor-general, Prince G. S. Golitsyn (who had been wounded by Hnchakist assailants), and his replacement by Count I. I. Vorontsov-Dashkov as viceroy. Since by the end of 1904 much of Transcaucasia was close to open revolt and there was trouble also among its Georgians, Muslims, and Russians, the viceroy advised conciliating the Armenians. In August 1905 Nicholas rescinded the confiscation decree and managed by declarations of friendship for his Armenian subjects and by punitive expeditions to pacify them and Transcaucasia by 1907. A combination of concessions, stern measures, and exhaustion brought peace to the area.

Most Armenians, and especially the substantial middle class, welcomed the restoration of public order; its continued disruption would hinder their ability to assist their brothers in Turkey and open the road to the social radicalism of Dashnaktsutiun. That party's congress, held in Vienna in 1907, had adopted an explicitly socialist programme. Besides demanding cultural autonomy, the right to local self-government and the use of local languages, the Dashnaks called for communal ownership of land, the separation of church and state, and universal suffrage in a democratic Federal Republic of Russia. The liberation of Turkish Armenia nevertheless remained the Dashnaks' primary goal and that meant for them, as well as for their more conservative countrymen, a suspension of open hostilities against the Romanov empire. Truce turned into alliance when Russia went to war against Turkey in 1914 and Nicholas told the Catholicos, the head of their Church, that a brilliant future awaited the Armenians.

They could not have known the horrors that would befall their people at Turkish hands in 1915 and how little protection the tsar's army was able or willing to give them. But they had already had a taste of Russian ambivalence and of the ferocious hostility of their Muslim neighbours in Azerbaijan during the riots that began in the oil city of Baku in February 1905, spread to the rural areas, and were not finally or firmly put down until 1907. Responsibility for the Armenian lives and property lost to the violence of Azerbaijani peasants and workers was laid at the door of the tsarist regime. Russian officials may indeed have taken satisfaction in the lesson administered to the troublesome Armenians; they certainly moved too slowly and indecisively to avert or stop the misfortunes visited upon them. But proof is lacking that they organized or initiated this explosion of racial and religious hatreds, of social and economic rivalry, in order to divide and confuse their enemies. And if, in fact, they had thought by such desperate devices to neutralize the Muslims of Transcaucasia politically, they failed.

Instead, the uncertain behaviour of imperial authority in face of the assaults launched upon it from all quarters served to mobilize Muslims throughout Russia. Those of Transcaucasia petitioned in March 1905 for equal access to government service, for the right to organize zemstvos, and demanded that no more Russians be allowed to settle among them. A group of young intellectuals, some of them active with the Bolsheviks in 1905, organized the first Azerbaijani political party, *Musavat* (Equality), in Baku in 1911–12. Their programme stressed the unification of Muslims everywhere and sought the union of the people of eastern Transcaucasia with their coreligionists and fellow Turks of Turkey.

Neither the Turkic intellectuals who led *Musavat*, and even less the peasants and landowners who made up the bulk of Azerbaijan's 1.5 million Turkic inhabitants, thought of themselves as a nation or put forward national goals. The very name Azerbaijan, a purely geographical designation, was hardly used before 1917 and its Turkic Muslims were usually (if incorrectly) referred to as Tatars. None the less, they were part of the cultural awakening that had begun among the Muslims of European Russia in the 1880s and of the movement which in 1905 and after entered the political arena on their behalf: the liberal All-Russian Muslim Union and, in addition to *Musavat*, the regional parties of the Crimean and Volga Tatars that were close to the Russian Socialist Revolutionaries.

Muslims elected thirty deputies to the First and thirty-nine to the Second Duma where, in spite of ideological divisions between the liberal majority and the socialist minority, they formed a Muslim faction. These numbers were severely cut back by the electoral law of 1907 – to nine members in the Third Duma and six in the Fourth – which deprived approximately 8 million Muslims of Central Asia (i.e., the Steppe Region and Turkestan) of any representation.

The colonial administrators of this frontier, mainly military men, had wisely prohibited the missionary work that the Orthodox Church conducted among the Volga Tatars with great determination but modest results. They had also left undisturbed native laws and customs at the village and tribal level; abolished slavery and torture; introduced railroads and irrigation (for cotton); and reformed land tenure and taxation. Russian officials, none the less, were and remained alien conquerors, distrusted even for their benevolence. If they were not incompetent and corrupt, as an imperial commission of 1908–09 found many of them to be,[11] they were first and foremost devoted to the interests of the empire rather than to the welfare of their charges.

St Petersburg looked upon Central Asia as a market for goods which Russian manufacturers found it difficult to sell elsewhere; as a source of cheap labour to produce the cotton that was to replace the expensive American import; and as a place of settlement for the land-poor peasants of the interior. The latter accounted for 40 per cent of the population of the Steppe Region by 1911. The opening of Turkestan to Russian settlement in 1907 made native herders and peasants fear for their grazing lands and farms as well. The assembly of notables and intellectuals which met at Tashkent, the capital of Turkestan, in March 1906 voiced the fears aroused by Russian encroachments in its demands for guarantees of religious freedom, a Muslim Ecclesiastical Administration, the restoration of expropriated pasture lands, and an end to the taxation of landed property.

Sporadic local risings in the 1880s and 1890s had been the first signs of economic and religious protest. They were only pale forebodings of the great peasant and nomad revolt that broke out all over Central Asia in the summer of 1916. Triggered by a decree conscripting native males – heretofore exempt from military service – for labour duty in the Russian forces, the revolt claimed the lives of thousands of Russian settlers and officials. Still greater numbers of natives fell victim to the Russian army and to the reprisals of Russian colonists before the last flames of rebellion were put out at the end of the year.

It would be wrong to see this elemental outburst as the culmination of a steady growth of a common identity or will on the part of Central Asians; much less did it express a determination to expel Russian rule or to separate from it. No more than the other Muslims of the empire could those of Central Asia agree on what their status in the new post-Romanov state should be.

Delegates to their first regional council, held in Tashkent in April 1917, were united only on the need for a greater voice in determining their own affairs, for an end to Russian colonization, and the return of confiscated lands. At the Moscow All-Russian Congress of Muslims, the Central Asians supported the motion of an Azerbaijani representative which advocated territorial autonomy in a federal republic. It prevailed over the idea of a unitary democratic state with only cultural autonomy, which its backers thought to be less divisive of Muslim unity and power. But neither unitarists nor federalists supported secession. Only after the fall of the Provisional Government did Kazakhs and other Central Asians, as well as Bashkirs and Tatars, proclaim their autonomy and the Azerbaijanis their independence.

Political power and genuine self-determination eluded Russia's Muslims both before and after 1917, because they lacked the unity, the common history and territory that could alone have made them the formidable force that the Tatar Duma deputy S. N. Maksudov professed to see. With only a few exceptions, he declared in 1910, all Russia's 20 million Muslims were of the Turko-Tatar race who spoke dialects of a common Turkic language.[12] Their ethnic and linguistic bonds were much less strong, however, in fact and feeling, than their Islamic faith and culture, and upon both of these the secularism of their intellectuals and the westernizing influences of the Russian environment had made considerable inroads.

This was the case above all among the two million Tatars living in the middle-Volga region at the turn of the century. They had maintained their religion for more than 300 years and had also won from Catherine the Great religious and civic rights. With a substantial stake in the economy of the empire and a commercial and industrial middle class, they were the most advanced and prosperous of Russia's Turkic Muslims. Carrying on much of its business in Asian Russia and surrounded by Russians at home, the Tatar bourgeoisie doubted whether a movement of Turkic nationalism which joined nomadic Bashkirs and Kazakhs, fundamentalist clerics, liberal and radical secularists was either possible or desirable.

Wealthy Tatars had been generous in their support of the schools and pub-lishing enterprises that had in one generation spread far afield and produced a Muslim intelligentsia. But neither they nor the overwhelming majority of the country's politically conscious Turks and Muslims desired its break-up or Balkanization. They wanted the full civil and political rights for which their Russian fellow-citizens were striving, as well as security and greater scope for their religion, their culture, and their way of life. Although the government had not met their demands, they had not given up hope. In August 1914, in the nation's hour of crisis, the Muslims proclaimed their devotion to the common fatherland and through their Duma deputies vowed to fight for its honour and integrity.[13]

Whether a victorious Russia would have rewarded their loyalty is doubtful. The nationalism which the state fostered to rally its Russian subjects to its side would in all likelihood have been strengthened by success in war. In Russian society, too, including its liberal elements, nationalism was growing in the years before 1914. While they condemned the chauvinism of the professional patriots of the Right and the discriminatory practices of the state, liberal nationalists distrusted the claims non-Russians were making for recognition of their separate identities and needs as a retreat from the ideal of a common nationhood freely affirmed by all free citizens. They feared that a democratic Russia, no less than an authoritarian one, might become vulnerable to internal disunity and foreign enemies through national particularism.

On the Left, neither wing of Marxism approved of the federal structure the Socialist Revolutionaries envisioned for the Russian republic. In theory, and for tactical reasons, the Bolsheviks conceded the right of every nationality to self-determination, even secession. In practice they resisted it as bourgeois, a departure from proletarian internationalism and likely to weaken the workers' state and party. Like the liberals, the socialists preferred to regard the problem of the nationalities as an aspect of a far wider oppression and their emancipation as part and parcel of the general struggle for the liberation of all the peoples of Russia.

None of these suffered as much from popular and official prejudice as did the Jews. Both grew more virulent in the reigns of the last two tsars, seemingly reinforced each other, and contributed to the exodus of two million Jews abroad (mainly to America) between 1881 and 1914. The economic, legal, and social situation of no other ethnic or religious minority was as precarious or marginal as theirs, and none did Russian administrators view with as much suspicion or dislike. Even the more enlightened bureaucrats who favoured emancipation and the removal of the thicket of restrictions that hedged about the Jews, expected them to shed their 'peculiarities'. The very state that wanted to make the Jews less Jewish and to prepare them for acceptance by Russian society also rejected them. It did so by keeping them in the anomalous condition of citizens who were denied some basic attributes of citizenship yet expected to fulfil all its obligations.

With the Polish partitions a country which had known or admitted only a tiny number of Jews was suddenly faced with upwards of 600,000 people who were alien in almost every way. They belonged to no Christian church, spoke a strange language (Yiddish), and wore strange medieval dress. More than an ordinary religious minority, they were a self-contained 'nation-caste'[14] which lived on the fringes of Polish society under the protection of the crown or nobles and regulated its internal affairs through the *kahal* (community or gathering) without recourse to the general laws or administration. The vast majority of Poland's Jews were traders and middlemen, keepers of shops and inns, artisans and landlords' agents and strikingly different, therefore, in occupational and social structure from their hosts and neighbours who often saw them as parasites. Only one per cent were engaged in agriculture, and there were neither warriors nor nobles among them who could or would have served in Russia's armies or government, as did Ukrainians, Germans, and Georgians, and formed links to the larger community.

Heavily burdened though the relationship between Russians and Jews was fated to be by the deep-seated animosities of the former and the strangeness of the latter, Catherine the Great treated her new subjects with even-handed liberality. Like other inhabitants of the newly acquired territories, Jews were guaranteed all their former rights and privileges, specifically their communal institutions, their property, and the free exercise of their religion. Since the empress wished to promote trade, manufactures, and an urban middle class, she decided that Jews were to participate on an equal footing with Christians in the municipal governments she created and to be admitted to the two urban estates into which she divided the trading and manufacturing population: the merchant guilds and the category of townsmen (*meshchane*).

But what appeared to be a boon and was, in fact, an advance on Polish or West European practice, turned out to be for all but the more prosperous merchants a misfortune. Within a few years all Jews were enrolled in the two urban estates and became city dwellers in law, although most lived in villages or townlets – semi-rural settlements called *mestechki* in Russian or *shtetls* in Yiddish. Their presence in the country side where they traded with the peasants or leased from nobles the right to distil and sell spirits, thus became illegal. Russian officials soon began to see the Jews as the chief source of peasant poverty, drunkenness, and turbulence. The three evils would become associated in their minds with the Jews who were repeatedly ordered to remove to the towns. Such orders could not always be carried out, for economic as well as practical reasons, but they posed a constant threat to the livelihood of rural Jews and impoverished those who were driven into the crowded Jewish quarters of the cities. By 1900 only about 18 per cent of Jews were left in the countryside.

Nor did the status of merchant or townsman confer the right of residence or inscription in the urban communities of the Russian interior. Neither the government nor their competitors were willing to extend to Jews the freedom of movement which few Russians as yet enjoyed. As a consequence, Jews could live only in the so-called Pale of Permanent Settlement, consisting of ten provinces of the Kingdom of Poland and fifteen of Russia's western and south-western guberniias. And there most of them remained until the end of the tsarist regime. Beginning with the reign of Alexander II, a few categories of Jews who were deemed to follow useful occupations – merchants of the first guild, individuals with university degrees or medical training, dentists, pharmacists, certain craftsmen – were permitted to work and reside in Russia proper, not as a matter of right, which comparable categories of citizens had by then received, but as a revocable privilege.

The Pale reminded even those Jews who lived outside its borders – never more than 5 per cent of the total – of their precarious position, for it became a place of exile for those discovered through more stringent interpretations of the law to have settled beyond it illegally. Even inside the Pale Jews did not enjoy the rights of 'natives'. They could not live or work where they wished and when the *kahal* was abolished in 1844, they lost that modicum of self-government left to Siberian or Central Asian natives who were exempt, moreover, from many taxes and conscription. Jews were not, paid a variety of special levies, could not become officers in the army, and were virtually excluded from state employment.

Yet they had reason to think that as the government of Alexander II freed the serfs and loosened the bonds in which all Russians had been kept, their hour too would come in the not too distant future. The relaxation of residential restrictions and the opening of educational and economic opportunities did enable a small number of Jews to achieve success in banking and railroad development, in the sugar and textile industries, in the export of timber and grain, in the professions and the arts. The accomplishments of a few men of wealth or education, their adoption of Russian speech and culture, raised hopes that state and society would recognize the contributions Jews could make to both and that similar opportunities would be offered to the poverty-stricken masses of the Pale.

These hopes were cruelly disappointed when anti-Jewish riots – pogroms – broke out in numerous localities of the Pale in 1881 and 1882. They led not only to the loss of life and property, but also caused a hardening of official attitudes. In the aftermath of the assassination of Alexander II the authorities of St Petersburg were at first disposed to see in the excesses of the mob the sinister hand of revolution. That view soon gave way to a more comforting interpretation. For officials and publicists who deplored the liberalizing tendencies of the previous reign, pogroms confirmed their deepest fears. Their prejudices were now given a semblance of intellectual respectability by the new 'scientific' anti-Semitism of Western, mainly German, origin: Jewish financiers and intellectuals became the symbols and agents of all that challenged traditional authority and values. The case was stated by Ignatev, soon to be minister of interior, in a memorandum to Alexander III.

In Petersburg there exists a powerful group of Poles and Yids which holds in its hands direct control of banks, the stock-exchange, the bar, a great part of the press, and other areas of public life. Through many legal and illegal ways it exerts an enormous influence over the bureaucracy and the general course of affairs. Parts of this group are implicated in the growing plunder of the exchequer and in seditious activity . . . Preaching the blind imitation of Europe, . . . these people . . . recommend the granting of the most extensive rights to Poles and Jews, and representative institutions after the Western model. Every honest voice . . . is silenced by the shouts of Jews and Poles who insist that one must listen only to the 'intelligent' class and that Russian demands must be rejected as backward and unenlightened.[15]

Ignatev's fanciful conjuring up of a Polish-Jewish conspiracy betrays the feelings of vulnerability that lay behind much of the nationalities policy of the next two decades. The pogroms, in addition, raised the spectre of popular wrath which might not stop at the Jews but turn upon Russian merchants, landowners, and officials. The unruliness of the masses, like the political ambitions of Poles and the money power of the Jews, was seen as the unsettling consequence of the Great Reforms against which men like Pobedonostsev, Dostoevskii and Aksakov had warned: the coming of industry and capitalism, the dissolution of old loyalties and controls. A backward country like Russia, Pobedonostsev said, must erect barriers against the Jews, against the spirit of the century that supported them, and guard the most defenceless and backward of its people, the peasants, from both.[16]

It was easier, of course, to curb the Jews than the masses or the spirit of the century. The commune, even Pobedonostsev conceded, was doomed; railroads and factories had to be built. Russia could not return to a simpler age. It was the Jews, therefore, who in Ignatev's explanation of the riots figured as the only culprits and the Jews who were the sole objects of the remedies he proposed. The main reason he gave for the 'uncharacteristic' violence of the poorer classes was exploitation by the Jews who had in the previous twenty years taken over trade and manufactures as well as significant amounts of land through rent or purchase. They had done so not to increase the productive forces of the country, but for their own clannish purposes, and provoked the violence of their victims. Having put down the disorders, the government had now to remove the 'abnormal conditions which exist between Jews and natives and protect the latter from the pernicious activity . . . which was responsible for the disturbances'.[17]

Although Ignatev was minister of interior for only a little more than a year and the Committee of Ministers rejected most of his programme for checking the harmful influence of the Jews, its legacy survived in law and in the bureaucratic mind until 1917. His colleagues, who had warned of unthinkable damage to the economy if all of Ignatev's measures were adopted, none the less gave their partial assent. 'In the interests of the local population', Jews not already living in the villages were forbidden to do so, to acquire rural properties through lease, purchase, or any other device, and to conduct business on Christian holy days. Minor restrictions were also placed on their traffic in liquor.

Known as the May Laws of 1882, these rules were to be purely temporary. Together with all legislation bearing on the Jews, they were to be reviewed by a High Commission which the Committee of Ministers asked the emperor to appoint. The Commission was set up in 1883 and chaired by Count Kh. I. Pahlen, a member of the Council of State and former minister of justice. After five years, eight of its fourteen members recommended Jewish emancipation and the gradual removal of discriminatory laws and regulations. As justification for proceeding carefully, they cited what Ignatev had called the abnormality of the relationship between Russians and Jews – precipitate action might exacerbate tensions – and the complexity of the Jewish problem. Whatever its roots might be, and the treatment they suffered at the hands of the government was surely one of them, the Commission agreed, the Jews had innate vices that nourished the hostility of their neighbours, especially among the lower classes. It was this frightening complexity of the problem and the unpredictable consequences of its solution that continued to be invoked on behalf of caution, inaction, or new restraints.

Alexander III did not follow the recommendations of the Pahlen Commission's majority. He and his close advisers looked upon emancipation as a leap into the unknown. Instead of taking it, they decided to counteract what the official history of the State Council called the geographical spread and numerical increase of the Jews, of whom there were 4 million by 1881. 'Because of the difficulty of a radical solution of the Jewish question, it seemed desirable to take certain palliative steps to restrict the in many ways harmful Jewish population.'[18] There was a veritable flood of these steps between 1882 and 1901.

The army set a quota of 5 per cent on doctors and medical assistants. The Ministries of Transport and State Domains limited the number of Jews (and Poles). The country's only Jewish vocational school was closed, additional restraints were placed on landholding by Jews and Poles in nine provinces, and in several cities Jewish membership in stock exchanges was made more difficult and election to the chairmanship impossible. Families of men who failed to answer draft calls were made liable to heavy fines and exempt individuals could be called as replacements. Jewish mine owners were barred from state lands, their exploitation of mines and oil wells elsewhere was inhibited, and the admission of Jews to the bar was suspended for fifteen years. There were expulsions from the border zone, a number of townlets were declared villages, and the statutes on local government of 1890 and 1892 deprived Jews of the vote. In the cities of the Pale, Jewish councillors, not to exceed 10 per cent of the total, were appointed by the authorities. Regulations on residence outside the Pale were more strictly interpreted and enforced, leading in 1886 to large-scale expulsions from Kiev and in 1891 from Moscow. Jewish soldiers could not even spend their leave outside the Pale.

This was not all that was done, nor the end of what some members of the administration, notably Pleve, then assistant minister of interior, wished to do. But it was enough to give rise to protests outside of Russia, to swell the stream of emigration, and to embitter the younger generation. The quotas established in 1887 for secondary and higher schools — 10 per cent in the Pale, 5 per cent in the rest of the country, and 3 per cent in Moscow and St Petersburg — blocked for many young Jews the chief avenue of access to employment and Russian society.

Not a few of them responded by joining the revolutionary movement, and some played leading roles in its formation: Grigorii Gershuni and Chaim Zhitlovskii among the Socialist Revolutionaries, Iulii Martov and Lev Trotskii among the Social Democrats. They expected to gain their full human and civil rights by fighting with non-Jewish comrades for an egalitarian and socialist Russia, and in the process they submerged or abandoned their Jewish loyalties and identity. Others founded a specifically Jewish workers' movement in 1897, the Bund, which based itself on the 600,000 Jewish proletarians of the Pale and was the first Marxist party with a mass following in the empire. There were 25,000 men and women in its ranks in 1903 and as many as 35,000 by 1905.

The Bund's founders initially considered their organization to be an integral part of Russian Social Democracy. Their Marxist principles made them put the class interests of workers above those of the Jewish people who were, moreover, a dispersed minority without a national territory. In 1901 a Bund congress went beyond the goal of civil equality, however, to declare that the Jews were a nation. In the Russian federal republic they too would be entitled to full national autonomy wherever they resided, to have Yiddish, the speech of the Jewish masses, recognized as the national language, to set up secular Yiddish schools, to develop a Yiddish press and literature. The Bund's cultural demands might have been acceptable to other Social Democrats. Since they were coupled with federalism and the insistence that the Bund remain the exclusive representative of Jewish workers and a distinct entity within the party, rejection was swift.

Trotskii and Martov, no less than Plekhanov and Lenin, dismissed the Bund's ideas as un-Marxist, nationalistic, and impractical, a threat to the unity of the movement and working class. The rift which this disagreement opened, and which caused the Bund's temporary withdrawal from the RSDWP in 1903, was never fully closed. Plekhanov's gibe, that the Bundists were Zionists who were afraid of sea-sickness,[19] reflected an abiding hostility to Jewish nationalism on the part of Russian Marxists which was strongest among the Bolsheviks. Within a few years of coming to power they repressed both the Bund and Zionism.

The Bundists themselves were none too comfortable in their affirmation of Jewish nationality and it was at least in part designed to counter the appeals of Zionism. That the Bund was organized only weeks after the first World Zionist Congress met in Switzerland in August 1897 was a coincidence; that it recognized the existence of a Jewish nation in 1901 while also denouncing Zionism as bourgeois and the goal of a Jewish state as utopian, was not. Zionist ideas and groups had existed since the early 1880s, when the pogroms and the May Laws made it appear that Jews could cease being a persecuted minority only in a land of their own.

By the turn of the century Zionists had created a vital movement with wide appeal to all classes of Jews, and their Minsk conference of 1902 was attended by over 700 delegates. Unlike the clandestine Bund, with which it competed, Zionism was tolerated by the authorities, both because it shunned radical politics and because it directed most of its efforts to emigration or the preparation for it. Even so, its activities soon became suspect and Pleve banned them in June 1903 because, he said, the goal of Palestine had become more remote and that of strengthening Jewish ideas, solidarity, and organizations in Russia more immediate and menacing.[20]

Pleve inflated the menace and misread its sources. He believed, for example, that all the terrorist attacks of the previous years were based on Jewish instigation and that Jewish bankers were helping to subsidize the opposition. There can be no question, however, that Jewish anger and militancy were on the increase and reached new heights with the armed self-defence units formed by Bundists and Zionists after the pogrom of Kishinev in Bessarabia of April 1903. Kishinev sent shock waves of indignation throughout Russia and the world. It was bloodier than any of its predecessors and not unnaturally was blamed on a government (and Pleve in particular) which had not allowed similar outrages for twenty years. The suspicion which first surfaced with the pogroms of 1881–82, that extensive mob violence was inconceivable in a well-policed state like Russia without permission from above, now hardened into conviction.

Pleve plausibly denied instigating the Kishinev pogrom. Nor does available evidence support the accusation that he gave orders to let the rioters have their way until, at the end of two days, troops and police stopped them. Yet this was no spontaneous outburst, but the work of local anti-Semites who spread the story of a ritual murder to incite the populace and who enjoyed the favour of local authorities. The legal culpability of officials, both local and central, can no longer be established, but their moral guilt is beyond doubt. A state which by its laws and practices brands a minority as harmful fairly invites attacks upon it. The military and police of Kishinev had reason to expect the indulgence of their superiors for failing to act vigorously and with dispatch.[21]

Although the government condemned the Kishinev pogrom and some of its perpetrators were tried and punished, pogroms did not end with the assassination of Pleve. The worst of these took place in the fall of 1905, when over 600 Jewish communities were affected and about 1,000 Jews were killed. This time there was complicity by elements of the administration. There were men in the Police Department in St Petersburg who thought to identify revolutionaries and Jews in the public mind by printing pogrom proclamations which members of right-wing organizations helped to circulate. Pogroms ceased after 1906, as did other major disturbances, and the economic recovery that began soon thereafter gave some relief to those Jews who had gained at least a toehold in trade or industry. But the condition of Russian Jewry as a whole was not improved by the political changes the Revolution of 1905 had brought about. The demands of the Union for the Attainment of Full Rights for the Jewish People of Russia, which was formed in March 1905 and spoke for liberals and moderates, remained as far from realization as the revolutionary goals of the Bund.

Jews were allowed to take part in elections to the Duma and to sit in it, and twelve of them did so in 1906 – nine Kadets and three Labourites (*trudoviki*). Their numbers were reduced by electoral manipulation to four, two, and three in subsequent Dumas, where neither the majority of deputies nor the government wished to raise and much less to press an unpopular issue. Stolypin had tried to do so in the Council of Ministers in October 1906. Because 'the principles of civil equality bestowed by the Manifesto of October 17th gave the Jews the rightful expectation of full citizenship',[22] he had sought partial relief for them to mollify the non-revolutionary part of Jewry and the liberal parties. This effort was frustrated by the veto of Nicholas II. That signal from above and the strength of rightists and anti-Semites in the third and fourth Dumas precluded further initiatives on behalf of the Jews and caused existing disabilities to be applied more strictly. Stolypin himself, although he recognized the need to alleviate the situation of the Jews, specifically excluded them as electors or deputies from his western zemstvo bill of 1910.

The pathological dimension in Russian Judeophobia appeared most fully in the ritual murder trial of a Jewish clerk, Mendel Beilis, which took place in Kiev in 1913. Although it was established quite early in the criminal investigation that the supposed victim, a Christian boy, had been killed by a gang of thieves, the judicial and police authorities of a great empire, headed by Minister of Justice I. G. Shcheglovitov, persisted for two years in trying to prove Jewish fanaticism and depravity in a court of law. A jury of simple men acquitted Beilis, although it also found that a ritual murder, by unknown hands, had been committed.[23]

For Shcheglovitov and other reactionaries inside and outside of government, anti-Semitism had become a major ideological weapon. They would employ it again to explain to themselves and others their failures in the Great War that began in 1914 and in the Civil War that followed the Bolshevik seizure of power in 1917. While it had murderous consequences for tens of thousands of Jews in those conflicts, the weapon proved useless for those who wielded it and an embarrassment for more rational defenders of the monarchy.

REFERENCES

1. V. I. Lenin, 'On the question of national policy', *Collected Works* (London and Moscow, 1960–78), XX, p. 219.
2. *Webster's Third New International Dictionary* (1964).
3. S. I. Bruk and V. M. Kabuzan, 'Dinamika i etnicheskii sostav naseleniia Rossii v epokhu imperializma (konets XIXv.–1917 g.)', *Istoriia SSSR* 3 (May–June 1980), pp. 74–93.
4. R. E. Pipes, *The Formation of the Soviet Union*, rev. edn (New York, 1964), pp. 1–2.
5. Violet Conolly, 'The "nationalities question" in the last phase of tsardom' in E. Oberländer *et al.* (eds), *Russia Enters the Twentieth Century* (New York, 1971), pp. 160, 164.
6. M. T. Florinsky, *Russia* (New York, 1953), II, p. 947.
7. Edward Chmielewski, *The Polish Question in the Russian State Duma* (Knoxville, Tenn., 1970), p. 44.
8. P. S. Wandycz, *The Lands of Partitioned Poland, 1795–1918* (Seattle, Wash., and London, 1974), p. 299.
9. C. L. Lundin, 'Finland' in E. C. Thaden (ed.), *Russification in the Baltic Provinces and Finland, 1855–1914* (Princeton, NJ, 1981), p. 447.
10. M. H. Haltzel, 'The Baltic Germans' in Thaden, op. cit., pp. 127–9.
11. R. A. Pierce (ed.), *Mission to Turkestan. Being the Memoirs of Count K. K. Pahlen, 1908–1909*, trans. from the Russian by N. J. Couriss (London, 1964).
12. H. Seton-Watson, *The Russian Empire, 1801–1917* (Oxford, 1967), p. 672.
13. S. A. Zenkovsky, *Pan-Turkism and Islam in Russia* (Cambridge, Mass., 1960), p. 124.
14. R. E. Pipes, 'Catherine II and the Jews', *Soviet Jewish Affairs* 5 (1972), p. 7.
15. From P. A. Zaionchkovskii, *Krizis samoderzhaviia na rubezhe 1870–1880 godov* (Moscow, 1964), p. 338.

16. H. Rogger, 'Russian ministers and the Jewish question, 1881–1917', *California Slavic Studies* VIII (1975), p. 26.

17. Iulii Gessen, 'Graf N. P. Ignatev i "Vremennye pravila" o evreiakh 3 maia 1882 goda', *Pravo* 30 (1908), col. 1632.

18. *Deiatelnost Gosudarstevennogo Soveta za vremia tsarstvovaniia Gosudaria Imperatora Aleksandra Aleksandrovicha, 1881–1894* (St Petersburg, 1900), p. 135.

19. Jonathan Frankel, *Prophecy and Politics* (Cambridge, 1981), p. 255.

20. Rogger, 'Russian Ministers', p. 42.

21. H. Rogger, 'The Jewish policy of late tsarism: a reappraisal', *The Wiener Library Bulletin* 25 (1971), pp. 44–6. On the pogroms of 1881 also see I. M. Aronson, 'Geographical and Socioeconomic Factors in the 1881 Anti-Jewish Pogroms in Russia', *Russian Review* 39 (Jan. 1980), pp. 18–31.

22. 'Perepiska N. A. Romanova i P. A. Stolypina', in *Krasnyi Arkhiv* 5 (1924), p. 106.

23. H. Rogger, 'The Beilis case: anti-semitism and politics in the reign of Nicholas II', *Slavic Review* 25 (Dec. 1966), pp. 615–29.

CHAPTER TEN

The ambiguous revolution

In few countries was belief in the possibility of revolution as widely held, in fear or hope, as in Russia at the beginning of this century. For the rulers, the spectre had been held at bay by the failure of peasant riots, workers' strikes, the constitutional and nationalities' movements to join or coincide, and by their trust in the efficacy of minor concessions and physical force to keep the opposition divided. This had allowed Pleve and his predecessor Sipiagin to steer an unchanging course even after they admitted to themselves and the tsar that the danger of a revolutionary rising could not be dismissed.

The revolutionaries' certainty that the autocracy was bound to be driven from power rested more on a reading of historical trends than on a day-to-day assessment of the balance of forces. Plekhanov's prophecy that the Port Arthur debacle would shatter to its foundations the regime of Nicholas II as the Sevastopol defeat had uprooted that of Nicholas I,[1] was more rhetorical than realistic. It was not the fall of Port Arthur that galvanized the political opposition and brought about its coalescence with the mass movement of social protest, but Bloody Sunday.

The opening event of what would become the Revolution of 1905 was not initiated by the socialist parties or their leaders – most of whom did not return to Russia until late in the year – but by a former prison chaplain and the Assembly of Russian Factory Workers of St Petersburg which he had founded with official encouragement and permission. In January 1905 Father Gapon was no longer trying to pacify the workers. He had become their instrument and ready to lead them in violent struggle if a peaceful appeal to the tsar should fail. The ambiguous character of the *Gaponovshchina* enabled liberals as well as Marxists to view 9 January as the first engagement of a larger and longer battle. The petition which the demonstrators had in vain tried to present to an absent Nicholas on that day incorporated parts of the liberal programme: a constituent assembly, universal and secret suffrage, the full range of civil liberties, responsibility of ministers 'before the people', equality of all before the law, along with calls for the eight-hour day, a progressive income tax, better pay, the right to organize and to strike, workers' insurance, and an end to the war.

The revulsion with which students, professors, and lawyers, organizations of doctors, teachers, and agronomists, associations of merchants and manufacturers reacted to the shooting down of 800–1,000 demonstrators (with about 150 killed) was given a special edge by the fact that many of the rights for which the workers asked were the goal also of respectable society. It is that which explains the support given in the next months to the non-economic demands of striking workers by their employers; that, and the wish to be freed from the tutelage of a state which in sponsoring Zubatov and Gapon had demonstrated its readiness to calm the workers at the expense of their bosses, and on Bloody Sunday its ineptitude. The phrase launched in a New Year's article by the arch-conservative *Novoe Vremia* ('New Times') became a constantly reiterated refrain: 'It is no longer possible to live in this way.'

The appearance in the political arena of the working masses of St Petersburg and, following 9 January, of more than two dozen other cities, was joyously greeted abroad by the men who looked to the proletariat as the advance guard of revolution. Mensheviks and Bolsheviks had played no part in the organization of the workers' march to the Winter Palace and little in the virtually general strike that followed it. But they proclaimed the event as the beginning of revolution. The logic of history, wrote Plekhanov, had placed the question of an armed clash between the workers and tsarism on the agenda of the day. Martov described the heroic proletariat as the 'liberator of the fatherland' and Social Democracy as its strongest political force. 'In the memorable summer of 1903 we had 200,000 men behind us. Now in this grand proletarian uprising we have a million. . . .' Lenin, too, concluded that the revolution had begun,[2] but neither faction of Social Democracy was leading it or certain of its ability to do so. It was a priest who had built a police-sponsored organization of 8,000 men and gathered a following many times that number, when in St Petersburg both branches of the RSDWP had only about 2,000 worker-members between them. For the moment the émigré Marxist leaders could only exhort their comrades inside Russia to involve themselves in the workers' movement while they defined for themselves the nature of that involvement, of the revolution, and their party's role in it.

However much 9 January had agitated the Russian body politic and stirred the urban masses, it failed to pressure the government into adopting measures capable of ending either the political or the social crisis. What the liberal opposition wanted was not reforms but transformation of the political order, a constitution, and representative government. Liberal determination was stiffened by the continuing militancy of the workers which was, in turn, heightened by their receptivity to liberal slogans and by their realization that the existing regime would not meet their economic grievances. That was made clear by the government's inept response to the strikers. St Petersburg was placed under martial law and the man entrusted with its pacification, General D. F. Trepov, in a matter of days restored an outward calm to the capital. He was also charged with carrying out the suggestion of Finance Minister Kokovtsov that the tsar show his benevolent interest in the welfare of the working men. To that end Trepov arranged for the reception of thirty-four loyal and well scrubbed deputies from a number of factories at the palace of Tsarskoe Selo, where they were given lunch and an imperial speech telling them that their striking brothers had been misled and deceived, but that forgiveness and compassion would be extended to all who remained faithful to church, to country, and to tsar. When the delegates reported back to their places of work they were met with indifference or contempt; some were threatened with beatings.[3]

A potentially more fruitful approach to labour was the decision taken on 29 January to set up a commission of inquiry to determine the causes of industrial unrest in St Petersburg and propose remedies. Named after its chairman, a member of the Senate and Council of State, the Shidlovskii Commission would consist of officials, employers and, in a radical innovation, of elected worker representatives. These were to be chosen by electors for whom the workers actually voted on 13 February. When the 372 electors met five days later the majority, influenced by Menshevik agitation, had made it a condition of their further participation (which the Bolsheviks opposed) that the worker members of the Commission be granted freedom of speech and personal inviolability for the duration of its sittings, that these be open to the public, and that similar bodies be instituted in other industrial centres.[4]

Because the government refused to meet these conditions, no delegates were selected and the Commission was disbanded, supplying further evidence for Social Democratic charges of official insensitivity and a stimulus to what was becoming an epidemic of strikes. As their numbers grew, so did efforts, aided or prompted by the radical intelligentsia, to form as yet illegal trade unions and strike committees. Councils, or soviets, of strikers appeared in April in the Urals and in the textile centre of Ivanovo-Voznesensk in May. They were the first of about sixty such workers' assemblies – the most famous being the St Petersburg Soviet of October – which arose during 1905 to coordinate strike action and assumed quasi-governmental functions wherever the authorities were temporarily in retreat. Social Democrats and Socialist Revolutionaries alike saw the soviets as living proof of the toilers' power and their ability to act independently of party tutelage, which did not keep them from seeking to use and as far as possible direct this new weapon of mass militancy.[5]

Rural turbulence was later in coming and more sporadic. But inflamed by the example of the cities, by bad news from the battlefields, by economic distress, by SR speakers and pamphlets, and by nationalism in the borderlands, it grew in scope and ferocity as the year wore on. Even this most dispersed and least politicized part of the population, which expressed its inchoate anger by the burning and looting of manors, developed an unprecedented degree of organization and political articulateness.

The villagers who assembled in Moscow in May 1905 did not, as had been hoped, declare their support of tsar and country. Instead, they complained of their lack of land and rights, declared the bureaucratic administration of the state incapable of answering these needs, and made plans for a nationwide organization. The All-Russian Peasants' Union, meeting in secret congress in Moscow in late July, could hardly claim to speak for the vast numbers and diverse sentiments of peasant Russia. Yet its one hundred or so delegates from twenty-two provinces represented a substantial body of opinion. Even if some of the resolutions they adopted reflected the positions of socialist and other radical intellectuals, the receptivity to such influence was a new factor in the life of the peasantry. Determined though they were to limit the role of non-peasants in the Union, its leaders also recognized their community of interests with the radicals by setting up 'bureaus of cooperation' with them.

That the issue of land dominated a congress of peasants was natural; that it led them directly to questions of government showed their waning isolation and traditionalism. Land, the delegates concluded, was the property of all the people and should be given to those who worked it – some private lands with compensation to its owners, lands belonging to church, state, or crown without. Details were to be worked out by a constituent assembly elected by secret, direct, equal, and universal suffrage which excluded only officials and clerics. A national legislature would be chosen on the same basis and democratically elected local governments were to have wide authority. Although it did not call for abolition of the monarchy, the congress demonstrated that the peasants might not be the solid, conservative majority to which the emperor and some of his advisers still looked as a counter-weight to urban workers and disgruntled intellectuals.[6]

Illusions of the essential soundness of rural Russia persisted among the state dignitaries who, under the tsar's chairmanship, discussed in July how to carry out his promise of 18 February, contained in a rescript to Interior Minister Bulygin, that 'the most worthy persons enjoying the confidence of the people and elected by them take part in the preliminary . . . consideration of legislative projects'.[7] Even when it was offered, the sop of a purely consultative assembly was ill-received – the more so since it was accompanied by an imperial manifesto condemning troublemakers, reaffirming autocracy, and asking loyal subjects to defend it. There was a further erosion of trust in the regime's sincerity and its ability to perceive the seriousness of its predicament. The liberal historian Miliukov considered the promise of the rescript illusory,[8] while the conservative journalist Lev Tikhomirov noted in his diary that neither the emperor nor Bulygin had the slightest intention of keeping it.[9]

The Union of Liberation and the Union of Unions, the latter headed by Miliukov and formed in May of fourteen organizations (unions of the professions, a union of railway workers and employees, another of clerks and book-keepers, unions for the emancipation of women and of Jews, and the Union of Zemstvo-Constitutionalists) now demanded the Constituent Assembly elected by universal, direct, equal, and secret vote, the so called 'four-tail' franchise. These demands were embraced by the Peasants' Union. Meetings of zemstvo and municipal representatives – some defying police prohibitions on their gatherings, yet still shying away from the revolutionary call for a Constituent Assembly – also adopted the four-tail formula to elect a legislature and set up a constitutional regime.

By 6 August, when the law for the election and convocation of a consulta-

211

tive assembly, the State Duma, was at last published, it offered so little and came so late as to inflame public opinion by its ignoring of the country's mood. The vote for the 'Bulygin' Duma would be indirect and most unequal. It discriminated against non-Russians, the poor, and urban dwellers and it excluded women, Jews, and men under 25. Peasants would make up 43.4 per cent of the electors, landowners 33.4 per cent, and propertied townsmen 23.3 per cent.[10]

The announcement of the Bulygin Duma satisfied no one. The moderate wing of liberalism accepted the new institution in order to use it as well as all other legal means, to obtain broader civil and political rights. The Union of Unions decided to boycott the Duma elections and continued to agitate for a constituent assembly and the four-tail franchise. The socialists refused participation in a body from which the urban masses were excluded by high property qualifications and, to disrupt the elections, called for a general strike which would also be the prelude to an armed uprising and the democratic revolution.

To bring about mass insurrection the socialists had neither sufficient numbers, unity, nor weapons. They did, however, meet with a new readiness among the workers to listen to their agitators and arguments. Mensheviks in particular were successful in having their slogans and advice accepted by the unions and strike committees springing up in September and October, because they were more willing than the Bolsheviks to follow the spontaneous action of the workers and their non-party leaders. In the end no political group controlled or led the workers, and revolution was not yet for the majority a conscious goal. But they had come to see the achievement of political rights as part of their struggle for a better life and human dignity. That point the socialists had tried to impress upon the workers for years and their experience of the last few months had at last driven it home.

The great October strike which forced the government into retreat and major concessions became general precisely because the workers had adopted the slogans which liberals and radicals had been the first to launch. Begun in Moscow on 7 October by the Union of Railway Workers – who demanded in addition to better wages, hours, and the right to strike an amnesty, civil liberties, and a democratically elected constituent assembly – the strike spread quickly, paralysing the railways and the government's ability to shift reliable troops. Postal employees, telegraphers, printers and industrial workers followed the example of the railwaymen, as did doctors, students, professors, lawyers, teachers, actors and dancers of the imperial theatres. In some cities there were barricades, in others fire fights between police and strikers, and everywhere innumerable meetings at which radical orators, striking workers, students, and solid citizens came together as they had never done before and seemingly spoke with one voice.

In Moscow medical personnel of the city's hospitals pledged financial aid to the strikers; several town dumas did likewise and invited spokesmen of the workers to take part in their sittings or, where they remained neutral, asked the military and the police to exercise restraint. A few employers even permitted strike meetings in their factories and continued to pay the strikers' wages; the Union of Unions took an active part in calling out employees and members of the professions, and the founding congress of the Constitutional Democratic Party declared its solidarity with the strikers and their aims.

They were divided as to ultimate goals; their crossing of class lines was a temporary phenomenon induced by the euphoria of the moment; their uncontested domination of the political arena and of public debate was the result of indecision and disarray in governmental and conservative circles – but for a brief moment the forces clamouring for liberty and social justice felt as one as they faced the state.

At the heights of power, the problem was still viewed as being one of physical security, of how to end this madness by the sobering application of force. But no one could be certain how much force was required or available, with most of the army still in the Far East and some of its units infected by the country's rebellious mood. There was one man in government who saw the issue facing it in broader terms, and even he was a reluctant convert to the necessity of fundamental changes in the constitution of the state. The liberal movement, Witte had said in February, was overrated; the introduction of representative government would mean anarchy and red terror; what was needed was a dictator to impose both order and reforms. But an indecisive Nicholas would not appoint a strong dictator or himself assume that role.[11] When at last he turned for advice to the man he had sent to negotiate peace with Japan, he was again admitting the seriousness of his predicament and the failure of his policies.

On 13 October Witte submitted to the emperor a survey of the situation and suggestions for dealing with it. His report reflected how much the political scene had been transformed since the early part of the year. Witte no longer talked of the insubstantiality of the opposition and circumventing it by a combination of rigour and reform. Now he almost sounded like a member of that liberal intelligentsia which not so long ago he had described as unrepresentative of the country.

The unrest that has seized the various classes of Russian society cannot be regarded as the consequence of partial imperfections of the political or social order, or as the result only of the activities of organized extremist parties. The roots of unrest lie deeper, in the imbalance between the ideals of thinking Russians and the reality of their lives. Russia has outgrown the existing regime and is striving for an order based on civic liberty. Therefore, the forms of Russian public life must be brought into conformity with the ideas animating the reasonable majority of society.[12]

To close the breach between state and society Witte proposed a series of steps which echoed parts of the liberal programme. To begin with, there was to be a dismantling of extraordinary security regulations and the introduction of guarantees for the personal inviolability of citizens, freedom of speech, conscience, assembly, and association. Henceforth all Russians must be equal before the law, irrespective of religion or nationality. Next, the government was to establish and respect institutions and legislative principles in keeping with the ideals of most of society. The state had to work diligently for their realization, prove its sincerity by maintaining strict neutrality in elections, and exact adherence to the new order from all branches of the bureaucracy through a cabinet of uniform political complexion. Equally important was acceptance of the promised Duma and its decisions which would not, Witte was confident, conflict with the national interest. Details could and should be worked out gradually, but proclaiming the general principles he had enunciated was the only way of gaining time and the cooperation of the non-revolutionary elements. 'We have faith in the political tact of the Russian people, for it is unthinkable that it wants anarchy which threatens, besides all the horrors of civil strife, the dismemberment of the state.'[13]

There was no talk here of a constitution, no belief, on Witte's part, in the absolute supremacy of the legislature. Even so, his baldly stated notion that the autocracy had been left behind by Russian society, that it had now to catch up and seek its confidence, was distasteful to Nicholas. He wavered for a few more days, exploring the alternative of repression, but when his most trusted military advisers were either sceptical of the efficacy of drastic measures or unwilling to apply them, he yielded. On the seventeenth of the month he signed the brief 'October Manifesto' which would, he hoped, put an end to disturbances and the general strike. On 18 October it was published together with a shorter and revised version of the political analysis prepared by Witte. A decree of 19 October re-established the Council of Ministers with broadened powers and Witte as Chairman.[14]

Russia now had, in effect, a premier, appointed not because he was liked by the tsar, but because he expressed the mood of the country, and a cabinet whose policies the first minister was to coordinate and unify along the lines of the report and the manifesto. The latter granted the full range of civil liberties, extended the franchise to those classes of the population excluded from it by the Bulygin law, and established the 'unshakable principle' that no law could take effect without approval of the people's elected representatives who would also be given an opportunity to see to it that the crown's officials kept within the law. Subjected to public scrutiny and legislative control, bureaucratic arbitrariness and absolutism would be no more.

The Manifesto, an historian has written,[15] transformed Russia into a constitutional monarchy, and the jubilant crowds who greeted its publication seemingly thought likewise. Their joy, however, was less the celebration of a final triumph than of a first battle won in a continuing campaign. In a matter of days they realized that the authorities did not necessarily interpret the Manifesto as limiting their powers or their responsibilities for the maintenance of public order which was indeed threatened by the boisterous mood or revolutionary acts of the urban crowds who held mass meetings, seized public buildings, demanded the release of political prisoners, or exhorted soldiers to join them. In the non-Russian areas in particular the Manifesto was viewed as a capitulation and provoked attacks on the symbols and agents of tsarism. After their initial confusion, the latter resisted wherever and whenever they felt strong enough to do so, dispersing even peaceful meetings, and assisted in many localities by more or less organized bands of 'patriots', the so-called Black Hundreds, who saw their tsar, country, and religion threatened by revolutionaries and liberals, students and *intelligenty*, Jews and foreigners.

The contradictions which marked the Russian state's structure and conduct during what has been called its constitutional, semi-constitutional, or pseudo-constitutional period, were rooted in confusion as to the meaning of Nicholas's Manifesto and the accompanying Witte report. The confusion began with the manner in which the country learned of them; it was compounded by their lack of specificity and clarity, and by the mixed motives which had inspired their promulgation. Since the regular institutions of government had not been involved in the decisions of October, most of their agents learned of the Manifesto from the press. Several governors, believing it to be a hoax, confiscated newspapers in which it appeared or prevented its being read in public; others, awaiting guidance from St Petersburg, withdrew police and troops to their quarters or government buildings for from one to four days.

The October Manifesto, one governor complained, bestowed many blessings, but did not indicate how they were to be realized or harmonized with existing legislation. 'One thing only was clear – there will be a representative regime with freedom of conscience, of speech, and of assembly. But when will these blessings become reality? When representative institutions are actually set up or now, immediately?'[16] In the face of such perplexity, lesser citizens could be forgiven for putting the most varied interpretations on the emperor's promises or for remaining dubious that he meant what he said or knew what was said and done on his behalf by an administration whose members were no clearer about the meaning of the 'constitution', if there was one, than the general public. Lev Tolstoi found no difficulty in assessing the Manifesto: 'There's nothing in it for the people.'[17] The peasants who vainly came to ask their land captain for more meadows and woods on its basis would have agreed. But what was in it for society, for the politically active and conscious, whom Witte had hoped to reach?

Since the Manifesto and the Witte report were but collections of general principles for whose enactment no certain date had been set, there was cause to wonder and to be suspicious. A meeting between Witte and St Petersburg publishers and editors on 18 October demonstrated the depth of distrust and how mistaken it was to think that well-meant words would quiet the revolutionary storm which was rising rather than subsiding. The newspapermen, beginning with a conservative editor, asked for a political amnesty as indispensable to the restoration of public order and confidence. Witte was evasive, promised to try, but asked for time and pleaded with his visitors to help him by being reasonable and keeping the press toned down. Pacification, another editor suggested, must start with ending the state of siege or exceptional protection imposed on most of the country, and with setting an early date for the removal of troops and Cossacks from St Petersburg. 'There is a revolution going on', Witte was told. 'What the country needs is not promissory notes, but hard currency.' He would not or could not issue it, prompting one of his visitors to exclaim, 'You do not trust society', and a liberal journalist to add, 'The country does not believe the promises of the government.'[18]

That state of affairs could not be changed overnight; certainly not by a Witte who had spent his life in the service of the autocracy and depended on it for his power. The coming weeks and months would reveal how conditional was his commitment to liberal institutions and civil liberty, how restricted his freedom of action by the fear of revolution from below and disavowal from above.

The radical Left's reaction to the Manifesto was predictable. Lenin and Trotskii, the vice-chairman of the St Petersburg Soviet, called it a scrap of paper. *Izvestiia*, the Soviet's newspaper, commented what a strange constitution it was that proclaimed the freedom of assembly and speech while meetings were surrounded by troops and the press was censored, a constitution that left intact an autocracy served by Witte as well as by General Trepov and his soldiers. 'Everything has been given, but nothing has been received.'[19]

The response of the liberals was not too different. Miliukov, leader of the Kadets, warned his party to take a sober second look at the documents of 17 October, to ask whether they represented a change of heart or simply a new tactic. They did not even contain the minimum concessions needed at the moment: the immediate introduction of universal suffrage, of full civil rights, and a complete amnesty for political prisoners – not to speak of a constituent assembly without which the tsar could take away what he had given. The more moderate liberals, who would soon form the Union of 17 October, accepted the Manifesto and wished to support the government. Yet they agreed with the Kadets that neither words nor Witte gave adequate proof of official sincerity. Until the majority of the Duma could furnish a cabinet, the old ministers had to make way for new men, either neutral 'experts' or members of the zemstvo congresses. As the Kadet V. D. Nabokov put it: 'We do not believe that yesterday's wolves can be miraculously transformed into today's lambs.'[20]

Witte realized that as long as there were neither new laws nor new institutions, new men were doubly essential to reassure the country. He dismissed some of the most unpopular ministers, including Pobedonostsev, and tried to include moderate public figures in his cabinet. He invited the widely respected zemstvo leader Shipov to become state comptroller, but as the latter pointed out, events had left him behind and he now represented only a minority on the right wing of zemstvo constitutionalism. The post he had been offered was hardly of great importance, and he advised Witte to offer the liberals several ministries, especially interior. But in that key position Witte was determined to have P. N. Durnovo whose ten years as head of the Department of Police made him valuable at that critical moment and acceptable to the emperor, but a political liability. Neither Kadets nor future Octobrists were willing to serve alongside a man so clearly a product of the most odious part of the old order. Durnovo's conduct, over which Witte had little control, justified their apprehensions. 'We are being invited,' one of their number remarked, 'to play the role of hired children for ladies of easy virtue.'[21]

Then and later, the doctrinaire intransigence of the liberals – particularly of the left-leaning Kadets – was blamed for Witte's failure and for that of the constitutional experiment he initiated. Sincere though Witte was in wanting to broaden the basis and appeal of his administration, he was unwilling to do so on any terms but his own, that is, without a genuine sharing of power with any of the political forces mobilized by 1905. Perhaps he thought that until quiet was restored he had no choice but to manœuvre without organized public support between the liberals on one hand and a suspicious tsar and reactionary bureaucrats on the other.

Even if Witte had been willing to concede it, the emperor was sure to veto the constituent assembly demanded by the Kadets. Witte also rejected their other conditions for serving in his ministry: civil rights, universal suffrage, and a full amnesty; such basic reforms must await the meeting of the Duma. His resistance was stiffened by the spread of violence, by the socialist call for insurrection, and by signs of recognition among some liberals that a mass rising which threatened them too would force them to seek the shelter of the state. This was, in fact, happening in the rural regions of the Polish and Baltic provinces and in south-central Russia, where the peasants were intermittently in open revolt from late October 1905 until August 1906. Emboldened by the general confusion, by the talk of freedom, and unimpressed by the remission of redemption dues, they burned or plundered noble estates, cut noble timber, or refused to pay taxes and rents.

The rebelliousness of the proletariat did not match that of the peasants in duration. In the two capitals it was a direct if brief challenge to the authorities. Fortunately for them the St Petersburg Soviet called off the general strike on 19 October, aware that the hungry workers would not sustain it for purely political ends. To maintain their militancy, the Soviet on 29 October approved a spontaneous movement for the eight-hour day by men walking off their jobs after that length of time. Employers answered with wage cuts, lock-outs, and black-lists, showing that the unity of the opposition had been breached. The Soviet then resumed the offensive against the government. The summons to another general strike on 1 November met with a mixed reception from the workers and a hostile one from the public. For declaring a fiscal boycott of the government the police on 26 November arrested the head of the Soviet's Executive Committee, the radical lawyer G. S. Nosar, without difficulty and a week later his successor Trotskii and 256 Soviet delegates. A third strike, called as a protest by the revolutionary parties, collapsed after four days.

Only in Moscow did it turn under Bolshevik urging into a poorly armed rising. The local garrison, on whose adherence the insurgents counted, and a guards regiment from St Petersburg levelled the workers' barricades with artillery and by 18 December their revolution was over, at a cost of 500 to 1,000 lives. The government gradually recovered both nerve and strength. It extended martial law to forty-one provinces, sent punitive expeditions to the countryside, and was heartened by evidence that most of society wanted no part of a revolution that went beyond political liberation and, at best, social reforms. As early as 8 December Nicholas observed that the public's state of mind had changed. 'The old heedless liberals, always critical of firm measures, are now clamouring loudly for decisive action.'[22] He was proved right when the Moscow city duma sided with the authorities against the workers and the

Octobrists in February condemned open rebellion. 'We are against those', wrote Miliukov, 'who pronounce the revolution "continuous", because . . . a continuous revolution serves only the aims of reaction.'[23]

Against this background of violence and fear of violence, of division in the oppositionist camp, of the workers' exhaustion and their employers' uniting to oppose them, the bureaucracy prepared the laws that were to ratify the liberals' revolution and, as it turned out, to limit it. The press rules of 24 November ended preliminary censorship but provided fines or imprisonment for publishing matter the censors, who interpreted their mandate broadly, considered seditious or criminal. Thus they confiscated all the capital's dailies which had carried the Soviet's appeal to the population to stop paying taxes and debts and to demand payment of accounts in gold. Although the regulations were temporary and could be circumvented by changing a newspaper's name or editor, they were a straw in the wind. More stringent ones were issued in March and April 1906. The rules governing public meetings, unions, societies, and parties that were 'not dangerous or illegal', also left a great deal of discretion to the authorities which had to approve them. Still, it was the people's Duma that would adopt permanent legislation to assure true freedom of the press, of assembly, and association. How it was to be elected and organized, and what were to be its rights and duties, therefore became of the greatest importance.

The electoral law of 11 December carried out the promise of the Manifesto to extend the suffrage to all classes without, however, making it direct, equal, or universal. Everyone under the age of twenty-five, women, workers in plants employing fewer than fifty men, certain categories of labourers and artisans, students and servants, landless peasants and soldiers remained without the vote which was still cast and counted by class and property groups (curias). In only twenty cities were Duma deputies elected directly. Elsewhere in European Russia they were chosen by electors, chosen in their turn by curias of industrial workers (151 electors), landowners (1,955), townsmen (1,352), and peasants (2,532). The latter were still regarded as a stronghold of monarchism, unlike the workers, nearly two thirds of whom did not receive the vote. The vote of one landowner was equal to that of 3.5 townsmen, 15 peasants, and 45 workers.

Witte worried that the new law would satisfy no one; Shipov criticized it strongly; and Miliukov called it the source of all future conflicts.[24] It was, none the less, an improvement over the Bulygin law and more liberal than the Prussian and Austrian ones. The men elected under its provisions could do fruitful work if the institution in which they were to serve made that possible. When the date (27 April) and the structure of the new legislature were announced on 20 February 1906 that prospect was dealt its first blow.[25]

What emerged from the official deliberations was not a parliament nor even the implementation of the principles proclaimed on 17 October. The Duma was restricted in a variety of ways. It was denied any constituent functions; the executive was obliged to call it for only two months in the year; and there was to be an upper house, the Council of State, of two hundred members, half appointed by the emperor, the rest elected by the Orthodox clergy, the zemstvos, the universities, the corporations of the nobility, and associations of trade and industry. Designed to be a brake upon the more democratic lower house, the Council fully answered that purpose and became known as the graveyard of liberal hopes. No bill could become law without its consent and that of the emperor whose veto was absolute.

The liberals could do little more than protest – and protest they did, from Shipov on the right to Miliukov on the left – unless, like the socialist parties, they wanted to continue the revolution and boycott the elections. Since the electoral and parliamentary struggle was the only one in which they could hope to prevail, the liberals could not give it up before it had begun, however unfavourable the terms of combat. When on 23 April 1906, four days before the nation's elected spokesmen were to meet, the new Fundamental Laws were made public, all the contradictions and limitations of the new order became visible.[26]

The monarch retained the title 'autocrat', without the adjective 'unlimited', as well as extensive and, in foreign and military affairs, absolute authority. He possessed the initiative in all legislative matters, the sole right to initiate changes in the Fundamental Laws, remained the only source of executive power, and under article 87 could issue emergency decrees when the legislature, which had subsequently to approve them, was not in session. Although its assent was required for all laws, the Duma was seriously handicapped in its law-making powers. No longer a purely advisory body, its primary function was still the discussion, amendment, and approval of proposals which would normally originate in the ministries. Legislation could indeed originate in the lower house (or the Council of State), but it required at least thirty of its members to introduce a bill, the chamber to agree that it deserved consideration, and a ministry to prepare the necessary project. Only if that was not forthcoming would the Duma draft, debate, and possibly pass its own laws. The power of the purse was blunted by exempting military, naval, and imperial court expenditures – one third of the total – from control by the legislature. If it should actually turn down the money requests of the executive, the prior year's budget or that approved by the upper house could be enacted.

The only other check on the administration and the legality of its actions was the Duma's right to question ministers who were not absolutely obliged to respond and could not be made to resign by a vote of censure. They served at the pleasure of the emperor and were individually responsible to him, not to the Duma or the head of a supposedly unified cabinet. Even as a device to expose bureaucratic abuses, the right of interpellation was difficult to use. It was not given to individual deputies but to the whole house. A majority had to approve the request for an interpellation signed by at least thirty members before it could be put on the agenda.

Their critics should not, perhaps, have measured the new laws and institutions by the standards and long experience of mature democracies and prejudged their workability. But however they were viewed there can be no disagreement that they fell short of the high hopes of October. The emperor and his advisers may not have planned such an amputation in advance, but it revived doubts of their willingness to carry out the promises they were thought to have made. Nor did the government always adhere to the spirit or the letter of its Fundamental Laws. Miliukov called them a 'worsening of the worst parts of the worst European constitutions',[27] and the author of a pamphlet pointed out that what the tsar had bestowed on his people was no better than the constitution Abdul Hamid had given the Turks in 1876 and had let lapse a year later.[28]. A constitutional regime of sorts had come into being and the Fundamental Laws defined the boundaries the Sovereign had set for it. Both inside the Duma and in the larger political arena the opposition would try to expand those boundaries, confident that it spoke for the people and the future.

That confidence was borne out by the elections which returned a decidely oppositionist and largely radical majority,[29] making even more likely a clash between the Duma and what was still, in many ways, an old regime. Witte, the architect of its partial renovation, was let go just before the Duma convened and just after he had obtained a French loan to make the government independent of it. Nicholas, who thanked him for that achievement, also regarded him as the author of his misfortunes and blamed him for the results of the election. Goremykin, the aged bureaucrat who became Chairman of the Council of Ministers, had neither talent nor inclination for an accommodation with the Duma. All but two members of his cabinet lacked sympathy for the results of October 17 and even they agreed that the government must not give in to pressure.

Goremykin thought of the Duma as little better than a revolutionary assembly and was determined not to be frightened into surrender by 'all this incredible nonsense'.[30] He tried to deal with the Duma by ignoring it, and when that was no longer possible by lecturing it on its rights and duties. From the start he and Nicholas agreed to let the people's representatives know their place. They worried excessively whether the inaugural ceremony was to be held in the Duma's quarters, the Tauride Palace of Catherine's favourite Potemkin, or in the Winter Palace; whether the emperor himself should come before it or send Goremykin, who had few concrete legislative proposals to counter those the Duma was certain to make.

On 27 April 1906 Nicholas received its deputies, state dignitaries, and members of his court in the throne room of the Winter Palace where he read his brief address from the throne. Its barely two hundred colourless words had only one paragraph which contained more than vague generalities. In it the emperor promised to protect the new institutions and urged them to 'clarify' the needs of the peasantry and promote popular enlightenment.[31] The 'Duma of National Hopes' could not have lived up to the voters' expectations if it had quietly proceeded to the implementation of such a timid programme. It would have meant leaving the field to the revolutionary socialists and proving their contention that the bourgeois liberals were spineless compromisers. Tactics and principle alike dictated a bold response.

It came in the Duma's 'Reply to the Address from the Throne' which insisted once again on direct elections and universal suffrage, demanded strict guarantees for civil liberties and denounced their violation by the arbitrary acts of officials. There must be an end to pogroms and firing squads, to imprisonment and capital punishment, to exceptional and martial law. Only if ministers were made responsible to the Duma and their subordinates subjected to public control could respect for the law and civil peace be assured. The State Council must be abolished and restrictions on the law-making power of the Duma removed. It would submit urgent legislation to charge the judiciary with the protection of individual freedoms and to ensure the equality before the law of all citizens, regardless of class, nationality, religion or sex.

The Duma considered its most immediate task to be the satisfaction of peasant land hunger and asked for the requisitioning of church, crown, and state lands and the compulsory expropriation of some privately owned estates. In addressing the problem of the wage labourer, it asked merely for 'measures to protect his position' and his right to organize. There were rather more general calls for free universal education, for the reform of local government, and for allowing the non-Russians to follow their own ways of life. The reply concluded with a plea for amnesty to all who had been convicted for political or religious offences or for violating the agrarian laws. 'Sire, the Duma awaits from you a full political amnesty as a first pledge of understanding and agreement between tsar and people.'[32]

The counter-address was a challenge and sure to be rejected, at least in its totality. Its framers were confident, however, that the government would recognize their strength and seek common ground. But when the Duma's president asked for an audience to present the reply, three days went by before he and the country were told that Nicholas refused to receive him and that the address should be presented to the cabinet through ordinary channels. The insult seemed so studied, the political blunder so great, that there was disbelief at first or the assumption of an effort at provocation. The Duma did not, as the Trudoviki wished, call for civil disobedience. Miliukov warned its members against picking a quarrel with the government before they had even tried to achieve land and liberty; urged by the Kadets to offer no pretext for dissolution, they awaited a response.

On 13 May Goremykin, in a barely audible monotone, read a declaration to a tense and silent house. He characterized its demands as inadmissible or untimely because they violated either the Fundamental Laws, the imperial prerogative, or the security of the state. The Duma, he said, had not demonstrated the need for a change in the franchise, the ministers were working to solve the peasant problem and would consider the request for educational and tax reforms. On the key issues – expropriation, amnesty, ministerial responsibility, legal accountability for civil service offences – not a single conciliatory word had been spoken.

The Duma had been told that it was not a co-equal branch of government and that it should stick to its subordinate role. It refused to do so, passed a vote of censure on the cabinet, and demanded that it be replaced by one enjoying the confidence of the legislature. Secret negotiations to bring public figures, notably Shipov and Miliukov, into the cabinet came to nothing. They foundered on the opposition of the emperor, the unwillingness of ministers to surrender key positions, and the intransigence of Kadets who felt too sure of victory to make the government more palatable to the country.

The cabinet neither resigned, submitted substantial legislation, nor responded to most of the interpellations put to it. In a public statement it asked the peasants to look to the government for the satisfaction of their needs and ruled out expropriations of private land. The Duma addressed the country in a statement of its own which was made the occasion of its closing on 8 July. New elections were expected to produce a more tractable assembly. Some two hundred deputies, mostly Kadets, signed the Vyborg Manifesto (after the Finnish city where they met) urging the population to give the state not a single kopek or recruit until the Second Duma met. Their appeal was a futile gesture, recognized as such by its signers, disregarded by the people, and of no danger to the state. The revolutionaries, who called for a resumption of armed struggle and strikes, took it as a further sign of waning liberal determination. Government and socialists alike wondered what tactics the Kadets, so intransigent in the First Duma, would follow in the Second.

There were those in the Kadet party, the lawyer Vasilii Maklakov foremost among them, who disapproved of its programme as too radical and of its tactics as revolutionary. It is true that the party platform (constituent assembly, land expropriation, the right to strike, the eight-hour day)[33] was a radical-democratic rather than a liberal one, and that many Kadets were as unbending as their adversaries in the government; true also that it was naive for men who had so little confidence in the latter to believe that it would abide by the judgement of elections, parliamentary motions, and the pressure of public opinion. And it was to maintain that pressure that the Kadets did not completely disavow the Left although they denounced its revolutionary methods. Yet they dropped the appeal for a constituent assembly, refused an electoral alliance with the SDs on that basis and, unlike the Left, they wanted to compensate owners of expropriated land and to guarantee private possession once redistribution had taken place. Above all they wanted to keep to parliamentary means of struggle.

Caught between the masses who looked to the Duma to cure their ills and a reactionary regime, most Kadets saw no gain in still greater moderation. Their success in the first elections confirmed this stand; to abandon it might lose them the mass following they needed to be more than a minority speaking only for a thin stratum of intellectuals and professionals, for a few liberal landowners and businessmen. Miliukov, whom Maklakov held largely responsible for the Kadets' lack of political realism and inflexibility, was painfully aware of their dilemma and compared them to the Gironde, the unlucky middle destroyed by the extremes of Right and Left. He pleaded with the Trudoviki and the SDs in the First Duma not to destroy by revolutionary acts or rhetoric what chance it offered for peaceful parliamentary action. He tried even more anxiously to ensure the survival of the Second Duma.

That task was made more difficult by socialist participation in the elections and by their outcome. When the new Duma met on 20 February 1907 it contained 54 SDs (18 of them Bolsheviks), 37 SRs, 104 Trudoviki, and 16 Popular Socialists. The Kadets returned with only 98 members to a house which they could no longer dominate. They were uncomfortably dependent either on the Left or on the 114 deputies to their right (54 Octobrists, moderate and extreme rightists, non-party conservatives) most of them friendly to a government which had supported them during the elections. The Kadets' campaign had been harried in legal and extra-legal ways, several of their candidates being debarred on some pretext or other.

Stolypin, the new premier, was neither a reactionary nor opposed to collaboration with the Duma if it showed itself to be reasonable. He was unable, however, to bridge the gulf between the government and the non-revolutionary opposition. As Goremykin's minister of interior, a post he retained, he had carried out the dissolution of the Duma and was known to favour changing electoral laws to tame it. Administrative interference in the elections had the same purpose, as did subsidies to organizations and newspapers of the extreme Right. The agrarian and other decrees he issued were designed to create accomplished facts which it would be difficult for the Duma to undo when, as required by the Fundamental Laws, they were submitted for its ratification. All this raised doubts of his respect for the rule of law, for representative institutions, and the rights of citizens.

The field courts-martial set up in August 1906 – possibly at the behest of Nicholas – after an attempt to blow up Stolypin's residence injured two of his children, were particularly detested for their disregard of legal procedures. Composed of senior military officers, whose names, like the proceedings themselves, were kept secret, these courts dealt with anti-governmental crimes brought before them not by judicial but by administrative officials. Cases had to be tried within twenty-four hours and concluded in two days. The judges saw the record only on the day of trial which was conducted without defence counsel. Death sentences had to be carried out within twenty-four hours and could not be reviewed or appealed. The tsar instructed commandants of military districts not to transmit telegraphed pleas for pardon. In February 1907 he also opposed Stolypin's recommendation for terminating the work of the courts.[34]

In public the premier said nothing to indicate his disapproval before the decree establishing them expired in April and 1,144 persons had been executed. Over 2,000 civilians more were executed by sentence of ordinary courts-martial during 1905–08. In the year following the October Manifesto, 7,000 persons (according to official figures) were fined, 2,000 expelled from regions under exceptional law, and 21,000 banished to distant provinces – all by administrative fiat. Such violations of due process seemed justified as a matter of self-preservation to a government which reckoned that more than 4,000 of its servants, from policemen to governors, had been killed or wounded in 1906 and 1907.[35] There were those who condemned violence yet argued that official terror had to end before that of the Left (mainly by the combat organization of the SRs) could be contained and that the state had legal means to deal with it. When the Octobrists declared their support for Stolypin and the field courts-martial, Shipov and his followers left the party in protest. Maklakov too found the premier's conduct contradictory, especially his 'merciless struggle against the Kadets',[36] if his aim was to divide the opposition, seek the aid of the liberals, and implement reforms.

It was a hostile Duma to which Stolypin on 6 March 1907 presented a programme with which he hoped to persuade a majority of the deputies of the government's seriousness, form them into a cooperative centre, and lead them to practical tasks. Besides proposing land and tax reform, workers' insurance (as well as their right to organize and strike for economic goals), the extension of local self-government, compulsory primary education and improved courts and police, a vigorous and self-assured Stolypin set forth his view of the state that had emerged from the revolution. 'The fatherland, transformed by the will of the monarch, . . . must become a government of laws.'[37] Freedom of speech, press, assembly, and conscience had to be defined and protected; the inviolability of persons, of home and correspondence had to be safeguarded and bureaucrats be made to bear civil and criminal responsibility for official misconduct. He did not proclaim his adherence to parliamentary government, but he accepted the idea of a *Rechtsstaat* (*gosudarstvo pravovoe*) in which the supremacy of the law would serve as surrogate for the supremacy of the people or their elected representatives.

On these terms, which would preserve the preponderance of power and initiative in the hands of government, Stolypin was willing to extend the hand of cooperation to the Duma's moderates. He wanted their advice and approval without which he would remain isolated and subject to reactionary pressures. But he made no immediate concessions to smooth the road to cooperation and none that the Kadets made for fear of yielding basic positions, falling into the camp of the government's clients, or risking disintegration and loss of public support.

The Kadets were divided over whether and how to test Stolypin's intentions and escape the charge of obstructionism. Wishing to protect the Duma, they received the premier's statement in silence rather than joining the Left in a vote of censure or the Right in applause. If this was a signal, Stolypin ignored it. He did allow the courts-martial to expire in April but defended them when the Kadets brought in a bill for their abolition on 13 March. In private he offered to legalize the Kadet party if it denounced political terror by the Left. Miliukov was willing, but was overruled by party comrades who thought it compromising and immoral to treat for what was theirs by right. Unlike the Octobrists and the right-wing Union of Russian People, the Kadets never became a registered and recognized party.

It was Stolypin's agrarian decrees of 9 November 1906 that stood in the way of an arrangement with the Kadets, caused angry outbursts from a Left which used the Duma as a revolutionary forum, and led to its dissolution. All opposition projects for land reform had one thing in common: confiscation. And it was that forcible transfer of private property, whether compensated or not, that Stolypin found unacceptable.[38] It was contrary to his intention of strengthening individual peasant ownership. By allowing easy withdrawal from the village commune, he wanted to divert the peasants' gaze from noble lands and to turn it to that owned by the commune itself, to the share held by its less fortunate or able members which more ambitious villagers would now be able to purchase. The Kadets knew that there could be no satisfactory outcome to the agrarian debate and wished to postpone it. But with other opposition parties having brought in land measures and 200 peasants in the Duma, it was impossible to evade the issue for long.

There was no middle ground between Stolypin's programme and the plans for the socialization (Trudoviki and SRs), municipalization (Mensheviks), or nationalization and direct seizure (Bolsheviks) of land offered on behalf of peasants who were themselves to distribute it equitably to those who worked it. The government countenanced only the voluntary redistribution of gentry land, by sale to the Peasant Land Bank on terms favourable to the seller. It also assigned certain state and crown lands to the Bank for resale to peasants, with loans made readily available at reduced rates of interest. For the rest, it relied on the consolidation of scattered strips into individual holdings and migration to Siberia to relieve rural property and create a satisfied class of agriculturalists who would make for stability and economic progress in the countryside.

The modified Kadet project did not propose confiscating and distributing estate land to all who wanted it. Excess land only was to be taken from the larger private owners – except those cultivating valuable industrial crops, such as sugar beets – and given to those who actually lived and worked on it. Questions of price and other matters were to be settled by joint committees of peasants and landlords, the former sharing with the state the burden of compensating the latter. But the principle of expropriation remained, and with it a source of conflict between government and opposition, a part of which was not interested in parliamentary solutions.[39]

Nicholas and Stolypin complained that the Duma was being used to issue calls to riot and rebellion. A well-orchestrated campaign of letters and telegrams sent to the tsar by monarchists and rightists urged dissolution. On 1 June the premier demanded the exclusion of Social Democratic deputies and the lifting of their parliamentary immunity on charges that they had conspired to kill the tsar and to subvert the armed forces. Even before the committee examining this request had reported back to the house that the government's evidence did not establish criminal guilt, the order of dissolution was issued on 3 June 1907.

It was accompanied by an arbitrary and complicated electoral law which reduced the rights of whole categories of voters yet served its purpose of producing a cooperative legislature.[40] The number of electors in the peasants' and workers' curias was reduced by about half; in the landowners' assembly it was increased by nearly a third. From now on one per cent of the population, mainly the well-to-do, chose close to two thirds of the Duma's electors and controlled almost 300 of 442 seats (cut down from 524). When the Third

Duma, the only one to last its full term of five years, met in November 1907, the opposition consisted of 19 Social Democrats, 13 Trudoviki, and 54 Kadets. They were often joined by 28 Progressives and 26 representatives of non-Russian nationalities whose strength too had been severely diminished. The government's principal supporters were 154 Octobrists and their adherents as well as 97 conservatives and moderate rightists who in 1910 formed the Russian National Union. Th extreme Right, which was more autocratic than the tsar and often fought Stolypin, had 50 members.

Stolypin's *coup d'état*, so called because it violated the Fundamental Laws, was a bold move which as much reflected as created a realignment of political forces. Ever since October 1906 the masses and the classes had been drifting apart. Many of the latter had come to see the revolutionary energies which the temporary disarray of authority had released as a threat to themselves or to the possibility of peaceful reform. The appearance of a radical Right and the danger from that quarter also made for second thoughts on how far and how fast to push for further changes. Zemstvo elections in 1906/07 showed the extent of the retreat from liberalism. The Kadets lost 14 of 15 zemstvo board presidencies they had held; the Octobrists gained 6 (from 13 to 19); the Right went from none to 11.[41] The shift to the right of the Octobrists and their absorption of the Trade-Industrial Party in late 1906 prefigured their emergence as Stolypin's allies. Even believers in the armed struggle of the masses had to admit that under existing conditions it was hopeless. Checked first in its proletarian, then in its peasant, and finally in its parliamentary phase, the revolution was over. Stolypin had both sensed and hastened its end.

REFERENCES

1. S. H. Baron, *Plekhanov: The Father of Russian Marxism* (Stanford, Cal., 1963), p. 262.
2. For the reactions of Plekhanov, Martov, and Lenin to Bloody Sunday see J. L. H. Keep, *The Rise of Social Democracy in Russia* (Oxford, 1963), p. 187.
3. V. N. Kokovtsov, *Out of My Past* (Stanford, Cal., and London, 1935), pp. 38–41; S. M. Schwarz, *The Russian Revolution of 1905. The Workers' Movement and the Formation of Bolshevism and Menshevism*, trans. from the Russian by G. Vakar (Chicago and London, 1967), pp. 75–83.
4. Ibid., pp. 86–128.
5. Ibid., pp. 167–95; and Oskar Anweiler, *The Soviets. The Russian Workers' Peasants' and Soldiers' Councils, 1905–1921*, trans. from the German by R. Hein (New York, 1974), pp. 20–96.
6. E. I. Kiriukhina, Vserossiiskii krestianskii soiuz v 1905 g. *Istoricheskie zapiski* 50 (1955), pp. 95–191.
7. *Istoriia SSSR* VI, p. 125.
8. T. Riha, *A Russian European: Paul Miliukov in Russian Politics* (Notre Dame, Ind., and London, 1969), p. 72.
9. '25 let nazad. Iz dnevnikov L. Tikhomirova', *Krasnyi Arkhiv* 39 (1930), p. 68.

10. G. Vernadsky *et al.* (eds), *Source Book for Russian History* (New Haven, Conn., and London, 1972), III, pp. 702–4; and Marc Raeff (ed.), *Plans for Political Reform in Russia, 1730–1905* (Englewood Cliffs, NJ, 1966), pp. 142–52.

11. Witte's conversation with an unnamed German diplomat is reported in the German Foreign Ministry's Political Archive, Abteilung A, Russland, No. 61, Heft 1811, under date 4 March 1905.

12. Vernadsky, op. cit., III, p. 704; S. Iu. Witte, *Vospominaniia* (Moscow, 1969), III, pp. 4–5.

13. Ibid., p. 7.

14. For the English texts of the October Manifesto and the accompanying Witte Report see H. D. Mehlinger and J. M. Thompson, *Count Witte and the Tsarist Government in the 1905 Revolution* (Bloomington, Ind. and London, 1972), pp. 331–5.

15. M. T. Florinsky, *Russia* (New York, 1953), II, p. 1177.

16. I. F. Koshko, *Vospominaniia gubernatora* (Petrograd, 1916), p. 11.

17. Henri Troyat, *Tolstoy* (Garden City, NY, 1967), p. 590.

18. 'Interviu S. Iu. Vitte s predstaviteliami pechati', *Krasnyi Arkhiv* 11–12 (1925), pp. 100–5.

19. Leon Trotsky, *1905* (New York, 1972), p. 123.

20. Quoted by M. J. Morse, 'The political career of P. N. Miliukov, 1905–1917', Ph.D. Diss., University of Wisconsin (1950), p. 87; 'Soiuz 17 Oktiabria v 1905 g', *Krasnyi Arkhiv* 35 (1929), pp. 151–75.

21. G. V. Adamovich, *V. A. Maklakov: politik, iurist, chelovek* (Paris, 1959), p. 109; Maurice Baring, *A Year in Russia* (2nd edn., New York, 1917), p. 126.

22. E. J. Bing, *The Secret Letters of the Last Tsar* (London, 1937; New York, 1938), p. 198.

23. Riha, op. cit., p. 101.

24. Ibid., p. 103; Morse, op. cit., p. 109.

25. Manifesto of 20 February in Vernadsky, op. cit., pp. 769–70.

26. Ibid., pp. 772–4, for 'The Fundamental State Laws of April 23, 1906'. Also see Mehlinger and Thompson, op. cit., pp. 336–44, for a comparison with earlier drafts. Cf. G. S. Doctorow, 'The Fundamental State Law of 23 April 1906', *Russian Review* 35 (Jan. 1976), pp. 33–52.

27. D. A. Davies, 'V. A. Maklakov and the Problem of Russia's Westernization', Ph.D. Diss., U. of Washington, 1968, p. 242; Adamovich, op. cit., p. 148.

28. N. A. Rubakin, *Dve konstitutsii; turetskaia i rossiiskaia: istoricheskii parallel* (St Petersburg, 1906).

29. The number of Duma members, which never reached its full complement of 524, fluctuated, as did their party or 'fractional' affiliations. The house of 484 deputies divided as follows in June 1906. The Social Democrats, who had boycotted the elections almost everywhere, held 17 seats (3.5 per cent). The Trudoviki (or Labourites), a coalition of leftist deputies of populist sympathies, a number of peasants among them, counted 95 members (19.5 per cent). More radical than the Kadets on the question of land, which they wanted socialized, they yet collaborated with them and often followed their tactical lead. The Kadets, with 183 deputies (38 per cent), were the largest, most cohesive and vocal group, owing their success to a well-organized, well-financed campaign, to official disapproval, and to the abstention of the SDs and SRs. There were 44 deputies (9 per cent) of different nationalities who did not adhere to other parties. Moderates and centrists to the right of the Kadets had sent 38 deputies (8 per cent) under different

labels; most of them soon merged in the Union of 17 October. The monarchist Right had only 7 members (1.5 per cent). There were 100 members (20.5 per cent) who had run without party labels and belonged to no caucus or fraction in the Duma. This group included about half of 200 peasants whose insistence on land expropriation strengthened the left wing and betrayed Witte's hopes in their conservatism. See W. B. Walsh, 'The composition of the Dumas', *Russian Review* 8 (April 1949), pp. 111–16; and 'Political parties in the Russian Dumas', *Journal of Modern History* 22 (June 1950), pp. 144–50.

30. Kokovtsov, op. cit., p. 124.

31. The emperor's speech from the throne and the reply of the State Duma are in T. Riha (ed.), *Readings in Russian Civilization* (2nd rev. edn. Chicago and London, 1969), II, pp. 445–9.

32. Ibid., p. 449.

33. Programme of the Constitutional Democratic Party in Sidney Harcave, *The Russian Revolution of 1905* (London, 1970), pp. 292–300. On the Kadets' call for a constituent assembly and its modification, see J. E. Zimmerman, 'The Kadets and the Duma, 1905–1907' in C. Timberlake (ed.), *Essays on Russian Liberalism* (Columbia, Mo., 1972), pp. 119–38.

34. On the courts-martial, their origination and termination, see V. I. Gurko, *Features and Figures of the Past* (Stanford, Cal., and London, 1939), p. 499; Hans Heilbronner, 'P. Kh. von Shvanebakh and the dissolution of the first two Dumas', *Canadian Slavonic Papers* 11 (1969), pp. 39, 52; Alfred Levin, *The Second Duma* (New Haven, Conn., 1940), pp. 267–9; A. A. Polivanov, *Iz dnevnikov i vospominanii . . . 1907–1914* (Moscow, 1924), pp. 18–19.

35. S. Kucherov, *Courts, Lawyers and Trials under the Last Three Tsars* (New York, 1953), pp. 205–12; G. T. Robinson, *Rural Russia under the old Regime* (New York, 1937), p. 198; 'V gody reaktsii', *Krasnyi Arkhiv* 8 (1925), pp. 242–3.

36. V. A. Maklakov, *Memoirs* (Bloomington, Ind., 1964), p. 232.

37. From 'Vospominaniia F. A. Golovina o II Gosudarstvennoi Dume', *Istoricheskii Arkhiv* 4 (1959), p. 153.

38. Stolypin's speech to the Duma of 10 May 1907 in Riha, *Readings*, II, pp. 456–64.

39. Ingeborg Fleischhauer, 'The agrarian program of the Russian Consitutional Democrats', *Cahiers du monde russe et sovietique* 20 (April–June 1979), pp. 173–201.

40. S. N. Harper, *The New Electoral Law for the Russian Duma* (Chicago, 1908).

41. G. A. Hosking, *The Russian Constitutional Experiment* (Cambridge, 1973), pp. 29–30.

CHAPTER ELEVEN

Hopes and fears 1907–1914

That the government had reasserted control and imposed a quiet that was not effectively challenged for a decade posed for contemporaries the question whether what had happened between 1905 and 1907 was indeed a revolution. For Nicholas, the spread of conservatism and apoliticism in society, the fact that with few exceptions the armed forces had remained loyal, and that the revolutionaries were incapable of rousing the masses, supported an accidental interpretation of events. If only, Nicholas and his consort believed, he had listened to his inner voice rather than Witte, the shameful retreat before mobs and demagogues could have been avoided. The emperor's increasing stubbornness and his conviction that a few carefully-selected peasant deputations or the loyal addresses of right-wing organizations spoke for the nation, were rooted in the feeling that he had been unnecessarily weak in 1905.[1] He had not kept his vow to pass on to his heir the fullness of power inherited from his father. He would be weak no more and never again listen to the warnings of politicians that his regime was out of step with the country or seek its confidence to avoid another revolution. There had been no revolution and there would be none.

Evaluating the results of 1905 before a London conference of his party in 1908, the leader of the Socialist Revolutionaries, Victor Chernov, expressed at least partial agreement with Nicholas.[2] Another, a full-scale, revolution was a certainty, but the first victory over tsarism had been incomplete and won, Chernov said, on credit. It had resulted not from revolutionary strength, but from autocracy's weakness, from its loss of nerve brought on by the Japanese War, by unpreparedness, and by much of the upper class deserting it. Unlike the Social Democrats, who had been blinded by the success of the October general strike into thinking that the proletariat could alone carry the struggle against a shaken and distraught enemy, the SRs had advocated defensive tactics. They had wanted to strengthen the liberties already won and to use them for organizing and involving in the movement the bulk of the popular masses as yet untouched by it. It had seemed essential to postpone the decisive battle until the peasantry would enter it alongside the proletariat. But in the whole vast peasant world there had been only bursts of flame, no conflagration. In consequence of the illusions induced by its easy initial gains, the Left had miscalculated the enemy's strength. Unable to defeat him, it could not even preserve the concessions forced from him. What had taken place in 1905, clearly, had not been The Revolution; but for a brief time, Chernov said, Russia had been transformed into a gigantic revolutionary university. Its teachings were certain to bear fruit.

What lessons did Chernov draw for himself and his party? He urged his comrades not to blink the fact that they had been beaten, but also to beware of despondency by recognizing the cause of their defeat: the illusion that the proletariat and the intelligentsia could topple autocracy by themselves. Yet he saw hope in the impact the SRs had made among the peasants in a brief period of relative freedom and in the support their agrarian programme had received from more than one hundred Duma deputies. What had been defeated was not their appeal to the masses but their organization which would have to be adjusted to work again under conditions of police repression. The party must become more centralized, more conspiratorial, more disciplined, but without losing touch with the people whose political consciousness could be developed in such mass organizations as unions, cooperatives, and peasant brotherhoods. This was all the more necessary, Chernov and others pointed out, as Stolypin tried to strengthen individualism by the break-up of the commune, which the peasants were urged to resist by refusing to leave it and by boycotting those who set up individual farms.

When they reported on their activities to the Socialist International in 1910 and 1914, the SRs admitted that in spite of continuing efforts to organize the peasantry, prospects for revolutionizing it were remote. The party had been discredited in 1908 by the revelation that Evno Azef, the head of its political terror arm, the Combat Organization, was a double agent and police spy; it had been decimated in Russia by the police and split by divisions abroad; it was disheartened by evidence of some government success in undermining the communal solidarity of the peasantry. The view of the village commune as a nucleus of socialism which was to be preserved at all costs was no longer tenable. The peasants' attachment to it, Chernov realized, stemmed not from the commune's supposed collectivism, but from the assurance it gave them of equal rights to land. The party remained socialist, but its agrarian programme became less so as it stressed expropriation, equal land use, and cooperation rather than communal tenure which was not, in fact, a universal peasant goal. This adjustment to reality stood the party in good stead when the peasants, in 1917, were once more able to express their political preferences openly, and when the SRs, afraid of rushing too far ahead of their constituency, became more cautious than they had been in 1905.[3]

The Mensheviks also interpreted 1905 as a case of premature extremism. It had resulted in their political isolation and warned them to secure the democratic revolution before advancing to the socialist one. Carried away by the pace of events into believing a seizure of power possible, Menshevism returned to more orthodox positions with the defeat of the Moscow rising in December 1905. Martov warned that autocracy alone would benefit from renewed attacks on the bourgeoisie which had still to complete its task of dismantling the old regime. In this, the proletariat should help rather than hinder the liberals. When Stolypin further curtailed representative government in June 1907, the Mensheviks thought it all the more important to support the liberals' struggle against his system, to enter into agreements with them in order to maintain the offensive against tsarism and broaden the current of revolution. Resolutions to that effect were introduced at the April 1907 (London) Congress of the Social Democratic Party which had been nominally reunited at Stockholm a year earlier. Although the Menshevik motions called for a relentless fight against liberal parties if they should display conciliatory tendencies towards tsarism, they failed. They were defeated by the Bolsheviks who taxed their authors with placing too much reliance on an unreliable middle class and investing too much energy in parliamentary and legal activities at the risk of 'liquidating' the underground party, weakening working class militancy, and ignoring the revolutionary potential of the peasantry.[4]

The Mensheviks did not so much ignore the peasantry as fear their political backwardness. A general rising of the villages to seize the land was to be welcomed and supported as a valuable blow struck against the feudal order. But a rising of millions of muzhiks who were neither socialists nor democrats would more likely be a *jacquerie* than a revolution. Much educational work was needed before the mass of peasants could be incorporated into a Marxist party. Part of that work would be performed by the economic evolution of the countryside away from feudalism, by the peasantry attending what Martov called 'the School of the capitalist bourgeoisie'.[5] Another part would fall to Social Democracy which, becoming broader and more open than either of its wings had been before 1905, would link to its central core of conscious revolutionaries the mass of workers and all the 'healthy elements of society' awakened by the revolution.[6]

The idea of shifting emphasis from illegality to open involvement in the work of trade unions, cooperatives, and other mass organizations had arisen in Menshevik ranks in 1905. When prospects for a new upheaval became remote, such steady and close participation by party activists in the education and organization of the masses seemed to hold out the best promise of preparing them for the long struggle and the final battles ahead. There was no unanimity among Mensheviks on this point, nor any abandonment of Marxist revolutionary perspectives. There was, none the less, a stress on the democratic goals that Russia had still to reach, on democratic ways of reaching them, and on opening the party to the masses.[7]

Stolypin's 'Third of June Regime' was hardly the best environment for building a broad-based democratic or labour movement. But most Mensheviks saw no other way of avoiding the isolation and sectarianism from which 1905 had briefly rescued them. The experience of that year had convinced Martov that the preconditions for the victory of the proletariat did not yet exist. To attempt the seizure of power in their absence was a form of revolutionary adventurism, a denial of Marxism and its European roots that came dangerously close to the peasant anarchism of Bakunin and the narodniks. To that view Martov adhered in 1917, even though he was not, like other Mensheviks, carried by it into cooperation with the pro-war liberals. He opposed the Bolsheviks in October 1917 not so much because their regime was a dictatorship but because it was dictatorship imposed by a minority of the country's revolutionary-democratic forces and would, he warned, provoke counter-revolution and civil war.

If Mensheviks and Socialist Revolutionaries were made more cautious by the events of 1905, Lenin was heartened. How far the lessons he drew from them diverged from those of his socialist rivals did not become manifest until the breakdown of the old regime made possible their application. But the mere fact that a revolution had taken place and that millions had been caught up in it was proof that revolution speeded up the processes of history, that it could be the teacher of the masses rather than being the end product of their political education. The events of 1905 had achieved what Bolshevism, for all its organizing and agitating, had not: the spectacular growth of Social Democracy, the struggle of the proletariat for its political and economic rights, the spread of that struggle to the peasantry and even to the army.[8]

In a temporary accommodation with liberals for the sake of preserving and expanding the few concessions wrested from autocracy, Lenin saw a triple threat: the waning of radicalism in the party, confusion among its followers, and betrayal once the selfish aims of the bourgeoisie were attained and it made common cause again with reaction. Yet the proletariat was too weak to fight autocracy alone and had to seek allies in the peasantry. Such advice was eminently practical in a peasant country but for Marxists this turning from the liberals to the politically immature peasantry required theoretical justification, assurance that the workers would not drown in a peasant sea, and some answer to the question: what kind of revolution would two such ill-matched and unequal partners produce?

In *The Two Tactics of Social Democracy in the Democratic Revolution* (1905) and in *The Agrarian Programme of Social Democracy in the First Russian Revolution* (1907),[9] Lenin restated his adherence to the Marxist scheme by disavowing the possibility or wish of going beyond the bourgeois-democratic limits of the Russian revolution. A socialist revolution was out of the question; socialism could not be reached by insurrection alone, only by political democracy, by the experience of open class struggle of the masses against the bourgeoisie. Having given orthodoxy its due, Lenin suggested that the bourgeois revolution could be extended and radicalized (nationalization and redistribution of landed property to the peasants, the establishment of a republic, extensive social welfare) by taking it out of the hands of the bourgeoisie. Only in that way could it prevail over tsarism, only if it were carried out by the workers and peasants who would secure their victory by setting up their joint democratic dictatorship, a provisional revolutionary government.

What of the peasantry's petty-bourgeois attachment to property, its political backwardness and instability, its indifference or hostility to socialism? Lenin did not envision the alliance as one of equals, much less that the peasantry would set its tone or course. The proletarian party would remain strictly a class party. Because of its discipline and doctrinal firmness, it could afford to enter such a coalition without fearing that the tail would wag the dog. Another factor made possible the proletariat's adoption of the peasantry as an auxiliary: in the given conditions it was a revolutionary force which by aiming at the confiscation of gentry lands challenged existing property relationships and the political order. The rural masses were the lever with which the old regime could be unseated and the way opened for the advance to socialism. Much as they might distrust the petty bourgeois character of the peasant movement – and they were right to do so, Lenin granted – Marxists must support it for the sake of putting an end to the old feudal past and sweeping clear the whole way for capitalism, for the growth of productive forces, for the free and open struggle of classes'.[10]

Seizure and distribution of lands would also further the development of capitalism in the countryside, lead to the division of the peasantry into poor and rich, and to the growth of a rural proletariat. Thus, by the force of objective circumstances and by propaganda, growing numbers of peasants would come to see the advantages of socialism and join its advocates. Lenin recognized a danger pointed out by Trotskii, that the 'revolutionary-democratic dictatorship of the proletariat and peasantry' might consolidate itself and under pressure of its peasant component stop with the achievement of bourgeois democracy.[11] But that was a remote danger from which, Lenin believed, the European socialist revolution, set off by that in Russia, would rescue the Russian proletariat. The prior task was and remained to complete the bourgeois-democratic revolution at home with the help of the peasantry. In 1917 Lenin saw that task accomplished sooner than most of his comrades and was readier than they to enter upon the next stage. His revolutionary determination was then, as earlier, nourished by the view he had formed in 1905 of the villages as a reservoir of recruits to revolution.

The different lessons drawn by the revolutionaries from the experiences of 1905 and 1906 had little bearing and less impact on the course of events. For most of ten years, radical politics again became exile politics, and belief in the resumption of the forward march to revolution was sustained more by faith or temperament than concrete evidence. Lenin may not have been the only man, as the Menshevik Pavel Akselrod said in 1910, who still gave his whole life to the revolution, who dreamed and lived for nothing else.[12] But he was definitely one of a small and declining number. The country appeared to be tired of upheavals. This was reflected in the virtual ending of industrial and agrarian strikes and disorders, in the effectiveness of police repression, in the Mensheviks' involvement in parliamentary and legal activity (even the Bolshevik Duma deputies grew more moderate in their speech and conduct), and most clearly in the declining membership of the Social Democractic Party. In early 1907 its various constituent sections had reached the impressive figure of 150,000. By 1910 the total number of members was down to 10,000, with no more than five to six Bolshevik committees regularly active inside Russia.[13]

The very idea of revolution, so long embraced or approved by the intelligentsia, seemed to have fallen into disrepute. It was attacked in the *Vekhi*

('Signposts') symposium published in 1909 whose contributors, including former Marxists, called upon the intelligentsia to abandon the 'tyranny of politics' for spiritual and cultural duties.[14] For a few short years that call was heeded. The arena of politics was greatly narrowed and its temperature lowered. Political initiative passed to the government while the main burden of opposing it was carried not by the revolutionary parties or the masses but by the parliamentary opposition of which the Kadets formed the most numerous and vocal part.

The Kadets too were divided over how to assess the revolution and how to conduct themselves in the future. The right wing felt with Maklakov that by rejecting compromises with an admittedly unreformed government, the party had failed the cause of liberalism. Instead of using whatever chance there was for the evolution of a law-abiding administration whose enlightened members would need the support of a moderate public opinion, the Kadets had relied on the revolutionaries to help them gain their goals. With the October Manifesto and the Fundamental Laws, Maklakov thought, the liberals should have stopped to consolidate their gains. They should have modified or postponed their ultimate aims – a parliamentary regime, ministerial responsibility, the universal franchise – and recognized that if they prevailed with the help of revolution they would be swept away by it and in the case of failure would create a powerful reaction in government and society.[15]

Much of Maklakov's criticism was the product of hindsight, of a sense of opportunities missed, and less applicable to Miliukov than to Kadets who stood to the left of their leader. Speaking for the party's centre and trying to preserve its unity, Miliukov had moderated its programme after the dissolution of the First Duma. He had warned against making hopeless demands and had urged orderly and constitutional methods in the struggle with government. When the Third Duma met in November 1907 a reduced delegation of fifty-four Kadets entered it as a 'responsible opposition', repudiated the Left's tactics of obstructionism and boycott, and pledged to take an active part in the legislative process. Two years later Miliukov described himself to an English audience as a member of His Majesty's Opposition, not of the opposition to His Majesty.[16] The left Kadets considered this a capitulation to the government.

That was hardly the case and Miliukov remained its constant and courageous critic. Yet he and the party had moved closer to Maklakov and adjusted their goals and tactics to the limited opportunities offered by the changed suffrage law and the country's changed mood. Maklakov, for his part, discovered that the administration remained impervious to the liberals' show of reason. It did not, he complained in 1909, live by the rules it had proclaimed in 1905 and continued to employ police methods of rule; since it did not trust society, it could hardly expect society's cooperation or trust. The Duma had condemned terror without speaking out against official terror; it had accepted Stolypin's agrarian programme, worked for strengthening Russia's military power, as the ministry had asked. But the hand of collaboration had not been offered in return. Even if it came, Maklakov feared, it might not conciliate society. 'Confidence is a tender plant. Perhaps the government is better than its deeds, perhaps it is merely powerless. But having gained a reputation for insincerity, it has lost the confidence and respect of the country – and therein lies the tragedy of its fate.'[17]

The Kadets' own tragedy lay in the fact that they could do little to make the government change its ways. Like Maklakov, Miliukov had become fearful of calling up the anger of the masses – now silent but more deeply rooted, he thought, than ever before – to launch a new offensive against the regime. There remained only the Duma and the hope that its moderate parties would work together to safeguard the gains of October, to achieve what melioration they could in the conditions of workers and peasants, and thus to establish the legislature as an integral part of the constitutional order to which the nation would look as the advocate of its interests and eventually as the real government. Although they professed confidence that Russia's liberalization would continue, if more slowly, and that they still voiced the people's aspirations, the Kadets were pessimistic and aware of their isolation. The weakened liberals, Miliukov observed in 1908, had been displaced as mediators between state and people. Other, more conservative parties, closely linked with the autocracy and the nobility, now played that role, creating a situation of extreme instability. 'In short, wherever we look, we only meet with new trouble to come, nowhere with any hope for conciliation or social peace.'[18]

The revised electoral law had indeed given Stolypin willing allies in the Third Duma. If the bulk of 150 Octobrist votes were joined to those of members sitting to their right (Nationalists and Moderate Rightists) he could count on a comfortable majority. If the Octobrists voted with the moderates to their left – Progressives and Kadets – they could embarrass the ministry even without the nationality groups or socialists. Events had made Octobrism more conservative and less constitutional. The landowners and businessmen who dominated the Union of 17 October had acquiesced in the many violations of the rights of citizens and of the Fundamental Laws as regrettable but necessary to stop the revolution. A basis was thus laid for collaboration with the premier. It rested on a shared belief in the utility of governmental institutions responsive to the people and responsible to the tsar, as well as on a common interest in the preservation of law and order, private property, the pre-eminent position of the Great Russian nationality at home and in the energetic pursuit of national interests abroad.

What had looked like a solid community of interests disintegrated quickly. Stolypin would have preferred to govern with the help of a friendly and stable Duma majority, formed around an Octobrist core, which would have strengthened him against reactionaries in the Council of State, at court, and in his own cabinet. But even such use as the essentially conservative Octobrists made of the opportunities offered by the legislature were resisted by Stolypin and rebuffed by the emperor. Friction arose when in 1908 the Octobrists, who stood for a strong military establishment, criticized its leadership, and when Nicholas, early in 1909, angrily returned a naval appropriations bill to the Duma because it had not merely approved but debated it, thus infringing the imperial prerogative. The minister of war was not only forbidden henceforth to appear in the Duma; he was instructed not to discuss military expenditures with the minister of finance.[19]

There was still common ground between Stolypin and the Octobrists; most importantly, they backed his agrarian programme, the amputation of Finnish autonomy, and his efforts to extend local self-government. But conflicts multiplied over educational matters, foreign affairs, the rights of Old Believers and non-Orthodox Christians, police involvement with right-wing extremists, persecution of labour unions, and the curtailment of the Duma's budgetary rights. At their congress of October 1909 the Octobrists complained of the government's illegalities and abuses. Their leader, Alexander Guchkov, who had in 1907 hailed Stolypin as Russia's saviour, rose in the house in March 1910 to say that the country had been patient while 'pacification' was delaying reforms, but that these were now overdue. When he was elected President of the Duma in the same month he pronounced the phrase – 'constitutional monarchy' – which three years earlier he had described as controversial.[20]

The break came in 1911. A year after assuming it, Guchkov resigned the Duma presidency in protest against Stolypin's high-handed treatment of the legislature. A bill to set up elective zemstvos in six western border provinces was approved by the Duma with the help of Guchkov but defeated in the Council of State. The upper house, giving precedence to class over nationality and hostile to Stolypin, did not like the preferential weight which the measure gave to the votes of small landowners and 'Russian' peasants (in effect, Orthodox Ukrainians and Belorussians) over those of Polish nobles. Stolypin, after threatening to resign, prevailed upon the tsar to discipline two reactionary members of the Council and to prorogue both houses for three days. The Western Zemstvo Bill was then issued as an emergency decree in violation of the Fundamental Laws. The premier passed this test of strength, but in doing so he alienated the emperor and destroyed the basis for a centrist majority in the Duma which declared his action unconstitutional and his explanation for it unsatisfactory. He now had the backing neither of the emperor nor of the legislature. If an assassin's bullet had not killed him in September 1911 he would in all likelihood have been dismissed.[21]

Guchkov's devotion to constitutional legitimacy was not the sole reason for his resignation. There was the difficulty of keeping his followers together. On the Finnish issue, thirty of them had voted against the party and sixteen had protested against the religious and national discriminations of the zemstvo bill. There were defections also to the right. Above all, Guchkov realized that aiding Stolypin had not obliged the latter to reciprocity and that he was against the military expenditures and forward foreign policy favoured by the Octobrists. Beginning in 1910, moreover, Stolypin came to rely on the Russian Nationalists, formed in 1909 out of a fusion of Nationalist and Right fractions in the Duma, as his legislative allies. By doing so he distanced himself from the Octobrists and their commitment to representative government and reform. In joining forces with a party which had an even more restricted constituency than the Octobrists, western landowners who were unabashed defenders of noble privilege and property and of their supremacy over Jews and Poles, Stolypin showed the limitations of the system as well as the limits of his tolerance for the give and take of politics when it was his turn to give.

There was no wholesale movement of Octobrists into the opposition or lasting cooperation with it; the Octobrists' social and economic conservatism prevented that. But on political issues they became more critical and vocal. M. V. Rodzianko, the Octobrist who succeeded Guchkov as president of the lower house, declared at the opening of the Fourth Duma in 1912 that its 'first and most urgent task must be the implementation of the great Manifesto of 17 October'.[22] The reduced Octobrist delegation of ninety-eight members which the election of 1912 had returned even softened the Great Russian chauvinism which had been one of the party's trademarks. A motion it proposed and the Duma adopted in May 1913 cut the budget of the Interior Ministry, criticized its refusal to introduce reforms that would at last establish a legal order and respect for the law, and condemned its nationalities policy for dividing and weakening the nation.

In November Guchkov spoke to his party of its failure 'to reconcile these two eternally hostile forces, the state and society', and of his fears for the future. Reaction, an incompetent government, and renewed unrest among the working class reminded him of 1905. This time the chief danger came not from the disorganized and impotent revolutionaries, but from a government whose actions were revolutionizing society and the people. 'With every day, people are losing faith in the state and in the possibility of a normal, peaceful resolution of the crisis' whose probable outcome was 'a sad, unavoidable catastrophe'.[23] Guchkov's intention to galvanize the Octobrists into unified opposition and bring the government to its senses did not succeed.

Although the sense of crisis was widespread and seized even some of the regime's staunchest partisans, it was not universal or translated into action; neither in the Duma nor in the country at large, was it shared by the gentry deputies of the centre and right. They saw little evidence in their rural districts of the social unrest afflicting the cities. After the death of Stolypin and the containment of the reformist challenge that he and like-minded bureaucrats had posed for the nobility's supremacy in the countryside (by their unsuccessful attempts, for example, to broaden local self-government), that class took a more sanguine view of the future and of the government. It dominated the Duma, and through its Congress of Representatives of Nobles' Associations (the 'United Nobility'), through personal influences at court and in the administration, was able to protect its interests.[24]

The tsar and his chief advisers were also confident that the country's tensions and troubles were caused or exaggerated by the opposition, that they were superficial and would pass. Stolypin's successor Kokovtsov gave it as his opinion in a Berlin press interview of November 1913 that there was no real discontent in Russia, least of all an inclination to revolution. The newspapers and the Duma corridors did not reflect the general state of mind. What the country needed was not extensive political reforms but a sound economy and good government, the attainment of which was the chief goal of his administration. If there was a revolutionary mood or movement, it could not be found outside of the industrial centres of Petersburg, Moscow, Kharkov, Kiev, Odessa or Saratov. It was a rather large exception to make for a man who had lived through 1905 and who should have remembered the part played then by the urban working class. Nor was Kokovtsov merely trying to reassure Russia's suppliers of credit abroad. In the memoirs he wrote in emigration he still insisted on the correctness of his appraisal: without war, without the February Revolution, with ten more years of peace and sensible rule, Russia would have survived and prospered.[25]

The profoundly different assessments that Kokovtsov and Guchkov made almost simultaneously of their country's condition opened a debate which continues to the present day. Was Russia in 1914 on the brink of another revolution which the coming of the war merely postponed and in the end made more certain and more profound by deepening existing political and social discord? Or did the war interrupt a gradual and peaceful evolution towards greater social harmony and stability, economic well-being, political liberalization or, at least, accommodation. Soviet scholars have always viewed the revolution which gave birth to their regime and legitimized it as inevitable: it was the result of a historical necessity created by Russia's capitalist development and her participation in the economic and territorial competition of the great powers.

Western historians are not as certain as their Soviet colleagues of the outcome of the trends and tensions visible in the last decade of the old regime. Yet there are those among them who see social instability and polarization, the political distemper of the classes and the sense of exclusion of the masses – exacerbated by an unresponsive state authority – as leading to another and probably more violent explosion than that of 1905. They dispute the optimists who point to instability as an unavoidable and healthy by-product of change, to the partnership between Duma and government on practical matters (e.g., education), to cultural and economic advance, to improvements in the state's administration and personnel as favouring its reconciliation with society. The acceptance by both of the need for compromise and the avoidance of confrontation if the gains already made were to be consolidated and the nation strengthened, boded well, the optimists believe, for a continued development of liberty, responsible and effective government, and the successful integration of the masses into society and economy. It was the war, and for most optimists the war alone, that overwhelmed these hopeful beginnings and led to collapse and revolution.[26]

The historical record does indeed show successes as well as failures, or what are thought to be such. But even the most careful and judicious account of these cannot, as in a balance sheet, yield a certain answer to the question whether a revolution was inevitable with or without war; even less can it tell us what the nature and outcome of a revolution might have been. Russia is believed by many to have been in a revolutionary situation when the outbreak of war thoroughly transformed the scene. Much of the country was certainly in a highly agitated state. A disturbed or even a revolutionary situation, however, may or may not turn into revolution and do so for reasons less compelling, more accidental than an international conflict.

It is possible to conceive of an inconclusive outcome to the pre-war strife which would have ended or suspended it for years without a decisive resolution for better or for worse. Inertia and fear of the unknown are powerful forces and they favour endurance. In the absence of war and its ruinous impact, revolution might have been forestalled or contained, even without the 'Westernizing' social and political changes foreseen by the optimists. An historian who regards the question as open, although he inclines more to the pessimists' perception of the Russian condition, can do no more than to review that condition in its chief aspects and ask how war affected and measured it.

The political contest between the government and its critics, which looked so menacing in 1914, was, as Kokovtsov believed, confined largely to the Duma. Since the death of Stolypin it had been growing more troublesome in face of the government's disregard. Ministers refused to appear before it for months on end; they tried to whittle away its rights of interpellation, of budgetary control, of legislative initiative, and of immunity for statements made from its rostrum. The reactionary minister of interior, Nikolai Maklakov, even favoured the idea, taken up by Nicholas, that the legislature be reduced to submitting minority and majority opinions for the emperor's decision.[27] Yet for all its restiveness, the Duma's basic alignment of forces remained unchanged. The right third of the house, its parties and press receiving increased subsidies from the administration, was safely on the government's side; the left third was oppositionist, while the centre was wavering and unpredictable. The Fourth Duma, elected in 1912 on a restricted franchise and dominated by men of property and privilege, was not likely to lead an assault on the regime.

Even its oppositional wing, convinced that the government was embarked on a perilous course, was of divided mind as to how to respond to the signs of renewed rebelliousness by the urban workers and of political protest in society, such as student unrest and the resignations of professors over violations of university autonomy. This uncertainty was reflected in the many splits and shifts that took place within and between the Duma parties and their failure to build a unified opposition. It also reflected their weakness. The 98 Octobrist deputies were hopelessly splintered, the Kadets (59) had only nine branches in the provinces, and the Progressives, with 48 members in the Duma, did not, as their leader admitted, exist outside of it. Social Democrats (14) and Trudoviki (10) were too few to matter.

Disunity, weakness, and reluctance to overstep the bounds of parliamentary struggle condemned the opposition to ineffectiveness and allowed the government to ignore it. There were left Octobrists and Kadets for whom the conduct of their parties was much too cautious and Progressives who found that the liberals had too quickly abandoned their common front with revolutionaries and workers in 1905. There were deputies who talked of resigning their mandates because they found their work within the Duma futile, and some who thought of provoking the government into dissolution in order to bring the crisis to a head. They had not done so by the time the two chambers adjourned for the summer in early July 1914. Nor had the cabinet, meeting that month, adopted the idea of reducing the Duma to a consultative body. There was not enough determination on either side for a full-fledged confrontation; both were restrained by apprehensions of military conflict abroad and workers' risings at home. The battle remained one of words.

Industrial strife, which had almost ceased in 1907 and was barely noticeable in 1911, became explosive after February 1912 with the shooting of unarmed strikers in the Lena goldfields, where about 200 had been killed and nearly twice as many wounded. The parliamentary opposition's fear that such behaviour on the part of the authorities would exacerbate class hatred and strengthen the appeal of the revolutionary Left was borne out by Bolshevik gains (largely at Menshevik expense) in the trade unions of the capital, in elections to the Duma and of labour representatives to insurance boards set up by a law of 1912. In the first six months of 1914, 1.4 million workers downed tools, half the total recorded for all of 1905. In July St Petersburg was almost paralysed by a great strike which grew out of sympathy demonstrations for striking comrades in Baku and protests against the police firing on a meeting of workers of the Putilov plant. The Petersburg strikers revealed a degree of exasperation and aggressiveness which surprised even their sympathizers. Troops were required to keep them out of the centre of town and to restore order. The strike ended just days before Germany declared war on July 19.

Clearly the workers' grievances had not been removed by the right to organize granted in 1906, by the industrial boom which began in 1909, or by the laws of 1912 which provided accident insurance and set up sick benefit funds to which workers and employers began to contribute in 1913.

The formation of trade unions, as well as of employers' associations, was permitted in March 1906, but the former were restricted in a variety of ways. Although strikes were not proscribed, dozens of unions which engaged in them, especially if they were said to have political aims, were shut down and their leaders exiled. Prohibitions on two or more local unions combining or forming regional and national organizations, the requirement of registering with the authorities, and of using only 'peaceful' means to achieve strictly economic ends, deprived labour of the means to carry on genuine collective bargaining. Police harassment and the resistance of owners, who joined in lock-outs, blacklisting, and closings of factories, made the unions' existence precarious and reduced their numbers and effectiveness. They had had 245,000 members in 1907, almost a tenth of the factory workforce; in 1913, after a year of growth, there were only between 30,000 and 40,000 organized workers.[28]

Wages rose, but barely kept up with living costs, and the work day remained long, an average of ten hours in 1913. Housing conditions in the industrial centres deteriorated with the dramatic increase in the workforce by about a third between 1910 and 1914. In the working-class districts of Moscow the average apartment accommodated 9 persons in 1912, and four couples were crowded into one room of a model barracks at one factory. In Petersburg the number of factory workers grew from 158,000 in 1908 to 216,000 in 1913. Many of them were fresh arrivals from the villages whose frustration at finding again the privations they had hoped to leave behind made them particularly prone to violence. They placed an intolerable strain on the public services of a city which lacked adequate transport and sanitation, had a higher death rate from infectious diseases than any other European capital, was the most expensive place in the empire, and the one most beset by labour strife.[29]

The unions could not channel this almost anarchic turbulence into disciplined solidarity and steady pressure on government and industrialists. They were also too few and weak to provide the cultural, social, and educational outlets that absorbed the energies of many workers in Western Europe and prepared them for 'revisionist', non-violent forms of social action. Nor were the socialist parties strong enough to translate the sporadic outbreaks of worker discontent into revolution.

The Bolsheviks, who were most eager to do so, lacked the organization and funds to consolidate their gains in St Petersburg or to rebuild their party in the rest of the country. Their radicalism had won adherents for them, but they were unable to guide the intransigence of the workers which outran their control. Lenin had realized this even before the Petersburg strikers ignored an appeal by the city's Bolsheviks to return to work. A premature rising was not part of their plans. It would most probably be confined to the capital, it could not count on sympathy or assistance from the liberals, and it was certain to be defeated by the massive force on which the state could still rely. What Lenin was in 1915 to call the 'crisis of the heights', (*krizis verkhov*)[30] – a crisis of the governmental apparatus, of its allies in society, and of its moderate critics – was not yet so deep as to divide them and undermine their will and powers of resistance.

The substantial economic improvements taking place in the five pre-war years, most strikingly in the industrial sector, came to the government's aid by moderating complaints from the business and professional class. Whether the recovery was sufficiently broad and deep to sustain continued expansion and reach the masses, remains a subject of intense controversy. On the positive side it is possible to record significant gains: favourable trade balances; budget surpluses; a rise in gold reserves; the development of savings banks and deposits, of credit unions and consumer cooperatives; increased sales of consumer goods, of sugar and tea, beer and vodka. There were high rates of growth and investment in industry and improvements in the productivity of labour. To the hopeful they proved that native capital, enterprise, and skills were coming into their own, that the end of Russia's dependence on foreign capital and expertise was near. A rising standard of living would lift up all her people and give enough of them a stake in the future to assure it.[31]

Less sanguine observers question whether the industrial boom can be taken as a sign of economic maturity or even take-off. Was it a self-generated response to the formation of a strong internal market, or did the stimulus of government orders launch the renewed expansion? The purchasing power of the agricultural population, still about three quarters of the total, also grew, as did the output of consumer goods – by a third, as compared with 84 per cent for producers' goods between 1908 and 1913. But the rural economy still absorbed only a third of industrial output; its ability to do so rested as much on the weather (several excellent harvests) and rising prices for cattle and grain in foreign markets as on the capacity of its peasant majority to produce surpluses.[32]

Extraordinarily high expenditures to strengthen the army and the navy were indeed responsible for the flourishing of the engineering, metallurgical, and shipbuilding industries. They also benefited, if less dramatically, the manufacturers of textiles and the providers of food and fodder. Railroad building, which had supplied the impetus for the industrial spurt of the 1890s, slowed considerably between 1910 and 1914. The home market could not sustain development by its own unaided efforts. The formation of syndicates and monopolies to regulate production and maintain prices (of sugar, for example), revealed its weaknesses, as did the calls of industrialists for a state agency to coordinate chaotic economic policies.[33]

After a French loan of January 1909, the government was able for five years to do without borrowing abroad. But private foreign investment in industry, banks, and municipalities continued to play an indispensable role in the Russian economy. The 55 per cent share accounted for by foreign capital in 1908–13 was not much lower than the 63.5 per cent recorded during the Witte years. Not only was 54.1 per cent of heavy industry and mining, 45 per cent of the chemical, and 85 per cent of the electrical industry in foreign hands – the military build-up, especially of capital ships, would have been unthinkable without the technical assistance which came from abroad and the sub-contracts placed there.[34]

Whether, with all these handicaps, the gap with the developed countries could have been closed, can never be known. A French economist predicted in 1913 that if the European nations continued to develop as they had between 1900 and 1912, Russia would by the middle of the century dominate the continent politically as well as economically.[35] We now know that the gap, instead of narrowing, widened, because the advanced economies grew even faster than the Russian one, and that per capita income, which had in 1860 been half the Western average, fell to one third (102.2 rubles) in 1913.[36]

Much, perhaps everything, it is generally agreed, depended upon the performance of agriculture. Its backwardness and low productivity had to be cured in order to overcome the economy's structural imbalance, the limitations of the domestic market, and the shortage of capital. As long as the rural sector, employing three quarters of the population, produced just over half the nation's wealth, it would hinder growth. There is little agreement, however, on how far the modernization of agriculture had proceeded when war halted it, how soon it would have been completed without that interruption, and whether it could have assured social stability in the countryside.[37]

Animated by the conviction that the solution of the agrarian problem required a thoroughgoing transformation of the economic as well as legal situation of the peasantry, Stolypin rejected as harmful the expropriation of all or some of the country's 130,000 large and medium-sized estates of which 107,000 belonged to the nobility. Even if all this land were shared out, he told the Second Duma, the peasants' land hunger would not be satisfied by the minimal additions to their allotments. The temporary relief they might gain from such a redistribution would soon be overwhelmed by their inexorably growing numbers. Nor was there any likelihood that increased acreage would mean improved productivity. There was the danger, rather, of recreating existing conditions after having eliminated the suppliers of marketable surpluses. Forty per cent of usable crop land belonging to non-peasant owners was already being leased by peasants and what Stolypin feared was made all too obvious when they actually seized and divided up all the land in 1917 and after. Total production fell by only 5 per cent, but the share of grain which reached the cities declined by half. There were political reasons, as well, for not violating the property rights of private owners, especially the 30,000 noble proprietors of large estates who were a power in local and national politics. On the contrary, respect for the sanctity of private property should be strengthened among the peasants by weakening the hold of the commune and persuading its members to assume individual ownership of their allotments.

The ending, in 1903, of joint responsibility for the payment of arrears on taxes and redemption dues in most repartitional communes had been a first step towards loosening communal bonds. Another was the manifesto of 3 November 1905 which forgave half the redemption dues for 1906 and cancelled them altogether after that year. In that same month peasant families were allowed to sell their share of communal land and leave the village. Thus, more than fifty years after the emancipation, a beginning was at last made to carry out the original intention of that act — to eliminate joint tenure and make the peasant the absolute owner of his land.

The Stolypin land reform was a complicated series of measures, promulgated over the course of five years and requiring decades for their implementation. Stolypin himself could not have been aware of their full reach and impact when he embarked on them. But he had a clear conception of the direction in which he wished to move and the determination to begin what he too realized was an experiment of uncertain issue. It was, he said, a wager, a 'wager not on the needy or drunken but on the strong and sturdy', a wager also that time would allow for the emergence of that new class of self-reliant, well-off farmers, settled on their own homesteads, who would be a strong and loyal foundation for the monarchy. It was a gamble that the dislocations caused by the reforms would not endanger their execution, that the displacement of the poor and shiftless would not create new conflicts, and that making the peasants redistribute and rearrange their own lands would make them less interested in seizing those of the gentry.

The Stolypin reform was initiated by an emergency decree of 9 November 1906 which was sanctioned and completed by the Duma in 1910 and 1911.

Its first and easiest step was the establishment of individual title to allotments previously vested in the commune. This could be requested by individual householders for their family's holding, or by a two-thirds vote of the village assembly (and subsequently by a simple majority) for all households. Where tenure had long been hereditary or where no general partition had taken place since 1887, heads of households were considered by the law of 1910 to have become owners of their allotments without the formality of an application. Although legally separated from the commune, the individual proprietor none the less retained the right to use its meadows, woods, and pastures. On the other hand he could not subdivide his land among his heirs, sell it to non-peasants, or mortgage it.

Much the more important and difficult aspect of the reform, however, and its ultimate goal, was the elimination of the strip system of farming, with or without the dissolution of the commune. The dispersal of a family's allotment in different locations, sometimes at considerable distance from its dwelling, was wasteful of time and labour and made impossible the use of machinery and modern methods of cultivation. To combine these scattered strips into compact and enclosed farms the decree of 1906 provided that if the separator demanded it, he be given a 'consolidated holding in so far as possible in one place'; it also made consolidation conditional upon a two-thirds vote of the village meeting. The laws of 1910 and 1911 made consolidation easier, with the latter requiring that it proceed simultaneously with the confirmation of title. Even pasture and woodland became subject to enclosure.

There were 12.3 million peasant households in European Russia in 1905, 9.5 million on communal tenure. The incomplete and not always comparable figures that record how the latter fared in the reform have led to contradictory appraisals of its success and to questions whether it was achieved by governmental fiat or voluntary participation. The two-thirds of households which are reckoned by the most generous interpretation to have obtained title before 1917 are cited to demonstrate the peasants' desire to possess and manage their own land. Their initial response does indeed suggest that the government's plans met deep-seated aspirations.

The largest number of exits from the commune took place in 1907–09, but a sharp decline in applications began in 1910. By 1915 approximately one third of household heads had filed for separation and about a quarter, or 2.4 to 2.6 million, completed the process. Some 9 per cent withdrew their applications because, Soviet researchers believe, they feared conflict with their fellow villagers more than the pressure of the land captain. An additional 3.7 million members of communes with hereditary tenure (1.7 million according to another estimate) were declared by the law of 1910 to be individual owners and may account for the two thirds total mentioned above. For most of them, conversion was nominal and only 625,000 requested the issuance of title-deeds.

Since that juridical change could not by itself bring about better agricultural techniques, the creation of independent farmsteads is a better indication of how the reform was received. About ten per cent of the total – 1.25 million families – actually set up consolidated farms, enclosing 8.85 per cent of all allotment lands. Only 320,000 of these consolidators left the communal village to move onto their own homesteads. They tended to have more draft horses and cattle, to produce larger crops, and to be more open to innovation than their communal neighbours. Yet there were too few of them to end the prevalence of subsistence farming among the bulk of the peasantry. Nor did all the consolidators become part of a surplus-producing rural bourgeoisie. Some failed because they were poor managers; others because, even with government assistance and loans, they still had too little capital or land or because they no longer had access to the common resources of the village, such as water, woods, and pasture.

The possibility of losing the human and material assistance of the commune was a deterrent to leaving it. This explains why the reform was least successful in the poorest and most crowded provinces, and especially those of the Central Agricultural Region. They were the very ones in which poverty and rebelliousness went hand in hand and where opposition to dissolving the commune created additional tensions. Between 1908 and 1916, 1.1 million families sold all or part of their allotment land: 3.4 million desiatinas to separators and 600,000 to consolidators. How many were driven to do so by need and how many for other reasons (settlement or repurchase elsewhere; the surrender of ownership by those who had abandoned farming earlier), is not known. Nor is there enough information to judge how much this transfer benefited the village bourgeoisie and met expectations for its strengthening.

The six million households which held their land in hereditary private tenure in 1915 may have represented the wave of the future and signalled the waning of the communal principle. That is doubtful, however, in view of its surprising vitality in 1917 and the renewed levelling that took place then. But it is certain that the economic results of the agrarian reform were modest or, at best, mixed. Although land under the plough expanded by 10 per cent, four fifths of all arable belonged to peasants, and ten million households were in cooperatives of various kinds, 80 per cent of peasant land remained in strips, most was still cultivated under the three-field system and remained short of capital, cattle, and draft animals.

The time given the reform was too short, the numbers affected too small, the gains too far in the future to change the condition or outlook of most peasants or to give the state and the economy a large enough group of efficient producers who were attached to property and the existing order. Not even the best effort the government had ever made – including the expanded operations on easy terms of the Peasant Land Bank, the subsidized settlement of 2.5 million peasants beyond the Urals, and the generous provision of agronomic assistance – could keep pace with the growing rural population.

Twenty-five million births in the nine years after 1905 and the formation of over three million new households suggest that vastly greater resources and more time were needed to solve the problems of the countryside. It is almost beside the point to ask whether it could have been done in twenty undisturbed years, as Stolypin thought, or whether forty-five or a hundred were required as others believed. No fundamental reorganization of the lives of so many people can expect to proceed in perfect tranquillity; it is likely, rather, to give birth to new and unforeseen difficulties. To say so is no indictment of the effort made or a prejudgement of its effects. A problem so long neglected and of such magnitude is not, as other nations have learned, amenable to quick and total solutions. Yet partial ones can help to relieve distress and discontent and hold out hopes of betterment.

Flawed as the Stolypin settlement was, it gave the government a breathing-space which might have been prolonged but for the war. It was not impossible, Lenin worried, that if it continued for a very long time, the agrarian structure might become completely bourgeois, with the stronger peasants acquiring most allotment land and the countryside ceasing to be a revolutionary factor.[38] Chernov was closer to the mark when he said that as long as the estates of the nobility were excluded from the reform, they would be a source of trouble in the villages.[39] But trouble did not begin there and not until the monarchy had fallen and the instruments of rule no longer commanded fear or respect.

The weakening of the political structure under the blows that war inflicted on the armies and the home front was prepared by the confusion of purpose and authority that reigned at the centre of government. It began when the emperor diminished the power of Stolypin's successor Kokovtsov – not, in any case, a strong figure – by separating the office of premier from that of minister of interior. It continued with the appointment of the lackadaisical and pliant Goremykin who had no interest or ability for giving leadership to a cabinet which contained ambitious men who worked at cross-purposes with one another yet felt they had the backing of the emperor.

Disarray and reactionary influences in the highest echelons of government overshadowed and, many believed, negated the positive developments of the pre-war years. A decree of 5 October 1906 had brought improvements in the legal status of the peasantry – equal rights to state service with other classes; free choice of residence; limitations on the authority of the land captain to fine or punish (corporal punishment had ended in 1904). Cooperation between Duma and certain ministries had led to greater budgetary discipline on the part of the latter, to the renovation of the armed forces, and to the spread of primary (though not compulsory) education (law of 1908). In 1912 the elected justices of the peace, removed in 1889, were restored, land captains lost their judicial functions, and workers' insurance was introduced. There were better relations between state and zemstvos, their introduction in nine provinces, improvements in the economy, greater technical competence in many agencies of government, and a reduction in the area in which exceptional or martial law facilitated abuses of citizen's rights.

But measured against the high hopes of 1905, the programme of Stolypin, and what still needed to be done, these achievements left much room for dissatisfaction. Even an optimistic interpreter of the Duma monarchy's record and prospects agrees that the liberal projects prepared for the Second Duma by Stolypin never became law in their original form or failed altogether because there was no commitment to reform on the part of the emperor, his ministers, or his appointees to the State Council.[40] That constellation of anti-liberal forces, joined on important issues by the right wing of the Duma, prevented the extension of the zemstvos to additional provinces and to the volost; it retained the land captain in his administrative capacity as well as separate class justice for the peasants; it added to Jewish disabilities rather than ending them; it defeated projects for making civil servants responsible before the law, for democratizing the franchise in the district zemstvos, enlarging the legislature's budgetary rights, and establishing firm legal guarantees of personal inviolability and religious toleration. The Lena shootings, the Beilis case, the Rasputin scandal, the dismissals and suspensions of professors and students, deepened the impression of a regime which lacked wisdom, steadiness, and firm control.

'Our government is not talented,' the Moscow manufacturer P. P. Riabushinskii exclaimed before a congress of industrialists in May 1914. 'If this goes on, even the broad masses will lose respect for authority . . . This will be sad, this is intolerable, this can lead to unfortunate consequences . . . A blind state, an orphaned people. One can only hope that our great country will outlive its petty government.'[41]

Of the major governments of Europe, none had so little credit with the people it would shortly have to lead in war as that of Nicholas II.

REFERENCES

1. See, for example, E. Narishkin-Kurakin, *Under Three Tsars* (New York, 1931), p. 189; A. F. Girs, 'Svetlye i chernye dni', *Chasovoi* [Brussels], March 1953, p. 9; Gustav von Lambsdorff, *Die Militär-bevollmächtigten Kaiser Whilhelms II. am Zarenhofe* (Berlin, 1937), p. 350.

2. V. M. Chernov, *Pered burei. Vospominaniia* (New York, 1953), pp. 281–4.

3. M. Perrie, *The Agarian Policy of the Russian Socialist-Revolutionary Party . . .* (Cambridge, 1976), pp. 185–95; D. S. Anin, 'The February Revolution: was the collapse inevitable?', *Soviet Studies* 18 (April 1967), p. 450.

4. I. Getzler, *Martov* (London, 1967), pp. 111–19; cf. Akselrod's speech at the Fourth Party Congress, April–May 1906, in Abraham Ascher (ed.), *The Mensheviks in the Russian Revolution* (London, 1976), pp. 59–64.

5. Quoted in Thornton Anderson (ed.), *Masters of Russian Marxism* (New York, 1963), p. 97.

6. Ibid., p. 95.

7. H. Shukman, *Lenin and the Russian Revolution* (London, 1966; New York, 1967, 1981), p. 129.

8. Rodney Barfield, 'Lenin's utopianism: state and revolution', *Slavic Review* 30 (March 1971), pp. 55–6.

9. V. I. Lenin, *Collected Works* (London and Moscow, 1960–78), IX, pp. 15–140; XIII, pp. 217–429.

10. Ibid., XV, p. 147.

11. A. G. Meyer, *Leninism* (Cambridge, Mass., 1957), p. 142.

12. Shukman, op. cit., p. 131.
13. Ibid., p. 126.
14. B. Shragin and A. Todd (eds.), *Landmarks. A Collectionof Essays on the Russian Intelligentsia. 1909* (New York, 1977); Leonard Schapiro, 'The Vekhi group and the mystique of revolution', *Slavonic and East European Review* 34 (Dec. 1955), pp. 56–76.
15. V. A. Maklakov, *The First State Duma* (Bloomington, Ind., 1964), pp. 8–11.
16. T. Riha, *A Russian European: Paul Miliukov in Russian Politics* (Notre Dame, Ind. and London, 1969), p. 178.
17. Interview with Maklakov in *Russische Korrespondenz* [Berlin] 43, 3 Nov. 1909.
18. Paul Milyoukov, *Constitutional Government for Russia* (New York, 1908), p. 26; and Riha, op. cit., pp. 161–2.
19. Edward Chmielewski, 'Stolypin and the Russian ministerial crisis of 1909', *California Slavic Studies* IV (1967), pp. 1–38.
20. Ben-Cion Pinchuk, *The Octobrists in the Third Duma* (Seattle, Wash., and London, 1974), pp. 58–9, 106–7.
21. Edward Chmielewski, 'Stolypin's last crisis', *California Slavic Studies* III (1964), pp. 95–126.
22. A. A. Kizevetter, *Na rubezhe, dvukh stoletii: vosipominaniia, 1881–1914* (Prague, 1929), p. 516.
23. A. I. Guchkov, *Rechi . . . 1908–1917* (Petrograd, 1917), pp. 106, 111; M. C. Brainerd, 'The Octobrists and the gentry in the Russian social crisis of 1913–1914', *Russian Review* 38 (April 1979), pp. 160–79; Louis Menashe, 'A Liberal with spurs: Alexander Guchkov, a Russian bourgeois in politics', *Russian Review* 26 (Jan. 1967), pp. 38–53.
24. N. B. Weissman, *Reform in Tsarist Russia* (New Brunswick, NJ, 1981), pp. 168–202; L. H. Haimson (ed.), *The Politics of Rural Russia, 1905–1917* (Bloomington, Ind., and London, 1979).
25. V. N. Kokovtsov, *Out of My Past* (Stanford, Cal., and London, 1935), p. 388.
26. A convenient sampling of the conflicting assessments made of Russia's prospects is provided by R. H. McNeal (ed.), *Russia in Transition* (New York, 1970). It does not, however, contain the most important article by L. H. Haimson, 'The problem of social stability in urban Russia, 1905–1917', nor the debate to which it gave rise in *Slavic Review*. See chapter bibliography for detailed references. McNeal has also surveyed the treatment Soviet historians have given 'The fate of imperial Russia', in S. H. Baron and N. W. Heer (eds),*Windows on the Past. Essays on Soviet Historiography Since Stalin* (Columbus, Ohio, 1977), pp. 122–38.
27. Raymond Pearson, *The Russian Moderates and the Crisis of Tsarism, 1914–1917* (London and New York, 1977), p. 12.
28. A. Ia. Avrekh in McNeal, op. cit., p. 38; S. P. Turin, *From Peter the Great to Lenin. History of the Russian Labour Movement* (London, 1935, 1968), pp. 93–117; V. Ia. Laverychev, *Tsarizm i rabochii vopros v Rossii 1861–1917* (Moscow, 1972), pp. 219–69; Siegfried Kohler, *Die russische Industriearbeiterschaft von 1905 bis 1917* (Leipzig, 1921), pp. 78–84.
29. Diane Koenker, 'Urban families in D. L. Ransel (ed.), *The Family in Imperial Russia* (Urbana-Chicago and London, 1978); and *Moscow Workers in the 1917 Revolution* (Princeton, NJ, 1981) pp. 54–6; J. H. Bater, *St Petersburg: Industrialization and Change* (London, 1976), pp. 326–53, 393–411.
30. 'What, generally speaking, are the symptoms of a revolutionary situation?' Lenin asked in 'The Collapse of the Second International' (*Collected Works*, XXI,

pp. 205–59). 'We shall certainly not be mistaken if we indicate the following three major symptoms: (1) when it is impossible for the ruling classes to maintain their rule without any change; when there is a crisis, in one form or another, among the 'upper classes', a crisis in the policy of the ruling class, leading to a fissure through which the discontent and indignation of the oppressed classes burst forth. For a revolution to take place, it is usually insufficient for 'the lower classes not to want' to live in the old way; it is also necessary that 'the upper classes should be unable' to live in the old way; (2) when the suffering and want of the oppressed classes have grown more acute than usual; (3) when, as a consequence of the above causes, there is a considerable increase in the activity of the masses, who uncomplainingly allow themselves to be robbed in 'peace time',but, in turbulent times, are drawn both by all the circumstances of the crisis *and by the 'upper classes' themselves* into independent historical action' (pp. 213–14).

31. S. S. Oldenburg and A. Gerschenkron in McNeal, op. cit., pp. 71–9, 94–101.
32. D. Geyer, *Der russische Imperialismus* (Göttingen, 1977), p. 199; J. Nötzold, *Wirtschaftspolitische Alternativen der Entwicklung Russlands in der Ära Witte und Stolypin* (Berlin, 1966), p. 188.
33. Eberhard Müller, 'Agrarfrage und Industrialisierung in Russland, 1890–1930', *Geschichte und Gesellschaft* 5 (1979), pp. 308–9; Heiko Haumann, *Kapitalismus im zaristischen Staat, 1906–1917* (Königstein, 1980), pp. 51–8.
34. Nötzold, 'Agarfrage und Industrialisierung' in D. Geyer (ed.), *Wirtschaft und Gesellschaft im vorrevolutionären Russland* (Cologne, 1975), pp. 239–42; Geyer, *Imperialismus*, p. 201.
35. S. S. Oldenburg, *Tsarstvovanie Imperatora Nikolaia II* (Munich, 1949), II, p. 115.
36. Nötzold, *Alternativen*, pp. 133, 194–202; P. R. Gregory, 'Economic growth and structural change in tsarist Russia: a case of modern economic growth?', *Soviet Studies* 23 (Jan. 1972), p. 420.
37. The literature on the Stolypin reform of peasant agriculture is large and growing. An as yet incomplete survey is provided by A. Moritsch, 'Neuere Literatur zur Stolypinschen Agrarreform', *Jahrbücher für Geschichte Osteuropas* 24 (1976), pp. 230–49. Besides the works cited in the chapter bibliography, I have made use of the following: Dorothy Atkinson, 'The statistics on the Russian land commune, 1905–1917', *Slavic Review* 32 (Dec. 1973), pp. 773–87; A. M. Anfimov and P. N. Zyrianov, 'Nekotorye cherty evoliutsii russkoi krestianskoi obshchiny v poreformennyi period (1861–1914gg.)', *Istoriia SSSR* 4 (July–August 1980), pp. 26–41; W. E. Mosse, 'Stolypin's villages', *Slavonic and East European Review* 43 (June 1965), pp. 257–74; George Tokmakoff, 'Stolypin's agrarian reform: an appraisal', *Russian Review* 30 (April 1971), pp. 124–38; G. L. Yaney, 'The concept of the Stolypin land reform', *Slavic Review* 23 (June 1964), pp. 273–93; Nötzold, *Alternativen*, pp. 51 ff.; G. T. Robinson, *Rural Russia under the Old Regime* (New York, 1932, 1957), pp. 225 ff; D. W. Treadgold, *The Great Siberian Migration* (Princeton, NJ, 1957), pp. 48–50; A. N. Antsiferov *et al.*, *Russian Agriculture During the War* (New Haven, Conn. 1930), pp. 9–115.
38. Lenin did think, however, that 'The success of Stolypin's policy would involve long years of violent suppression and extermination of a mass of peasants who refuse to starve to death and be expelled from their villages. History has known examples of the *success* of such a policy. It would be empty and foolish democratic phrase-mongering for us to say that the success of such a policy in Russia is

"impossible". It is possible! But our business is to make the people see clearly at what a price such a success is won, and to fight with all our strength for another, shorter and more rapid road of capitalist agrarian development *through* a peasant revolution. A peasant revolution under the leadership of the proletariat in a capitalist country is difficult, very difficult, but it is possible, and we must fight for it.' From 'On the beaten track', in *Collected Works*, XV, p. 44.

39. O. H. Radkey, *The Agrarian Foes of Bolshevism* (New York, 1958),p. 83.
40. M. Szeftel, *The Russian Constitution of April 23, 1906* (Brussels, 1976), pp. 391–431.
41. I am grateful to Dr Lewis Siegelbaum of La Trobe University for the Riabush-inskii quotation from *Zhurnal zasedanii vos'mogo ocherednogo sezda predstavitelei promyshlennosti i torgovli . . . 2, 3, 4 maia 1914 g.* (Petrograd, 1915), pp. 100–1.

CHAPTER TWELVE

The last act: July 1914 to February 1917

The bloody fighting that ravaged Europe for four years seemed to Lenin, as he observed it from neutral Switzerland, to be the predictable outcome of the world's imperial rivalries. It was 'Imperialism, the Highest Stage of Capitalism' (written in 1916) that had inexorably driven the great powers to 'frictions, conflicts, and struggles in every possible form'.[1] In 1913 he had not been so sure, demonstrating that the forecasting of wars, as of revolutions, is a chancy business for even the most astute analyst of social and international conflict. A war between Russia and Austria, Lenin had written then, would be a very useful thing for the revolution throughout eastern Europe, 'but it is hardly possible that Franz Josef and Nicky would give us this pleasure'.[2]

In relating the alarms and crises of the pre-war decade as a linked sequence issuing in the explosion of 1914, it is important to bear in mind that what appears in retrospect to be a fated drift into the abyss was seen by contemporaries in a less ominous light. There were, it is true, warnings and presentiments on all sides of the irreparable damage war would do to the fabric of European society; yet few of its leaders thought it would come to that and fewer still expected that if hostilities broke out they would last more than weeks or months.

Crises had long been endemic in the concert of powers, and their disputes had usually been composed or contained. The Austro-Hungarian and Russian empires, in particular, had every reason not to subject their internal weaknesses to the pitiless judgement of war, which, in spite of deep differences and sharp discords, they had always managed to avoid. It was, none the less, the two states which had most to fear from the disruptions caused by a resort to arms which set in motion the chain of events leading to the First World War. It was their very weaknesses that hardened resolution, the need to display strength and firmness lest they be thought by the world and their peoples no longer capable of defending their position as great powers. To abandon their claim to that status seemed a greater risk than war itself.

In the case of Russia, the forceful reaffirmation of her importance in international affairs had to be postponed for several years after the defeat by Japan and the revolution at home. Although neither her political nor military elites

251

considered withdrawing into isolation, both realized that an inadequacy of means commanded restraint for the moment and left to diplomacy alone the defence of interests considered vital. As Stolypin put it to the cabinet in February 1908: the country needed a breathing spell to recover its strength before it could once again occupy its rightful place as a great power.[3] The advisability of pursuing that goal instead of concentrating on pressing domestic problems was rarely questioned outside the Left. The overwhelming majority of the Duma gave unstinting support to the enormously costly programmes of military reorganization and rearmament which were scheduled for completion in 1917 and which Kokovtsov resisted as much and as long as he could.

Government and political society – from most Kadets to Octobrists, Nationalists and the moderate Right – discovered common ground in an assertive and vigorous foreign policy.[4] The discovery was facilitated by the termination of the imperialist venture in Asia and the return to Europe and the Near East as the traditional theatres of Russian concern. Here emotional and practical reasons came together to elicit a large measure of public sympathy for the actions taken by Russian diplomacy: the backing given to the Balkan states against Austria or a weakening Turkey; resistance to the penetration of the latter by Germany; and efforts to increase Russia's influence and economic opportunities in areas close to her in geography and sentiment.[5]

The two German states were increasingly viewed as the most likely disturbers of the peace and the greatest threats to Russia and her friends. That Britain became one of these distressed extreme conservatives and rightists who would have preferred alignment with the conservative monarchies rather than with republican France and liberal England. But the German option was no longer available. Taking it up, as Nicholas was told in 1905 when he signed an abortive agreement with William II without the knowledge of his foreign minister, would mean the end of the French alliance and of financial and diplomatic help from that quarter. Besides, there was unhappiness with the commercial treaty concluded with Germany in 1904 on the part of Russian exporters of grain and anger at Austrian expansionism in the Balkans even on the part of conservatives.

It was the German challenge to her naval, colonial, and commercial supremacy that led Britain to seek understandings with France in 1904 and with France's ally Russia in 1907. The English gave no such binding military commitments as the French and Russians had made to each other, but the agreements reached developed into the Triple Entente which in 1914 became an alliance facing that of the Central Powers, Austria and Germany, who were joined by Turkey two months after war began. The Anglo-Russian accords of 1907 divided Persia into northern (Russian) and southern (British) spheres of influence, with a neutral zone in the centre; recognized Britain's preponderance in the Persian Gulf and Afghanistan, from which Russia was excluded; and pledged to respect the territorial integrity of Tibet under Chinese suzerainty. The reduction of the hazardous enmity with Britain in regions of secondary importance and doubtful value freed Russian diplomacy to attempt the realization of a long-cherished goal.

As part of the negotiations leading up to the settlement, Foreign Minister A. P. Izvolskii had obtained from the British a vague promise to consider a revision of the international treaties which closed the Straits of the Bosphorus and Dardanelles to the naval vessels of all nations. Closure, in fact, gave a measure of protection to Russia's Black Sea coast and did not hinder her considerable commerce through its ports. Yet it was rightly seen as an infringement of her sovereign rights and an inhibition of her freedom of action. Although Turkey could, under certain conditions, allow the warships of friendly powers to transit the Straits in time of peace, she had refused a Russian request to do so during the war with Japan. By bottling up the Black Sea fleet, Turkey had contributed to the Russian defeat, and she was even less likely to be forthcoming in conflicts closer to home.

Revision of the Straits Conventions of 1841 and 1871, whatever its practical benefits for a country which at the time had no navy to speak of, would have been a great psychological victory. It would have helped to repair Russia's tarnished image and to restore her confidence; it would also have shown that she had powerful friends who needed and valued her. Encouraged by what he chose to regard as British assurances, Izvolskii sought similar concessions from his Austrian counterpart, Count A. L. von Aehrenthal, in difficult bargaining over Balkan matters.

Since 1897 Russia and Austria had collaborated to maintain the status quo in south-eastern Europe, keeping their antagonisms in check and their interests in balance. That fragile adjustment was strained after 1903 by Serbia's encouragement or toleration of movements which envisioned the unification of all Southern Slavs under her aegis or, at a minimum, the detachment of Serbs and Croats from the Habsburg Empire and their absorption by Serbia. This was a threat to the very existence of the Dual Monarchy in which Germans and Magyars ruled over large numbers of Slavs – Czechs and Poles as well as Serbians, Croats and Slovenians. To counter that threat Austria had started a tariff war against Serbia in 1903. Two years later, without prior consultation with Russia, she announced her intention of building a railway across the peninsula to drive a wedge between Serbia and Montenegro and improve Austria's ability to contain South Slav irrendentism with military force.[6]

The Sanjak railroad project, opposed by Russia as a violation of the status which both powers were pledged to uphold, demonstrated Austria's determination to stave off the disintegration of her disparate lands. Aehrenthal saw another chance to secure Austria's Balkan possessions and presence when Turkey was distracted by revolution in July 1908.

The Turkish provinces of Bosnia and Hercegovina had been given to Austria to occupy and administer by the Congress of Berlin in 1878. They and their Croatian and Serbian populations were a prime target of nationalist agitation and policy in neighbouring Serbia. Aehrenthal, who had earlier been approached on the Straits question by Izvolskii, was prepared, when the two ministers met in September 1908, to grant Russia's wishes in return for her agreement to Austrian annexation of Bosnia and Hercegovina. Both parts of the bargain required the assent of the other powers, but before it could be obtained or discussed, Austria declared the incorporation of the provinces to be an accomplished fact (24 September/7 October). Serbia, Russia, and Izvolskii were the losers, and there was little they could do but protest. Austria, backed by Germany, refused to submit the dispute to a conference of the powers who intervened to prevent a war between Serbia and Austria which might involve them all. A German demand that Russia abandon support of the Serbs and recognize the annexation – irresistible in view of Russia's military weakness – completed her diplomatic defeat.[7]

Izvolskii had been incautious, he had exceeded his authority, he had gained nothing, and he was soon replaced by Stolypin's brother-in-law S. D. Sazonov. This did not, however, change the fact that Russia had suffered a deep humiliation; press and politicians likened it to the naval disaster of Tsushima.[8] Compromises became more difficult because they would be interpreted as further retreats. In 1910 there was a renewed understanding with Austria not to disturb the Balkans and an agreement with Germany reducing differences over northern Persia and German railroad concessions (the Baghdad Railway) in Turkey. But fronts had hardened and Russian suspicions increased.

The efforts of Russian diplomats to obtain from Turkey the opening of the Straits denied by friends and adversaries alike failed, as did their hopes that a league of Balkan states which Russia sponsored but could not control would serve as a bulwark against Austria. Instead of presenting a common front against the Dual Monarchy, Bulgaria, Serbia, and Greece fought against Turkey in the First Balkan War (1912) and against each other in the Second (1913). In both conflicts Russia disappointed the Slavs – the Bulgarians by opposing, *inter alia*, their seizure of Constantinople; the Serbians by not standing up for all their territorial demands in the face of Austrian ultimata and the possibility of war. An alliance with Bulgaria, drafted in 1909, was now out of the question and in 1915 she aligned herself with the Central Powers. If a nervous Serbia was not to drift out of the Russian orbit as well, another abandonment had to be avoided. The maintenance of Russian credibility demanded it, as did domestic opinion and strategic considerations.[9]

The latter came into play in the so-called Liman von Sanders crisis – the appointment of a German general to the command of Turkish forces at Constantinople in late 1913. This time the Germans yielded to Russian protests and assigned Liman von Sanders to a less provocative post, but they had confirmed Russian fears and strengthened the hand of those who argued for a more forceful policy. For the moment, the opinion of foreign minister Sazonov prevailed that the status of the Straits was satisfactory to Russia and that it would be a mistake to let 'abstract dreams and missionary enthusiasm' tempt her into unilateral action. At a ministerial conference held in February 1914 he agreed with Navy Minister I. K. Grigorovich that another power in possession of the Straits would have a stranglehold over South Russia's economic life, hegemony over the Balkans, and the key to Asia Minor. The conference concluded that while it must be a basic Russian goal to prevent the establishment of a third power in Constantinople and the Straits, their seizure was impossible without a general European war – and for that, it was agreed, Russia was not yet ready.[10]

War came not over the Straits but the Balkans. On 15/28 June 1914 a member of the secret Serbian society 'Union or Death' – which had for several years engaged in terror, sabotage, and propaganda against Austria – assassinated the Archduke Francis Ferdinand, heir to the Habsburg throne, in the Bosnian city of Sarajevo. Austria blamed the Serbian government and after receiving firm promises of German support, presented the Serbians with an ultimatum. To its harsh and bullying demands the Serbians gave a conciliatory reply which the German emperor thought had removed all reasons for war.[11] The Austrians, feeling that they must seize what might be their last chance to pluck the Serbian thorn from their side, thought otherwise. On 15/28 July they declared war on Serbia. All efforts to localize the conflict failed. To demonstrate her resolve and prevent the annihilation of Serbia, Russia mobilized. Germany demanded that Russia rescind her preparations and when she failed to do so, declared war on Russia (19 July/1 August) and two days later on France. The German invasion of Belgium, dictated by the necessity of striking quickly at France before Russian forces could assemble in strength, brought England into the conflict on the side of Russia and France.

The circumstances of Russia's involvement in the war and the fact that she would fight it alongside the Western democracies helped to win acceptance for it in broad circles of Russian society. In Russia, as elsewhere, there was a surge of patriotic enthusiasm all across the political spectrum and a closing of ranks behind the government. The Duma politicians who had only yesterday deplored its recalcitrance and incompetence seemed almost relieved to be rescued from the impasse in which their isolation and irresolution had landed them. They welcomed the tsar's wish 'to be at one with his people in defence of Russia and her Slav brothers against an insolent foe' and greeted the unity of purpose war made necessary as a portent of lasting collaboration and mutual trust. The war, commented a liberal review, had brought the nation to its senses. 'What had appeared unattainable in time of peace, was achieved.'[12]

The achievement was, in fact, the government's alone. It became even less dependent on the goodwill of society and freed itself for most of the war from Duma criticism and control by summoning that body for only brief periods and adjourning it when it became an inconvenience or an embarrassment. During the one-day session of 26 July, the majority of its members practically invited the administration to ignore them and exacted no promises or concessions for their loyal support. The Duma's Octobrist president, Rodzianko, told a minister, 'We shall only hinder you; it is better, therefore, to dismiss us altogether until the end of hostilities.'[13] The Kadet leader Miliukov asked his party's friends and followers to suspend their quarrels with the government and to remember that their first duty was to preserve Russia one and indivisible and to defend her position as a great power. 'In this struggle we are all as one; we present no conditions or demands; we simply throw upon the scales of battle our firm determination to overcome the aggressor.'[14]

Only the minuscule deputations of the Left – 5 Bolsheviks, 6 Mensheviks,

255

and 10 Trudoviki – refused to issue the government a blank cheque and denounced the ruling classes of all countries for the suffering and bloodshed they had brought upon workers and peasants. They did not, however, call for the defeat of tsarism as the lesser evil, as Lenin would shortly do. Their spokesmen – A. F. Kerenskii for the Trudoviki and V. I. Khaustov for the Social Democrats – vowed that the Russian democracy and proletariat would defend the native land from any attacks, whatever their source; and having defended it, would set it free. When the Duma voted approval of the government's actions and credits for the war, the leftists, perhaps to avoid accusations of disloyalty if they opposed them, walked out or abstained. Even if they had been determined to 'make war on war', they could not have been sure that the people would follow them. Mobilization went off smoothly, for the most part; there was little resistance to it either in the villages or the cities where strikes ceased almost completely for nearly a year.[15]

Some of the most famous figures of the revolutionary movement – including the grand old men of anarchism and Marxism, Kropotkin and Plekhanov – called upon their comrades to make the defeat of German militarism their first duty. There had been nothing like it in the Japanese war but, with Germany the enemy, it was different. Lenin might fume but even among his Bolsheviks patriotism or 'defencism' took their toll. The story among the Socialist Revolutionaries was much the same. What remained of uncompromising defeatism, pacifism, or internationalism was silent or barely managed to survive abroad.[16]

That the patriotic intoxication might be neither deep nor lasting, least of all among the masses who would bear the brunt of the burdens of war, was apparent to fearful conservatives even before hostilities began. In February 1914, P. N. Durnovo, now a member of the Council of State, pleaded with the emperor for an accommodation with Germany in order to avoid war. He predicted social revolution, the disintegration of the army, and hopeless anarchy in the likely event of military setbacks.[17] Maklakov, the reactionary minister of interior, feared a repetition of what had happened in 1905. When he was brought the mobilization order for his signature he said: 'War cannot be popular among the broad masses of the people who are more receptive to ideas of revolution than of victory over Germany.'[18] V. I. Gurko, an ex-assistant minister of interior, was close to the mark with his observation that although the war aroused neither patriotism nor indignation among peasants or workers, it deeply stirred the patriotic sentiments of the educated classes.[19]

The reverses suffered by the armies in the opening months of the war were not yet so grave as to exhaust the sturdy endurance of the soldiers or the goodwill articulate society had extended the country's leaders. The great battles at Tannenberg and the Masurian Lakes of August and September, which caused the Russians to be driven out of East Prussia at a loss of 170,000 men in prisoners and casualties, were not decisive. They proved to be costly to the victorious Germans; they served to weaken the German front in the West, where Paris may have been saved by the shifting of troops to meet the unexpectedly rapid Russian onslaught; and they were balanced by the successes which Russian forces scored over the the Austrians in Galicia and Bukovina, advancing as far as Cracow and northern Hungary by the beginning of November.[20]

Yet victories and defeats alike revealed defects and created problems which reached an unprecedented magnitude with the offensives launched by the Central Powers in April 1915. When the Russians ended their retreat in September and were able to stabilize their defences on a line running from just west of Riga in Livland south to Czernowitz (Chernovtsy) in Bukovina, they had given up not only the conquests of the previous year, Galicia and Bukovina, but also all of Poland, with its industries and coalmines, as well as Kurland, Lithuania, and much of White Russia. And against the Turks, who had entered the war in October 1914, the Russian high command had to send twenty-two badly needed divisions to the Caucasian front.

The vaunted Russian steamroller, the nightmare of an endless flood of men which had haunted the German General Staff, turned out to be neither unstoppable nor inexhaustible. During the five months of the Great Retreat of 1915 there were almost a million dead and wounded and another million taken prisoner. In the campaigns of 1914 the losses had been nearly as great. The rate at which trained conscripts and reserves had then been expended contributed to the later débâcle and to the manpower crisis in a country which put fewer men into uniform than did Germany and barely more than France with their much smaller populations. Of the nearly 15 million men who served in the forces during three years of the war, about half were eliminated by enemy action: 2.4 million prisoners; 2.8 million wounded and sick; 1.8 million killed.

The reasons for this carnage and Russia's failure to make better use of her human resources are many, and they have been examined in detail in two studies which are indispensable to an understanding of events at and behind the eastern front.[21] Before the war lack of money restricted the annual intake of conscripts to about one third of the available manpower; as a result much less of it was trained than in Germany or France. The shortage of officers and noncoms was another factor keeping that proportion down and it got worse when high casualty rates among the regulars caused them to be replaced by inexperienced men who were often as disaffected as the soldiers they were supposed to lead, yet rarely gained their respect.[22] Difficulties of supply and support services over great distances, poor roads and railways, also limited the number of troops who could be put into the front lines when and where they were needed.

An erratic and inequitable system of exemptions and deferments allowed many to escape conscription which was, in any case, unable to reach into every corner of the vast empire. And what a more determined effort at mobilization could lead to among people who were indifferent or hostile to the Russian war effort was shown in the Central Asian revolt of 1916. Thus, technical constraints and prudence made less of Russia's manpower available as trained combat soldiers than mere numbers would suggest. The deficiency became critical because the extraordinary wastage of men and *matériel* had not been anticipated. No country was prepared for the kind of bloodletting or for the enormous expenditure of weapons and ammunition that occurred. But Russia faced more and greater obstacles in repairing the material, moral, and political damage those losses inflicted.

The shortages of artillery, machineguns, rifles, shells, and bullets that caused such havoc and demoralization – although poor generalship bears a large part of the blame for the defeats and casualties of 1914 and 1915 – were remedied most easily. By the end of 1916 the Russians were at least as well provided as their adversaries, perhaps better. Industry, and especially the larger and more modern firms which had not used their full capacity before the war, was able to supply most of the army's needs. Allied help, previously blocked by Turkey's barring of the Straits, began to arrive by way of newly built or expanded rail lines to White Sea and Pacific ports and could be expected to increase in 1917.

In spite of the fact that Russian industry performed better than has generally been thought – Stone attributes its problems to rapid modernization, not backwardness – there were economic as well as non-economic limits to the maintenance and even more to the bettering of its performance. Whether it could have continued to meet the demands of the military as well as other essential requirements is far from certain. Output in such important sectors as iron ore and coal, pig iron and steel, began to drop in 1916, before the catastrophic declines of revolutionary 1917. Scarcities of fuel and raw material were aggravated by the disruption of foreign trade and domestic transport, the latter caused by the disrepair of rolling stock and the loss of key railways in enemy-occupied territory. Labour productivity declined with the employment of unskilled hands, including large numbers of women. Not until 1915, when it was too late for many of them, were workers in critical occupations exempted from conscription. With 80 per cent of the labour force engaged in war production, little if any improvement could be obtained by adding to it and further cutting back the manufacture of consumer goods which were already in short supply.[23]

Industry's impressive record in supplying the armies was achieved by guaranteeing huge profits and neglecting needs which turned out to be as imperative as those of the military. By the end of 1915 the production of agricultural machinery had fallen by half; together with the requisitioning of horses and the cessation of imports, this had obvious and predictable consequence for the ability of agriculture to feed workers and soldiers and keep food prices from soaring. The lack of machinery (as of chemical fertilizer) was much less damaging, however, for the bulk of the peasantry than for the owners of estates and prosperous farms who were the chief users and purchasers of both. With the virtual ending of shipments abroad and the introduction of prohibition in 1914, there should have been enough grain for the armies and cities.

Peasant producers were, in fact, able to better their output and incomes, thanks to good weather, the relative abundance of labour, state payments for soldiers' dependants and requisitions, and the expansion of ploughland. If the marketed share of harvests declined from 25 per cent pre-war to 15 per cent in 1916/17, the explanation lies once again in the disorganization of transport, but more importantly in the failure of industry to produce common items of consumption – such as tools, boots, cloth, and nails – in quantities and at prices that would have induced the peasants to part with their grain. Since the scissor, as Trotskii was to call it a few years later, between what they had to pay and what they received was constantly widening, the peasants preferred to eat their produce themselves, to feed it to their animals, or to withhold it in expectation of better terms of trade. Profiteers and speculators made matters worse, while neither the state monopolization of the grain trade in October 1916 nor the setting of allotment and delivery quotas in November improved them. By that time the cities, their populations swollen with six million newcomers, were getting less than half the foodstuffs they required. In the last two weeks of January 1917 food shipments to Moscow fell 60 per cent short of need; the northern capital, renamed Petrograd in 1914, had only a few days' grain reserves when bread riots broke out in February.

The army was beginning to feel the pinch as well. At the end of 1916 the bread ration was cut from three to two pounds and then to one. Soldiers so thoroughly detested the lentils which were issued to supplement it that they 'can almost be accounted as a major cause of the Revolution'.[24] There were, of course, others of equal or greater importance and the revolution did not start at the fronts, which were holding, but in the rear. The grumbling about poor food – what kind of government was it that could not assure its fighting men of enough coarse rye bread to fill their stomachs? – was only one manifestation of the discontent which had been growing among the troops from the very beginning of hostilities.

The obvious superiority of the German enemy in the skills and engines of war, the devastating casualties he inflicted, and the woeful inadequacy of their medical and supply services robbed the men of what little patriotic fervour there was among them. They very quickly became convinced that what had happened in Manchuria would be repeated all over again, that the war could not be won, and that even if it could, they would not survive it. Whether they blamed incompetent generals, cowardly and cruel officers, greedy landlords, Jewish spies, or German influences at court and in government, they had spiritually opted out of a war they never considered theirs long before they deserted it physically.

That the armies had more and better weapons in 1916, that dressing stations and field hospitals were much improved thanks to the Unions of Towns and Zemstvos, made little difference to men who feared that the slaughter would only be prolonged. The Russian offensives of 1916 on the northern, south-western, and Turkish fronts, and in particular the spectacular advance of General A. A. Brusilov against the Austrians in Volynia, Galicia, and Bukovina proved them right; they cost another million casualties and brought no lasting or decisive gains. Brusilov's advance was stopped with the aid of fifteen German divisions brought from France. The Roumanians, who had been encouraged by his success to enter the war on Russia's side in August, were hard pressed by the Central Powers and instead of relieving the Russians, needed their help.

Towards the end of 1915 there had already been conscription riots in several cities and attacks on the police who did not have to serve. A year later mutinies involving several combat regiments were reported. Such incidents were still few and they were quickly dealt with, but more passive and subtle forms of insubordination were widespread: from the sullen and half-hearted execution of orders to malingering, voluntary capture, individual desertions to the rear, and self-mutilation, the so-called 'finger wounds'. They gave clear warning that the front-line units, whose ranks were being replenished with hastily trained raw youths and angry family men in their forties, were not immune from the war-weariness and disgruntlement that infected the garrison towns of the rear. The unwilling warriors who filled them – replacements, trainees, and recovering wounded – represented half the army's strength in 1916 and proved to be its weakest link in 1917.

The letters and rumours that reached the soldiers in the field telling of conditions at home contributed to their demoralization and the feeling that it was they and their worker and peasant families who suffered most of the privations. There were, it is true, jobs to be had as well as higher wages in the burgeoning war industries, on the railroads, in mines, and on landowners' estates to make up for the closing of many cottage and consumer goods industries and the earnings of men who had gone to war. But for much of the unskilled labour which replaced them there was also lower pay, compulsory overtime, the lifting of restrictions on night work for women and children, and beginning in 1915 the inflation which soon wiped out the gains even of favoured workers in defence plants. The scarcity of consumer goods and food and the government's fiscal policy combined to make Russia's inflation worse than that of other warring countries. In the second half of 1916 the price index was almost three times above the level of 1913; by the beginning of 1917 the paper ruble had lost two thirds of its pre-war value. High rents and prices, long lines for food and fuel, and terrible crowding in the working-class quarters of the urban centres led to the revival of the strike movement, which in 1916 approached the scope of the immediate pre-war period. In Petrograd the first case of soldiers refusing to fire on strikers occurred in October. A month later 5,000 troops demonstrated in sympathy with striking workers in a Ukrainian town.

Efforts to control prices and guarantee the provisioning of the cities were late and ineffective. The sporadic rationing of certain commodities did not begin until the autumn of 1916 when sugar cards were introduced in Moscow. The measure did not fill the stores which issued them: it drove up prices in the open market to which supplies were now diverted, and it heightened anxieties. The rationing of flour and bread in Moscow on 20 February 1917 caused panic buying, shortages, and rumours of worse to come which spread to Petrograd and led to riots there. It was beyond the capacity of the government to enforce or win acceptance for a comprehensive and equitable system of rationing, price controls, and procurements. The millions of suspicious peasants who had reverted to a subsistence or barter economy would hardly be affected by it and the larger producers and traders successfully opposed it by threatening, more or less openly, to withhold deliveries unless they could be sure of what they considered an adequate return.

The minister of agriculture, who happened also to be a leader of the United Nobility, an agrarian pressure group, justified the raising of grain prices in September 1916 by saying, not incorrectly, that without such an inducement production would decline. A state project for the procurement of coal at fixed prices and its planned distribution was turned down by a solid front of mine owners and other industrialists as an unwarranted infringement of the freedom of enterprise. Fiscal policy was similarly hampered by considerations of feasibility and politics. To pay for the war and to make up for lost income from the liquor monopoly, railways, and customs duties, indirect taxes were raised; but there were limits to what the sorely tried consumer could be made to pay. Income and excess profits taxes, finally adopted in 1916, were kept ridiculously low to avoid drying up sources of capital and alienating its owners; they yielded little revenue and were useless as demonstrations that the rich were paying a fair share of the war's costs. These had to be met for the most part by loans and recourse to the printing press with the inflationary results already described.

The liberality the government thought it wise or necessary to extend to powerful economic interests was not matched in the political arena. It served, on the contrary, to divide and weaken an opposition which was beginning to revive in 1915. In that desperate year, as news of military bungling and disasters reached the public, small gestures of goodwill and the sacrifice of unpopular ministers were offered to society and answered their purpose of forestalling a concerted assault on the regime. In January the recall of the Duma appeased for a time the increasingly restive politicians who were allowed to reaffirm their unity with the government in the prosecution of the war and, as agreed in advance, to pass its budget. With Mensheviks and Trudoviki abstaining – the Bolshevik deputies, in violation of their parliamentary immunity, had been arrested – there was no opposition. After three days the Duma was recessed; its members dispersed without protesting, at least in public. During the session only Kerenskii and a Progressive deputy questioned the wisdom of their uncritical and undemanding compliance.

The worsening situation at the fronts and pressure from their constituents made it impossible for the leaders of the moderate parties to continue their silent endorsement of the administration. It was now proving what had been feared all along – that the bureaucracy was incapable of organizing itself for war. Tacitly admitting its inadequacy, it allowed a larger role to organizations and individuals it had previously kept at arm's length.

The Unions of Towns and Zemstvos, formed in 1914 for war relief, were suspect because of their liberal leanings and tolerated rather than welcomed. In June 1915 they were none the less permitted to join forces in Zemgor to enlist light industries and rural artisans in the filling of state orders for army supplies. A Central War Industries Committee, headed by Guchkov, was established at the same time to coordinate the activities of larger enterprises. Both organizations were represented on the Special Councils for Defence, Food, Fuel and Transportation set up in August where they sat side by side with deputies of the Duma and State Council and representatives of the ministries who were in the majority.

The economic importance of the voluntary or public organizations was modest; their share of war production, it has been estimated, was no more than 5 per cent of the total, the rest being furnished by state-owned firms (15 per cent) or the giants of heavy industry and the syndicates (80 per cent) which the government found less troublesome and more efficient.[25] They did, however, contribute to the rising chorus of demands that the regime show greater trust in society and seek its help by recalling the Duma. Nicholas was persuaded of the advisability of doing so by the moderate members of his cabinet. In order to avoid an open confrontation with the legislature, he parted with four of the more offensive of their colleagues, including Shcheglovitov (Justice), whose name was connected with the shameful Beilis affair, and Maklakov (Interior) who insisted to the last that the Duma posed a threat to the emperor's power and should become a purely consultative organ. But the retention of Goremykin as head of the cabinet spelled trouble, as did the politicians' realization that their continued silence would be interpreted as surrender.

Six weeks after it was convened on 19 July 1915, the Duma was prorogued (3 September). A few weeks later the tsar refused to receive a delegation of the Unions of Towns and Zemstvos on the grounds that they were political in nature; his wife urged him to get rid of Guchkov and the War Industries Committee. There had obviously been no change of heart, only a cosmetic correction of course that was reversed when the Duma and especially the public organizations proved to be less tractable than expected and to have allies in the cabinet and at army headquarters.

The Duma had, in fact, offered very reasonable terms for its collaboration in hopes of prolonging its own life and keeping more militant forces from supplanting it. A Nationalist resolution, adopted on the first day of the session and calling for a ministry enjoying the confidence of the nation (instead of the Progressives' 'ministry responsible to the Duma'), became the basis on which a broad spectrum of some 300 out of 430 members joined with a group from the State Council to form the Progressive Bloc.[26]

In late August confident that their numbers, their moderation, the sympathy of most ministers, and the government's loss of popularity would convince the tsar to accept it, they presented the Bloc's programme. It asked for no structural changes in the institutions of state, merely for a united cabinet able and willing to cooperate with the legislature and to gain its confidence and that of the country by a strict observance of legality in its dealings with society. To unify the nation for victory a number of immediate conciliatory steps, as well as agreement on future legislation, were deemed essential: imperial clemency for persons charged with or exiled for religious and political offences; an end to the persecution of religious groups and workers' organiz-ations; submission of bills for Polish autonomy and of a programme 'begin-ning the abolition of restrictions on the rights of Jews'; relief for Finns and Ukrainians; equalization of peasants' rights with those of other classes; the introduction of zemstvos in the volost, Siberia, and the Caucasus, and a less-ening of bureaucratic control over all organs of local government.

Goremykin, who was a prime target of the Bloc, which would not have found him acceptable in a reformed ministry, easily persuaded Nicholas to reject its overtures and to adjourn the Duma. Dismissals of several ministers favourable to the Bloc followed in short order. They, indeed the entire cabinet with the exception of Goremykin and the service ministers, had already incurred the emperor's displeasure by a collective plea (and tender of resig-nation) that he reverse his decision of taking the place of the Grand Duke Nikolai Nikolaevich as commander of the armies at headquarters (*Stavka*) in Western Russia. They feared that henceforth the monarch and the monarchy would be held directly responsible for military reverses; that the emperor's absence from the capital would only compound the existing confusion and conflicts of authority between Stavka and government, generals and ministers, front and rear; and that the empress's meddling in high politics against the Duma and its ministerial allies would get worse, as it did.[27]

'Had you given in now in these different questions,' Alexandra wrote to her husband, 'they would have dragged out yet more of you.'[28] Judging by their reactions, neither the ministers nor the leaders of the Bloc were likely to do so. The former, told by the emperor to stay at their posts and follow his and Goremykin's orders, obediently awaited their dismissals; the latter, although stunned and angered by the unexpected turn of events, carried out none of their threats of boycotting the war effort, appealing to the tsar, or taking their case to the country. Failure, the lack of any response, would advertise their impotence, as had happened with the futile Vyborg Appeal after the dissolution of the First Duma. Success would transfer the battle from parliament into the streets. That would defeat one of the chief purposes of the Bloc, the very one which had given it such broad support. As expressed by the Nationalist deputy V. V. Shulgin, it was 'to replace the discontent of the masses, which might easily turn into revolution, with the discontent of the Duma'.[29] Shulgin and others were beginning to wonder whether they were not fanning rather than dampening the fires of revolution and the thought kept them from pressing their attack.

The dilemma of the moderates was most pronounced and painful for the liberal wing of the Bloc which was torn and ultimately paralysed by contrary pulls to left and right. On the one side, favoured by the Progressives and Left Kadets, there lay common action with radical groups, mass movements, and the more militant of the public organizations towards a seizure of power; on the other, preservation of the Bloc and of the alliance with its conservative members, pressure on the government to mend its ways, and the maintenance of social peace, for revolution invited defeat. If organizing Russia for victory required organizing her for revolution, the Kadet leader Miliukov told a special session of the Duma in March 1916, he would wish to leave her as she was, unorganized, while the war lasted.[30]

By November 1916, with victory nowhere in sight, with Goremykin replaced (in January) by the inept B. V. Stuermer who was close to the empress and Rasputin and wrongly suspected of pro-German leanings, Miliukov accused the government of claiming that to organize the country meant to organize a revolution. He charged that it preferred chaos and disorganization to joining forces with society and asked, 'what is this, stupidity or treason?', repeating the question each time he listed one of the administration's sins of omission or commission. The implication of sinister and treacherous influences working behind the scenes for a separate peace with Germany gained credibility from Stuermer's name and the empress's German birth. Miliukov's speech, which the censor deleted from press accounts of the Duma sitting, circulated in mimeographed and typewritten copies, inflaming popular hatred of 'that German woman' and more vaguely all who were held responsible for the miseries of war, from ministers to policemen.[31]

Intemperate and offensive as his language had been, Miliukov had not departed from constitutional propriety. He had asked for no more than what the Bloc had demanded for over a year: the replacement of a cabinet which he called incapable and ill-intentioned by one acceptable to the Duma majority. His denunciations did not achieve even that limited goal, although they were echoed all across the house to the benches of the far right. They merely persuaded the tsar, over the objections of his wife, to part with Stuermer and to entrust the chairmanship of the Council of Ministers to A. F. Trepov, minister of transport. The mentally unbalanced and universally detested A. D. Protopopov, a protégé of Alexandra and Rasputin, retained the ministry of interior to the very end. Until the next round of 'ministerial leapfrog' only one other portfolio, that of agriculture, changed hands.[32]

Trepov had been chosen because he had better relations with the Duma than Stuermer; having secured its quiet adjournment on 17 December to 14 February 1917 – even Miliukov did not really want to rouse a storm lest it 'break out in a form we do not desire'[33] – he was asked by Nicholas to resign after six weeks in office. His successor was an outsider to government, Prince N. D.Golitsyn, who had no political experience, influence, or ambitions. He was the last occupant of the post which he had accepted with the utmost reluctance and held for only two months.

The spectres of a mass rising and a lost war which Miliukov had hoped to banish by his verbal attack drove other men to still more desperate stratagems. Guchkov had come to feel that the only way to save the country and the monarchy was to remove the monarch. In August 1916 he began to lay the groundwork for a plot which would with the help of a group of young cavalry officers and elements of the Petrograd garrison depose Nicholas and install a new government. Some generals were sympathetic but unwilling to commit themselves in advance. Guchkov's illness delayed preparations for the coup, planned for the middle of March, until it was too late. Its success would not, in all probability, have changed the course of history profoundly.[34]

The murder on 16/17 December of Rasputin, the supposed author of Russia's misfortunes, had little impact on the course of events. He fell victim to a conspiracy which three men had entered to rid the dynasty of its evil genius: Grand Duke Dmitrii Pavlovich, Prince Iusupov (a nephew by marriage of the tsar), and the head of the proto-fascist Union of the Archangel Michael, Purishkevich, who had denounced Rasputin in the Duma as a 'filthy; vicious, and venal muzhik'. Their deed had no political effects and if it was welcomed by some citizens; others, ever ready to believe the worst of their 'masters', were sure he had been done in because he was a simple peasant who worked for peace.[35]

All three attempts to improve the nation's chances for victory by changes of personnel at the heights of power betrayed an inability to recognize or admit how wide was the gulf in late 1916 between the mass of ordinary Russians and respectable society – all those who would soon be categorized as the bourgeoisie. The former were no longer interested in victory, if they had ever been, and more and more often they blamed society, represented in the Duma and the voluntary organizations, as much as the tsar and his officials, for prolonging their hardships. Hostility to the war had grown so much among the workers that their representatives at a December conference of War Industries Committees (WICs) felt compelled to voice it by criticizing the Duma for its refusal to discuss German peace feelers.

The Workers Groups of the Central WIC at Petrograd and of its provincial branches were the only legal channels, with the closely watched exception of factory sick benefit and insurance funds, for the expression of labour's views and wants. They were virtually its only channels, and a privileged one at that, because the police had disrupted the work of the trade unions and the radical parties. In order to secure the collaboration of the workers and the support of their leaders, Guchkov and the industrialists of the WICs had in the summer of 1915 obtained the grudging assent of the government to the election of worker delegates to the committees. The first group, chosen in the factories of Petrograd in November 1915, was followed by others and by May 1916 worker representatives had been elected to 20 regional and 98 district WICs. Their uniquely protected status allowed them not only to defend the workers' material interests and to encourage their organization; they also made use of their access to the factories to raise political issues bearing on the conduct and goals of the war.[36]

Anti-war socialists – Bolsheviks, Maximalist SRs, and Internationalist Mensheviks –, although they differed over the tactics to be followed in resisting the imperialist conflict, denounced collaboration with the bourgeoisie as treason to the working class and 'social chauvinism'. They were unable, however, to overcome the arguments of defencist or pragmatic Mensheviks and SRs that membership in the WICs offered unique opportunities for organizing the working class, protecting its rights, and articulating its political demands. The Mensheviks in particular saw the Workers' Groups as the nucleus of a broad-based labour movement which could, in guarded cooperation with the liberal bourgeoisie, fight a reactionary regime for the democratization of the political order and capital for the satisfaction of workers' needs.

That their entry into the WICs did not mean cooptation by the bourgeoisie, or wholehearted support of the war, the workers'representatives made clear from the very beginning. They declared that an irresponsible government had taken Russia into a war for capitalist markets – a far cry from making Prussian militarism the chief culprit; that this government was making war on its own people; and that it bore the guilt, in which Duma politicans shared, for all the disasters which had befallen the country. A constituent assembly elected by universal suffrage; the immediate granting of full civil and religious liberty; the right of self-determination for the non-Russian nationalities; comprehensive social legislation, the eight-hour day, and land for the peasants were the most important demands put forward by the Petrograd Workers' Group in November 1915. It also embraced the central tenet of 'revolutionary defencism', which Kerenskii and the Menshevik N. S. Chkheidze had advanced in the Duma in August: a democratic peace without annexations or indemnities.

Yet for a year the Workers' Group urged caution upon the proletariat of the capital, warning against premature and isolated strikes, and recommending common action with other classes against the tsarist government. By the end of 1916 the workers' impatience and the competition of a growing number of Bolshevik and other militants made such restraint appear inadvisable, and the Workers' Group joined in a strike call for the anniversary of Bloody Sunday on 9 January 1917. It was answered by 140,000 or 40 per cent of Petrograd's workers and was followed on 14 February by another strike of 84,000 which the Workers' Group had called for the reopening of the Duma. By that time its leaders had been arrested (27 January) and the strike movement, sometimes egged on, sometimes held back for tactical reasons by the militants, had assumed a life of its own. Strikes were still confined to individual shops and plants, moving from one to another without becoming general, and still concerned, for the most part, with wages, hours, and food supplies.[37]

But on Thursday, 23 February, which was International Women's Day, there began the unplanned and unforeseen transformation of uncoordinated strike action into a revolutionary rising. A week later (2 March) it had led to the abdication of Nicholas and the end of the Romanov dynasty when his brother, the Grand Duke Michael, renounced the throne (3 March). What distinguished the events of the first day of the Second Russian Revolution from those immediately preceding it was the determination of the strikers to take their grievances beyond the workplace to the centre of the capital. Their purpose was to enlist its citizens in demonstrations which demanded on this and more insistently on subsequent days not only bread or even peace but the overthrow of the government and of autocracy.

As the strikes and marches gained momentum, they were aided by agitators and organizers of all socialist factions making the round of the factories – from members of the Workers' Group who were still at liberty to a thousand or more militant anti-war Mensheviks, SRs, and some 3,000 Bolsheviks. The demonstrators' biggest accretion of strength, however, came from the women of Petrograd and the soldiers of its garrison. The former, exasperated by hours of mostly futile waiting in bread lines, took to smashing bakeries and food shops; the latter followed them into open defiance of authority from which there was no turning back. The soldiers' sympathies were with the crowds, not with those who were going to send them to the front to be maimed or killed.

The soldiers' revolt was decisive in converting the workers' and women's angry protests into revolution. It was precipitated by an order Nicholas issued from GHQ (Stavka) on the night of 25 February. Told for the first time of the extent of the disorders and of the general strike which had paralysed Petrograd that day, he instructed the authorities, who hoped until then to confine the disturbances to the factory districts, to put them down with whatever force was required. When troops were ordered to fire on the demonstrators on the 26th and 27th, their occasional disregard of officers' commands on previous days became a full-fledged mutiny, with soldiers joining the crowds in attacks on the hated police who were disarmed and went into hiding if they were not beaten or killed. By the 28th, Petrograd was in full insurrection and there were no longer any substantial units of loyal troops in the capital or in the nation's second city, Moscow, which fell to the insurgents on 1 March.

There was, in fact, no longer a government in Russia. Late on the 27th the members of the cabinet, in their own timid version of mutiny or desertion, had resigned their posts. Knowing that the situation was out of control and that their lives were in danger, they covered their retreat by recommending to Nicholas that he appoint the Grand Duke Michael as temporary dictator. The tsar rejected their suggestion as well as their resignation. The ministers chose discretion over obedience to their sovereign and so, in a matter of days, did the commanders of the armed forces in the field and at GHQ. They abandoned plans to march on the insurgent capital, backed the Duma leaders' demand for the abdication of Nicholas, and acquiesced in the demise of the monarchy because they were unsure whether it would help to preserve the loyalty of their men or be the cause of further disaffection.

The generals were also held back from an immediate commitment to counter-revolution by the misleading assurances they received from the president of the Duma, Rodzianko, that he and the politicians of the Progressive Bloc could control the revolution, halt the disintegration of army and country, and save the dynasty if the tsar appointed a responsible ministry chosen from their midst. When Nicholas acceded, it was already too late, as Rodzianko, the politicians, the generals, and the emperor himself quickly realized. The mood of the masses was so implacably anti-monarchist that the removal of Nicholas became a necessity and his replacement by Michael, either as regent for the young tsarevich or as tsar in his own right, an impossibility. The moderates were thus deprived of the symbol of authority, continuity, and legitimacy they craved and thought necessary for the nation's acceptance of their rule and the return of stability.

Formation on 27 February by leaders of the Progressive Bloc of a Temporary Duma Committee to 're-establish order in the capital and for liaison with persons and institutions', was their first hesitant step towards the assumption of governmental responsibility. It was taken in response to the prorogation of the Duma, which had been the last premier's last act on the 26th, and to the revolution of the streets which the Bloc's members had neither wanted nor made. Yet it was to them, meeting unofficially and in the greatest perplexity in the Duma's Tauride Palace, that much of the city's populace looked for leadership when the agencies of the tsar's government ceased to function or were no longer obeyed. Although it had been elected on a most restricted franchise and was felt to represent property and privilege, the Duma was the only established institution which enjoyed a measure of public respect because it had been critical of the regime of which it was a part. The mere fact that some of its members continued to meet after prorogation was taken as an act of defiance which ranged them on the side of revolution.

The leaderless soldiers who came to pledge support for the Temporary Committee and thereby to gain approval for their rebellion also found installed in the Tauride Palace the Executive Committee of the Petrograd Soviet of Workers' and (subsequently) Soldiers' Deputies which had been formed almost simultaneously with Duma Committee. It was the creation of socialist intellectuals and politicians, for the most part Mensheviks and members of the Workers' Group released from prison by the crowds, who appealed to workers and soldiers to send delegates from their factories and units to the Soviet's first session to be held on the evening of the 27th. That meeting, at which there were as yet few worker and soldier delegates, elected the Menshevik Duma deputy Chkheidze as chairman of the Soviet, Kerenskii and another socialist Duma member (M. I. Skobelev) as vice-chairmen, and a regular Executive Committee on which all the socialist parties were represented.

In spite of the fact that the Soviet claimed to speak for the 'Russian democracy', the revolutionary masses, and although it organized district committees, a workers' militia, and a military commission, it did not lay claim to sole leadership of the revolution or the state. The Soviet's leaders were not setting up an alternative government to the one they expected the bourgeoisie to establish but an organ for watching over it and for defending and deepening the gains of the revolution.

The moderates none the less perceived the Soviet as a competitor for power, which at this time only a few of the most radical socialists wished it to be. Fear of the Soviet and of the growing anarchy finally pushed even the most reluctant members of the Temporary Committee of the Duma to form a Provisional Government on 2 March and to announce it to the country on the next day. They did so as the presumptive legatees of the Duma which had ceased to function, without the stamp of continuity and legality that a ruler or regent might have supplied, but with the half-hearted agreement of the Soviet to accept the new government in so far as it continued to struggle against the old regime and acted to realize the reforms it had promised.

These included an immediate and complete amnesty, the full range of civil liberties, the abolition of all national and religious restrictions, and the 'immediate preparation for the convocation of the Constituent Assembly

. . . which will determine the form of government and the constitution of the country'.

The complexion of the new government – it contained six Kadets, two Progressives, two Octobrists, one non-party liberal and one nominal socialist – was to the left of the Duma Committee and the Progressive Bloc. Its make-up reflected an awareness of how far the moderate opposition had been left behind by the radicalization of the masses. Yet in their eyes the cabinet, with the exception of Kerenskii (who now declared himself a Socialist Revolutionary), was still too closely identified with the old order and the upper classes. G. E. Lvov, the non-party liberal who had been head of the Union of Zemstvos, became premier and minister of interior; he was a large landowner and bore the unfortunate title of prince. There were two wealthy industrialists among the ministers, A. I. Konovalov and M. I. Tereshchenko; Guchkov, the minister of war and navy, was suspect because of his monarchism and because he, like Miliukov at the Foreign Ministry, was known to favour the vigorous prosecution of the war. Whether a government committed to that end, however it was composed, would be able to maintain the quiet which was gradually returning to the streets of Petrograd remained to be seen.

REFERENCES

1. V. I. Lenin, *Collected Works* (London and Moscow, 1960–78), XXII, p. 295.
2. *Lenin and Gorky. Letters. Reminiscences. Articles*, trans. from the Russian by B. Isaacs (Moscow, 1973), p. 100.
3. I. V. Bestuzhev, *Borba v Rossii po voprosam vneshnei politiki, 1906–1910* (Moscow, 1961), p. 151.
4. I. V. Bestuzhev, 'Borba v Rossii po voprosam vneshnei politiki nakanune pervoi mirovoi voiny, 1910–1914', *Istoricheskie zapiski* 75 (1965), pp. 45–85; and Horst Jablonowski, 'Die Stellungnahme der russischen Parteien zur Aussenpolitik der Regierung . . .', *Forschungen zur osteuropäischen Geschichte* 5 (1957), pp. 60–92.
5. On the pre-history of Russia's entry into the First World War see, *inter alia*, B. Jelavich, *A Century of Russian Foreign Policy 1814–1914* (Philadelphia and New York. 1964), pp. 249–79; Joachim Remak, *The Origins of World War I* (New York, 1967); D. Geyer, *Der russische Imperialismus* (Göttingen, 1977), pp. 189–238, 251–8; V. M. Khvostov, *Diplomatiia v novoe vremia, 1871–1914* (Moscow, 1963), chs 17–21; R. E. McGrew, 'Some imperatives of Russian foreign policy' in T. G. Stavrou (ed.), *Russia Under the Last Tsar* (Minneapolis, Minn., 1969), pp. 202–29, and I. V. Bestuzhev, 'Russian Foreign Policy February–June 1914' in Walter Laqueur and G. L. Mosse (eds), *1914: The Coming of the First World War* (New York, 1966), pp. 88–107.
6. W. S. Vucinich, *Serbia Between East and West, 1903–1908* (Stanford, Cal., 1954).
7. B. E. Schmitt, *The Annexation of Bosnia, 1908–1909* (Cambridge, Mass., 1937).
8. *Istoriia SSSR*, V, pp. 483–4.
9. E. C. Thaden, *Russia and the Balkan Alliance of 1912* (University Park, Penn., 1965).
10. A. M. Zaionchkovskii, *Podgotovka Rossii k pervoi mirovoi voine v mezhdunarodnom*

otnoshenii (Leningrad, 1926), pp. 314–328; S. D. Sazonov, *Fateful Years 1909–1916* (New York, 1928), pp. 125–6.

11. Remark, op. cit., p. 115.

12. *Vestnik Evropy* (Jan. 1915), cited by S. S. Oldenburg, *Tsarstvovanie Imperatora Nikolaia II* (Munich, 1949), II, p. 160. Reactions to the coming of war are described in H. Rogger, 'Russia in 1914', *Journal of Contemporary History* 1 (Oct. 1966), pp. 104–14.

13. Raymond Pearson, *The Russian Moderates and the Crisis of Tsarism, 1914–1917* (London and New York, 1977), p 13.

14. F. A. Golder, *Documents of Russian History, 1914–1917* (New York and London, 1927), p. 35.

15. Ibid., pp. 33–4, for Kerenskii's speech. Also see O. H. Gankin and H. H. Fisher (eds), *The Bolsheviks and the World War. The Origin of the Third International* (Stanford, Cal., 1940), pp. 134–7.

16. Ibid., pp. 267–8; O. H. Radkey, *The Agrarian Foes of Bolshevism* (New York, 1958), pp. 88–9, 111–26; Oldenburg, op. cit., p. 153; Bertram Wolfe, 'War comes to Russia', *Russian Review* 22 (April 1963), pp. 123–38.

17. Durnovo's memorandum to Nicholas II in T. Riha (ed.), *Readings in Russian Civilization* (2nd rev. edn. Chicago and London, 1969), II, pp. 465–78 and, in full, in Golder, op. cit., pp. 3–23.

18. E. D. Chermenskii, *Istoriia SSSR; period imperializma* (Moscow, 1959), p. 414.

19. V. I. Gurko, *Features and Figures of the Past* (Stanford, Cal., and London, 1939), p. 538.

20. Alexander Solzhenitsyn's *August 1914* is a brilliant reconstruction of the opening campaign in East Prussia.

21. See the books by Stone and Wildman listed in the chapter bibliography.

22. Peter Kenez, 'Changes in the social composition of the officer corps during World War I', *Russian Review* 31 (Oct. 1972), pp. 369–75.

23. On the economic history of the war see, besides Stone: H. Haumann, *Kapitalismus im zaristischen Staat, 1906–1917* (Königstein, 1980), pp. 72–137; A. M. Anfimov, *Krupnoe pomeshchiche khoziaistoo evropeiskoi Rossii* (Moscow, 1969); K. I. Zaitsev et al., *Food Supply in Russia during the World War* (New Haven, Conn., 1930); and Antsiferov, Kohn, Michelson, and Nolde, in chapter bibliography.

24. A. K. Wildman, *The End of the Russian Imperial Army* (Princeton, NJ, 1979) p. 108.

25. Haumann, op. cit., pp. 98–9. Cf. Lewis Siegelbaum, 'Russian industrialists and the First World War: the future of the national bourgeoisie', in *Slavic and Soviet Series [Tel-Aviv University]* 2 (1977), pp. 31–48, and 'Moscow industrialists and the War Industries Committees during World War I', *Russian History* 5 (1978), pp. 64–83, esp. pp. 81–2; Thomas Fallows, 'Politics and the war effort in Russia: the Union of Zemstvos and the organisation of the food supply, 1914–1916', *Slavic Review* 37 (March 1978), pp. 70–90.

26. Thomas Riha, 'Miliukov and the Progressive Bloc in 1915: a study in last chance politics', *Journal of Modern History* 32 (March 1960), pp. 16–24; M. F. Hamm, 'Liberal politics in wartime Russia: an analysis of the Progressive Bloc', *Slavic Review* 33 (Sept. 1974), pp. 453–68. See the programme of the Progressive Bloc in G. Vernadsky et al. (eds), *Source Book for Russian History* (New Haven, Conn., and London, 1972), III, pp. 845–7 and Golder, op. cit., pp. 134–6.

27. M. Cherniavsky (ed.), *Prologue to Revolution* (Englewood Cliffs, NJ, 1967), pp. 76–116, 153–67.

28. B. Pares (ed), *The Letters of the Tsaritsa to the Tsar, 1914–1916* (London, 1923), p. 114.
29. V. V. Shulgin, *Dni* (Leningrad, 1927), pp. 113–14.
30. T. Riha, *A Russian European: Paul Miliukov in Russian Politics* (Notre Dame, Ind., and London, 1969), p. 248.
31. Ibid., pp. 264–70. Text of Miliukov's speech in Golder, op. cit., pp. 154–66; excerpts in Vernadsky, op. cit., III, p. 870. Cf. George Katkov, *Russia 1917* (New York, 1967), pp. 187–195.
32. Disarray in the government was not limited to its central organs. There was gubernatorial as well as ministerial leapfrog. Only 38 governors and vice-governors serving before the war kept their posts through 1916; 12 new ones were appointed in 1914; 33 in 1915; 43 in nine months of 1916. V. S. Diakin, 'K voprosu o "zagovore tsarizma" nakanune fevralskoi revoliutsii' in N. E. Nosov (ed.), *Vnutrenniaia politika tsarizma* (Leningrad, 1967), p. 385.
33. Riha, *Miliukov*, p. 274.
34. Pearson, op. cit., pp. 128–9; Katkov, op. cit., pp. 173–7.
35. Ibid., pp. 196–210; Bernard Pares, *The Fall of the Russian Monarchy* (New York, 1961) pp. 398–411; V. S. Diakin, *Russkaia burzhuaziia i tsarizm v gody pervoi mirovoi voiny* (Leningrad, 1967), pp. 298–310.
36. On the Labour Group of the War Industries Committee see Katkov, op. cit., pp. 16–22; and Tsuyoshi Hasegawa, *The February Revolution* (Seattle, Wash., and London, 1981), pp. 123–32.
37. Hasegawa, op. cit., pp. 202ff.; and Pearson, op. cit., pp. 140–73 for the events leading up to the formation of the Provisional Government.

CHAPTER THIRTEEN

Epilogue: February to October
1917

The most authoritarian of Europe's monarchies had proved, in its hour of greatest need, to be the state least capable of giving firm and unified direction to the nation's war effort. The possibility of vesting a 'super-minister' with dictatorial powers was considered in June 1916.[1] But there was never in Imperial Russia the near-militarization of labour and industry imposed in Germany or the large measure of political cooperation and economic coordination achieved in France and Britain, no such far-reaching control as General Ludendorff exercised in the Reich, no Ministry of Munitions or coalition cabinet as Lloyd George headed in England, no 'sacred union', with its inclusion of socialist ministers, as in the French government. The erosion of trust in the authority and competence of the state had advanced so far in Russia that there was little hope and much fear of what a truly centralized and effective command of the home and military fronts might accomplish.

When in March 1917 ten liberal politicians found themselves forced to pick up the reins of government by a revolution they had not made and some of them feared, the crisis of authority which had plagued the old regime was prolonged rather than solved. And the related questions of the legitimacy and efficacy of state power, of the degree to which consensus and coercion, those twin pillars of authority, could be counted on by the country's new rulers, grew more rather than less pressing. The Provisional Government, although it was subject to no formal restraints in its exercise of all the administrative, legislative, and executive functions of state – Duma and State Council ceased to operate, the monarch had abdicated –, was, in effect, weaker than its predecessor had been. As its very name implied, it was a temporary body, to be approved or removed at an early date by a Constituent Assembly which was to settle the country's permanent form of government and constitution. But the regime's provisional character was not the most serious hindrance to the exercise of full political responsibility; it was the inhibitions placed upon the government by the Petrograd Soviet and the government's inability or reluctance to call upon the military and the police to enforce its will.

The very formation (on 27 February) and conduct of the Soviet were tantamount to a declaration of limited confidence in the middle- and upper-class politicians, professionals, and businessmen who made up the first cabinet of the Provisional Government. Led by Mensheviks and Socialist Revolutionaries, the Petrograd Soviet represented the workers and soldiers of the capital. With the emergence of hundreds of soviets elsewhere (they met in an all-Russian conference on 29 March and held their first congress in June), the soviets could claim, with some justification, to speak for the previously disfranchised masses, 'the toiling democracy', and to be the guardians of their interests. Having rejected socialist participation in a 'bourgeois' cabinet, the Petrograd Soviet gave the new government's ministers its qualified support. Only in so far and for as long as they carried out the promises they had made, worked to secure the gains of the revolution, and continued to fight the old order, would they have the backing of the Soviet.[2]

At the same time, and upon the urging of soldiers who had burst into a general meeting of the Soviet, the latter adopted a resolution which became known, when it was published on 2 March, as 'Order No. 1'.[3] Addressed to the soldiers and sailors of the Petrograd garrison for 'immediate and strict execution',the order circulated within days among front-line troops and had effects which the Soviet leaders had not expected or intended.

It called for the election in all units of committees by the lower ranks and asked these committees, rather than officers, to take charge of weapons; it granted full civil and political rights to servicemen; it subordinated the military to the Soviet 'in all political actions' and declared that orders had to be obeyed only if they were not in conflict with those of the Soviet. A direct challenge was thus posed to the commanders of the armed forces and to their civilian superiors. The soldiers and sailors who demanded assurances of more humane treatment and guarantees that they would not be punished for their insurrectionary acts, disarmed by their officers, or used by them against the revolution, did not object to that part of the order which prescribed that in the performance of their service duties they were to observe the strictest military discipline. Nor had the Soviet leaders wished to undermine the defence of the nation.[4]

Yet by issuing an order directly to the troops the Soviet had played a quasi-governmental role, and so it was viewed by General Alekseev, the new Commander-in-Chief and by Minister of War Guchkov. The Soviet's 'Order No. 2', designed to explain the limits of the previous one – it had not, for example, meant to sanction the election of officers by the men – did not reassure the general. He protested against its dissemination, refused to announce it to the troops, and declared that the Executive Committee of the Soviet of Workers' and Soldiers' Deputies which had issued it was unknown to him and did not belong to the framework of governmental authority. Guchkov complained as early as 9 March that the Provisional Government had only the appearance of authority, that real power over the army, the railroads, the posts and telegraph was in the hands of the Soviet which determined whether decrees of the government were to be carried out or not.[5]

'Order No. 1' did not cause the acts of insubordination, the lynchings of officers, and the desertions that sapped and finally destroyed the effectiveness of the army and the fleet. In fact, for a time in the early part of the year and with the help of the committees which the order had caused to be formed, it served to delay a process of disintegration that had deeper and more compelling sources: class hatred, the yearning for peace and for the land that the peasant soldiers expected from the revolution, inadequate supplies of food and clothing, epidemics of scurvy and typhus. For many servicemen the order did, however, justify the rejection of orders and commanders they disliked. To them and to the worker masses it made the Soviet appear more popular and more responsive than the government with its patriotic appeals to keep working and fighting until the final victory.

Thus they looked to the Soviets, if they looked anywhere, for guidance, approval, and the satisfaction of their demands. It was the Petrograd Soviet, not the government, which on 10 March reached an agreement with the city's manufacturers for the introduction of the eight-hour day and the election of factory committees.[6] And it was to the Soviet that the troops of the Petrograd military district turned in April when they were directed by its commander, General Lavr Kornilov, to put down popular demonstrations against the war in which several regiments had joined. The Soviet revoked the general's orders and persuaded the protesting regiments to return to barracks. Its appeals succeeded where commands had failed. In May it was once again leaders of the Petrograd Soviet who convinced the recalcitrant Soviet of the Kronstadt naval base to recognize the government.[7]

This situation, in which the government could not and the Soviet would not rule, has been known since then as 'dual power'. What that arresting description overlooks is the powerlessness from which both bodies suffered, the limitations that were placed upon their ability to act decisively by the limits of popular acceptance and obedience. It soon became evident that workers, soldiers, and peasants (who were forming their own soviets) accepted no authority they considered to be remote and alien. When they had no understanding or sympathy for what was asked of them or felt betrayed and disappointed in their hopes for peace, for social and economic betterment, the masses withheld their allegiance from socialist leaders and parties as they denied it to liberal ministers, officers, and landlords.

The power of the Soviet was largely a negative one, the ability to veto or to paralyse; it could not mobilize or energize the people on behalf of its own contradictory and confused programme and initiatives. The masses found it hard, for example, to understand the theoretical reasons given by the Mensheviks and Socialist Revolutionaries who dominated the Soviet for their refusal to join the government in March: that the liberals must be allowed to complete the bourgeois transformation of the country before it would be ready for socialism; harder still to comprehend why in May the Soviet permitted socialists to enter the government and why, in seeming deference to their bourgeois fellow-ministers, they failed to distribute the land and endorsed the ill-fated June offensive ordered by the minister of war, A. F. Kerenskii, who called himself a Socialist Revolutionary but accepted neither the party's programme nor discipline.

Kerenskii had joined the Provisional Government in March – as minister of justice and self-appointed 'hostage of democracy' – without the express agreement of Soviet or party. His past as a leftist Duma deputy and lawyer who had courageously defended many victims of the tsarist regime made him the 'persuader-in-chief' for a cabinet in which he was the only, if nominal, socialist. But as the country grew more radical Kerenskii became less so. Becoming prime minister in July and supreme commander in August, he called for iron discipline among the troops and denounced the strikes of railway workers as crimes in time of war. The loss of prestige and credibility he and his government suffered as a result confirmed the warnings of those who had predicted compromise and failure should socialists take power or be too closely identified with it.[8]

In view of what was happening throughout the vast empire – the withdrawal of obedience from all established authorities or their collapse – such caution was well-advised. Even members of the government who had no doctrinal reservations about the necessity to maintain law and order while they removed the old regime's arbitrariness and repression, realized that persuasion and performance would play a greater part in determining their capacity to rule than compulsion. The abolition of the Corps of Gendarmes, the *okhrana*, and the Police Department, the removal of provincial governors, vice-governors, and land captains within one week of the government's formation were more than symbolic or well-meant concessions to the universal odium which attached to these agents and agencies of the old order. They were a sober if unhappy recognition of what was, in fact, happening everywhere.[9]

Prince Lvov reported to the cabinet on 4 March that local administrators, from governors to the lowliest policeman, had either fled or been arrested by revolutionary and public committees, 'completely unknown people', who were now, in the middle of a war, in control of large areas of the country. The ministers were stunned by the news and wondered what to do.[10] The provincial commissars they appointed, in most cases chairmen or vice-chairmen of zemstvo boards, were unable to take effective control of provincial administration. They were checkmated, ignored, or removed by local soviets, factory and peasant committees. These and other organizations were filled or formed from below by people who were paying less and less attention to a remote and ineffectual central authority that was unable to arrest the continuous economic decline and to secure either victory or peace. In face of these failures neither the government's genuine commitment to the liberties and legal equality of all citizens, nor its best efforts to organize production and distribution with the help of the specialist civil servants it had inherited, could prevent the social polarization and administrative disorganization that were pulling Russia apart.

The country's enormous problems and tensions, made worse by years of neglect and war, could not possibly have been solved in a short time. Yet the revolution had created expectations that they would, at last, be solved, as well as the conditions for the forceful expression of discontent if they were not. It was this, as much as the Marxist teaching of historical stages, that motivated the socialists' abstention from power in March. As late as 28 April, just three days before it was to reverse itself and allow five socialists to enter the government, the Executive Committee of the Petrograd Soviet again opposed doing so, but this time by the narrow margin of one vote. The position of the Committee's majority was expressed by its chairman, the Menshevik N. S. Chkheidze. Non-participation made it easier for the Soviet both to support and to watch over the actions of the government, whereas the assumption of ministerial offices under existing conditions would raise hopes on the part of the masses which no one could possibly meet. To disappoint them would lead to the Soviet's loss of influence over its following and therefore over the government.[11]

The decision to join a coalition with representatives of the bourgeoisie, of 'privilege' Russia, was approved by 44 votes and opposed by 12 Bolsheviks, 3 Menshevik-Internationalists, and 4 SRs.[12] The Menshevik and SR leaders of the Soviet who favoured it gave a variety of reasons for their change of mind and strategy. There were extremist demands for the immediate confiscation of land and factories which might, if not resisted, lead to a counter-revolution from the right; there was the frightening growth of anarchy; there was the need to extend government controls over the economy to prevent its collapse and protect the welfare of the workers. Most importantly, there was the issue of the war and the necessity of defining a policy towards it that would be acceptable to a war-weary people yet not invite defeat, Germany's triumph, and charges of disloyalty against the socialists.[13]

The war overshadowed everything else. The conservatives and liberals, generals and industrialists, who had accepted the revolution did so because they believed that freed of the incubus of the monarchy they might have a better chance of organizing and rallying the nation for victory. For them, waging and winning the war was a matter of national honour and interest, of loyalty to Russia's allies, and of dependence upon their aid; it was also a way of containing the revolution, a justification for limiting it to the political sphere and postponing fundamental social and economic reforms until success had been achieved in the field, at which time the forces of order and moderation would be able to turn their attention to the home front.

Socialists in and out of the Soviet had few illusions about prospects for a vigorous continuation of military operations. Most of them had denounced the conflict as a quarrel of competing imperialisms, a fight between the grasping ambitions of the ruling classes of all the belligerent states; the more militant among them had suffered imprisonment or exile for their opposition. None the less, in the first heady days of the revolution, when patriotism was on the lips and banners of many regiments and citizens who hailed it, most socialists were uncertain what their stand was to be. Their fear of political isolation made them proceed cautiously, as did their abhorrence of German militarism which posed a greater and more immediate threat to Russia than did the territorial aims of her liberal allies Britain and France.

That the distaste of the Left for Germany was stronger than its hatred of war became evident in the appeal which the Petrograd Soviet addressed to 'the peoples of all the world' on 14 March. In this, its first statement on the 'horrible butchery' which had been raging for nearly three years, it called upon the 'comrade proletarians and toilers' of all countries to join Russia's workers and soldiers in common action for peace and against the policy of conquest of the ruling classes. But it was the German proletariat in particular that they exhorted to throw off the yoke of semi-autocratic rule as their Russian brothers had cast off the tsarist autocracy. They also made clear that the Russian revolution would not retreat before the bayonets of the conquerors or permit itself to be crushed by foreign military force.

In spite of its revolutionary rhetoric and the summons to the proletarians of all countries to unite, the appeal's defencist and even nationalist notes were clearly audible. They dominated the speech Chkheidze had made in the debate preceding its adoption. 'If the Germans pay no attention to our appeal, we will fight for our freedom till the last drop of blood. We are making this proposal with guns in our hands. The slogan for the revolution is "Down with Wilhelm!"'[14] The revolutionary defencism of the Soviet's leaders, summed up in the formula 'peace without annexations or indemnities', was bound to clash with the official policies of the government as enunciated by its foreign minister. Miliukov charged that the formula gave an advantage to the Central Powers by undermining the unity of the Allies and the Russian will to fight. Only if Russia remained a determined combatant to the end and true to the obligations she had undertaken would the Western powers assist her and allow her to reap the promised rewards of their common effort. These included the annexation of the Bosphorus, the Sea of Marmora, the Dardanelles, and Constantinople. Russia's territorial claims, Miliukov insisted, were not imperialistic in the traditional meaning of the word; possession of the Straits was a vital and basic necessity for defence and economic development. He refused to be swayed by the Soviet's appeal and dismissed it as the expression of a minority view.[15]

The appeal's failure to bring about a revision of Russia's war aims and foreign policy, as well as its lack of specific demands and recommendations, made it unsatisfactory as a guide to action and even as a statement of principles. Some of the most prominent internationalist socialists, returning from Siberian or foreign exile, felt that the appeal could only be given meaning and effect if the government were pressured to accept the Soviet's view on peace and repudiated the foreign policy of Miliukov. Some wished to do so by open agitation, the Georgian Menshevik Iraklii Tsereteli, who now took a leading role in the Soviet, by agreement and negotiation. Tsereteli's approach was successful on 27 March in getting the Provisional Government to issue a declaration in which defence and liberation of the fatherland from the invading enemy were coupled with a renunciation of all acquisitive goals and conquests. Free Russia, the declaration stated, wanted neither domination over other peoples nor their territories and possessions. Yet that disclaimer was weakened by a pledge that the undertakings assumed towards the Allies would be faithfully carried out and that the final solution of all problems connected with the war and its termination would be left to the will of the people, i.e., the Constituent Assembly.[16]

The ambiguities of the declaration enabled Miliukov to disregard it and made the Soviet's success less than complete. Tsereteli himself told the All-Russian Conference of Soviets (29 March) that the Russian government must go further and make its allies too abandon their annexationist ambitions in a general revision of war aims. Other delegates demanded the publication of secret treaties and an international socialist conference to force the hands of all the powers. Martov for the Menshevik-Internationalists and Chernov for the Socialist Revolutionaries berated the Soviet majority for not taking a firmer line with the government. Both men agreed that if the revolution did not end the war, the war would put an end to revolution.[17] Martov, caught in Switzerland until early May, had to confine himself to letters and cables. Chernov, reaching Petrograd on 8 April, told the Soviet's Executive Committee that the declaration was bound to be ineffectual as long as it was only a statement of good intentions to the Russian people. He convinced the Soviet and ultimately the cabinet to send it as an official, diplomatic note to the Allies. When Miliukov dispatched it on 18 April he accompanied it with a covering note that reiterated Russia's intention of fully observing her treaty obligations and her people's determination to bring the war to a decisive victory.

The angry protests and street demonstrations that broke out a few days later against the war and Miliukov resulted in his and Guchkov's resignations and the formation of the first coalition cabinet on 5 May. From now on the socialist parties, their representatives in the cabinet – Chernov and Tsereteli among them – and the Soviet which authorized their joining it would share responsibility and blame for losing both the war and the peace.

Martov had foreseen precisely that hazard and he had warned against it before and after his return to Russia. Participation in a coalition ministry was inadmissible, he told a meeting of Mensheviks, for it would turn them into a governmental party rather than a revolutionary one. Like Lenin, he was proved right in rejecting as futile the efforts of the Soviet's majority leaders – Chernov, Chkheidze, and Tsereteli – to obtain peace through a conference of socialist parties to be held in neutral Stockholm in July and an inter-Allied conference that was to follow it. Unlike Lenin, Martov did not, however, believe that a general revolutionary assault on European capitalism and imperialism was either possible or necessary to extricate Russia from her predicament. If she were to present an ultimatum to the Allies, not merely resolutions or diplomatic notes, and threatened to cease fighting, they would be forced to seek peace; if they rejected it, Russia might indeed face Germany alone, as the moderate socialists feared. But this need not mean a separate peace and the strengthening of Germany. It might lead to a separate, a truly defensive, war if the Germans launched another offensive, a war in which Russia would stand as a beacon of revolution and anti-imperialism to the peoples of the world.[18]

The complexities of Martov's argument on the questions of power and peace were in sharp contrast with the 'April Theses' Lenin presented to his party on 4 April.[19] Only a day after he arrived in Petrograd from Switzerland – after crossing Germany in a train provided for him and thirty-one other anti-war socialists by that country's government in hopes that they would weaken the eastern front – Lenin attacked the defencism of SRs and Mensheviks and their support, however conditional, for the government of 'Lvov and Co.'. Its capitalist nature, the inseparable connection between capitalism and imperialism, made it unavoidable that Russia's part in the war retained its predatory character and impossible to end it with a really democratic, non-oppressive peace. Only if power were transferred to the proletariat and the poorest peasantry, and exercised by the Soviet, 'the only form of revolutionary government', could there be a genuine break with capitalism, imperialist war, and hope for a democratic peace; only then would defencism be justified. Lenin demanded that these views be widely propagated among the armies in the field and fraternization with enemy soldiers encouraged.

He managed to put nearly as great a distance between himself and the Menshevik-SR bloc on other issues as well: abolition of the police, the standing army (to be replaced by the 'universal arming of the people'), and the bureaucracy, with the soviets assuming its functions at every level of administration; officers to be elected and subject to recall; private land to be confiscated, all land to be nationalized, and large estates to be converted into model farms; all banks merged, nationalized, and like most of production and distribution put under Soviet control.

Lenin's theses were only gradually accepted by his own party, and they widened the breach between Bolsheviks and Mensheviks, as he had intended. He had always preferred a clear and bold line, freedom of action and flexibility, whatever the risk, to unity based on compromise and concession. Although he had been careful not to depart so far from doctrine as to advocate the immediate introduction of socialism, and had specifically disavowed that goal, he had none the less put it before his party. Calling for 'All Power to the Soviets' meant, in effect, pushing on towards the next, the socialist, stage of the revolution only a month after its bourgeois phase had begun.

More cautious Marxists in the movement which had now been irrevocably split, with the Bolsheviks increasingly emphasizing their distinctness, wondered whether their fractious comrade was in his right mind. Some decried Lenin's programme as revolutionary adventurism; others, an anarchist reaching for the impossible, especially for a party which was, by Lenin's own admission, a small minority in the soviets.[20] Most socialists were convinced that neither they nor the masses were yet ready for soviet power and that members of the old elite who accepted the new order were still needed to run the country and the war. A premature bid for power was certain to drive them into passive resistance or counter-revolution, with chaos at home and collapse of the fronts the predictable consequence. To preserve Russia's national independence and new-won liberties – even Lenin admitted that she was now the freest of the belligerent countries[21] – and to allow her workers and peasants to mature and organize politically, the more moderate socialists, for all their differences with the liberals on the shape of the future, agreed with them on the needs of the moment: the rule of law, the acceptance of governmental authority, and the postponement of major reforms until the Constituent Assembly could ascertain the popular will.

Lenin was not and could not be certain that his uncompromising militancy on the war and on collaboration with the bourgeoisie would bring the masses to his side. Indeed, as late as November, when the Bolsheviks were already in power, the elections to the Constituent Assembly gave them only a quarter of the popular vote to 58 per cent for the SRs.[22] But his staking out for the Bolsheviks of the most radical position on a broad range of issues made the party which was untainted by support for the war or the Provisional Government the beneficiary of growing popular anger and frustration. This was particularly the case among soldiers of the Petrograd garrison and sailors of the Baltic fleet, in factory committees, trade unions and urban soviets – the very groups and places that provided the key to the Bolsheviks' victory in October.

The 'April Theses' and the deepening of the revolution from below which appeared to validate them also brought new recruits into the Bolshevik Party in large numbers. No reliable figures are available, but the membership – variously estimated at from 23,000 to 45,000 in February – grew about tenfold in the next eight months.[23] Many of the new recruits were former Mensheviks, SRs, and anarchists and they were clearly attracted by Bolshevik intransigence. The most important convert to Bolshevism was Trotskii who hailed the 'April Theses' as a confirmation of his theory of permanent revolution, joined the party with a group of his followers, and became a member of its Central Committee. In Trotskii, the chairman of the St Petersburg Soviet during its final days in 1905, Lenin found an invaluable ally who was his equal as a Marxist theoretician and practitioner of revolutionary politics and who surpassed him as an orator and popular tribune. The two men were at one in their determination to drive forward the proletarian revolution in Russia, to spread it to the army, the countryside, and to the rest of Europe.[24] 'The Russian revolution', Lenin proclaimed on 29 April, 'is only the first stage of the proletarian revolutions which are the inevitable result of war'.[25]

The Bolsheviks' campaign to discredit the other socialist parties as vacillating helpers of the bourgeoisie, win over the masses, and capture the soviets experienced difficulties and setbacks. They were hurt by charges that Lenin was a German agent[26] and they failed to break SR-Menshevik dominance of the soviets. When the latter met in June for their first national congress, the bloc had 533 delegates to the Bolsheviks' 105. In early July the Bolsheviks were thrown onto the defensive by government measures against their leaders and press. Later that month the party's VI Congress (26 July to 3 August) renounced the slogan 'All Power to the Soviets' and substituted for it the vague formula of preparing for the ultimate seizure of power by the revolutionary classes. Yet each reversal was followed by a swift recovery. It was made possible by the steady deterioration of the economy, the worsening military situation, and by the heightened antagonism of workers, soldiers, and peasants for all authorities and institutions that would not meet their needs and wishes.

Inflation and the inability of the country's crippled transporation system to deliver grain to the cities negated the gains that workers had made in the early part of the year: the eight-hour day, the minimum wage, and nominal pay increases averaging 50 per cent. The government's efforts at economic regulation – the introduction of state monopolies for grain and coal, formation of an Economic Council, increased income and war profits taxes – were defeated by the weakness of its control mechanisms and the resistance of the population. Like its predecessor, the Provisional Government had to resort to the printing press which fed the rampant inflation. From January to August the ruble lost half its value; by October the real wage of an unskilled worker had fallen by 57 per cent while the price of bread had nearly tripled. When the fixed grain price was doubled in late August to stimulate deliveries, the actual market price was still higher by 75 per cent. Shortages, black markets, and speculation grew apace and with them class hatreds and cleavages.

Inflation and scarcity drove the workers to demand not only higher wages but also control of the workplace. Distrust of the bosses, not syndicalist ideas of having labour own and run the instruments of production, led factory committees to ask for 'workers' control' of their enterprises. They were suspicious of owners' explanations that shortages of fuel and raw materials made necessary the closing of factories and believed that locking workers out, particularly if they struck, was a tactic to tame or starve them into submission.[27] The Moscow industrialist Riabushinskii confirmed their suspicions when he said publicly in early August that it would, unfortunately, require the 'bony hand of hunger and national destitution'[28] to bring the false friends of the people in various committees and soviets to their senses. In Moscow alone some 231 enterprises were shut down in August and September and 61,000 workers were thrown out of work. When the Menshevik minister of labour in early August restricted the rights of factory committees, he underlined the accusations of the Bolsheviks (who had embraced 'workers' control') that he and his party were betraying the workers and serving the bourgeoisie. There was other evidence that the authorities were heeding employers' arguments for taking a firm stand against unruliness and unreason.[29] As a result the government and the parties represented in it shared in the workers' enmity and loss of trust which were reflected in a leftward shift and growing Bolshevik influence in city soviets, trade unions, and town councils.

The fragile accommodation that had been reached after February between the officers and men of the armed forces, and between their commanders and the government, was also breaking down in the summer. The issuance on 11 May of the Declaration of Soldiers' Rights by Kerenskii as minister of war was the high point of the concessions made to the enlisted men.[30] It was followed in the same month by efforts to tighten military discipline and to transfer from the rear to the front units considered unreliable and infected by Bolshevik propaganda. Four front-line regiments were disbanded for refusing to go into action, incitement to disobedience was made liable to prosecution, and extra-ordinary penalties, including penal servitude and the denial of rations to families, were decreed for desertion and refusals to carry out orders in combat.[31]

For men, particularly those in rear garrisons, who had hoped that the revolution would save them from being sent or returned to the battlefield, these measures were a further inducement to regard the war and those who declared its continuation necessary with the utmost hostility. The Military Organization of the Bolsheviks, with its dozens of branches throughout the army and navy, found increasing acceptance for its agitators, leaflets, and newspapers. Most of the Latvian Rifle Brigades, responding to the Bolsheviks' advocacy of the seizure of landed estates, peace without annexations, fraternization, and self-determination for national minorities, went over to them in May. In June a rebellious Black Sea Fleet removed its commander, Admiral Kolchak, and in the cities of the interior, *frontoviki*, front-line soldiers who were recuperating or on leave contributed to the radicalization of local politics.[32]

The demonstrations of workers and soldiers which the Congress of Soviets, meeting in the capital, had called for 18 June in support of the government and the offensive which began that very day on the Galician front, turned against its organizers. Bolshevik slogans against the war, against the ten 'capitalist ministers' and for soviet power, predominated among the banners and placards carried by the 400,000 marchers. After initial advances the offensive, and with it the South-Western Front, collapsed before a German counterattack, with a loss of 60,000 killed and wounded. The socialist leaders who had hoped that a Russian victory in the field would bring the Allies to the council table for a revision of war aims, suffered nearly as great a defeat as did the generals and the government.

The armed protest which was started against the latter on 3 July by a machinegun regiment in Petrograd and joined the next day by Kronstadt sailors and large crowds did not, in the short run, help the Bolsheviks. Their Central Committee, urged by members of the Military Organization, decided only belatedly and hesitantly to take the leading part in an insurrectionary move for which Bolshevik numbers and organization were inadequate and of whose success and ultimate direction there were serious doubts. These were shown to be well founded. The government, aided by allegations that Lenin was in the pay of the Germans, managed to muster enough force to put down the disorders and turn back the challenge of the most turbulent military units and their Bolshevik allies. The party's press and agitators were temporarily curbed and several of its leaders arrested; Lenin went into hiding in Finland. In the long run, however, the Bolsheviks profited from their identification with the impatient and even anarchistic desires of the soldiers and workers who had taken to the streets. The Soviet and the government were unable to translate their temporary success in the 'July Days' into greater stability or popularity.[33]

The military débâcle in Galicia and massive desertions coincided with a cabinet crisis which was not solved until Kerenskii, who had become prime minister on 8 July, two weeks later formed the second coalition in which seven other socialists shared responsibility with seven liberals. The increased presence of the Left in government brought no fundamental changes in policy, only ever louder cries from fearful liberals and authoritarian conservatives for law and order. As early as May the Kadet Maklakov had said that the revolution had given Russia more freedom than she could manage.[34] A receptive Kerenskii on 12 July restored the death penalty at the front[35] and appointed as commander-in-chief General Kornilov who wanted also to apply it to reserve units in the rear. Tsereteli, one of only four ministers to oppose reimposition of the death penalty (as did the Soviet), none the less responded to the government's critics on the right by declaring, in his capacity as acting minister of interior, that it would not tolerate appeals to civil war, violence or arbitrary actions that threatened the country's survival.[36] His successor and Kerenskii were empowered by their colleagues to close public meetings and assemblies.[37] On 9 August elections to and convocation of the Constituent Assembly, originally scheduled for that month, were postponed to November.

Tsereteli's declaration and a circular to local commissars that the 'entire land fund' was to be kept inviolate until the Constituent Assembly disposed of it,[38] was only a reiteration of earlier official condemnations of 'plunder and violence' in the countryside. Land committees had been set up in March to study and prepare an agrarian reform with the participation of peasant delegates; in April the use of troops to end agrarian disorders had been authorized and a law for the protection of crops had been adopted. These measures had little effect on the rising curve of rural unrest – the seizures of public, church, and private lands (including the holdings of Stolypin's 'separators'), the expropriation of timber and forests, the destruction of estates and their inventory. The government had neither enough physical force nor moral authority to impose restraint on the peasants and it was unable to pay them enough in money or goods to make them part with their grain. As it temporized, peasant soviets came increasingly under the influence of the SRs whose leader, Chernov, had proclaimed to the Congress of Peasant Soviets in May that only those who laboured on the land had a right to own it.

That principle had long been cherished by the peasants themselves. Realizing that it would not be enacted soon, they began to fear that they would not receive the land they considered rightfully theirs without having to fight or pay for it. They therefore wanted all of it placed immediately under the control of local land committees, a demand which the Peasants' Soviet had adopted at its May Congress and the SRs supported. Unable to get even his fellow-socialists in the cabinet to agree with him, Chernov resigned from it on 20 July. He had failed to secure an absolute prohibition on the selling or mortgaging of land – a device some owners used to guard it from the expected general redistribution – or to win agreement for the immediate confiscation of landed estates. The last agrarian bill prepared for the Provisional Government in mid October by its SR minister of agriculture, S. L. Maslov, still did not bring all the land under the control of land committees. It also provided for the payment of rental on confiscated properties and excluded from the land reserve it proposed to establish for the peasants those portions of estates cultivated by the owners themselves as well as acreage under specialized crops.[39]

'Maslov's bill may have reflected popular sentiment in the spring, by fall it was a long way out of step.'[40] Lenin called the measure a complete betrayal of the peasants by the SRs, Kadets denounced it as too radical and pre-empting the decisions of the Constituent Assembly.[41] They and others pointed out, correctly, that it would further disrupt administration and production in the countryside. Such considerations carried little weight with the rural masses who were determined to carry out the revolution in land relations they had expected as a result of the tsar's fall. They had, in fact, accomplished it by the time the Bolsheviks took power; in spite of Lenin's conviction that small peasant farming was backward and inefficient, he and his party ratified the inevitable.

What made the rural revolution irresistible was its close connection with the break-up of the army and the ways in which the two processes reinforced each other.[42] The soldiers, since the vast majority of them were peasants, could not be used at home to repress fellow-peasants and they became increasingly unreliable at the fronts because they were straining to get back to their villages to take part in the sharing out of the land. The many desertions and mutinies, the arrests and lynchings of officers, the involvement of soldiers in estate seizures in areas near the front, were forceful manifestations for the agrarian revolution and against the war that was preventing or delaying it. The relationship between the two phenomena was as obvious to the peasant soldiers as it was to men in government and the military who opposed radical changes in rural policy and elsewhere because they would make it impossible to supply the army and hold it together as a fighting force.

In August, with peasant unrest reaching new heights and a German break-through at Riga (which fell on the 21st) threatening Petrograd, General Kornilov appeared, especially to his conservative admirers, to be the only man capable of stabilizing the rear and strengthening the government. The latter put the capital under his jurisdiction and he was authorized to dispatch a cavalry corps to the city against the possibility of a Bolshevik rising. Negotiations conducted through an inept intermediary led Kornilov to believe that he was to enter the government and Kerenskii to suspect that the general wanted to remove him and establish a dictatorship. Instead, it was Kornilov who was dismissed as commander-in-chief and who entered upon a short-lived mutiny (27–30 August) against the Provisional Government and the Soviet. His cavalry, intercepted by railwaymen and exhorted by Soviet delegates, melted away before it reached Petrograd. Kornilov was arrested on 1 September.[43]

His revolt was a decisive turning-point in the history of the Russian Revolution. It lent substance to the spectre of counter-revolution and discredited all those who had collaborated or sympathized with the general or were merely suspected of having done so by virtue of belonging to the upper classes. Kornilov's foolhardy adventure undermined what remained of discipline and respect for officers in the forces and ended the Bolsheviks' political isolation in which their role in the July Days had landed them. Against the danger from the Right represented by Kornilov, the Left called for a closing of ranks and admitted Bolsheviks to the Committee for the People's Struggle Against Counterrevolution set up by the Soviet. Trotskii and other Bolshevik leaders were released from jail by Kerenskii who was frantically trying to refurbish his radical credentials and proclaimed Russia a republic on 1 September. At the same time he was engaged in efforts to build a third coalition acceptable to the Soviet yet including Kadets and non-party specialists who were still believed to be needed to preserve the unity of all democratic forces and a functioning administration. The cabinet, announced at last on 25 September, contained three SRs, four Mensheviks, one Radical Democrat and five non-party men. Impotent and ignored, it survived for a month.

The Bolsheviks were neither asked to join it nor would they have done so. For a brief moment Lenin, still in hiding in Finland, considered a compromise with the majority socialists for a government of SRs and Mensheviks responsible to the soviets.[44] But their continued support of Kerenskii made it impossible and Bolshevik successes in local soviets and town councils made it unnecessary. On 31 August the Petrograd Soviet for the first time passed a Bolshevik resolution; it condemned the policy of conciliation with the bourgeoisie and called for a government, representing the proletariat and the revolutionary peasantry, which was to abolish the private ownership of landed estates, establish workers' control of production and distribution, end the death penalty, guarantee the right of self-determination to the national minorities, summon the Constituent Assembly immediately, and secure a general democratic peace without delay. Within the week the Moscow and Kiev Soviets followed suit; on 24 September the Bolsheviks were victorious in elections to the municipal Duma in Moscow and on the 25th Trotskii was elected chairman of the Petrograd Soviet.

'All Power to the Soviets' once again became the watchword of the Bolsheviks who were confident that the Second All-Russian Congress of Soviets, scheduled to meet in Petrograd on 20 October but postponed until the 25th, would give their party a majority and validate its claim to power. Some leading Bolsheviks, fearful that the fiasco of the July Days might be repeated, were even prepared to wait until November and the Constitutent Assembly to confirm that the masses had, in fact, come over to their side.

Not so Lenin. Beginning in mid September, he bombarded his comrades in Petrograd with letters and appeals for the immediate seizure of power in the name of the soviets. The party, having obtained a majority in those of both capitals, could and should take state power into its hands without delay, organize an insurrectionary headquarters and armed forces, occupy key positions, and arrest the General Staff and the government. To wait for a formal majority in the Congress of Soviets he dismissed as naiveté, idiocy, or treason. The time was ripe, the enemy's forces were disorganized, the party had the support of a majority of Russia's workers, soldiers, and peasants, the wave of revolution was rising in the rest of Europe. To wait would be criminal, to expose a near-certain and bloodless victory to the risks of an uncertain election, the recovery of the government's nerve, or the chance that it would surrender Petrograd to the advancing Germans.

With all my might I urge comrades to realize that everything now hangs by a thread; that we are confronted by problems which are not to be solved by conferences or congresses (even Congresses of Soviets) . . . If we seize power today, we seize it not in opposition to the Soviets but on their behalf. The seizure of power is the business of the uprising; its political purpose will become clear after the seizure. It would be a disaster or a sheer formality to await the wavering vote of 25 October. The people have the right and are in duty bound to decide such questions not by a vote but by force . . .[45]

On 10 October, with Lenin present, ten members of the Bolsheviks' Central Committee agreed to an armed rising, but without setting a date. Three members were absent, two in opposition. They questioned whether the party was yet strong enough to carry the country with it. Their doubts were strengthened by reports from lower party organs that even if the workers of Petrograd did come out into the streets – and that was far from certain in their mood of weariness and disenchantment with all forms of revolutionary rhetoric – those of other cities and, above all, the peasants could not be counted on to follow them. It became all the more necessary, therefore, to take more time with preparations for a rising, especially in the garrison of the capital, and to make them appear to be a defence of the soviets rather than an attack upon them or the government.

The not very real German threat Lenin had invoked to stir his comrades to action was also used by Kerenskii to remove the danger which unreliable troops of the Petrograd Military District posed to his regime. He ordered its commandant to transfer them to the Northern Front, ostensibly to strengthen the defences of Petrograd. As had been true in February and July, they rebelled and gave credence to Bolshevik charges that another Kornilov was planning under the guise of military necessity to disperse the Congress of Soviets and to disarm and crush the revolution. The soldiers and sailors now either declared their loyalty to the Bolshevik-dominated soviet of the city or, in the majority of cases, remained neutral and therefore useless to the government.

On 16 October the Petrograd Soviet created a Military Revolutionary Committee (MRC) for the defence of the city against the Germans and of the Congress of Soviets from the counter-revolution. With Trotskii in effective charge of the Committee, the Bolsheviks acquired a command centre which allowed them in a matter of days to wrest control of the garrison from its chief and to extend it also over the workers' militias, the Red Guards, which had been formed earlier in the year and rearmed at the time of the Kornilov revolt. Trotskii now disposed of a force to carry out his own plan: an insurrection timed to coincide with the convocation of the Second Congress of Soviets on 25 October. Lenin still pleaded and pushed for greater speed. He wanted to confront the Congress with an accomplished fact which would be its own legitimation and, having been created by the Bolsheviks alone, would force the other socialists to accept it on Bolshevik terms or demonstrate the weakness of their revolutionary commitment.

On 23 October, the very day on which Trotskii's personal appeal had won over the garrison of the fortress of Saints Peter and Paul whose cannons commanded the Neva River and the Winter Palace, Kerenskii came inadvertently to Lenin's aid. He prevailed upon the cabinet to authorize the removal of the

MRC's commissars, the arrest of leading Bolsheviks, the closing of two of their newspapers, and the calling of loyal troops from the suburbs. Early the next morning, a Tuesday, detachments of government soldiers seized the presses and premises of the Bolshevik papers, leading the MRC to declare that the Petrograd Soviet was in danger. The MRC put all units on battle alert, gained the adherence of the crew of the cruiser *Aurora* which was anchored in the Neva, by countermanding a government order that it put to sea, and sent pro-Bolshevik units to reopen the closed printing shops. Later that day and the next, soldiers, sailors, and Red Guards occupied the central telegraph and post offices, the telephone exchange, railway stations, and other strategic points. At ten o'clock on Wednesay morning the 25th, the MRC proclaimed that power had passed to the Petrograd Soviet and before that body Trotskii, in the afternoon, announced that the Provisional Government had been over-thrown. The final assault on the Winter Palace, where the cabinet refused to surrender, came during the night; it was taken with surprising ease and few casualties. The ministers were arrested at 2 a.m. on the 26th.

At the II Congress of Soviets which had opened on the previous evening about 300 Bolsheviks and 90 Left SRs, who sided with them, were in the majority.[46] Most of the other 260 delegates were willing to accept the situation which had been created while they were assembling. But they wanted the new Soviet government to be a coalition of all socialist parties. The Bol-sheviks were saved from having to share power when, after an acrimonious exchange over their unilateral seizure of it, Mensheviks and SRs of the centre and right walked out.

In the early hours of 26 October the Congress overwhelmingly approved a manifesto written by Lenin which proclaimed that the Provisional Govern-ment had been deposed, that the Congress of Soviets had taken power into its own hands and that it would at once propose peace and an armistice. It also promised the transfer of all land to peasant committees, democratization of the army, workers' control in industry, bread for the cities, manufactured goods for the villages, self-determination for national minorities, and the call-ing of the Constituent Assembly as scheduled. Local authority and the main-tenance of 'revolutionary order' were entrusted to soviets of workers', soldiers', and peasants' deputies. After a recess, the new government was presented to the Congress on the evening of the 26th and confirmed. It consisted only of Bolsheviks, for even the Left SRs would not yet join them. After having adopted a Decree on Peace and a Decree on Land, the Congress adjourned and left the business of governing to the Council (Soviet) of People's Commissars as Lenin, its chairman, and his fellow-ministers called themselves.[47]

* * * *

To depose a government which could barely be said to exist or govern proved to be the easiest part of the Bolsheviks' task. To carry out their programme and hold together a country whose disintegration had created the conditions for their rise and triumph was vastly more difficult. The editors of *Izvestiia*, the Soviet's newspaper, pointed out, just before they were replaced, that the

Bolsheviks had only seized Petrograd, not the rest of Russia, and warned prophetically of the threat of civil war. 'Bloodshed and pogroms – this is what we must prepare ourselves for. This can only be averted . . . if a democratic government recognized by all democratic elements and parties is formed anew, and if the Bolsheviks agree to submit to such a government. The entire responsibility for the future of the country now falls on them alone.'[48]

Convinced that they were moving in history's direction they were prepared and, in Lenin's case, eager to accept that responsibility. Lenin believed that such an excellent opportunity for determined Marxists to make a revolution should not be missed; even if it failed, it would serve to heighten the socialist consciousness of the proletariat and leave a rich legacy of inspiration and practical experience. There were good reasons for Lenin's confidence in the success and staying power of the revolution. Since February the Bolsheviks had steadily grown in numbers, adherents, and influence. Worker support gave them domination of the urban soviets and they compensated for their weakness in the countryside by adopting (in the Decree on Land) the agrarian programme of the SRs, thereby gaining the benevolent neutrality of most peasants and soldiers. If this did not make them a majority party, as the elections of November would show, they were much more numerous than the Mensheviks, more unified and better organized than the SRs.

Whether he had the majority of the country's voters behind him was not, in any case, of primary concern to Lenin. If 130,000 landlords, he said, had been able to govern Russia after 1905, 240,000 Bolsheviks should certainly be able to do so, the more so as they would rule in the interests of the poor against the rich, of the many against the few.[49] The point of the conquest of state power, Lenin wrote after it had taken place, was not the introduction of 'pure' democracy, but the revolutionary overthrow of the bourgeoisie, the establishment of the dictatorship of the proletariat and its employment for winning the sympathies of a majority of the toilers for the building of socialism.[50]

This was, of course, an admission that in October 1917 the majority of Russia's lower classes had not been converted to socialism, certainly not to its Bolshevik variant. They had, in fact, a very confused understanding of socialist doctrines and goals. But they did understand that the socialists and the soviets stood and spoke for them against leaders, now called bourgeois, who still asked them to be patient and law-abiding and patriotic. That is why the socialist parties garnered 87 per cent of the vote in the elections to the Constituent Assembly and that is why the Bolsheviks took power not in their own name but in that of the soviets and as their defenders against the forces of reaction. It was not so much that Russia and her people were moving towards Bolshevism as that the Bolsheviks were moving towards a country convulsed by a powerful worker-peasant revolt. Besides its proximate causes in war and hunger, that revolt had deep roots in the social divisions, enmities, and grievances of the old order, grievances the Bolsheviks expressed, mobilized and exploited. In that sense the 'Great October Socialist Revolution' is the last chapter in the history of the old regime which fell in February; it is also the beginning of the history of the Soviet Union and of still greater convulsions to come.

REFERENCES

1. V. S. Diakin, 'K voprosu o "zagovore tsarizma" nakanune fevralksoi revoliutsii in N. E. Nosov (ed.) Vnutrenniaia politika tsarizma (Leningrad, 1967), p. 367 and R. Pearson, The Russian Moderates and the Crisis of Tsarism, 1914–1917 (London and New York, 1977), pp. 100–102.

2. T. Hasegawa, The February Revolution (Seattle, Wash., and London, 1981), pp. 313ff. For a Soviet view of the soviets in 1917 see: A. M. Andreev, The Soviets of Workers' and Soldiers' Deputies on the eve of the October Revolution, trans. from the Russian by J. Langstone (Moscow, 1971).

3. J. R. Boyd, 'The origins of Order No. 1', Soviet Studies 19 (Jan. 1968), pp. 359–72.

4. Texts of Army Orders No. 1 and No. 2 in F. A. Golder, Documents of Russian History 1914–1917 (New York and London, 1927), pp. 386–90; and P. R. Browder and A. F. Kerensky (eds), The Russian Provisional Government, 1917: Documents (Stanford, Cal., 1961), II, pp. 848, 851–2.

5. Ibid.; A. K. Wildman, The End of the Russian Imperial Army, (Princeton, N.J., 1979), pp. 228–34; J. M. Thompson, Revolutionary Russia, 1917 (New York, 1981), p. 33.

6. J. L. H. Keep, The Russian Revolution (New York and Toronto, 1976), p. 69.

7. Thompson, op. cit., p. 62. Alexander Rabinowitch, Prelude to Revolution (Bloomington, Ind., and London, 1968), p. 53.

8. Kerenskii has given his own version of the role he played in the events of 1917. See, for example, Russia and History's Turning Point (New York, 1965).

9. Golder, op. cit., pp. 313–14; Browder and Kerensky, op. cit., I, pp. 243–9, 192, 205–8, II, p. 524.

10. Kerenskii, op. cit., pp. 226–7.

11. Reinhard Wittram, Studien zum Selbstverständnis des 1. und 2. Kabinetts der russischen Provisorischen Regierung (Göttingen, 1971), p. 48.

12. Browder and Kerensky, op. cit., III, pp. 1267–71.

13. Golder, op. cit., pp. 361–3; 368–70; 457–9.

14. Browder and Kerensky, op. cit., II, pp. 1077–8.

15. W. G. Rosenberg, Liberals in the Russian Revolution (Princeton, N.J., 1974), pp. 74–8.

16. R. A. Wade, The Russian Search for Peace: February–October 1917 (Stanford, Cal., 1969), pp. 26–50.

17. O. H. Radkey, The Agrarian Foes of Bolshevism, (New York, 1958), p. 476; I. Getzler, Martov (London, 1967), p. 153.

18. Getzler, op. cit., pp. 149–52.

19. V. I. Lenin, Collected Works (London and Moscow, 1960–78), XXIV, pp. 21–5; Browder and Kerensky, op. cit., III, pp. 1205–7.

20. S. H. Baron, Plekhanov: The Father of Russian Marxism (Stanford, Cal., 1963), pp. 347–348; A. Ascher, Pavel Axelrod and the Development of Menshevism (Cambridge, Mass., 1972); p. 323; N. N. Sukhanov, The Russian Revolution, 1917, tr. and abridged from the Russian by Joel Carmichael (London, 1955), p. 289;

D. A. Longley, 'The divisions in the Bolshevik Party in March 1917', *Soviet Studies* 24 (July 1972), pp. 61–76.

21. Lenin, op. cit., XXIV, p. 22.

22. Thompson, op. cit., p. 176; O. H. Radkey, *The Elections to the Russian Constituent Assembly of 1917* (Cambridge, Mass., 1950), pp. 12–22, 80.

23. Robert Service, *The Bolshevik Party in Revolution* (London and New York, 1979), p. 43.

24. Irving Howe, *Leon Trotsky* (New York, 1978), pp. 39–41.

25. Lenin, op. cit., XXIV, p. 310.

26. Adam Ulam, *The Bolsheviks* (New York, 1965), writes that 'there can no longer be any doubt that the substance of the charges, as distinguished from some details, was correct: the Bolsheviks were getting money from the Germans' (p. 349). There remains, none the less, some doubt as to the weight to be assigned to that assistance in the Bolsheviks' ultimate success. For further discussion of this question see, especially, G. Katkov, *Russia 1917. The February Revolution* (New York, 1967) pp. 63–115; H. Shukman, *Lenin and the Russian Revolution* (New York, 1967), pp. 167–70; and Z. A. B. Zeman (ed.), *Germany and the Revolution in Russia, 1915–1918. Documents from the Archives of the German Foreign Ministry* (London, 1958).

27. P. H. Avrich, 'Russian factory committees in 1917', *Jahrbücher für Geschichte Osteuropas* 11 (1963), pp. 161–82; and 'The Bolshevik Revolution and workers' control in Russian industry', *Slavic Review* 22 (March 1963); Keep, op. cit., pp. 78–89.

28. Diane Koenker, *Moscow Workers and the 1917 Revolution* (Princeton, NJ, 1981). p. 132.

29. Browder and Kerensky, op. cit., II. pp. 721–4, 758.

30. Ibid., pp. 880–3.

31. Ibid., pp. 887–8.

32. D. J. Raleigh, 'Revolutionary politics in provincial Russia: the Tsaritsyn "Republic" in 1917', *Slavic Review* 40 (Summer 1981), pp. 194–209.

33. On the July Days, see Rabinowitch, *Prelude to Revolution*.

34. N. G. Rosenberg, *Liberals in the Russian Revolution* (Princeton, NJ, 1974), p. 119.

35. Browder and Kerensky, op. cit., II, pp. 982–4.

36. Ibid., III, pp. 1439–40.

37. Ibid., p. 1440.

38. Ibid., II, p. 563. On the government's land policy and the situation in the countryside, see G. J. Gill, 'The failure of rural policy in Russia, February to October 1917', *Slavic Review* 37 (June 1978), pp. 241–58, and the same author's *Peasants and Government in the Russian Revolution* (London and New York, 1979).

39. Browder and Kerensky, op. cit., II, pp. 577–9.

40. Gill, op. cit., p. 248.

41. Browder and Kerensky, op. cit., II, 580–2.

42. M. S. Frenkin, *Russkaia armiia i revoliutsiia, 1917–1918* (Munich, 1978).

43. A. F. Kerenskii, *The Prelude to Bolshevism. The Kornilov Rebellion* (London and New York, 1919); George Katkov, *The Kornilov Affair: Kerensky and the Break-Up of the Russian Army* (London and New York, 1980; Alexander Rabinowitch. *The Bolsheviks Come to Power* (New York, 1976), pp. 94–150.

44. Rabinowitch 'The Petrograd garrison and the Bolshevik seizure of power' in *Rev-*

olution and Politics in Russia. Essays in Memory of B. I. Nicolaevisky (Bloomington, Ind., and London, 1972), p. 182.

45. Lenin, op. cit., XXVI, pp. 234–5.
46. These figures are only an approximation. The exact number of delegates and their party allegiances are unknown and fluctuate considerably in the counts taken at the time and since. The figure that appears most often in the sources is 390 Bolsheviks (90 of whom may have been Left SRs voting with them) out of a total of 650 delegates.
47. Browder and Kerensky, op. cit., III, pp. 1793–8.
48. Ibid., p. 1801.
49. Lenin, op. cit., XXVI, p. 25.
50. Ibid., XXX, p. 262.

Selected bibliography

This section, arranged by chapters, contains recommendations for further reading and titles of works which I have found particularly useful or important. With few exceptions, only materials in English have been included. Bibliographies of primary and secondary sources in other languages, including Russian, may be found in several of the following general works and source collections. See especially the handbooks edited by Auty and Hellmann.

Akademiia Nauk SSSR, Institut Istorii, *Istoriia SSSR*. First series, vols. V–VI. Moscow, 1968.

Auty, R., and Obolensky, D. (eds), *Companion to Russian Studies*. Vol. I: *An Introduction to Russian History*. Cambridge, 1976.

Billington, J. H., *The Icon and the Axe: An Interpretative History of Russian Culture*. New York, 1968.

Black, C. E. (ed.), *The Transformation of Russian Society*. Cambridge, Mass., 1960.

Bruford, W. H., *Chekhov and His Russia: A Sociological Study*. London, 1947.

Charques, R., *The Twilight of Imperial Russia*. London and New York, 1958; repr. 1974.

Crankshaw, E., *The Shadow of the Winter Palace: Russia's Drift to Revolution, 1825–1917*. New York, 1976.

Florinsky, M. T., *Russia. A History and an Intrepretation*, 2 vols. New York, 1953.

Geyer, D. (ed.), *Wirtschaft und Gesellschaft im vorrevolutionären Russland*. Cologne, 1975.

Harcave, S. S., *Years of the Golden Cockerel: The Last Romanov Tsars, 1814–1917*. New York, 1968.

Hellmann, M., *et al*. (eds), *Handbuch der Geschichte Russlands*. Vol. III: G. Schramm (ed.) *Von den autokratischen Reformen zum Sowjetstaat*. Stuttgart, 1982.

Istoriia SSSR (see under Akademiia Nauk SSSR).

Kochan, L., *Russia in Revolution, 1890–1918*. London, 1966.

Oberländer, E., *et al*. (eds), *Russia Enters the Twentieth Century*. New York, 1971.

Pares, B., *Russia and Reform*. London, 1907; repr. as *Russia Between Reform and Revolution*. New York, 1962.

Pipes, R. E., *Russia Under the Old Regime*. London and New York, 1974.

Riasanovsky, N. V., *A History of Russia*. New York, 1963; 3rd edn, 1977.

Salisbury, H. E., *Black Night, White Snow: Russia's Revolutions, 1905–1917*. New York, 1978.

Seton-Watson, H., *The Decline of Imperial Russia, 1855–1914*. London, 1952; repr. New York, 1966.

Seton-Watson, H., *The Russian Empire, 1801–1917*. Oxford, 1967.

Simmons, E. J. (ed.), *Continuity and Change in Russian and Soviet Thought*. Cambridge, Mass., 1955.

Stavrou, T. G. (ed.), *Russia Under the Last Tsar*. Minneapolis, Minn., 1969.

Thaden, E. C., *Russia Since 1801: The Making of a New Society*. New York, 1971.

Troyat, H., *Daily Life in Russia Under the Last Tsar*. London, 1961; repr. Stanford, Cal., 1979.

Von Laue, T. H., *Why Lenin? Why Stalin? A Reappraisal of the Russian Revolution, 1900–1930*. Philadelphia, Penn., 1964.

Vernadsky, G., *et al.* (eds), *A Source Book for Russian History*. Vol III: *Alexander II to the February Revolution*. New Haven, Conn., and London, 1972.

Walkin, J., *The Rise of Democracy in Pre-Revolutionary Russia: Political and Social Institutions Under the Last three Tsars*. New York, 1962.

Wallace, D. M., *Russia*. London, 1877 and 1912; repr. New York, 1961.

Wieczynski, J. L. (ed.), *The Modern Encyclopedia of Russian and Soviet History*, 24 vols (incomplete). Gulf Breeze, Fla., 1976–

A visual introduction to the late imperial and early revolutionary periods is provided by:

Allshouse, R. H., *Photographs for the Tsar*. New York, 1980.

Fitzlyon, K., and Browning, T., *Before the Revolution. A View of Russia Under the Last Tsar*. London, 1977; Woodstock, NY, 1978.

Obolensky, C., *The Russian Empire: A Portrait in Photographs*. New York, 1979.

Salisbury, H. E., *Russia in Revolution, 1900–1930*. New York, 1978.

CHAPTER ONE

Adams, A. E., 'Pobedonostsev and the rule of firmness', *Slavonic and East European Review* 32 (Dec. 1953), pp. 132–9.

Baddeley, J. F., *Russia in the Eighties*. London, 1921.

Byrnes, R. F., *Pobedonostsev: His Life and Thought*. Bloomington, Ind., 1968.

Chicherin, B. N., *Vospominaniia: Zemstvo i Moskovskaia Duma*. Moscow, 1934.

Eckhardt, J. W. A., *Von Nikolaus I. zu Alexander III*. Leipzig, 1881.

Feoktistov, E. M., *Vospominaniia*. Leningrad, 1929.

Heilbronner, H., 'The administrations of Loris-Melikov and Ignatiev, 1880–1882'. Ph.D. Diss., University of Michigan, 1954.

Heilbronner, H., 'Alexander III and the reform plan of Loris-Melikov', *Journal of Modern History* 33 (Dec. 1961), pp. 384–97.

Katz, M., *Mikhail N. Katkov: A Political Biography, 1818–1887*. The Hague, 1966.

Leontovitsch, V., *Geschichte des Liberalismus in Russland*. Frankfurt, 1957.

Liwoff, G., *Michel Katkoff et son époque*. Paris, 1897.

Lowe, C., *Alexander III of Russia*. London, 1895.

Lukashevich, S., 'The Holy Brotherhood: 1881–1883', *American Slavic and East European Review* 18 (Dec. 1959), pp. 491–509.

Lukashevich, S., *Ivan Aksakov, 1823–1886. A Study in Russian Thought and Politics*. Cambridge, Mass., 1965.

Mosse, W. E., *Alexander II and the Modernization of Russia*. London and New York, 1958.

Pipes, R. E., 'Russian conservatism in the second half of the nineteenth century', *Slavic Review* 30 (Mar. 1971), pp. 121–8.

'Pobedonostsev and Alexander III' *Slavonic and East European Review* 7 (June 1928), pp. 30–54.

Pobedonostsev, K. P., *Reflections of a Russian Statesman* (trans. from the Russian by R. C. Long). London, 1898; repr., Ann Arbor, Mich., 1965.

Raeff, M. (ed.), *Plans for Political Reform in Russia, 1730–1905*. Englewood Cliffs, NJ, 1966.

Raeff, M., 'A reactionary Liberal: M. N. Katkov'. *Russian Review* 11 (July 1952), pp. 157–67.

Rogger, H., 'Reflections on Russian conservatism', *Jahrbücher für Geschichte Osteuropas* 14 (June 1966), pp. 195–212.

Samson-Himmelstjierna, H. von, *Russia under Alexander III* (Trans. from the German by J. Morrison). London, 1893.

Thaden, E. C., *Conservative Nationalism in Nineteenth-Century Russia*. Seattle, Wash., 1964.

Tiutcheva, A. F., *Pri dvore dvukh imperatorov*. Moscow-Leningrad, 1928–29.

Whelan, H. W., *Alexander III and the State Council. Bureaucracy and Counter-Reform in Late Imperial Russia*. New Brunswick, N.J., 1982.

Zaionchkovskii, P. A. *The Russian Autocracy in Crisis, 1878–1882* (Trans. from the Russian by G. M. Hamburg). Gulf Breeze, Fla., 1979.

CHAPTER TWO

Bing, E. J. (ed.), *The Secret Letters of the Last Tsar*. London 1937; New York, 1938.

Bogdanovich, A. V., *Tri poslednikh samoderzhtsa. Dnevnik*. Leningrad, 1924.

Daudet, E., *L'avant dernier Romanoff: Alexandre III*. Paris, 1920.

Flourens, E. L., *Alexandre III, sa vie, son oeuvre*. Paris, 1894.

Gurko, V. I., *Features and Figures of the Past. Government and Opinion in the Reign of Nicholas II* (trans. from the Russian by L. Matveev). Stanford, Cal., and London, 1939.

Hanbury-Williams, J., *The Emperor Nicholas II as I Knew Him*. London, 1922.

Kilcoyne, M., 'The political influence of Rasputin'. Ph.D. Diss., University of Washington, 1961.

Kokovtsov, V. N., *Out of My Past. The Memoirs of Count Kokovtsov* (trans. from the Russian by L. Matveev). Stanford, Cal., and London, 1935.

Lowe, C., *Alexander III of Russia*. London, 1895.

Massie, R. K., *Nicholas and Alexandra*. New York, 1967.

Mossolov, A. A., *At the Court of the Last Tsar (1900–1916)*. London, 1935.

Narishkin-Kurakin, E., *Under Three Tsars* (trans. from the German by J. E. Loesser). New York, 1931.

Pares, B. (ed.), *The Letters of the Tsaritsa to the Tsar, 1914–1916*. London, 1923.

Polovtsov, A. A., *Dnevnik gosudarstvennogo sekretaria A. A. Polovtsova*, 2 vols. Moscow, 1966.

Seraphim, E., *Russische Porträts*, 2 vols. Zürich-Leipzig-Vienna, 1943.

Stead, W. T., *Truth About Russia*. London and New York, 1888.

Szeftel, M., 'The form of government of the Russian Empire prior to the constitutional reforms of 1905–1906', in J. S. Curtiss (ed.), *Essays in Honor of G. T. Robinson*. New York, 1963.

Szeftel, M., 'Personal inviolability in the legislation of the Russian absolute monarchy', *American Slavic and East European Review* 17 (Feb. 1958), pp. 1–24.

Von Laue, T. H., *Sergei Witte and the Industrialization of Russia*. New York, 1963.

Vitte, S. Iu., *The Memoirs of Count Witte* (trans. from the Russian and abridged by Avrahm Yarmolinsky). New York and London, 1921.

Vitte, S. Iu., *Vospominaniia*, 3 vols. Moscow, 1969.

Vulliamy, C. E. (ed.), *The Letters of the Tsar to the Tsaritsa, 1914–1917*. London and New York, 1929.

Youssoupoff [Iusupov], F. F., *Lost Splendor*. London and New York, 1954.

Youssoupoff, F. F., *Rasputin*. New York, 1927.

Zaionchkovskii, P. A., *The Russian Autocracy under Alexander III* (trans. from the Russian by D. D. Jones). Gulf Breeze, Fla, 1976.

CHAPTER THREE

Bock, M. P., *Reminiscences of My Father, Peter A. Stolypin*. Metuchen, NJ, 1970.

Golovin, K. F., *Meine Erinnerungen* (trans. from the Russian by V. von Rauterfeld). Leipzig, 1911.

Izvolskii, A. P., *Recollections of a Foreign Minister: Memoirs of Alexander Iswolsky*.

(trans. from the Russian by C. L. Seeger). Garden City, NY, and Toronto, 1921.

Sazonov, S. D., *Fateful Years, 1909–1916*. London and New York, 1928.

Struve, P. B., 'Witte und Stolypin' in P. R. Rohden and F. Ostrogorsky (eds), *Menschen die Geschichte machten*. Vol. III. Vienna, 1931.

Suvorin, A. S., *Dnevnik A. A Suvorina*. Moscow-Petrograd, 1923.

Taranovski, T., 'The aborted counter-reform: the Muravev Commission and the judicial statutes of 1864', *Jahrbücher für Geschichte Osteuropas* 29 (April 1981), pp. 161–84.

Yaney, G. L., *The Systematization of Russian Government*. Chicago and London, 1973.

Zacek, J. C., 'Champion of the past; D. A. Tolstoi as Minister of the Interior, 1882–1889', *The Historian* 30 (May 1968), pp. 412–38.

Zaionchkovskii, P. A., *The Russian Autocracy in Crisis, 1878–1882* (trans. from the Russian by G. M. Hamburg). Gulf Breeze, Fla., 1979.

Zaionchkovskii, P. A., *The Russian Autocracy under Alexander III* (trans. from the Russian by D. D. Jones). Gulf Breeze, Fla., 1976.

CHAPTER FOUR

Amburger, E., *Geschichte der Behördenorganisation Russlands von Peter dem Grossen bis 1917*. Leyden, 1966.

Armstrong, J. A., 'Old-regime govenors: bureaucratic and patrimonial attributes', *Comparative Studies in Society and History* 14 (Jan. 1972), pp. 2–29.

Balmuth, D., *Censorship in Russia, 1865–1905*. Washington, DC, 1979.

Bennett, H. A., 'Evolution of the meanings of Chin: an introduction to the Russian institution of rank ordering and niche assignment from the time of Peter the Great's table of ranks to the Russian revolution', *California Slavic Studies* **X** (1977), pp. 1–44.

Curtiss, J. S., *Church and State in Russia. The Last Years of the Empire, 1900–1917*. New York, 1940.

Edeen, A., 'The civil service: its composition and status' in C. E. Black (ed.), *The Transformation of Russian Society*. Cambridge, Mass., 1960, pp. 274–92.

Fainsod, M., 'Bureaucracy and modernization: the Russian and Soviet case' in J. LaPalombara (ed.), *Bureaucracy and Political Development*. Princeton, NJ, 1963, pp. 233–67.

Immekus, Erwin, *Die russische orthodoxe Landpfarrei zu Beginn des XX. Jahrhunderts nach dem Gutachten der Diözesanen Bischöfe*. Würzburg, 1978.

Kennan, G., *Siberia and the Exile System*, 2 vols. New York and London, 1891; repr. Chicago, 1958.

Kucherov, S., *Courts, Lawyers and Trials under the Last Three Tsars*. New York, 1953.

Orlovsky, D. T., 'Recent studies on the Russian bureaucracy', *Russian Review* 34 (Oct. 1976), pp. 448–67.

Pinter, W. M., and Rowney, D. K. (eds), *Russian Officialdom*. Chapel Hill, NC, 1980.

Polner, T. I., *et al.* (eds), *Russian Local Government During the War and the Union of Zemstvos*. New Haven, Conn., 1930.

Raeff, M., 'The bureaucratic phenomena of imperial Russia, 1700–1905', *American Historical Review* 84 (April 1979), pp. 399–411.

Raeff, M., 'The Russian autocracy and its officials', *Harvard Slavic Studies* 4(1957), pp. 77–91.

Robbins, R. G., *Famine in Russia 1891–1892. The Imperial Government Responds to a Crisis*. New York and London, 1975.

Rowney, D. K., 'Higher civil servants in the Russian Ministry of Internal Affairs: some demographic and career characteristics, 1906–1916', *Slavic Review* 21 (March 1972), pp. 101–10.

Simon, G., 'Church, state and society' in E. Oberländer et al. (eds), *Russia Enters the Twentieth Century*. New York, 1971, pp. 199–235.

Sliozberg, G. B., *Dorevoliutsionnyi stroi Rossii*. Paris, 1938.

Thurston, R. W., 'Police and people in Moscow, 1906–1914', *Russian Review* 39 (July 1980), pp. 320–38.

Urusov, S. D., *Memoirs of a Russian Governor* (trans. from the Russian by H. Rosenthal). London and New York, 1908.

Vassilyev, A. T., *The Ochrana: The Russian Secret Police*. Philadelphia and London, 1930.

Vinogradoff, P., *Self-government in Russia*. London, 1915.

Vucinich, A., 'The state and the local community' in C. E. Black (ed.), *The Transformation of Russian Society*. Cambridge, Mass., 1960, pp. 191–209.

Weissman, N. B., *Reform in Tsarist Russia. The State Bureaucracy and Local Government, 1900–1914*. New Brunswick, NJ, 1981.

Yaney, G. L., *The Systematization of Russian Government*. Chicago and London, 1973

CHAPTER FIVE

Brutskus, B. D., *Agrarnyi vopros i agrarnaia politika*. Petrograd, 1922.

Czap, P., 'Peasant class-courts and peasant customary justice in Russia, 1861–1912', *Journal of Social History* 1 (Winter 1967), pp. 149–78.

Emmons, T., 'The Russian landed gentry and politics', *Russian Review* 33 (July 1974), pp. 269–83.

Gerschenkron, A., 'Agrarian policies and industrialization: Russia, 1861–1917' in *Cambridge Economic History of Europe*, vol. VI, part 2. Cambridge, 1965, pp 706–800.

Hamburg, G. M., 'The crisis in Russian agriculture: a comment', *Slavic Review* 37 (Sept. 1978), pp. 481–6.

Hamburg, G. M., 'The Russian nobility on the eve of the 1905 revolution', *Russian Review* 38 (July 1979), pp. 323–38.

Hause, T. S., 'State and gentry in Russia, 1861–1917'. Ph.D. Diss., Stanford University, 1974.

Korelin, A. P., *Dvorianstvo v poreformennoi Rossii, 1861–1904 gg.* Moscow, 1979.

Korelin, A. P., 'Institut predvoditelei dvorianstva', *Istoriia SSSR* 3 (May–June 1978), pp. 31–48.

Liashchenko, P. I., *History of the National Economy of Russia* (trans. from the Russian by L. M. Herman). New York, 1949.

Maynard, J., *The Russian Peasant and Other Studies.* London, 1942.

Nötzold, J., *Wirtschaftspolitische Alternativen der Entwicklung Russlands in der Ära Witte und Stolypin.* Berlin, 1966.

Pavlovsky, G., *Agricultural Russia on the Eve of the Revolution.* London, 1930; repr. New York, 1968.

Robbins, G. B., *Famine in Russia, 1891–1892: The Imperial Government Responds to a Crisis.* New York, 1975.

Robinson, G. T., *Rural Russia under the Old Regime.* New York, 1932, 1957.

Shanin, T., *The Awkward Class. Political Sociology of Peasantry in a Developing Society: Russia 1910–1925.* Oxford, 1972.

Simms, J. Y., 'The crisis in Russian agriculture at the end of the 19th century: a different view', *Slavic Review* 36 (Sept. 1977), pp. 377–98.

Simms, J. Y., 'On missing the point: a rejoinder', *Slavic Review* 37 (Sept. 1978), pp. 487–90.

Solovev, Iu. B., *Samoderzhavie i dvorianstvo v kontse XIX veka.* Leningrad, 1973.

Treadgold, D. W., *The Great Siberian Migration. Government and Peasant in Resettlement from Emancipation to the First World War.* Princeton, NJ, 1957; 2nd edn. London, 1967.

Volin, L., *A Century of Russian Agriculture. From Alexander II to Khrushchev.* Cambridge, Mass., 1970.

Vucinich, W. S. (ed.), *The Peasant in Nineteenth-Century Russia.* Stanford, Cal., 1968.

Watters, F. M., 'Land tenure and financial burdens of the Russian peasant, 1861–1905'. Ph.D. Diss., University of California, Berkeley, 1966.

CHAPTER SIX

Bater, J. H., *St Petersburg: Industrialization and Change.* London, 1976.

Bill, V. T., *The Forgotten Class. The Russian Bourgeoisie From the Earliest Beginnings to 1900.* New York, 1959.

Blackwell, W. L., *The Industrialization of Russia.* New York, 1970.

Crisp, O., *Studies in the Russian Economy Before 1914.* London and New York, 1976.

Crisp, O., 'Labor and industrialization in Russia' *in Cambridge Economic History of Europe*, vol. VII, part 2. Cambridge, 1978.

Falkus, M. E., *The Industrialization of Russia, 1700–1914*. London, 1972.

Fedor, T. S., *Patterns of Urban Growth in the Russian Empire During the Nineteenth Century*. Chicago, 1975.

Gerschenkron, A., 'Agrarian policies and industrialization, Russia 1861–1917' in *Cambridge Economic History of Europe*, vol. VI, part 2. Cambridge, 1966.

Gerschenkron, A., 'The early phases of industrialization in Russia' in W. W. Rostow (ed.), *The Economics of Take-Off into Sustained Growth*. London, 1963.

Gerschenkron, A., *Economic Backwardness in Historical Perspective*. Cambridge, Mass., 1962.

Gindin, I. F., 'The Russian bourgeoisie in the period of capitalism', *Soviet Studies in History* 6 (Summer, 1967), pp. 3–50 (trans. from *Istoriia SSSR*, 2 and 3, 1963).

Girault, R., *Emprunts russes et investissements français en Russie, 1887–1914*. Paris, 1973.

Glickman, R., 'The Russian factory woman, 1880–1914', in D. Atkinson *et al.* (eds), *Women in Russia*. Stanford, Cal., 1977.

Goldsmith, R. W., 'The economic growth of tsarist Russia, 1860–1913', *Economic Development and Cultural Change* 9 (1961), pp. 441–75.

Gorlin, R. H., 'Problems of tax reform in imperial Russia', *Journal of Modern History* 49 (June 1977), pp. 246–65.

Gregory, P. R., 'Russian industrialization and economic growth: results and perspectives of western research', *Jahrbücher für Geschichte Osteuropas* 25 (1977), pp. 200–18.

Gregory, P. R., 'Economic growth and structural change in tsarist Russia: a case of modern economic growth?", *Soviet Studies* 23 (Jan. 1972), pp. 418–34.

Hamm, M. F. (ed.), *The City in Russian History*. Lexington, Ky., 1976.

Hildermeier, M., 'Sozialer Wandel im städtischen Russland in der zweiten Hälfte des 19. Jahrhunderts. Anmerkungen zur neueren Literatur', *Jahrbücher für Geschichte Osteuropas* 26 (1977), pp. 525–66.

Johnson, R. E., *Peasant and Proletarian: The Working Class of Moscow in the Late Nineteenth Century*. New Brunswick, NJ, 1979.

Kahan, A., 'Capital formation during the period of early industrialization in Russia, 1890–1913' in *Cambridge Economic History of Europe*, vol. VIII, part 2. Cambridge, 1978.

Kahan, A., 'Government policies and the industrialization of Russia', *Journal of Economic History* 27 (Dec. 1967), pp. 460–77.

Kaser, M. C., 'Russian entrepreneurship' in *Cambridge Economic History of Europe*, vol. VIII, part 2. Cambridge, 1978.

Liashchenko, P. I., *History of the National Economy of Russia to the 1917 Revolution* (trans. from the Russian by L. M. Herman). New York, 1949.

McKay, J. P., *Pioneers for Profit: Foreign Entrepreneurship and Russian Industrialization, 1885–1913*. Chicago and London, 1970.

Miller, M. S., *The Economic Development of Russia, 1905–1914*. London, 1926; repr. 1967.

Nötzold, J., *Wirtschaftspolitische Alternativen der Entwicklung Russlands in der Ära Witte und Stolypin.* Berlin, 1966.

Owen, T. C., *Capitalism and Politics in Russia: A Social History of the Moscow Merchants, 1855–1905.* Cambridge, 1981.

Portal, R., 'The industrialization of Russia' in *The Cambridge Economic History of Europe,* vol. VI, part 2. Cambridge, 1966.

Pospielovsky, D., *Russian Police Trade Unionism: Experiment or Provocation?* London, 1971.

Roosa, R. A., 'Russian industrialists and "State Socialism", 1906–17', *Soviet Studies* 23 (Jan. 1972), pp. 395–417. (See J. D. White below.)

Roosa, R. A., '"United" Russian industry', *Soviet Studies* 24 (Jan. 1973), pp. 421–425.

Sablinsky, W., *The Road to Bloody Sunday. The Role of Father Gapon and the Assembly of Russian Factory Workers in the Petersburg Massacre of 1905.* Princeton, NJ, 1976.

Schneiderman, J., *Sergei Zubatov and Revolutionary Marxism: The Struggle for the Working Class in Tsarist Russia.* Ithaca and London, 1976.

Tolf, R. W., *The Russian Rockefellers. The Saga of the Nobel Family and the Russian Oil Industry.* Stanford, Cal., 1976.

Tugan-Baranovsky, M. I., *The Russian Factory in the Nineteenth Century* (trans. from the Russian by A. Levin, C. Levin and G. Grossman). Homewood, Ill., 1970.

Von Laue, T. H., *Sergei Witte and the Industrialization of Russia.* New York, 1963.

Westwood, J. N., *A History of Russian Railways.* London, 1964.

White, J. D., 'Moscow, Petersburg and the Russian industrialists. In Reply to R. A. Roosa', *Soviet Studies* 24 (Jan. 1973), pp. 414–20.

CHAPTER SEVEN

Anderson, T. (ed.), *Masters of Russian Marxism.* New York, 1963.

Ascher, A., *Pavel Axelrod and the Development of Menshevism.* Cambridge, Mass., 1972.

Baron, S. H., *Plekhanov: The Father of Russian Marxism.* Stanford, Cal., 1963.

Billington, J. H., *Mikhailovsky and Russian Populism.* Oxford, 1958.

Dan, F. I., *The Origins of Bolshevism* (ed. and trans. from the Russian by J. Carmichael). New York, 1964.

Deutscher, I., *The Prophet Armed: Trotsky, 1879–1921.* Oxford, 1954.

Emmons, T., 'The Beseda Circle, 1899–1905', *Slavic Review* 32 (Sept. 1973), pp. 461–90.

Emmons, T., 'Russia's banquet campaign', *California Slavic Studies* X (1977), pp. 45–86.

Emmons, T., 'the statutes of the Union of Liberation', *Russian Review* 33 (Jan. 1974), pp. 80–85.

Fischer, G., *Russian Liberalism: From Gentry to Intelligentsia*. Cambridge, Mass., 1958.

Fischer, L., *The Life of Lenin*. New York, 1964.

Freeze, G. L., 'A national liberation movement and the shift in Russian liberalism, 1901–1903', *Slavic Review* 28 (March 1969), pp. 81–91.

Galai, S., *The Liberation Movement in Russia, 1900–1905*. Cambridge, 1973.

Getzler, I., *Martov: A Political Biography of a Russian Social Democrat*. London, 1967.

Haimson, L. H., *The Russian Marxists and the Origins of Bolshevism*. Cambridge, Mass. 1955: repr. Boston, 1966.

Hildermeier, M., *Die Sozialrevolutionäre Partei Russlands – Agrarsozialismus und Modernisierung im Zarenreich (1900–1914)*. Cologne-Vienna, 1978.

Karpovich, M. M., 'Two types of Russian liberalism: Maklakov and Miliukov' in E. J. Simmons (ed.), *Continuity and Change in Russian and Soviet Thought*. Cambridge, Mass., 1955.

Keep, J. L. H., *The Rise of Social Democracy in Russia*. Oxford, 1963.

Kindersley, R., *The First Russian Revisionists: A Study of 'Legal Marxism' in Russia*. Oxford, 1962.

Knei-Paz, B., *The Social and Political Thought of Leon Trotsky*. Oxford, 1978.

Lane, D. S., *The Roots of Russian Communism. A Social and Historical Study of Russian Social-Democracy 1898–1907*. London and University Park, Pa., 1975.

Lenin, V. I., *Collected Works* (English edn, 46 vols). London and Moscow, 1960–78.

Lenin, V. I., *The Lenin Anthology* (ed. R. C. Tucker). New York, 1975.

Lenin, V. I., *The Lenin Reader* (ed. S. T. Possony). Chicago, 1966.

McNeal, R. H., *Bride of the Revolution. Krupskaya and Lenin*. Ann Arbor, Mich., 1972.

Mendel, A. P., *Dilemmas of Progress in Tsarist Russia: Legal Marxism and Legal Populism*. Cambridge, Mass., 1961.

Meyer, A. G., *Leninism*. Cambridge, Mass., 1957.

Perrie, M., *The Agrarian Policy of the Russian Socialist–Revolutionary Party from its Origins through the Revolution of 1905–1907*. Cambridge, 1976.

Pipes, R. E., *Social Democracy and the St Petersburg Labor Movement, 1885–1897*. Cambridge, Mass., 1963.

Pipes, R. E., *Struve. Liberal on the Left, 1870–1905*. Cambridge, Mass., 1970.

Plekhanov, G. V., *Selected Philosophical Works* (English edn in 5 vols). Moscow and London, 1961–81.

Pomper, P., *Peter Lavrov and the Russian Revolutionary Movement*. Chicago and London, 1972.

Pomper, P., *The Russian Revolutionary Intelligentsia*. New York, 1970.

Raeff, M., 'Some reflections on Russian liberalism', *Russian Review* 18 (July 1959), pp. 218–30.

Riha, T., *A Russian European: Paul Miliukov in Russian Politics*. Notre Dame, Ind., and London, 1969.

Schapiro, L., *The Communist Party of the Soviet Union*. New York, 1959.

Scheibert, P., Über den Liberalismus in Russland', *Jahrbücher für Geschichte Osteuropas* 7 (1959), pp. 34–48.

Shub, D., *Lenin: A Biography*. Baltimore, Md, and London, 1966.

Shukman, H., *Lenin and the Russian Revolution*. London, 1966; New York, 1967, 1981.

Theen, R. H. W., *Lenin: Genesis and Development of a Revolutionary*. Princeton, NJ, 1973.

Timberlake, C. (ed.), *Essays on Russian Liberalism*. Columbia, Mo., 1972.

Treadgold, D. W., *Lenin and His Rivals: The Struggle for Russia's Future, 1898–1906*. New York, 1955.

Trotsky, L. D., *My Life*. New York, 1930; repr. 1960.

Tucker, R. C., *Stalin as Revolutionary, 1879–1929. A Study in History and Personality*. New York, 1973.

Ulam, A., *The Bolsheviks*. New York, 1965.

Venturi, F., *Roots of Revolution: A History of the Populist and Socialist Movements in Nineteenth-Century Russia* (trans. from the Italian by F. Haskell). London and New York, 1960; repr. 1968.

Walicki, A., *The Controversy over Capitalism. Studies in the Social Philosophy of the Russian Populists*. Oxford, 1969.

Walicki, A., *A History of Russian Thought from the Enlightenment to Marxism* (trans. from the Polish by H. Andrews-Rusiecka). Stanford, Cal., 1979.

Wildman, A. K., *The Making of a Workers' Revolution: Russian Social Democracy, 1891–1903*. Chicago, 1967.

Wolfe, B. D., *Three Who Made a Revolution*. Boston, Mass., 1948; repr. 1958.

Wortman, R., *The Crisis of Russian Populism*. Cambridge, 1967.

Yarmolinsky, A., *The Road to Revolution. A Century of Russian Radicalism*. New York, 1959.

CHAPTER EIGHT

Dallin, D. J., *The Rise of Russia in Asia*. New Haven, Conn., 1949.

Geyer, D., *Der russische Imperialismus. Studien über den Zusammenhang von innerer und auswärtiger Politik, 1860–1914*. Göttingen, 1977.

Goldwin, R. A., *et al.* (eds.), *Readings in Russian Foreign Policy*. New York, 1959.

Hough, R. A., *The Fleet that Had to Die*. New York, 1961.

Hunczak, T. (ed.), *Russian Imperialism from Ivan the Great to the Revolution*. New Brunswick, NJ., 1974.

Jelavich, B., *A Century of Russian Foreign Policy, 1814–1914*. Philadelphia, Penn., and New York, 1964.

Jelavich, B., *The Ottoman Empire, the Great Powers, and the Straits Question, 1870–1887*. Bloomington, Ind., and London, 1973.

Jelavich, B., *St Petersburg and Moscow. Tsarist and Soviet Foreign Policy, 1814–1974*. Bloomington, Ind., and London, 1974.

Jelavich, C., *Tsarist Russia and Balkan Nationalism, 1879–1886*. Berkeley, Cal., 1962.

Kennan, G. F., *The Decline of Bismarck's European Order: Franco-Russian Relations, 1875–1890*. Princeton, NJ, 1979.

Khvostov, V. M., *Diplomatiia v novoe vremia, 1871–1914*. Moscow, 1963. Vol. II of *Istoriia Diplomatii*, eds. V. A. Zorin *et al.*

Kuropatkin, A. N., *The Russian Army and the Japanese War* (2 vols, trans. from the Russian by A. B. Lindsay). New York, 1909.

Langer, W. L., *The Franco-Russian Alliance, 1890–1894*. Cambridge, Mass., 1929.

Lederer, I. (ed.), *Russian Foreign Policy. Essays in Historical Perspective*. New Haven, Conn., and London, 1962.

Lensen, G. A., 'Japan and tsarist Russia: changing relationships, 1875–1917', *Jahrbücher für Geschichte Osteuropas* 10 (1962), pp. 337–48.

Lensen, G. A., *The Russian Push Toward Japan*. Princeton, NJ, 1959.

Malozemoff, A., *Russian Far Eastern Policy, 1881–1904*. Berkeley and Los Angeles, Cal., 1958.

Nolde, B., *L'alliance franco-russe*. Les origines du système politique d'avant guerre. Paris, 1936.

Pavlovsky, M. N., *Chinese Russian Relations* (trans. from the French by R. Krader). New York, 1949.

Petrovich, M. B., *The Emergence of Russian Panslavism*. New York, 1956.

Price, D. C., *Russia and the Roots of the Chinese Revolution, 1896–1911*. Cambridge, Mass., 1974.

Price, E. B., *The Russo-Japanese Treaties of 1907–1916 Concerning Manchuria and Mongolia*. Baltimore, Md, 1933.

Romanov, B. A., *Russia in Manchuria, 1892–1906* (trans. from the Russian by S. W. Jones). Ann Arbor, Mich., 1952.

Rosen, R. R., *Forty Years of Diplomacy*, 2 vols. London and New York, 1922.

Sumner, B. H., *Russia and the Balkans, 1870–1880*. Oxford, 1937.

Sumner, B. H., *Tsardom and Imperialism in the Far East and Middle East, 1880–1914*. London, 1942; repr. Hamden, Conn., 1968.

Warner, D., and Warner, P., *The Tide at Sunrise: A History of the Russo-Japanese War, 1904–1905*. New York, 1974.

White, J. A., *The Diplomacy of the Russo-Japanese War*. Princeton, NJ, 1964.

CHAPTER NINE

Allen, W. E. D., *The Ukraine*. Cambridge, 1941.

Allworth, E. (ed.), *Central Asia. A Century of Russian Rule*. New York and London, 1967.

Armstrong, J. A., 'Mobilized diaspora in tsarist Russia: the case of the Baltic Germans' in J. Azrael (ed.), *Soviet Nationality Policies and Practices*. New York, 1978.

Baddeley, J. F., *The Russian Conquest of the Caucasus*. London, 1908.

Becker, S., *Russia's Protectorates in Central Asia: Bukhara and Khiva, 1865–1924*. Cambridge, Mass., 1968.

Bilmanis, A., *A History of Latvia*. Princeton, NJ, 1951.

Blit, L., *The Origins of Polish Socialism, 1878–1886*. Cambridge, 1971.

Chmielewski, E., *The Polish Question in the Russian State Duma*. Knoxville, Tenn., 1970.

Curzon, G. N., *Russia in Central Asia in 1889 and the Anglo-Russian Question*. London, 1889; repr. 1967.

Demko, G. J., *The Russian Colonization of Kazakhstan, 1896–1916*. The Hague, 1969.

Dubnow, S. M., *History of the Jews in Russia and Poland* (3 vols, trans. from the Russian by I. Friedlaender). Philadelphia, Penn., 1916–20; repr. 1946.

Frankel, J., *Prophecy and Politics. Socialism, Nationalism and the Russian Jews, 1862–1917*. Cambridge, 1981.

Hodgson, J. H., 'Finland's position in the Russian Empire 1905–1910', *Journal of Central European Affairs* 20 (July 1960), pp. 158–73.

Hovannisian, R. G., *Armenia on the Road to Independence: 1918*. Berkeley and Los Angeles, Cal., 1967.

Hovannisian, R. G., *The Republic of Armenia*, 2 vols. Berkeley and Los Angeles, Cal., 1971–82.

Hovannisian, R. G., 'Russian Armenia: a century of tsarist rule', *Jahrbücher für Geschichte Osteuropas* 19 (1971), pp. 31–48.

Hrushevskyi, M., *A History of Ukraine* (trans. from the Ukrainian by W. Halich *et al.*). New Haven, Conn., 1941.

Juttikala, E., *A History of Finland*. London, 1962.

Kazemzadeh, F., *The Struggle for Transcaucasia, 1917–1921*. New York and Oxford, 1951.

Kirby, D. G. (ed.), *Finland and Russia, 1808–1920: From Autonomy to Independence. A Selection of Documents*. New York, 1976.

Lang, D. M., *The Last Years of the Georgian Monarchy, 1658–1832*. New York, 1957.

Lang, D. M., *A Modern History of Georgia*. London, 1962.

Leslie, R. F., *Reform and Insurrection in Russian Poland, 1856–1865*. London, 1963.

Löwe, H. D., *Antisemitismus und reaktionäre Utopie. Russischer Konservatismus im Kampf gegen den Wandel von Staat und Gesellschaft, 1890–1917*. Hamburg, 1978.

Mendelsohn, E., *Class Struggle in the Pale: The Formative Years of the Jewish Workers' Movement in Tsarist Russia*. Cambridge, 1970.

Morris, P., 'The Russians in Central Asia, 1870–1887', *Slavonic and East European Review* 53 (Oct. 1975), pp. 521–38.

Nalbandian, L. Z., *The Armenian Revolutionary Movement*. Berkeley and Los Angeles, Cal., 1963.

Nolde, B. E., *La formation de l'empire russe*, 2 vols. Paris, 1952–3.

Pierce, R. A., *Russian Central Asia, 1867–1909*. London, 1964.

Pipes, R. E., *The Formation of the Soviet Union: Communism and Nationalism, 1917–1923*. Cambridge, Mass., 1954; rev. edn New York, 1968.

Plakans, A., 'Peasants, intellectuals and nationalism in the Russian Baltic provinces, 1820–1890', *Journal of Modern History* 46 (Sept. 1974), pp. 445–75.

Raeff, M., 'Patterns of imperial policy towards the nationalities' in E. Allworth (ed.), *Soviet Nationalities Problems*. New York, 1971.

Rauch, G. von, *Russland: Staatliche Einheit und nationale Vielfalt*. Munich, 1953.

Reshetar, J. S., *The Ukrainian Revolution, 1917–1920: A Study in Nationalism*. Princeton, NJ, 1952.

Rogger, H., 'The Beilis case: anti-semitism and politics in the reign of Nicholas II', *Slavic Review* 25 (Dec. 1966), pp. 615–29.

Rogger, H., 'Government, Jews, peasants and land in post-emancipation Russia', *Cahiers du monde russe et sovietique* 17 (Jan.–March 1976), pp. 5–25; and 17 (April–Sept. 1976), pp. 171–211.

Rogger, H., 'Russian ministers and the Jewish question, 1881–1917', *California Slavic Studies* VIII (1975), pp. 15–76.

Senn, A. R., *The Emergence of Modern Lithuania*. New York, 1959.

Smith Jr, C. J., *Finland and the Russian Revolution, 1917–1922*. Athens, Ga., 1958.

Sokol, E., *The Revolt of 1916 in Russian Central Asia*. Baltimore, Md., 1954.

Starr, S. F., 'Tsarist government: the imperial dimension' in J. Azrael (ed.), *Soviet Nationality Policies and Practices*. New York, 1978.

Thaden, E. C. (ed.), *Russification in the Baltic Provinces and Finland, 1855–1914*. Princeton, NJ, 1981.

Tobias, H. J., *The Jewish Bund in Russia. From Its Origins to 1905*. Stanford, Cal., 1972.

Uustalu, E., *A History of the Estonian People*. London, 1952.

Vakar, N. P., *Belorussia: The Making of a Nation*. Cambridge, Mass., 1956.

Wandycz, P. S., *The Lands of Partitioned Poland, 1795–1918*. Seattle, Wash., and London, 1974.

Wittram, R., *Baltische Geschichte. Die Osteelande Livland, Estland, Kurland, 1180–1918*. Munich, 1954.

Wuorinen, J. H., *Nationalism in Modern Finland*. New York, 1931.

Zenkovsky, S. A., *Pan-Turkism and Islam in Russia*. Cambridge, Mass., 1960.

CHAPTER TEN

Conroy, M. S., *Petr Arkadevich Stolypin. Practical Politics in late Tsarist Russia*. Boulder, Col., 1976.

Floyd, D., *Russia in Revolt: 1905*. London, 1969.

Haimson, L. H. (ed.), *The Politics of Rural Russia, 1905–1914*. Bloomington, Ind., and London, 1979.

Harcave, S. S., *The Russian Revolution of 1906*. London, 1970 (originally published as *First Blood* in 1964).

Healy, A. E., *The Russian Autocracy in Crisis. 1905–1907*. Hamden, Conn., 1976.

Hennessy, R., *The Agrarian Question in Russia 1905–1917. The Inception of the Stolypin Reform*. Giessen, 1977.

Levin, A., *The Second Duma: A Study of the Social Democratic Party and the Russian Constitutional Experiment*. New Haven, Conn., 1940.

Levin, A., *The Third Duma: Election and Profile*. Hamden, Conn., 1973.

McNeal, R. H. (ed.), *Russia in Transition, 1905–1914. Evolution or Revolution?* New York, 1970.

Maklakov, V. A., *The First State Duma: Contemporary Reminiscences* (trans. from the Russian by M. Belkin). Bloomington, Ind., 1964.

Mehlinger, H. D., and Thompson, J. M., *Count Witte and the Tsarist Government in the 1905 Revolution*. Bloomington, Ind., and London, 1972.

Miliukov, P. N., *Political Memoirs, 1905–1917* (trans. from the Russian by C. Goldberg; ed. by A. P. Mendel). Ann Arbor, Mich., 1967. (Abridged from *Vospominaniia*, 2 vols, New York, 1955.)

Miliukov, P. N., *Russia and Its Crisis*. Chicago, 1905; repr. New York, 1962.

Riha, T., *A Russian European: Paul Miliukov in Russian Politics*. Notre Dame. Ind., and London, 1969.

Rogger, H., 'The formation of the Russian Right, 1900–1906', *California Slavic Studies* III (1964), pp. 66–94.

Rogger, H., 'Was there a Russian fascism? The Union of Russian People', *Journal of Modern History* 36 (Dec. 1964), pp. 398–415.

Scheibert, P., *Die russischen politischen Parteien von 1905 bis 1917. Ein Dokumentationsband*. Darmstadt, 1972.

Schwarz, S. M., *The Russian Revolution of 1905: The Workers' movement and the Formation of Bolshevism and Menshevism* (trans. from Russian by G. Vakar). Chicago, 1967.

Szeftel, M., *The Russian Constitution of April 23, 1906. Political Institutions of the Duma Monarchy*. Brussels, 1976.

Trotsky, L. D., *1905* (trans. from the Russian by A. Bostock). New York, 1972.

CHAPTER ELEVEN

Alston, P., *Education and the State in Tsarist Russia*. Stanford, Cal., 1969.

Avrekh, A. Ia., *Stolypin i tretia Duma*. Moscow, 1968.

Avrekh, A. Ia., *Tsarizm i treteiunskaia sistema*. Moscow, 1966.

Birth, E., *Die Oktobristen (1905–1913)*. Stuttgart, 1974.

Diakin, V. S., *Samoderzhavie, burzhuaziia i dvorianstvo v 1907–1911 gg*. Leningrad, 1978.

Dietze, C., *Stolypinsche Agrarreform und Feldgemeinschaft*. Berlin, 1920.

Edelman, R., *Gentry Politics on the Eve of the Russian Revolution: The Nationalist Party, 1907–1917.* New Brunswick, NJ, 1980.

Haimson, L. H. (ed.), *The Politics of Rural Russia, 1905–1917.* Bloomington, Ind., and London, 1979.

Haimson, L. H., 'The problem of social stability in urban Russia, 1905–1917', *Slavic Review* 23 (Dec. 1964), pp. 619–42; and 24 (March 1965), pp. 1–22. Comments by Mendel and Von Laue in 24, pp. 23–33 and 34–46.

Haumann, H., *Kapitalismus im zaristischen Staat, 1906–1917.* Königstein, 1980.

Hosking, G. A., *The Russian Constitutional Experiment: Government and Duma, 1907–1914.* Cambridge, 1973.

Johnson, W. H. E., *Russia's Educational Heritage.* Pittsburgh, Penn., 1950; repr. New York, 1969.

McKean, R. B., *The Russian Constitutional Monarchy, 1907–1917.* London, 1977.

McNeal. R. H, (ed.), *Russia in Transition, 1905–1914. Evolution or Revolution?* New York, 1970.

Owen, L. A., *The Russian Peasant Movement, 1906–1917.* London, 1937; repr. New York, 1963.

Pavlovsky, G., *Agricultural Russia on the Eve of the Revolution.* London, 1930; repr. New York, 1968.

Pinchuk, Ben-Cion, *The Octobrists in the Third Duma, 1907–1912.* Seattle, Wash., and London, 1974.

Pipes, R. E., *Struve, Liberal on the Right, 1905–1944.* Cambridge, Mass., 1980.

Rexheuser, R., *Dumawahlen und lokale Gesellschaft. Studien zur Sozialgeschichte der russischen Rechten vor 1917.* Cologne-Vienna, 1980.

Rodzianko, M. V., *The Reign of Rasputin. An Empire's Collapse. Memoirs* (trans. from the Russian by C. Zvegintzoff). London, 1927: repr. Gulf Breeze, Fla., 1973.

Rogger, H., 'Russia in 1914', *Journal of Contemporary History* 1 (Oct. 1966), pp. 95–119.

Sazonov, S. D., *Fateful Years, 1909–1916.* New York, 1928.

CHAPTER TWELVE

Antsiferov, A. N., *et al.*, *Russian Agriculture During the War.* New Haven, Conn., 1930.

Brussilov, A. A., *A Soldier's Notebook 1914–1918.* London, 1930.

Buchanan, G. W., *My Mission to Russia*, 2 vols. London and New York, 1923.

Florinsky, M. T., *The End of the Russian Empire.* New York, 1931, repr. 1961, 1971, 1979.

Golder, F. A. (ed.), *Documents of Russian History, 1914–1917* (trans. by E. Aronsberg). New York and London, 1927; repr. Gloucester, Mass., 1964.

Golovin, N. N., *The Russian Army in the World War*. New Haven, Conn., 1931.

Gronsky, P. P., and Astrov, N. I., *The War and the Russian Government*. New Haven, Conn., 1929.

Gurko, V. I., *War and Revolution in Russia 1914–1917*. New York, 1919.

Hasegawa, T., *The February Revolution*. Seattle, Wash., and London, 1981.

Katkov, G., *Russia 1917. The February Revolution*. New York, 1967.

Knox, A., *With the Russian Army: 1914–1917*. New York, 1921.

Kohn, S., *The Cost of the War to Russia: The Vital Statistics of European Russia During the World War*. New Haven, Conn., 1932.

Michelson, A. M., et al., *Russian Public Finance During the War*. New Haven, Conn., 1928.

Nolde, B. E., *Russia in the Economic War*. New Haven, Conn., 1928.

Odinets, D. M., and Novgorodtsev, P. J., *Russian Schools and Universities in the World War*. New Haven, Conn., 1929.

Paléologue, G. M., *An Ambassador's Memoirs, 1914–1917* (3 vols, trans. from the French by F. A. Holt). London and New York, 1923–25; repr. 1973.

Pares, B., *The Fall of the Russian Monarchy. A Study of the Evidence*. London and New York, 1939; repr. New York, 1961.

Pearson, R., *The Russian Moderates and the Crisis of Tsarism, 1914–1917*. New York and London, 1977.

Polner, T. I., et al., *Russian Local Government During the War and the Union of Zemstvos*. New Haven, Conn., 1930.

Rutherford, W., *The Russian Army in World War I*. London, 1975.

Smith, C. J., *The Russian Struggle for Power, 1914–1917; A Study of Russian Foreign Policy During the First World War*. New York, 1956.

Stone, N., *The Eastern Front, 1914–1917*. London and New York, 1975.

Struve, P. B., et al., *Food Supply in Russia During the World War*. New Haven, Conn., 1930.

Wildman, A. K., *The End of the Russian Imperial Army: The Old Army and the Soldiers' Revolt, March–April 1917*. Princeton, NJ, 1979.

Zagorsky, S. O., *State Control of Industry in Russia During the War*. New Haven, Conn., 1928.

CHAPTER THIRTEEN

Boll, N. M., *The Petrograd Armed Workers Movement in the February Revolution (February–July 1917)*. Washington, DC, 1979.

Browder, P. R., and Kerensky A. F. (eds), *The Russian Provisional Government. 1917: Documents*, 3 vols. Stanford, Cal., 1961.

Bunyan, J., and Fisher, H. H. (eds), *The Bolshevik Revolution, 1917–1918*.

Documents and Materials. Stanford, Cal., 1934.

Chamberlain. W. H., *The Russian Revolution, 1917–1921*. Vol. I: *1917–1918. From the Overthrow of the Czar to the Assumption of Power by the Bolsheviks*. New York, 1935; repr. 1952, 1965.

Chernov, V. M., *The Great Russian Revolution* (trans. from the Russian by P. E. Mosely). New Haven, Conn., 1936.

Daniels, R. V., *Red October: The Bolshevik Revolution of 1917*. New York, 1967.

Elwood, R. C. (ed.), *Reconsiderations on the Russian Revolution*. Cambridge, Mass., 1976.

Ferro, M., *October 1917. A Social History of the Russian Revolution* (trans. from the French by N. Stone). London and Boston, Mass., 1980.

Ferro, M. *The Russian Revolution of February 1917: The Fall of Tsarism and the Origins of Bolshevik Power* (trans. from the French by J. L. Richards). Englewood Cliffs, NJ, 1972.

Gankin, O. H., and Fisher, H. H. (eds), *The Bolsheviks and the World War: The Origins of the Third International*. Stanford, Cal., 1940.

Gill, G. J., *Peasants and Government in the Russian Revolution*. London and New York, 1979.

Katkov, G., *The Kornilov Affair: Kerensky and the Break-Up of the Russian Army*. London, 1980.

Keep, J. L. H., *The Russian Revolution: A Study in Mass Mobilization*. New York and Toronto, 1976.

Kerenskii, A. F., *The Catastrophe: Kerensky's Own Story of the Russian Revolution*. New York, 1927.

Kerenskii, A. F., *The Crucifixion of Liberty*. New York, 1934.

Kerenskii, A. F., *The Prelude to Bolshevism. The Kornilov Rebellion*. London and New York, 1919.

Kerenskii, A. F., *Russia and History's Turning Point*. New York, 1965.

Koenker, D., *Moscow Workers and the 1917 Revolution*. Princeton, NJ, 1981.

Lockhart, R. H. B., *The Two Revolutions: An Eyewitness Study of Russia, 1917*. London, 1967.

Mawdsley, E., *The Russian Revolution and the Baltic Fleet*. London, 1978.

Miliukov, P. N., *The Russian Revolution*. Vol. I: *The Revolution Divided: Spring 1917* (trans. from the Russian by T. and R. Stites). Gulf Breeze, Fla., 1978.

Mohrenschildt, D. von (ed.), *The Russian Revolution of 1917: Contemporary Accounts*. New York, 1971.

Pethybridge, R., *The Spread of the Russian Revolution: Essays on 1917*. London, 1972.

Pethybridge, R. (ed.), *Witnesses to the Russian Revolution*. London, 1964.

Rabinowitch, A., *The Bolsheviks Come to Power: The Revolution of 1917 in Petrograd*. New York, 1976.

Rabinowitch, A., *Prelude to Revolution: The Petrograd Bolsheviks and the July 1917 Uprising*. Bloomington, Ind., and London, 1968.

Radkey, O. H., *The Agrarian Foes of Bolshevism: Promise and Default of the Russian Socialist Revolutionaries, February to October 1917*. New York, 1958.

Reed, J., *Ten Days That Shook the World*. New York 1919; many reprints.

Rosenberg, W. G., *Liberals in the Russian Revolution. The Constitutional Democratic Party, 1917–1921.* Princeton, NJ, 1974.

Saul, N. E., *Sailors in Revolt: The Russian Baltic Fleet in 1917.* Lawrence, Kan., 1978.

Sobolev, P. N. (ed.), *The Great October Socialist Revolution* (trans. from the Russian by D. Skvirskii). Moscow, 1977.

Sukhanov, N. N., *The Russian Revolution 1917: A Personal Record* (ed., abridged, and trans. from the Russian by J. Carmichael). New York and London, 1955; repr. 1962.

Suny, R. G., *The Baku Commune 1917–1918. Class and Nationality in the Russian Revolution.* Princeton, NJ, 1972.

Thompson, J. M., *Revolutionary Russia, 1917.* New York, 1981.

Trotskii, L. N., *History of the Russian Revolution* (3 vols, trans. from the Russian by M. Eastman). New York and London, 1932; repr. 1967.

Wade, R., *The Russian Search for Peace: February–October 1917.* Stanford, Cal., 1969.

Maps

Map 1.   The Russian Empire, 1914

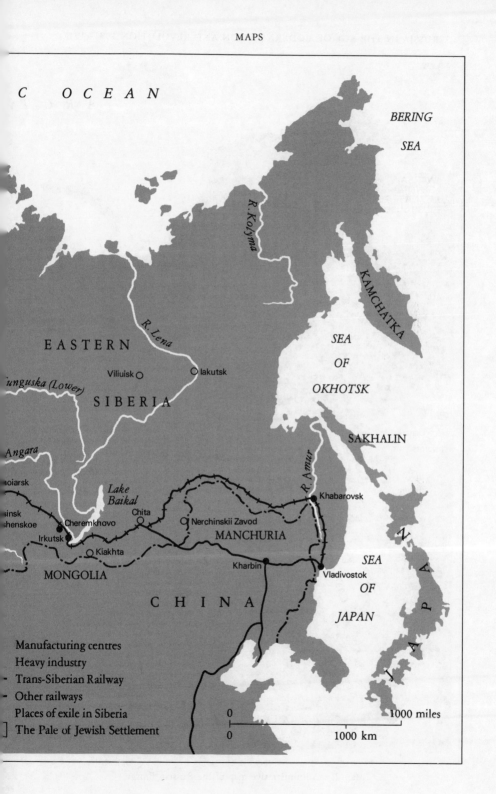

ARCT

NORWAY

WARSAW
GENERAL
GUBERNATORSTVO
(9 POLISH GUBERNIIAS)

FINNISH GENERAL
GUBERNATORSTVO
(8 GUBERNIIAS)

Helsinki
(Helsingfors)

3 Reval
2   1
Mitau
Riga   St.
Petersburg   4

KHOLM
GUBERNIIA
Grodno   Kovno
Vilna
Vitebsk   Pskov
Petrozavodsk
Arkhangelsk

Novgorod

5
Zhitomir   Minsk
Mogilev
Smolensk   Tver
Kaluga
Moscow   Iaroslavl   Vologda

Kamenets-
Podolsk
6 Kiev   Chernigov
Orel
Vladimir
Kostroma

Poltava   Tula
Riazan
Viatka
TOBOLSK
GUBERNIIA
R. Ob

Kishinev
Kherson   Kursk   Tambov   Nizhnii-Novgorod
Penza   Simbirsk   Kazan
Perm

7
8 Ekaterinoslav
Voronezh   Saratov
Ufa
Tobolsk

Simferopol
9
Samara

BLACK
Ekaterinodar   Novocherkassk   Uralsk
Orenburg
Omsk
TOMSK
GUBERNIIA
Tomsk

Novorossiisk
10   Stavropol
13   Kutais   Astrakhan   R. Ural   URAL
OBLAST   TURGAI
OBLAST   STEPPE
GENERAL
Semipalatinsk

SEA
Batum
11   Vladikavkaz

Kars
Tbilisi (Tiflis)
12   Derbent
TURKESTAN
ARAL
SEA
GUBERNATORSTVO
AKMOLINSK
OBLAST
Lake
Balkhash
SEMIRECHE
OBLAST

OTTOMAN   EMPIRE
Erevan
Elizavetpol
Baku
CASPIAN SEA
SYR DARIA OBLAST
GENERAL

14
Khiva
GUBERNATORSTVO
Tashkent
Vernyi

TRANSCASPIAN OBLAST
Bukhara
15
Samarkand
16
Skobelev
17

PERSIA
Ashkhabad

Map 2.   Administrative map of the Russian Empire

314

O C E A N

UTSK   GENERAL   GUBERNATORSTVO

KAMCHATKA
OBLAST
● Petropavlovsk

Iakutsk ●

IAKUTSK OBLAST

GUBERNATORSTVO

ERNIIA

18 ● Aleksandrovsk

GENERAL
MARITIME
AMUR OBLAST   MARITIME
OBLAST

oiarsk   Lake
Baikal
IRKUTSK   TRANSBAIKAL   Blagoveshchensk ●
GUBERNIIA   OBLAST   ● Khabarovsk
Irkutsk ●   Chita ●

SEA

OF

JAPAN

MONGOLIA

H I N A

1 ESTLAND GUBERNIIA   10 KUBAN OBLAST
2 LIVLAND GUBERNIIA   11 TEREK OBLAST
3 KURLAND GUBERNIIA   12 DAGESTAN OBLAST
4 OLONETS GUBERNIIA   13 BLACK SEA GUBERNIIA
5 VOLYNIA GUBERNIIA   14 KHIVA KHANATE
6 PODOLIA GUBERNIIA   15 BUKHARA KHANATE
7 BESSARABIA GUBERNIIA   16 SAMARKAND OBLAST
8 TAURIDE GUBERNIIA   17 FERGANA OBLAST
9 DON OBLAST   18 SAKHALIN OBLAST

0 _____ 1000 miles

0 _____ 1000 km

RUSSIA

R. Pruth

R. Dniester

R. Danube

Czernowitz

BUKOVINA

BESSARABIA

Budapest

AUSTRIA-HUNGARY

Jassy
(Iasi)

R. Drava

TRANSYLVANIA

R. Sava

Braila

Belgrade

ROUMANIA

BOSNIA

SERBIA

Bucharest

Silistra

BLACK

Sarajevo

SANDJAK OF
NOVIBAZAR

R. Danube

Shumla

HERCEGOVINA

Nish

BULGARIA

Varna

SEA

Mostar

Djakova

Sofia

Burgas

MONTE
NEGRO

Skoplje

EASTERN ROUMELIA

Philippopolis

ADRIATIC

ALBANIA

THRACE

Durazzo

Constantinople

SEA

MACEDONIA

ASIA

Saloniki

AEGEAN

MINOR

Yanina

Larissa

GREECE

SEA

••••• Ottoman boundary in 1815

—·— Ottoman boundary in 1908

|||||||||| Territory ceded to Roumania in 1856, retroceded to Russia in 1878

||||| Additional territory allotted to Bulgaria by Treaty of San Stefano 1878

············ Boundary between Bulgaria and Eastern Roumelia by Treaty of Berlin 1878

═══ Acquired by Roumania from Bulgaria 1913

——— Boundaries in 1913

0   200 miles

0   200 km

Map 3.   Russia, Austria, and the Balkans, 1856–1914

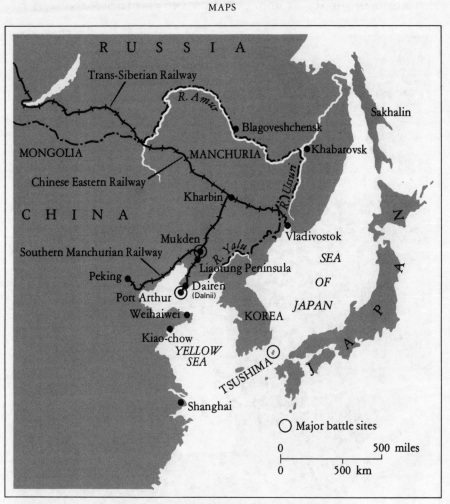

Map 4. Russia and the Far East

Map 5.   Russian fronts in the First World War

Index

319